Co-operation
Between the Sexes

Heinz L. Ansbacher, Professor Emeritus of psychology at the University of Vermont, has contributed numerous symposium chapters and encyclopedia articles on Alfred Adler, and edited Adler's *The Science of Living*. Rowena R. Ansbacher, his wife, has been his long-time associate as former editor of the *Journal of Individual Psychology*. Together, the Ansbachers have edited two books of Adler's writings, *The Individual Psychology of Alfred Adler* and *Superiority and Social Interest*.

ALFRED ADLER

Co-operation
Between the Sexes

Writings on Women, Love and
Marriage, Sexuality
and Its Disorders

EDITED AND TRANSLATED BY

HEINZ L. ANSBACHER AND

ROWENA R. ANSBACHER

WITH AN ESSAY BY HEINZ L. ANSBACHER

JASON ARONSON 𝒜
NEW YORK • LONDON

Doubleday Anchor Books edition: 1978
Aronson hardcover edition: 1980

ISBN: 0-87668-443-6
Library of Congress Catalog Card Number: 76–23804

CONTENTS

PREFACE

The theory of sexuality of Alfred Adler (1870–1937) is best characterized as the opposite of Freud's. Whereas Freud believed a person's sexuality determines his personality, Adler asserted that the total personality, the style of life, determines the sexuality.

The purpose of the present book is to gather Adler's writings on sex and all related matters such as feminism, love and marriage, and sexual disorders in one volume so that they can be examined as a whole.

Such a volume seems to be particularly called for at this time of heightened interest in sex and widespread rejection of Freud's theories, from members of women's liberation movements to psychoanalysts.

Adler considered sex one of the three great life problems every human being must meet, the others being work and social relations. Since Adler, furthermore, emphasized the unity of the personality, a presentation of his sexual theories will be practically an introduction to his theories of personality and psychological disorders as a whole.

The book is arranged in seven chapters, forming three parts. Part I, "Sociological and Theoretical Writings," presents in Chapter 1 Adler's views on the "woman question," which are strongly on the side of equality of the sexes. They most likely preceded Adler's psychological work, although they were not published in that order. Chapter 2 is the first full-length translation of Adler's critique of Freud's theory of sexuality, augmented by some further early theoretical writing.

Part II, "Sexuality and the Individual," deals in Chapter 3

with sexual development, women's and men's psychosexual attitudes, and sex education and puberty. Chapter 4 deals at length with problems of love and marriage, including reasons for disturbances, and the dynamics involved in preparation for love and marriage.

Part III, "Sexual Disorders," is concerned in Chapter 5 with homosexuality and in Chapter 6 with other deviations, dysfunctions, and prostitution. Adler generally counted prostitutes together with sexual deviates among the "failures of life," which included neurotics, psychotics, criminals, alcoholics, problem children, and suicides. In Chapter 7, seven cases of homosexuality are presented.

Since the material for this volume was gathered from many different sources, some overlapping was unavoidable, and there is also a certain unevenness of style. Some parts, written for the general public as they were, offer relatively easy reading, while others were addressed to more or less specialized professional readers.

A word regarding terminology is also indicated. Two terms most widely identified with Adler's psychology, "social interest" and "life style," appear relatively infrequently, although equivalents for "life style"—expressing the personality as a whole—are found throughout. These two terms were not introduced by Adler until 1918 and 1926, respectively, while most of his writings on the present subject matter were composed earlier. On the other hand, the term "masculine protest," which figures so large in these early writings, was later replaced by such concepts as striving for success, power, superiority, or simply a plus situation.

A great part of the material is here translated for the first time or retranslated, as indicated by footnotes to the various sections. Also, nearly all the headings and subheadings have been supplied by the editors.

An "Essay" by the first editor follows Adler's writings. It attempts to facilitate an understanding and evaluation of Adler by filling in the historical and biographical context, by referring to further pertinent writings of Adler, and by examining his contributions in the light of contemporary developments. Section 1 presents Adler's basic assumptions as the framework within which all his writings must be seen. Section 2, introducing Adler as the "Psychologist of Women's Equality," supplements Chapter 1. Section 3, "The Masculine Protest," deals with the quite technical theoretical issues involved in Chapter 2. Section 4, "Sexuality, Love and Marriage," refers to Chapters 3 and 4. Sections 5 and 6, "Sexual Disorders," referring to Chapters 5 to 7, are essentially a review of Adler's concepts on sexual disorders and psychotherapy, and their validation through contemporary psychiatric thinking. The Essay may well be read as an introduction to Adler's writings in this volume.

A "Bibliographical-historical Commentary" follows the Essay. In discussing the sources and circumstances of the selections from Adler it supplies further background material and contributes to Adler's biography.

Some readers may find fault with the absence of critical comments. The reason for such absence is that we thought it was essential that Adler's views on the subjects of this volume be first presented on his own terms in a positive light. We shall be satisfied if by doing so we may have provided a basis from which informed criticism by others may come forth. A second reason is that, frankly, we do not find much to criticize on basic matters.

Regarding Adler's procedure as a writer, however, we discussed critically two specific instances, of not indicating where an earlier statement was superseded by a later formulation (p. 283) and of not being very careful otherwise (p. 421). In general, we may add in accordance with Adler's own overruling principles: (a) Sweeping generalizations are to be understood as statements of probability only. (b) Dogmatic or blunt statements must be taken as maxims, working hypotheses, or therapeutic devices. (c) Apparent reifications must be read and revalued as statements of processes.

The present volume must be considered the last of a trilogy. The first, *The Individual Psychology of Alfred Adler* (New York: Basic Books, 1956; Harper Torch Books, 1964) is a systematic presentation of Adler's work in selections from all his writings. The second, *Superiority and Social*

Interest (Evanston, Ill.: Northwestern University Press, 1964; 3rd ed., New York: W. W. Norton, in preparation), is a collection of later writings presented in full length, and includes a biographical essay by Carl Furtmüller as well as a complete Adler bibliography.

* * *

Initial translation of the material in Chapters 5 to 7, most of Chapter 3, and the first two sections of Chapter 4 was supported by Public Health Service Research Grant No. MH-14330–01 from the National Institute of Mental Health. In this connection I wish to express sincere and lasting gratitude to my colleague at the University of Vermont, Donald G. Forgays, at that time chairman of the Department of Psychology. It was he who got me started on this book by encouraging my grant application and helping it along. He has always been a good personal friend, as well as a friend and supporter of Adlerian psychology.

Continued deep gratitude goes to my wife, Rowena R. Ansbacher, co-editor of the present volume as well as the two preceding. She gave particularly valuable help in selecting some of the material for inclusion and going over much of the translation.

I am very grateful to the faithful coworkers I had in typing —Sherrill Musty, who took down the first translations, Leslie Weiger, who was most helpful and supportive in the middle stages, and Hildegarde Bolsterle, who saw the manuscript through to a happy ending.

To return to Adler, he saw the solution to all of life's problems in rational co-operative effort among equals who, as responsible fellow human beings and respecting each other, would strive independently and interdependently toward commonly useful goals. He gained this perspective from his convictions and observations on psychological patients and embodied it in a theory which he took great pains to place on a scientifically sound foundation which adhered to the realities of life as closely as possible.

The particular message of the present book is that the life problem of sex and marriage is not to be solved on an individual basis—if humanity and in turn each individual is to benefit, even survive. As we are completing this book, we note a rising storm of voices pronouncing that such a message has become increasingly urgent. Adler saw the solution in a close co-operation between two individuals of different sex, committed not to a' mistaken "self-actualization" but an actualization of each other and, through children, the future of humanity. Hence the main title of the present collection: *Co-operation Between the Sexes.*

HEINZ L. ANSBACHER

University of Vermont
Burlington, Vermont
February 27, 1978

PART I
Sociological and Theoretical Writings

1

THE MYTH OF
WOMEN'S INFERIORITY[1]

DIVISION OF LABOR
AND SEXUAL DIMORPHISM[2]

The two factors that dominate all psychological processes are social interest (*Gemeinschaftsgefühl*) and striving for significance (*Geltungsstreben*). In constructing and securing the conditions of his life, in meeting the three main tasks of life—love, occupation, society—man always activates his social interest and effects his striving for significance, for power, and for superiority. Any psychological phenomenon must be evaluated by the quantitative and qualitative relationship of these two factors to each other to approximate a psychological understanding. The relationship of these factors will determine the extent to which a person will be capable of comprehending the logic of human living together, and of adapting himself to the division of labor that this logic enforces.

Division of labor is an absolute necessity for the preservation of human society. Consequently, every person must fill a specific place at some point. If a person does not participate in fulfilling this obligation, he denies the preservation of so-

[1] New translation of A1927a, Part 1, Chap. 7, *Das Verhältnis der Geschlechter* (The Relationship of the Sexes), except for the last two sections.
[2] A1927a, pp. 95–97.

cial life, of the human race altogether. He forgets his role as a fellow man and becomes a troublemaker. In lighter such cases we speak of bad manners, mischief, doing things your own way; in more difficult cases, of eccentricity, delinquency; and in later life, of crime. Such phenomena are condemned exclusively on account of their distance from and incompatibility with the demands of social life.

A person's worth is determined by how he fills the place that is assigned to him in the division of labor of the community. In his affirmation of the social life he becomes significant for others, and one of the links of a thousandfold chain on which the continuation of human life is based, and in which the absence of a certain number of these links would result in the collapse of social life. Ideally, it will be the individual's abilities that will assign to him his place in the total production process of human society. But quite some confusion has crept into this understanding and has disturbed the division of labor on this basis by setting false criteria for the evaluation of human worth. An individual may for some reason be unsuited for the place in which he finds himself; or difficulties may have arisen from the power craving or false ambition of certain individuals who in their own egotistical interest impede this kind of human living together and working together. Personal power or economic interests cause work to be distributed so that the more enjoyable positions, which give more power, are attained by certain groups of society, whereas others are excluded from them. Since the striving for power plays an enormous role in these matters, the process of division of labor never took place smoothly. Continuous violent intervention has rendered work a kind of privilege for some, and a kind of oppression for others.

Such a division of labor is also given through human sexual dimorphism [*Zweigeschlechtlichkeit* (division into two sexes)]. From the start this excludes one part, the female, from certain occupations according to her physique, while other jobs are not assigned to men because they can be employed better elsewhere. This division of labor should be carried through according to a completely unprejudiced criterion.

4

The woman's movement, insofar as it does not overdo things in the heat of battle, has accepted the logic of this viewpoint. It does not defeminize women nor destroy the natural relations of man and woman toward the work opportunities suited for them. In the course of human development the division of labor took the form that the woman takes over a part of those jobs that otherwise would also keep the man busy, while the latter can employ his powers more usefully. This division of labor is not quite unreasonable as long as labor resources are not thereby rendered idle and intellectual and physical resources are misused.

THE CULTURAL SITUATION

Male Dominance[3]

Through the development of culture in the direction of the striving for power, especially through the efforts of certain individuals or classes who wanted to secure privileges for themselves, the division of labor has been steered in favor of the men. This trend prevails to this day, with the result that human culture is characterized by the overtowering significance of man. The division of labor is such that the men are the group with guaranteed privileges. Due to their dominance, men influence the female position in the division of labor, in the production process, to their own advantage. Men prescribe to women their sphere of life and are in a position to enforce this; they determine forms of life for women that follow primarily the male viewpoint.

As matters stand today, men continuously strive for superiority over women, while women are constantly dissatisfied with the male privileges. Since, however, the two sexes belong closely together, there is tension, a constant upset of psychological harmony. This general psychological condition is experienced as extremely painful by both parts of the human race and leads to far-reaching disturbances.

[3] A1927a, pp. 97–100, with some omissions, covered later.

Male dominance did not originate as a natural fact, but had to be secured by a number of laws. Before that, there must have been periods when male dominance was not so certain. There is indeed historical evidence for a time of matriarchy, matrilineality (*Mutterrecht*), when the mother, the woman, played the more important role in life, especially toward the child, and all men of the tribe had a kind of obligation to her. Certain customs and traditions still point to this, as for example the usage of jokingly referring to every man as a child's uncle or cousin.

The transition from matriarchy to patriarchy was preceded by a great battle. Originally man did indeed not have the privileges that today he likes to describe as due him by nature, but had to fight for them. A good detailed description of this development is to be found in August Bebel (1885), *Woman and Socialism*. The victory of the men was tantamount to the subjugation of the women. Especially the records of the development of law testify eloquently to this process of subjugation.

Male dominance has not been a natural state, but became necessary only in the course of continuous fighting with neighboring peoples, when a significant role fell to man that he finally used to seize leadership definitely. Hand in hand with this went the development of private property and the law of inheritance as a foundation of male predominance, inasmuch as man is generally the earning and owning part.

The View of Women's Inferiority[4]

To justify his dominance, man generally argues that, in addition to his position being due him by nature, woman is an inferior being. The view of women's inferiority is so widespread that it appears as if it were common to all human beings. Together with this, a certain unrest is found in man, which probably stems from the time of the struggle against matriarchy, when woman indeed represented a disquieting factor for man.

[4] A1927a, pp. 103–7, with some omissions, covered later.

6

In history and literature we continually meet hints of this kind. Thus a Roman writer says, *"Mulier est hominis confusio."* [Woman is the confusion of man.] At Church councils the question of whether woman had a soul was the object of lively discussion, and learned treatises were written on the question of whether she was a human being at all. Witch hunting, with its witch burnings, lasted for centuries, and is sad testimony to the errors, to the enormous insecurity and confusion at that time, regarding this question.

Women often are presented as the cause of all evil in the world, as in the Bible story of original sin, or in Homer's *Iliad,* in which one woman was sufficient to plunge entire peoples into misery. Legends and fairy tales of all times refer to the moral inferiority of women, their depravity, malice, deceitfulness, fickleness, and unreliability. "Female frivolity" is even mentioned in support of laws. Similarly, women are depreciated regarding competence and performance. Figures of speech, anecdotes, proverbs, and jokes of all peoples are full of depreciating criticism of women. They are accused of quarrelsomeness, unpunctuality, pettiness, and stupidity.

Extraordinary acuity is mustered to prove woman's inferiority, to think only of persons such as Strindberg, Moebius, Schopenhauer, and Weininger. Their number is enlarged by many women who, in their resignation, came to share the view of woman's inferiority and her deserved subordinate role. The low esteem of women is also expressed in far lower pay for women than for men, even when their work is equal in value to men's work.

It is true that aptitude tests have shown that in certain subjects, such as mathematics, boys do better, and in other subjects, such as languages, girls do better. Boys show indeed more aptitude than girls for subjects that prepare for male occupations. But this speaks only apparently for their greater aptitude. If one looks more closely at the situation of girls, it turns out that the story of the lesser ability of women is a fable, a lie, which only looks like a truth.

A further argument against the prejudice of women's inferiority is the substantial number of women who have become outstanding in the most varied fields, especially literature, art,

7

technology, and medicine, whose accomplishments fully equal those of men. Incidentally, the number of men who show no accomplishments but a high degree of incompetence is so great that one could defend with an equal mass of evidence a myth of the inferiority of men—of course equally unjustly.

A serious result of this myth of the inferiority of everything female is a peculiar dichotomy of concepts. Masculine is simply identified with valuable, strong, and victorious, and feminine with obedient, servile, and subordinated. This manner of thinking has become so deeply rooted in our culture that everything excellent has a male tint, whereas everything that is less valuable and objectionable is represented as feminine. As is well known, for some men the worst insult is, "just like a woman," whereas in girls manliness does not mean derogation. The accent is always placed so that everything that reminds one of the female is represented as inferior.

Phenomena that frequently support this myth so clearly are upon closer observation nothing but the consequences of impeded development. We do not wish to claim that we could make of every child a person who in the usual sense can be considered "gifted" or very able. But we are confident that we could make of every child a person who would be considered *untalented*. We have of course never done this, but we know that others have succeeded in doing so. And it is very plausible that this is today more often the fate of girls than of boys. We have had occasion to see such "untalented" children who one day appeared so gifted that it seemed as if they had virtually been transformed.

EFFECTS ON THE CHILDREN

Boys[5]

All our institutions, traditions, laws, morals, and customs bear witness to the privileged position of the male toward whom they are oriented and by whom they are maintained.

[5] A1927a, pp. 98–103.

They penetrate as far as the nursery and have an enormous influence on the child's psyche. Though we cannot assume that the understanding of the child for these coherences is great, the child is sensitive to them. Consider the case of a boy who answered the demand to put on girl's clothing with a vehement temper tantrum. Such occurrences give us enough reason to investigate these coherences. This leads us again, from another side, to a consideration of the striving for power.

Once the boy's striving for significance has reached a certain degree, he will prefer to take the path that appears guaranteed by the privileges of his masculinity, which he sees everywhere. Present-day family education is very well suited to advance the striving for power and thereby the inclination to value male privileges highly and to aspire to them. The reason is that usually the man, the father, confronts the child as a symbol of power. By his mysterious comings and goings he arouses the child's interest much more than does the mother.

Very soon the child notices the overtowering role that the father takes; he sets the tone, makes arrangements, directs everything. The child sees how everybody defers to his orders and how the mother constantly refers to him. In every respect man appears to the child as the strong and powerful one. To some children the father appears so authoritative that they believe whatever he says must be holy, and in order to strengthen an assertion often reply only, "Father said so."

Even where the father's influence is not so clearly apparent, children will get the impression that the father is superior, because the entire burden of the family seems to rest on him, whereas actually only the division of labor gives the father the opportunity to employ his resources better.

The growing child does not need to read books on the subject. Even if he knows nothing of these matters, he will feel the result of the fact that man is the earning and privileged part, even when sensible fathers and mothers are gladly willing to renounce these old traditional privileges in favor of equal rights. It is extremely difficult to explain to a child that the mother, who performs the domestic work, is a partner who has equal rights with the father.

Imagine what it must mean for a boy to see before him from his first day everywhere the priority of man. Already at birth he is received much more joyfully than a little girl, and is celebrated as a prince. Everybody knows that all too frequently parents would rather have boys. The boy senses at every step how, as male progeny, he is preferred and considered more valuable. Various words addressed to him or occasionally picked up by him again and again suggest to him the greater importance of the masculine role.

The superiority of the masculine principle confronts a boy also in the form that the women living under the same roof with him are used for the less appreciated jobs, and finally that women in his environment are not always convinced of their equal value with men. They usually play a role that is presented as subordinated and inferior.

The child experiences all the situations that follow from this relationship. The result is innumerable pictures and opinions regarding the essence of woman, in which she generally emerges poorly. The psychological development of a boy thus receives a masculine cast. What he can sense as a desirable goal in his striving for power are almost exclusively masculine traits and attitudes.

From the described power relationships arises a sort of masculine virtue. Certain character traits that point to this origin are considered "masculine," others "feminine," without any basic facts justifying these valuations. When we compare boys and girls and find apparent confirmation of this classification, we cannot speak of natural facts. Rather, we note these phenomena in persons who are already tied to a certain frame, whose life plan, whose guiding line, is already narrowed down by one-sided power decisions. These power relationships have compellingly assigned to such persons the place on which they will have to seek their development.

The distinction of masculine and feminine character traits is thus not justified. We shall see that both kinds of traits can serve the demands of the striving for power, that one can exercise power also with "feminine" means—for example, through obedience and submission. Through the advantages that an obedient child enjoys, he may possibly move much more into the foreground than one who is disobedient, although in both cases the striving for power is at work. Our insight into a person is often made more difficult because the power striving resorts to the most varied character traits in order to prevail.

As a boy grows older, the significance of his masculinity almost becomes a duty. His ambition, his striving for power and superiority, are joined completely, become virtually identical with the obligation toward masculinity. Many children in their striving for power are not satisfied to carry the consciousness of masculinity merely within. They want always to show and prove that they are men and therefore must have privileges. On the one hand they try always to excel, and in doing so exaggerate their masculine character traits; on the other hand, they always try to demonstrate their superiority to the feminine environment, as all tyrants do, through defiance, or through tricky cunning, depending on the degree of resistance that they encounter.

Since every person is measured by the ideal of privileged masculinity, it is little wonder that this measure is always held up to a boy and that in the end he measures himself by it. He will ask himself and observe whether his bearing is always manly, whether he is already sufficiently manly, etc. All that is today presented as "manly" is familiar—first of all, something purely egotistical, something that satisfies self-love (that is, superiority), the pre-eminence over others—all this together with the help of active traits such as courage, strength, pride, memories of victories of all kinds (especially over women), the achievement of offices, honors, and titles, the inclination to harden oneself against "feminine" impulses, etc. It is a continuous struggle for personal superiority, because it is considered manly to be superior.

Thus a boy will adapt traits for which he can borrow the models only from adult men, especially his father. The traces of this artificially cultivated idea of grandeur can be followed everywhere. A boy is tempted early to secure for himself an excess of power and privileges. They mean to him as much as "manliness." In bad cases manliness often turns into the well-known phenomena of rudeness and brutality.

Girls[6]

The advantages that masculinity frequently offers are a great temptation, and thus many girls are guided by a masculine ideal. This may be expressed either as an unfulfillable yearning or as a criterion for the evaluation of their behavior, or as a manner of appearing and acting. "In matters of culture every woman will want to be a man." This includes the girls who in an indomitable urge prefer exactly those games and activities that according to physical aptitude would be more suitable for boys. They climb trees, like to move in the company of boys, and decline all feminine occupations as a disgrace. They find satisfaction only in masculine activity. All this is to be understood from the preference for masculinity. Here we see clearly how the struggle for an eminent position, the striving for superiority, extends more toward appearance than reality and the actual position in life.

A girl is told at every step, so to speak, daily, and in countless variations, that girls are incapable, and are suitable only for easier and subordinated work. Obviously, a little girl unable to examine such judgments for their correctness will regard female inability as woman's inevitable fate, and will ultimately herself believe in her own inability. Thereby discouraged, she does not meet such school subjects [as mathematics]—if she will ever have to do with them at all—with the necessary interest, or she loses interest in them. Thus she lacks external and internal preparation.

Under such circumstances the proof of woman's inability will of course seem correct. But it is an error for two reasons. The first reason is that the value of a person is still often judged on the basis of his performance from a business standpoint—that is, from a one-sided, purely self-seeking point of view. From this standpoint one can indeed overlook the question to what extent performance and aptitudes are connected with psychological development.

6 A1927a, first paragraph, p. 103; the remainder, pp. 105–7.

The second and main reason is that from childhood a girl encounters a myth that is very likely to shake her belief in her own value, her self-confidence, and to undermine her hope of ever performing competently. When she is reinforced in this by seeing that women are assigned only subordinated roles, it is understandable that she will lose courage, will no longer want to take a real hold, and will eventually pull back from the tasks of life.

Then, of course, she is really unfit and useless. When we face someone and impress him with the consensus, and in its name deny him all hope that he could amount to anything— when we undermine his courage in this manner, and find that he does not perform, then we are not justified in saying we were right, but we must admit that *we* have caused the whole misfortune.

It is not easy in our culture for a girl to have self-confidence and courage. Incidentally, even in aptitude testing, the strange fact was shown that a certain group of girls, aged fourteen to eighteen years, were superior to all other groups, including boys. These were all girls from families in which also the woman, the mother, or she alone, had an independent occupation. This means that these girls grew up in a situation in which they did not feel the myth of the lesser capability of women, or felt it to a lesser degree, because they could see for themselves how the mother advanced through her competence. Thus these girls could develop themselves more freely and independently, almost unhampered by this myth.

EFFECTS ON WOMEN

Rebellion Against the Feminine Role[7]

The primacy of men has brought a serious disturbance into the psychological development of women, which results in women's almost general dissatisfaction with their role. They move in the same paths and under the same conditions as all

[7] A1927a, pp. 107–11.

13

human beings who are likely to derive from their position strong inferiority feelings. The myth of their presumed natural inferiority is an additional aggravating factor in their psychological development.

If, nevertheless, a large number of girls find a halfway satisfactory compensation, this is due to their character development, their intelligence, and perhaps certain privileges which, however, show only that one error immediately entails others. Such privileges are exemptions, luxuries, gallantries, which at least have the semblance of preference, by feigning esteem for the female. Finally, women are also idealized which, however, results in the ideal of a woman created to the advantage of the man. One woman[8] noted aptly: "The virtue of women —that is a good invention of men!"

In the struggle against the feminine role in general three types of women can be distinguished. One type will develop in an active, "masculine" direction. These women become extremely energetic, ambitious, and struggle for crowning success. They try to surpass their brothers and male comrades, turn preferably to occupations that are reserved for the male gender, engage in all sorts of sports, etc. Often they also reject love and marriage relationships. If they do enter such a relationship, they disturb it by their effort here also always to be the dominating partner, the one who is somehow superior to the other. Toward all affairs of the household they manifest an enormous aversion, either directly by frankly stating so, or indirectly by denying any talent for them—and at times also by proving that lack of talent.

This type attempts to make up for the evil by a kind of masculinity. The defensive position against the female role is a basic trait of their nature. They are sometimes called "man-women." But this is based on the erroneous conception of an innate factor, a masculine substance, that compels such girls to their attitude. However, all of cultural history shows that woman's oppression and restrictions, to which she is still subjugated, are unbearable for a person and urge her to revolt. If the revolt takes a direction that one perceives as "masculine,"

8 George Sand (1804–76), pseudonym of the French woman novelist Amandine Dudevant.

this is due to the fact that there are after all only two possibilities to find one's way in this world—either according to the ideal manner of a woman or of a man. Thus any stepping out of the feminine role appears as masculine, and vice versa, not because of mysterious substances but because spatially and psychologically it is not possible otherwise. One must therefore keep in mind the difficulties under which a girl's development takes place. We cannot expect a complete reconciliation with life, with the facts of our culture, and the forms of our living together, as long as women are not granted equal rights with men.

Another type of woman goes through life with a kind of resignation and demonstrates an unbelievable degree of adaptation, obedience, and humility. Seemingly such women fit in anywhere, and go to work on everything, but they display such awkwardness and stupidity that they don't get anywhere, and one must become suspicious. Or they produce nervous symptoms, and emphatically present their weakness and claim for special consideration. Thereby they show how such artificial training in violation of their nature is generally punished by a nervous ailment and renders the person incapable for social life. They are the best persons in the world, but unfortunately they are ill and unable to meet the demands made on them. In the long run they are not able to satisfy their environment. Their submission, humility, and self-limitation are based on the same rebellion as in the case of the first type. They seem to say clearly: This is not a joyful life.

A third type seems to be those who, while not rejecting the feminine role, nevertheless carry within themselves the tormenting consciousness that as inferior beings they are condemned to take a subordinated role. They are fully convinced of woman's inferiority as well as the belief that only man is called upon for all the more competent performances. Thus they also advocate his privileged position. Thereby they strengthen the chorus of voices who attribute all ability only to man and demand a special position for him. They show their feeling of weakness so clearly it is as if they were seeking recognition for it and were asking for support. But this attitude also is the breaking out of the long-prepared rebellion.

15

It manifests itself often in a woman's marriage when she continuously turns all duties that she should fulfill herself over to her husband, admitting freely that only a man could accomplish them.

The dissatisfaction with the feminine role is even more extreme in girls who for certain "higher" reasons retreat from life by entering a convent, for example, or take up an occupation that is connected with celibacy. They belong with those who cannot be reconciled to their feminine role and in fact give up all preparations for their actual vocation. Many girls want to have a job very early to gain the independence that appears to them a protection against marrying too easily. In this attitude the disinclination toward the traditional kind of feminine role is again the driving factor.

Even when marriage is entered, where one should assume that the girl has voluntarily accepted this role, this is often no proof of reconciliation with the feminine role.

Such Women as Mothers[9]

Despite the myth of woman's inferiority, one of the most important and difficult tasks of life, the rearing of children, is left almost completely to women. This being so, what kind of parents will the three types just described make, and how will they differ?

The first type, with its masculine attitude toward life, will rule like a tyrant, will be busy with loud shouting and continuous punishment, and thus exercise strong pressure on the children, which they, of course, will try to escape. At best this will accomplish a drill that will be of no value whatever. Children usually regard such mothers as incapable of rearing them. The noise, the great uproar, and the fuss have a very bad effect, and there is the danger that the girls will be encouraged to imitate their mother, while the boys will be filled with enduring fear for the rest of their lives. Among men who were dominated by such a mother surprisingly many make a

9 A1927a, pp. 110–11.

16

great detour around women, as if inoculated with bitterness, and unable to have confidence in a female. Thus a permanent discord between the sexes arises that we consider clearly pathological. Yet even in such cases there are some people who talk foolishly of a "bad distribution of masculine and feminine substance."

The other two types of women are equally unsuccessful in bringing up children. One type tends to display such a skeptical manner that the children soon notice their mother's lack of self-confidence, and get out of hand. The mother will continually renew her efforts and warnings, also threatening to tell the father. However, by always looking to the male parent, she again discloses that she has no confidence in her ability to raise her children successfully. Thus also as a parent she has her eye on retreat, as if it were up to her to justify the view that man alone is competent and therefore also indispensable in raising children. Or, such women, feeling completely incapable, refuse any educational activity and turn this responsibility over to their husband, governesses, etc.

Older Women[10]

We want to mention in this connection still another phenomenon that also frequently gives occasion for a depreciating critique of women. It is the so-called dangerous age around fifty years when certain psychological phenomena and changes along the lines of a sharpening of some character traits occur. Physical changes may suggest to a woman that she will now lose the last reminder of the slim significance she had worked so hard to maintain. Under these aggravated conditions she will increase her effort to hold onto everything that helped her before, in reaching and maintaining her position.

In our present culture, with its prevailing belief in accomplishment, older people have a difficult time altogether, but this applies even more to women. Such damage, which undermines the value of older women completely, strikes in another

[10] A1927a, pp. 116–17.

form every one of us. A calculation or evaluation of our lives cannot be made on a day-to-day basis. What one has accomplished in the full power of his years should be credited to him when he has lost his strength and effectiveness. One cannot simply exclude a person from his psychological and material connections just because he is old. The manner in which this happens to older women is practically insulting. Imagine the anxiety with which a growing girl thinks of this time, which she too will have to face one day. Being a woman is not extinguished in the fiftieth year, and human dignity also continues undiminished after this point in time, and must be preserved.

A CASE[11]

A typical example of lack of reconciliation with the feminine role is the case of a thirty-six-year-old married woman who complained about various nervous ailments. She was the older child in a marriage of an aging man and a very domineering woman. The fact that the mother, a very pretty girl, married an aging man suggests that objections against the feminine role were involved and influenced the choice of a husband. And indeed the marriage was not a good one. At home the mother shouted when she talked and enforced her will without any consideration. The old father was always pushed into the corner. The patient says that her mother often did not allow her father even to stretch out on a bench in order to rest. She was always intent on conducting her household by a principle that she had arranged by herself and that had to be considered inviolable by all.

Our patient grew up a very capable child who was much pampered by her father. Her mother, on the other hand, was never satisfied with her and was always her opponent. Later, when a boy was born, the mother greatly favored him, and her relationship with her daughter became altogether unbearable. The girl knew, however, that she had a supporter in

[11] A1927a, pp. 111–16.

her father; as indolent and compliant as he was otherwise, he could offer very vehement resistance in matters concerning his daughter.

In her stubborn struggle with her mother, the girl virtually came to hate her. A preferred object of the girl's attack was her mother's cleanliness, which went so far, for example, as not to allow a housemaid to touch a doorknob without wiping it off afterward. The girl had fun in going around as dirty and slovenly as possible and getting everything dirty. Altogether she developed only those traits that were the direct opposite of what her mother expected. This speaks very clearly against the assumption of innate characteristics. If a child develops only such traits as must vex her mother to death, this must be based on a conscious or unconscious plan. The battle continues to this day, and there is hardly a more vehement hostility.

When the patient was eight years old, approximately the following situation existed: The father was always on the side of his daughter; the mother always had a severe and angry look, and made sharp remarks and reproaches; the daughter was snappish, quick on the repartee, and countered all the efforts by her mother with unusual wit. The situation was aggravated when her younger brother, mother's favorite and likewise pampered, fell ill with a heart-valve disorder. This caused his mother's care to become even more intensive. It should be noted that the parents' efforts with regard to their children were continuously at odds. These were the circumstances under which the girl grew up.

One day she seemingly became seriously ill of a nervous ailment that no one could explain. She was constantly tormented by evil thoughts directed against her mother, which she believed hindered her in everything. Suddenly she steeped herself in religion, but without success. After a while the evil thoughts receded, which was attributed to some medication; but probably the mother was somewhat forced into a defensive position. Only a remnant of the thoughts was left, a striking fear of thunderstorms. The girl believed that the thunderstorms came only on account of her bad conscience, and that someday they would become a disaster for her on account of her evil thoughts. One sees how the child herself endeavors to free herself from the hatred against her mother. Thus the child's development continued, and she seemed in the end yet to have a good future ahead of her. Once she was particularly impressed by one of her teachers saying, "This girl could do anything if she only wanted to." In themselves such words are insignificant. But for this girl they signified: "If she wanted to carry through something, she could do it." The result of this view was further greediness in the fight against her mother.

At the time of puberty she grew into a beautiful girl, became marriageable, and had many suitors. But through a particularly sharp tongue she again and again broke off all chances of a relationship. She felt particularly attracted only to an elderly man in the neighborhood so that one was always afraid she might marry him. But this man also went away after a while, and the girl remained without a suitor until the age of twenty-six years. This was very unusual in her circles, and no one could understand it, since they did not know her history. In the hard battle waged since childhood against her mother, she had become incompatible and quarrelsome. To fight was her victorious position. By her mother's behavior she had become irritated and led to chase constantly after triumphs. She liked nothing better than a heated argument. This showed her vanity. Her "masculine" attitude expressed itself also in her preference for games where the point was to win over an opponent.

At the age of twenty-six she met a very decent man who was not deterred by her quarrelsomeness and seriously courted her. He acted very humbly and submissively. Urged by her relatives to marry him, she declared repeatedly that she greatly disliked him and that a union with him could not end well. In view of her manner such a prophesy was not difficult. After two years' resistance she finally consented, firmly convinced to have found a slave with whom she could do what she wanted. Secretly she hoped he would be like a second edition of her father, who always gave in to her.

But soon she realized that she had been wrong. A few days after the wedding he would sit with his pipe in the living room comfortably reading his newspaper. In the morning he

20

disappeared in his office, came punctually for dinner, and grumbled when it was not ready on time. He demanded cleanliness, affection, punctuality—in her opinion, all unjustified demands for which she was not prepared.

The relationship that developed was not at all like that between her and her father. This was a rude awakening from her dreams. The greater her demands, the less did her husband fulfill her wishes; and the more he pointed to her role of a housewife, the less he got to see of it. She continuously reminded him that he had actually no right to make such demands, since she had warned him explicitly that she did not like him. But he was not impressed. He continued to make his demands relentlessly, so that she took a very dark view of the future. This righteous, conscientious man had courted her in an intoxicated state of self-forgetting, which soon dissipated once he considered himself in secure possession.

The disharmony between them was not changed when she became a mother. She had to take on new duties. The relationship to her mother, who definitely sided with her son-in-law, became increasingly worse. Since the incessant war at home was fought with such heavy guns, the husband was at times indeed unpleasant and inconsiderate and she was in the right. Yet his behavior was a consequence of her inadequacy in and lack of reconciliation with her feminine role. If she could always have played the role of the ruler walking through life with a slave by her side who would fulfill her every wish, the marriage might perhaps have worked.

What should she do now? Should she get a divorce, or return to her mother and declare herself defeated? She could no longer become independent, as she was not prepared for this. A divorce would have violated her pride, her vanity. Life was a torment. On the one side was her husband criticizing everything; on the other, her mother with her heavy guns, always preaching cleanliness and orderliness.

Suddenly the patient became cleanly and orderly. She started scrubbing and polishing all day long. She seemed finally to have learned the lesson that her mother had always dinned into her ears. At first her mother probably smiled, and her husband was also quite pleased with the sudden orderliness of his wife, who constantly straightened out the closets.

But such a thing can also be overdone. She washed and scrubbed until everything in the house was worn. Everybody disturbed her in straightening things out, and she on her part disturbed everybody else. When she had washed something, and somebody touched it, it had to be wiped off again, and only she could do this. Yet one could rarely find as much dirt as in this woman's home, since with her it was not really a matter of cleanliness but of causing a disturbance. It fits her case that she had no girl friend, could not get along with anybody, and knew no consideration.

This so-called washing compulsion is very frequent. Such women fight against their feminine role and want in a sort of perfection to look down on the others who do not wash as often. Unconsciously these efforts aim at exploding the home.

Culture must bring us in the near future methods for the education of girls that will accomplish a better reconciliation with life. As we see this today, such reconciliation can sometimes not be attained even under the most favorable conditions. In our culture woman's inferiority, although not existent in reality and denied by all reasonable persons, is still founded in law and tradition. We must always keep this in focus, recognize the whole technique of this erroneous attitude of our social order, and fight against it not from a pathologically exaggerated veneration of the female but because such conditions are destroying our social life.

REMEDIES[12]

All these phenomena are based on errors of our culture. Once a myth has permeated a culture, it will penetrate everywhere and can be found everywhere. Thus the myth of woman's inferiority and the related overbearance of man continuously disturb the harmony of the sexes. The consequence is an enormous tension, which especially enters all love rela-

[12] A1927a, pp. 117–21.

tionships, threatening all possibilities for happiness and frequently destroying them. Our entire love life is poisoned by this tension, dries up, and becomes barren.

This is why a harmonious marriage is so rare and children grow up in the belief that marriage is something unusually difficult and dangerous. The myth about women and similar thoughts frequently prevent children from attaining a true understanding of life. Consider the many girls who regard marriage only as a kind of escape, the men and women who see in marriage only a necessary evil. The difficulties that have grown from this tension between the sexes have today taken on gigantic dimensions. They are the greater, the stronger the girl's inclination from childhood to rebel against the role forced upon her or, respectively, the greater the man's desire to play a privileged role despite the illogic that this involves.

Comradeship

The characteristic sign of conciliation, of relaxation between the sexes, is comradeship (*Kameradschaftlichkeit*). Exactly in the relationship of the sexes subordination is as unbearable as in the lives of nations. The difficulties and burdens that arise from subordination for both parties are so great that everybody should pay attention to this problem. This area is so enormous that it comprises the life of each individual. It is so complicated because our culture has charged the child with choosing his attitude toward life in a kind of opposition to the other sex.

A calm upbringing probably could master these difficulties. But the hustle of our days, the lack of really tested educational principles, and especially the competition of our entire life, have their effects as far as the nursery and give there already the directives for later life. Many persons are afraid of entering love relationships. The danger is that it has become man's task to prove his masculinity under all circumstances, even through cunning, through "conquests." This destroys the open-mindedness and confidence in love. Don Juan is undoubtedly a person who does not believe he is sufficiently manly and therefore continuously seeks new proofs for this in his conquests.

The prevailing mistrust between the sexes undermines any confidence, and thus all humanity suffers. The exaggerated ideal of masculinity represents a demand, a continuous incentive, a permanent unrest, which results in nothing but demands of vanity, self-enrichment, and privileged position, which contradict the natural conditions of humans living together.

We have no reason to oppose the present goals of the woman's movement of freedom and equal rights. Rather, we must actively support them, because ultimately happiness and joy in the life of all humanity will depend on the creation of conditions that will enable women to become reconciled with their feminine role, and on how men will answer the problem of their relationship to women.

Coeducation

Among the attempts made so far to initiate a better relationship between the sexes, coeducation is the most important. This is a controversial practice; it has its opponents and friends. The latter mention as the main advantage that it affords the sexes an opportunity to get to know one another in time, so that harmful myths can be avoided. The opponents mention primarily that the difference between boys and girls is already so great when they enter school that common education would only widen it. The boys would feel oppressed, because girls are intellectually more advanced at this time. The boys, who had to carry the entire burden of their privilege and of proof that they were more competent, would now suddenly be confronted with the realization that their privilege is only a soap bubble that dissolves in the face of reality. Some scholars also claim to have found that through coeducation boys become timid toward girls and lose their self-esteem.

Undoubtedly there is some truth to these observations and

arguments. But the arguments are only valid if one regards coeducation in the sense of a competition between the sexes, for the victory of one being more competent than the other. If understood in this way by teachers and pupils, then it is naturally harmful. Unless teachers will attain a better understanding of coeducation—one of practice of and preparation for the future co-operation of the sexes on common problems —and base their vocational activity on this conception, experiments with coeducation will always fail, and the opponents will take these failures as confirmation of their standpoint.

To give here a complete picture would require the creativity of a poet. We must be satisfied to call attention only to the main points. Coherences with the above-mentioned types are always present, and many readers will remember that the same thoughts appear here as in the description of children born with inferior organs: The growing girl often behaves as if she were inferior. In that case what was said regarding the compensation of inferiority feelings is also valid for her. The difference is that the girl receives the belief in her inferiority also from the outside. Her life is so much drawn into this path that even insightful research persons succumb at times to this myth.

The general effect of this myth is that both sexes are in the end drawn into the whirlpool of prestige politics (*Prestigepolitik*) and are playing a role with which neither part can cope. It complicates the harmlessness of their lives, robs their relationships of spontaneity, and satiates them with prejudices in the face of which any prospect of happiness disappears.[13]

CONCLUSION[14]

Perhaps the most important problem in our society is the woman question (*Frauenfrage*). Since our life is oriented toward work and earning a living, it follows that in terms of money, men demand and receive a higher price than women.

[13] A similar paragraph will be found on p. 121.
[14] Original translation from A1914f, pp. 482–83.

This situation is reflected in the minds of most people as meaning that women exist for men and their service. But this is an unnatural presupposition, based on an artificial division of the natural coherence of the sexes. Yet this myth easily originates from the occasional impediments of women, and is borne by women as well as men, usually throughout life. One may seek this evaluation not in words and conscious thoughts, but in attitudes.

From a woman's low self-esteem it follows that she easily retreats from the tests and decisions of life, having lost belief in herself. Her efforts usually weaken too soon, or by their exaltation betray a lack of confidence. The inclination toward independent action usually vanishes as early as childhood, and an excessive need to lean on something, which can rarely be satisfied, marks her achievements as inferior. The weapons of the weak, detours toward excessively high goals, and traits of submission appear, which at first seem exaggerated and soon turn into lines of domineering.

The natural meaning of the body and its organs is falsified, and all impulses are changed and poisoned by the desired and at the same time undesired goals and by the compulsion of marriage. This is because the traits of natural womanhood have been depreciated and restored only conditionally. Some highly learned authors believe to have found "innate feminine" traits in the bad sense of the word, or a feminine nature, which would condemn a person to permanent inferiority. But this is only the unfortunate outcome that we have just described, which must occur when the little girl has interiorized a masculine superstition of the hopelessness of her intellectual strivings and now continuously attempts to talk with a masculine voice. All attempts at protest, initiated to regain the belief in herself, of which she was robbed already in the nursery, only detract from the spontaneity of experiencing. When a boy meets with difficulties in his achievements, he finds help at first in the recognition of this as a general inconvenience, retains his psychological equilibrium, and can go on with his work. A girl in such cases only hears from all sides, and also from the restlessness of her own heart, "because I am only a girl"—and easily considers her effort in vain. The human soul cannot find a point of rest in such self-depreciation. The outcome is generally a hidden, but easily decoded, strange hostility toward the seemingly preferred man.

The man, for his part, burdened since childhood with the obligation to prove his superiority over women, answers the secretly hostile nature of the female sex by increased suspicion and possibly by tyranny. In view of the obvious equality of value "of all human kind" it is understandable that both sexes, from their unnatural but almost inescapable attitudes, fall heir to a permanent struggle. In consequence, they are also prone to inescapable armaments, safeguards, and skirmishes for the sake of an unnecessary prestige. Furthermore, both sexes, with very disturbing caution and increased fear, face each other as enemies, both defying each other and fearing their own defeat.

These considerations outline the severest illness of our social organism and show that these erroneous perspectives of childhood become the executors of a tragic fate. In view of this it would be wrong to point to the life lie of the refinement of our sentiments, which supposedly emerges from the battle of the sexes. To those who want to search further, I wish to point out that proofs of superiority in the relationship between men and women are almost always only pseudoproofs that advance any actual "being higher" only little. It should also be added that this appearance is often attained by forbidden devices of cunning and imagination.

APPENDIX: THE PROBLEM OF ABORTION[15]

As in most questions, so when we examine the anti-abortion law we find that only from the viewpoint of Individual Psychology can all sides of the problem be seen in proper illumination and be recognized in their true significance.

Arguments generally advanced by those who are fighting the anti-abortion law appear to the psychologist not always as

---

[15] Original translation of A1925i.

27

the most valid. I do not wish to deal here with the medical necessity on the basis of which pregnancy is often interrupted. One may assume that any physician who is not committed by a prejudice in principles, will take the position that when the life of the mother is threatened, the saving intervention must be carried out. To assess the danger correctly remains then a matter of diagnostic certainty.

Often objections against continuation of a pregnancy achieve their apparently compelling character only through the pessimistic view of the persons in question. In most of the individual cases that we examine objectively, we will find that the situation could also be regarded otherwise, more courageously, and that then the compelling reasons for an abortion would fall away.

We are often told that a family could live quite well on its income with two children, but that with a third or fourth child it would be threatened with a considerable reduction in its standard of living. But we see on the other hand often enough that it was exactly the arrival of new children that gave the parents fresh impulses toward increased activity, inspired them with new ideas for sources of income, and that instead of the feared impoverishment, a new prosperity of the whole family took place. The special difficulties in finding work and the housing shortage of our time may, naturally, in some cases aggravate this situation.

In other cases, where perhaps a young girl is endangered as an unmarried mother to lose her social position and to get into an insoluble conflict with her parents, one may frequently be able to arrive at a solution other than abortion. We have often experienced that girls who anticipated their delivery in desperation, later on saw the highest value of their life in the child and knew how to solve the difficult question of unmarried motherhood excellently. Only by this were they urged to a fruitful career that guaranteed them independence from an oppressing environment. By the same token we often see that girls who succeeded in getting rid of the undesired pregnancy, later on deplored it bitterly and realized that there would have been ways to make motherhood possible that would have brought them consolation and joy. A courageous attitude of the unmarried mother is also rather likely to encourage the partner to enter marriage. But there are also cases where we see no other way for saving the existence of the girl than by interrupting the pregnancy, especially since we cannot influence the girl's entire environment, her parents, etc.

We see then that the most important reasons given for abortion are objectively not valid. The case is usually that the pregnant woman does not want the developing child. She does not want it because in the general lack of the female sex she is afraid to fail in her life. A child, after all, means much more than the responsibility for a hungry little mouth. It means primarily a great reinforcement of the tie to the father of the child. It means surrender of the boundless egotism, of the central position, which a number of women are accustomed to take in their environment. To become pregnant and give birth also means a defeat for many women who are altogether engaged in a struggle against the superiority of the masculine sex. It means the exposure of their natural disadvantages as a woman in the area of sexuality.

But only seldom will a woman admit to herself this rejection of motherhood, because she knows that this would be an admission of egotism and cowardliness. Thus we often enough see women who are in a situation well suited for the blessing with children who are married and in good circumstances, yet are creating an artificial arrangement through which they can escape this task that is approaching them. We see women guarding their domesticity with such painstaking, "exaggerated" care, and attributing such significance to the irregularity or any interruption of the accustomed order that their entire environment automatically arrives at the thought: "How lucky that this woman has only one child!" And we shall find again and again as the root of numerous nervous disturbances, the fear of having a child.

Should one force such a woman who so strongly rejects the idea of having a child to give birth against her will? For the legislator the problem may end with the birth of the child. But we know that the problem only begins with the birth, that such a woman will by no means come to terms without protest with the undesired fact of her motherhood. What kind of a mother will she be to the child?

How can she fulfill such a difficult task when it is forced upon her against her will? One is inclined to maintain that with the birth of the child mother love will set in unconditionally, like a chemical reaction. The psychologist knows, however, that this is not always the case. Enough women let their children feel in hundreds of ways that they were unwanted when they were born. The knowledge of being an unwanted child poisons the life of many individuals, plants the root for serious psychological disturbance, and is often the basic evil from which arise delinquents and all those psychopaths who for the rest of their lives cannot get rid of the curse of a youth without love. Alone in the interest of these children—and it is primarily with regard to the children that we are judging this question—I am in favor of telling every woman plainly: "You need not have children if you don't want to."

And I have often seen that the same woman who resisted motherhood with a hundred pretenses, suddenly wanted herself the child whom she had violently rejected, once she saw herself free to decide the outcome of her pregnancy. We must never forget how deep is in each woman the protest against the inequality with men. The compulsion of a law created by men through which women are robbed of the free decision regarding their fate must be felt by every woman as a humiliation. Within this law a woman plays less the role of a person than that of a function in the interest of progeny.

Compared to this argument all others take a secondary place: Only a woman who wants the child can be a good mother to him or her.

Some parties like to maintain that the abolition of the law against abortion would worsen still further our already deplorable condition of general morals. But the low level of morality has so many other, deeper-reaching reasons—especially our entire education, which is so little oriented toward social feeling and so much toward personal ambition—that it is absurd to apply the moral lever just at this place, where one part of mankind is hit so much harder than all others. We shall well have to share the great responsibility for the ethical living together of human beings, instead of turning the heaviest burden on the weakest shoulders.

It would be a real blessing for humanity if marriage-counseling centers were created at which Individual Psychologists would function and give information on all related questions.

2

MASCULINE PROTEST AND A CRITIQUE OF FREUD

MASCULINE PROTEST[1]

Facts of Psychological Hermaphroditism

Almost every investigator of human hermaphroditism has mentioned or emphasized that among the derived sexual characteristics one often finds psychological traits of the other sex. Krafft-Ebing, Dessoir, Halban, Fliess, Freud, and Hirschfield are among these.

Freud has studied particularly the phenomena of homosexuality in neurosis and found that every neurotic shows homosexual traits. This observation has been amply confirmed. [*Later replaced by:* I have been able to correct this observation as a frequent sign of the irreconcilability of neurosis with eroticism.] In a small paper (A1908f) I have pointed out the relationship of prostitution to homosexuality. Fliess believed earlier that the male neurotic suffered from suppression of his feminine traits; the female neurotic, from repression of her masculine traits. Sadger held similar ideas.

A careful study of the neuroses with regard to traits of hermaphroditism yields the following results:

[1] Translation of A1910c, "Psychological Hermaphroditism in Life and Neurosis: On the Dynamics and Therapy of Neuroses," as reprinted in A1914a, pp. 74–83; 1928 ed., pp. 76–84.

1. General physical phenomena of the opposite sex are found remarkably often—feminine habitus in male neurotics, and masculine habitus in female neurotics. Secondary characteristics of the opposite sex are likewise often found: in men —inferiority phenomena of the genitals, such as hypospadias [congenital opening of the urethra on the underside of the penis], para-urethral passages, small penis, small testicles, cryptorchidism [concealment of one or both testes within the abdomen], etc., and in women—large labium minus, large clitoris, infantilism of the sexual apparatus, etc. Additionally, we find as a rule inferiorities of other organs. (See A1907a.)

Whether these physical phenomena bear right from the start any genetic relationship to the opposite-sex psyche, as Fliess assumes and as Krafft-Ebing specified, so that in the man the feminine psyche, in the woman the masculine psyche would be more strongly developed, cannot be proven at present [*later added:* with certainty].

It can be shown, however, in children with inferior organs, organ systems, and glandular systems, that their mobility and physical development often deviate from the norm, that their growth and functioning show deficiencies, and that sickness and weakness are prominent, especially at the beginning of their development, although these may later on often give way to robust health and strength.

2. These objective phenomena frequently give rise to a subjective feeling of inferiority and thus hinder the independence of the child, increase his need for support and affection, and characterize the adult person, often until old age. Weakness, clumsiness, awkwardness, sickliness, childhood disorders such as enuresis, incontinence of the feces, stuttering, shortage of breath, deficiencies in the visual and auditory apparatus, innate or early acquired blemishes, and extreme ugliness, etc., may all give a deep foundation for the feeling of inferiority in relation to stronger persons and fixate it for life. This is especially true of the feeling toward the father. Significant traits of obedience, submission, and devoted love toward the father

characterize many children, especially those disposed toward neurosis.[2]

Such children are thus often placed in a role that appears to them as unmanly. All male neurotics as children were moved by doubt regarding their achievement of full masculinity. The renunciation of masculinity, however, appears to the child as synonymous with femininity. Thereby a wide area of originally childish value judgments is given: Any uninhibited aggression, activity, competence, power, and the traits of being brave, free, rich, aggressive, or sadistic can be considered as masculine; all inhibitions and deficiencies, as well as cowardliness, obedience, poverty, and similar traits, as feminine (see A1908b).[3]

3. The child plays a double role for a while. On the one hand, he shows tendencies of submission to the parents and educators, and on the other hand, some of his wishes, fantasies, and actions express a striving for independence, a will of his own, and significance ("the little would-be-great"). Since girls and women display more of the one tendency, and boys and men more of the other, the child arrives at value judgments similar to those of the adults: to regard inhibition of aggression as feminine, increased aggression itself as masculine. "To be bad" often means for the child to be masculine.

This inner disunion in the child is the example and foundation of the most important psychological phenomena especially of the neurosis, the [*later added:* falsely so-called] splitting of consciousness and [*later added:* starting point of] indecision, and may result in various outcomes in later life. As a rule one will find attitudes of an individual varying between the "feminine" and the "masculine" directions, together with tendencies to strengthen the unity of the picture from within. After all, males are impeded from complete merging into the feminine role, and vice versa. This leads usually to a compromise—that is [in men], feminine deport-

[2] See also C. G. Jung (1909). [Author's note, omitted from later editions.]

[3] Incidentally, this evaluation holds not only for the child, but also for the greater part of our cultural consciousness. [Author's note.]

34

ment with masculine means (for example, masculine shyness and submission, masculine masochism, homosexuality, etc.), and [in women] masculine role with feminine means (emancipation tendencies of women, polyandry, compulsion neurosis as disturbance of the feminine role, etc.). Or one finds an apparently haphazard side-by-side of "masculine" and "feminine" traits.

In neurosis, where we are always dealing with the incongruencies of such traits, their discernment and reduction are possible with the methods of Individual Psychology. The precondition, however, is that the therapist does not bring his own value judgments about masculine and feminine traits to the analysis but adapts himself to the feelings of the patient and follows these.

The Masculine Protest[4]

The starting point for the feminine tendencies of the neurotic is the child's feeling of weakness in the face of adults. From this arises a need for support, a demand for affection, a physiological and psychological dependency and submission. In cases of early and subjectively felt organ inferiority (motor weakness, clumsiness, sickliness, childhood disorder, slow development, etc.), these traits are intensified, whereby the dependency grows. This increased feeling of one's own smallness and weakness (the root of the delusion of smallness) leads to inhibition of aggression and thereby to anxiety. The uncertainty regarding one's competence releases doubts, a vacillation between the "feminine" tendencies (anxiety and related phenomena) and the "masculine" tendencies (aggression, compulsion phenomena). The structure of the neuroses (neurasthenia, hysteria, phobia, paranoia, and especially compulsion neurosis) shows the often ramified "feminine" lines carefully hidden and covered over by hypertrophied "masculine" wishes and tendencies.

[4] See Schiller, "The Dignity of Men": "I am a man. . . ." [Author's note.]

35

This is the masculine protest. It follows necessarily as over-compensation when the "feminine" tendency is valued negatively by the childish judgment, somewhat like a childhood disorder, and is retained only in sublimated form and on account of external advantages (love of one's relatives, freedom from punishment, praise for obedience, subordination, etc.).

Every form of inner compulsion in normal, and neurotic individuals may be derived from this attempt at a masculine protest. Where it succeeds, it naturally strengthens the masculine tendencies enormously; posits for itself the highest and often unattainable goals; develops a craving for satisfaction and triumph; intensifies all abilities and egotistical drives; increases envy, avarice, and ambition; and brings about an inner restlessness that makes any external compulsion, lack of satisfaction, disparagement, and injury unbearable. Defiance, vengeance, and resentment are its steady accompaniments. Through a boundless increase in sensitivity, it leads to continuous conflicts. Normal and pathological fantasies of grandeur and daydreams are forced by such overly strong masculine protest and are experienced as provisional surrogates of drive satisfaction. Dream life also comes entirely under the dominance of the masculine protest. Every dream, when analyzed, shows the tendency to move away from the feminine line toward the masculine line.

The masculine protest is equally valid for women as for men, only that in women it is usually covered and changed, and seeks to triumph with feminine means. Very often one finds during the analysis the wish to change into a man. Vaginism, sexual anesthesia [frigidity], and many well-known neurotic phenomena originate from this tendency.

If one follows the "dynamic approach" that I have suggested, one will soon recognize that all these phenomena have in common the striving somehow to gain distance from the feminine line and to gain the masculine line. Thus neurotic symptoms are sometimes more feminine, sometimes more masculine, and every neurotic symptom represents a hermaphrodite.

The neurotic compulsion shows the masculine protest; to

succumb to the compulsion is feminine—for example, in compulsive blushing (erythrophobia), the patient reacts with (masculine) rage and temper to felt or feared depreciation. But the reaction takes place with feminine means, with blushing or fear of blushing. The meaning of the attack is: "I am a woman and want to be a man."

Thus the neurotic safeguards himself from decisions that appear dangerous—for example, by substituting a compulsion of his own for one from without (Furtmüller, 1912).

If the patient finds himself cut off from all personal success, if the satisfaction of his usually overreaching masculine protest has failed in a main line, in which the sex drive, though always included, is only one of the components, then the neurosis, toward which steps have long since been taken, finally breaks out. The patient then tries to satisfy his masculine ambition on side lines through displacement onto other persons and goals; or, the inhibition and blocking become more intensive, and such transformations of the aggression drive result as I have described in my paper entitled "The Aggression Drive in Life and Neurosis" (A1908b).[5]

The aggression drive and its transformations play the most important role in neurosis. [But] this conception suffered from the defect of being biological and not suitable to a complete understanding of neurotic phenomena. To this end, one must consider a conception of the neurotic that is most highly personal and judges phenomena in a way that does not admit of definitions in biological terms, but only in psychological terms, or in terms of cultural psychology.

It is my proposition, then—consonant with that of Freud—that in every neurotic (in every human being) we find masculine as well as feminine traits, whether it be in mixed (compromise) formation, or one alongside the other. The sublimated form of this conception is the problem of freedom

[5] Aggression drive is used by Adler not exclusively in the sense of hostility, as is generally done today, but also in the sense of an active assertion. George A. Kelly (1963, p. 143) has since then made the similar distinction between hostility and aggression, where aggression is a dimensional trait, with inertia and initiative as the two poles.

or the determination of the will. Despite our inner conviction that the will is determined, we behave as if it were free; the fault lies in the posing of the problem. In a similar way, these two distinct conceptions are felt by the neurotic, and all character traits can be traced back to that fact.[6]

The Structure of Neurosis

For the structure of the neurosis all these variations gain great significance. The feminine, masochistic tendency (in the opinion of the patient) predominates and creates the feminine, masochistic picture of the neurosis, while at the same time the patient becomes endowed with extreme sensitivity against any sinking into "femininity," against any depreciation, oppression, curtailment, and defilement.

The weak point, the feeling of inferiority, the feminine lines are covered up or are masked by compromise formation, or are made unrecognizable through sublimation and symbolization. But they gain in breadth and intensity, continuously or occasionally, and become manifest in the form of abulia, ill humor, depression, anxiety, pain, feeling of anxious expectation, doubt, paralysis, impotence, insufficiency, etc.

The feeling of inferiority thus whips up the drive life, increases the wishes boundlessly, provokes oversensitivity, and creates a craving for satisfaction that tolerates no adaptation and results in continuous, overheated expectations and fears. In this hypertrophied craving, passion for success, frantic masculine protest, lies the germ of failure—but also the predestination for the achievements of the genius and the artist.

The neurosis breaks out when the masculine protest has failed in a main line. The feminine traits then apparently predominate, but only under continuous increase of the masculine protest and pathological attempts to break through along masculine side lines. Such attempts may succeed without bringing real satisfaction and harmony, or they may fail,

[6] This and the preceding paragraph reprinted from A1910n, p. 425 and pp. 425–26, respectively.

as often in neurosis, and force the patient further into the feminine role, apathy, anxiety, and mental, physical, and sexual insufficiency, etc., which are further exploited as means for power.

The investigation of full-fledged neurosis, in view of the above, will always reveal the following traits and note their dynamic valences:

    a. feminine traits [*later:* traits evaluated as feminine].
    b. hypertrophied masculine protest.
    c. compromise formation between a and b.

The failure of the masculine protest in the case of psychological hermaphroditism is favored, practically brought about, through the following factors:

1. Exaggeration of the protest. The goal is as such, or with regard to the patient's resources, unattainable.

2. Overestimation of the goal. Such overestimation (as by Don Quixote) is unconsciously purposeful, so as not to disturb the hero role of the patient. In this way disappointments are bound to result.

3. Feminine tendencies setting the tone and inhibiting aggression. Often at the crucial moment or before the intended action, the "feminine" feeling awakens in the form of exaggerated belief in authority, doubt, and anxiety, and leads to humiliation and submission under continuous protest formation, or it forges a weapon from doubt, anxiety, etc., and thus leads the submission to absurdity.

4. An active guilt feeling (see A1909a) [*later added:* a descendant of social interest] that is derived from childhood and [whose objects] can easily be shifted. It supports the feminine traits and frightens the patient with possible consequences of his deed (the Hamlet type).

Reinforcement of Feminine Lines

At this point I must mention further reinforcers of the feminine lines in the child that go more or less beyond the physiological measure and regularly represent the occasions for exaggerating the masculine protest. I was able to recognize the following origins and mechanisms in a considerable number of neurotics of both sexes, so that I may well speak of a general validity of these findings, all the more so since by their uncovering, the cure of the neurosis was initiated.

1. Fear of punishment. It is furthered by overreacting to pain and oversensitivity of the skin, strictness of the educators, and corporal punishment. To be taken as masculine reactions are: indifference toward punishment, defiant indifference, the bearing of pain, often seeking of tortures (apparent masochism, see Wexberg, 1914), and the patient's demonstrative assertions of how much he can stand, erection and active sexual behavior when threatened with punishment, which may sometimes be facilitated by individual physiological peculiarities (see Asnaourow, 1913).

2. Seeking sympathy by demonstrating one's weakness or suffering. Or, masculine protest: ideas of grandeur (in compensation for the feminine delusion of smallness), indignation about the sympathy of others, laughing instead of crying [later added: cynicism, fight against stirrings of affection], etc., making fun of oneself. Combinations occur regularly. Childhood disorders such as enuresis, stuttering, sickliness, headaches, lack of appetite, etc., may become fixated through counting on sympathy or out of defiance. Almost regularly, compromise formations occur. The masculine reaction uses weakness to annoy the parents and is defiant by retaining a disorder so as not to have to give in. All [later: Many] enuretic dreams show the attempt of the dreamer to act like a man (to urinate standing up, urinal for men, large arc of the urine stream, urinating figures in the sand). At the same time this is a masculine reaction against fear of punishment, often with use of fictions, as if the chamber pot or the toilet were available.

3. Erroneous conception of the sexual roles, ignorance of the difference between man and woman, and thoughts about the possibility of a transformation of boys into girls and vice versa. Frequently there is a dim feeling of being a her-

maphrodite. Physical attributes, errors in upbringing, misunderstood utterances from the environment (girls' clothing on boys, long hair on boys, short hair on girls, bathing together with the other sex, dissatisfaction of the parents with the sex of the child, etc.) awaken or increase the child's doubt as long as the sex differences are not clear to him. Similarly, fairy tales regarding the birth of children or false conceptions of it (birth through the anus; conception through the mouth, through a kiss, through poison, or through touching) create confusion. Deviating early sexual experiences or fantasies in which the mouth or the anus plays the role of the sex organ contribute to blurring the distinction between man and woman and may become fixated in a biased way.

Sexual Disorders

Homosexuality originates from the attempt to change the sexual role [*later:* from the uncertainty of one's sexual role]. Homosexual men had in childhood the talent to think themselves into a girl's role. If, as always, the masculine protest occurs, the transformation into a homosexual takes place as avoidance of the feared woman.

Altogether, understanding can be attained only if one follows the masculine attempts at protest, as for example in compulsory masturbation which, like any compulsion, means the attempt to do like a man and yet evade one's sexual role [*later:* one's task]. The same tendency is found in pollution and ejaculatio praecox. The haste as well as the accompanying phenomena (insufficient erection, sometimes homosexual dreams) betray the weak point hidden behind these. In the analysis of dreams one should look for nightmares, dreams of being prevented from something, and dreams of anxiety that belong to an elaboration of the feminine line, a defeat. Yet in these dreams almost regularly the masculine tendency breaks through (screaming, fleeing, awakening)—as protest.

Exhibitionistic traits are favored by the tendency to show oneself as a man [*later added:* despite the feeling of insecu-

41

rity]. In girls and women a renunciation of female modesty or the rejection of female garments seems to be sufficient for this purpose. The same tendency for power characterizes narcissism. In fetishism the unmanly line regularly becomes prevalent (preference for lingerie, blouses, aprons, jewelry, hairpieces, etc. [later added: instead of the partner]), but is always accompanied by the masculine tendency not to be dominated by the partner. Originally an expression of hermaphroditism like every autoeroticism, [glove and] shoe fetishism [are] directed toward the cover [later: the incidental thing] and [gain their] feminine, masochistic character through their distance from the masculine role. [Later added: The evasion from an assumed danger zone always becomes apparent.]

Originally masochistic traits, like hypochondriases and exaggerated sensitivity to pain, belong with the "feminine" traits of endurance. Like any psychological phenomenon, they never lack further incidental determiners to demonstrate the size of the suffering, etc. [later added: and to withdraw from fulfilling the life tasks in presentiment of a defeat].

It is very understandable that the child uses the traits of his mother to represent his feminine lines, and those of his father for his masculine lines. ("From father I have the stature. . . .") The masculine protest intensifies the desires of the child, who then seeks to surpass his father in every respect and comes into conflicts with him. Thus those secondary traits arise that correspond to desires aimed at the mother (Oedipus allegory).

Therapy

It is the task of education and psychotherapy to uncover this dynamic and make it conscious. Thereby the biased overgrowth of the "feminine and masculine traits" will disappear, and the childish valuation give room to a more mature world view; likewise, the dissociative processes, split consciousness, and *double vie* will stop. The oversensitivity gives way, and the patient learns to tolerate the tensions from the environment without becoming upset. Whereas he was before "a toy of dark unconscious stirrings, he becomes the conscious master or sufferer of his feelings" (A1905b) [reference later omitted].[7]

ANTITHETICAL APPERCEPTION AND DOGMATIZATION[8]

We consider the guiding force of the neurosis to be the desire for the enhancement of the self-esteem as the final purpose. This force always tries to assert itself with special strength. It is the expression of a striving and wanting, which is deeply rooted in human nature. This guiding thought could also be called "will to power" (Nietzsche). Its expression and deepening informs us that a particular compensatory force is involved to put an end to the general human insecurity.

By a rigid formulation, which usually rises to the surface of consciousness, the neurotic tries to gain a firm basis to unhinge the world. It does not really matter whether he is conscious of much or little of this driving force. In either case he neither knows the mechanism nor is he able by himself to uncover and break up his childish analogical behavior and apperception. This succeeds only with the method of Individual Psychology, which permits one to guess and to understand the childish analogy by means of abstraction, reduction, and simplification, and by the observation of the nearly content-free psychological movement.

It turns out that the neurotic apperceives always according to the analogy of an antithesis and usually even knows and admits only antithetical relationships. This primitive orientation in the world, which corresponds to the antithetical categories of Aristotle, as well as to the Pythagorean tables of opposites, originates in the feeling of insecurity and represents a

[7] The original reference actually reads: "The helpless toys of bad moods and depressions will become conscious opponents or sufferers of an imposed destiny."

[8] Translated from A1912a, 1928 ed. Most of these selections have appeared also in A1956b, pp. 246–50.

43

simple device of logic. What I have described as polar hermaphroditic opposites (A1910c), Lombroso[9] as bipolar, and Bleuler[10] as ambivalent, leads back to this mode of apperception, which functions according to the principle of antithesis.

One must not fall into the common error of regarding this as an essence of things, but must recognize in it the primitive working method, a point of view, which measures a thing, a force, or an experience by an opposite that is fitted to it.

Antithetical Apperception

The neurotically disposed individual has a sharply schematizing, strongly abstracting mode of apperception. Thus he groups inner as well as outer events according to a strictly antithetical schema, something like the debit and credit sides in bookkeeping, and admits no degrees in between. This mistake in neurotic thinking, which is identical with exaggerated abstraction, is also caused by the neurotic safeguarding tendency. This tendency needs sharply defined guiding lines, ideals, and bogeys in which the neurotic believes, in order to choose, foresee, and take action.

In this way he becomes estranged from concrete reality, where psychological elasticity is needed rather than rigidity—that is, where the use of abstraction is needed rather than its worship and deification. After all, there is no principle to live by that would be valid to the very end; even the most correct solutions of problems interfere with the course of life when they are pushed too far into the foreground, as, for example, if one makes cleanliness and truth the goal of all striving.

In the psychological life of the neurotic we find the inclination to stylize experiences and persons in the environment to a very pronounced degree, exactly as we find it in primitive thought, mythology, legend, cosmogeny, theogeny, primitive art, psychotic productions, and the beginnings of philosophy. In this process phenomena that do not belong together must,

[9] Cesare Lombroso (1836–1909), Italian psychiatrist.
[10] Eugen Bleuler (1857–1939), Swiss psychiatrist.

44

of course, be sharply separated by abstractive fiction. The urge to do this comes from the desire for orientation which, in turn, originates in the safeguarding tendency. This urge is often so considerable that it demands artificial dissection of the unity, the category, and even the self into two or several antithetical parts.

One of the pairs of opposites often becomes increasingly clear: inferiority feeling vs. enhancement of self-esteem. To resort to concrete pairs of opposites corresponds to the primitive attempts of the child to orient himself in the world and to safeguard himself. Among these pairs I have regularly found: (1) *above-below* and (2) *masculine-feminine*. In the sense of the patient, but not always in the general sense, memories, impulses, and actions are then always arranged by a classification of *inferior = below = feminine* vs. *powerful = above = masculine*. This classification is important. Because it can be falsified and advanced at will, it affords a distortion of the picture of the world by which the neurotic can always retain his standpoint of having been humiliated. It lies in the nature of things that here the patient's experiences of his constitutional inferiority come to his assistance, as does the increasing aggression of his environment, which is continuously irritated by his neurotic behavior.

The neurotic's striving for security, his very safeguards, can be understood when the original antithetic value-factor, namely that of insecurity, is taken into consideration. Both security and insecurity are the result of a dichotomizing judgment that has become dependent upon the fictional personality ideal and furnishes biased subjective value judgments. The feeling of security and its opposite pole, the feeling of insecurity, arranged according to the antithesis of inferiority feeling and personality ideal, are, like the latter, a fictional pair of values. They are the kind of psychological construction concerning which Vaihinger (1911) points out "that in them reality is artificially divided, that they have meaning and value only when together, but that, when taken singly, they lead through their isolation to meaninglessness, contradictions, and illusionary problems."

In the analysis of psychoneuroses it often becomes apparent that these antitheses are analogous to the antithesis of man—woman taken for real. The dynamics of the neurosis can therefore be regarded, and are often so understood by the neurotic, "as if" the patient wished to change from a woman to a man or wanted to hide his unmanliness. These tendencies, in their varied fullness, give the picture of what I have called the *masculine protest*.

Dogmatized Guiding Fiction

The neurotic carries his feeling of insecurity constantly with him. Therefore, "analogical thinking"—that is, the attempted solution of problems according to the analogy of former experiences—is more strongly and distinctly expressed in him than in normal individuals. His fear of the new (the *misoneism* of Lombroso) and of decisions and tests, which always confront one, originates from his deficient self-confidence. He has chained himself so much to guiding lines, takes them so literally, and seeks to realize them so much, to the exclusion of any alternative, that unknowingly he has renounced the unprejudiced, open-minded approach to questions of reality.

The feeling of insecurity forces the neurotic to a stronger attachment to fictions, guiding lines, ideals, and principles. These guiding principles are envisaged by the normal person also. But to him they are a figure of speech (*modus dicendi*), a device for distinguishing above from below, left from right, right from wrong; he does not lack the open-mindedness, when called upon to make a decision, to free himself from these fictions, and to reckon with reality. Neither are the world's phenomena for him divided into rigid antitheses; on the contrary, he strives constantly to keep his thoughts and actions detached from the unreal guiding line and to bring them into harmony with reality. The fact that he uses fictions at all as a means to an end arises from the usefulness of the fiction in casting up the accounts of life.

The neurotic, however, like the dependent child still removed from the world, and like primitive man, clings to the straw of his fiction, hypostasizes it—that is, arbitrarily ascribes reality to it, and seeks to realize it in the world. For this the fiction is unfit; it is still more unfit when, as in the psychoses, it is elevated to a dogma or anthropomorphized. "Act 'as if' you were lost, 'as if' you were the biggest, 'as if' you were the most hated." The symbol as a *modus dicendi* dominates our speech and thought. The neurotic takes it literally, and the psychotic attempts its realization. In my contributions to the theory of the neuroses this point is always emphasized and maintained.

More firmly than the normal individual does the neurotic fixate his god, his idol, his personality ideal, and cling to his guiding line, and with deeper purpose he loses sight of reality. The normal person, on the other hand, is always ready to dispense with this aid, this crutch. In this instance, the neurotic resembles a person who looks up to God, commends himself to the Lord, and then waits credulously for His guidance; the neurotic is nailed to the cross of his fiction. The normal individual, too, can and will create his deity, will feel drawn upward. But he will never lose sight of reality, and always take it into account as soon as action and work are demanded. The neurotic is under the hypnotic spell of a fictional life plan.

I readily follow here the ingenious views of Vaihinger, who maintains that historically ideas tend to grow from fictions (unreal but practically useful constructs) to hypotheses and later to dogmas. In Individual Psychology this change of intensity differentiates in a general way the thinking of the normal individual (fiction as an expedient), of the neurotic (attempt to realize the fiction), and of the psychotic (incomplete but safeguarding anthropomorphism and reification of the fiction: dogmatization).

An example of this progression would be the intensification of cautiousness into anxiety, and occasionally the reification of the anticipation of disaster into depression. These three steps of achieving security may be clarified as follows. Caution (normal, fiction): "as if" I could lose my money, "as if" I could be below. Anxiety (neurotic, hypothesis): "as if" I were *going* to lose my money, "as if" I were *going* to be below. Depression (psychotic, dogma): "as if" I *had* lost my

47

money, "as if" I were below. In other words, the stronger the feeling of insecurity, the more accentuated the fiction becomes through increasing abstraction from reality, and the more it approaches dogma. The patient nourishes and feigns within himself everything that brings him nearer to his guiding line, which in turn gives him security and thus is effective, albeit in a reduced circle. In this process reality becomes devaluated in various degrees, and the corrective paths that are adapted to society prove themselves increasingly insufficient.

CRITIQUE OF FREUD'S LIBIDO THEORY[11]

Less to be critical than to bring out my own viewpoint, may I separate from the fruitful and valuable contributions of Freud especially three of his fundamental views as erroneous, since they threaten to block progress in the understanding of neurosis.

Libido, Subject to Purpose, "Will to Power"

The first objection concerns the understanding of libido as the driving force in neurosis. Exactly neurosis, more clearly than normality, shows that a purpose forces the feeling of pleasure, its modification and its strength, into its own direction. Thus the neurotic can, so to speak, only with the healthy part of his psychological energy follow the allurement of attaining pleasure, whereas for the neurotic part "higher" goals are in operation. [*Later added:* If "libido" is translated into "love" with its many meanings, then by a clever use and expansion of these any event in the cosmos can be paraphrased by it—but not explained. By this paraphrasing many people get the impression that any human impulse is full of "libido," whereas in reality the lucky finder only extracts what he first put into it. Freud's latest interpretations seem as if his libido

[11] Translated from A1912a, 1928 ed., pp. 2–5.

48

theory moved rapidly toward our standpoint of social interest and the striving toward a personality ideal ("ego ideal"). In the interest of a growing understanding, this is to be greatly welcomed.]

We have found the neurotic purpose to be the enhancement of the self-esteem [*Erhöhung des Persönlichkeitsgefühls*], the simplest formula of which can be recognized in the exaggerated masculine protest. This formula, "I want to be a real man," is the guiding fiction [*later added:* so to speak the fundamental apperception (Jerusalem)[12]] in every neurosis, for which it claims greater reality value than the normal psyche. To this guiding idea are subordinated the libido, the sex drive, and any inclination to deviation, whatever their origin. Nietzsche's "will to power" and "will to seem" include much of our conception, which also touches in many points on the views of Féré[13] and older authors, according to whom the feeling of pleasure is rooted in the feeling of power, that of displeasure in the feeling of powerlessness.[14]

Sexual Etiology, a Metaphor

A second objection concerns Freud's basic view of the sexual etiology of the neurosis. Previously Pierre Janet (1894) had come precariously close to this view when he raised the question, "Should, then, the sexual feeling be the center, around which the other psychological syntheses are constructed?" The usefulness of the sexual metaphor leads many, especially the neurotic, to believe it to be an identity. [*Later added:* We frequently find among mystics—for example, Baader[15]—such expressions. Language also, with its incli-

12 Wilhelm Jerusalem (1854–1923), Austrian educator, philosopher, close to pragmatism, translator of William James' *Pragmatism*.

13 Charles S. Féré (1852–1907), French physician, student of Charcot.

14 Eventually Adler replaced "will to power" with "striving toward overcoming."

15 Franz Xavier von Baader (1765–1841), German mystic and professor of philosophy in Munich.

nation toward analogy, sets considerable traps for the unsuspecting investigator.] This usefulness must not deceive the psychologist.

The sexual content in the neurosis originates primarily in the conceived antithesis of "masculine-feminine" and is a change in form from the masculine protest. The sexual impetus in the fantasy and the life of the neurotic is oriented toward the masculine purpose; it is really no drive at all, but a compulsion. The entire syndrome of the sexual neurosis is a metaphor that reflects the patient's distance from his fictitious masculine final goal, and his attempts to overcome or perpetuate it.

It is strange that Freud, a connoisseur of the symbolic in life, was incapable of resolving the symbolic in the sexual apperception, to recognize the sexual as a jargon, as a *modus dicendi.*

Infantile Wishes Compelled by Goal

But we can understand this when we regard the third basic mistake, Freud's assumption that the neurotic is under the compulsion of infantile wishes [*later added:* especially the incest wish]. These wishes were assumed to come to life every night (dream theory), but also on certain occasions in reality. But in reality all infantile wishes themselves are already under the compulsion of the fictive final goal, have usually themselves the character of a guiding but co-ordinated thought, and for reasons of economy of thought are very well suited as symbols for calculating.

A sick girl who, feeling particularly insecure, leans on her father during her entire childhood, and thereby wants to be superior to her mother, can occasionally formulate this psychological constellation as the "incest parable," as if she wanted to be her father's wife. But thereby her final purpose is already given and effective: to have her insecurity contained by being with her father. Her growing psychomotor intelligence, her unconsciously affected memory answer all feelings of insecurity with the same aggression: with the preparatory attitude to seek refuge with her father as if she were his wife. There she finds the higher self-esteem that she has posited as her purpose and that she borrowed from the masculine ideal of her childhood, the overcompensation of her inferiority feeling.

When she is frightened by a courtship or marriage, insofar as these threaten new depreciations of her self-esteem [*later added:* insofar as she finds greater difficulties than with her father], she acts symbolically. Her readiness is purposefully turned against a feminine destiny, and lets her seek security where she has always found it—with her father. She applies a device, acts according to a nonsensical fiction, but thereby can certainly attain her purpose [*later added:* to avoid the feminine role].

The greater her feeling of insecurity, the more does this girl cling to her fiction and try to take it almost literally. Since human thinking is inclined toward symbolic abstraction, the patient sometimes—and with some effort, the analyst also— succeeds in capturing the neurotic striving for security in the symbol of an incest impulse [*later added:* to be superior as with her father].

In this purposeful process Freud had to see a revival of infantile wishes because he had assumed the latter as driving forces. We recognize in this infantile working method, in the extensive application of safeguarding working hypotheses as which we must regard the neurotic fiction, in this total longstanding preparation, in this tendency toward strong abstraction and symbolization, the appropriate means of the neurotic who wants to reach security, enhancement of his self-esteem, the masculine protest.

[*Later added:* The neurosis shows us the execution of erroneous intentions. All thinking and acting can be traced back to childhood experiences. Thus, regarding Freud's "regression," the psychologically ill person does not differ from one who is well. The difference is only that the psychologically ill person builds upon errors that go too far, and that he takes a poor attitude toward life. In itself, regression is the normal form of thinking and acting.]

SEXUALITY IN NEUROSIS[16]

Limited Role of Sexuality

The sex drive is of similar importance in everybody's life. Thus it would be an idle question to ask if a neurosis is possible without it. The question rather is, whether the sex drive is to be regarded as the beginning and end of everything, including the formation of all neurotic symptoms. To this I wish to reply with a brief description, not of the isolated sex drive, but of its development in the ensemble of all drives.

Biologically speaking, it would not be possible to maintain that every drive has a sexual component, including the drive to eat, the drive to see, and the drive to touch, etc. One must assume rather that organic evolution has led to developments that we must regard as the differentiation of originally present potentialities of the cell. Thus a nutritive organ has followed the will and need of assimilation; touch, auditory, and visual organs have followed the will and necessity to feel, hear, and see; a procreative organ followed the will and necessity for progeny.

The protection of all these organs became so necessary that it was approached from two sides: through the sensation of pain and that of pleasure. But these were not enough, and thus a third safeguard developed in the form of the organ of prudence, the organ of thinking, the brain. In the laboratory of nature, variations of all three safeguards can be found. Peripheral defects as well as heightened sensations of pain and pleasure in an inferior organ may occur. The most variable part, the central nervous system, takes over the final compensation.

The statement that the child is a polymorphous pervert, is a *hysteron proteron* [reverses the order of things], is a poetic license. The "sexual constitution" can be cultivated at will

[16] Translated with some omissions from A1911a as published in A1914a, 1928 ed., pp. 92–95. Parts of this translation have appeared in A1956b, pp. 56–60.

through experiences and education, especially on the basis of organ inferiorities. Even prematurity can be kept down or advanced. Sadistic and masochistic impulses are simply developments from the more harmless relationships of the regularly present need for support and the impulse toward independence once the masculine protest is involved with its intensification of rage, anger, and defiance.

Only the sexual organ, and it alone, develops the sexual factor in life in general and in the neurosis. As sexuality enters relations with the total drive life and its causes, so does every other drive. Approximately at the end of the first year of life—before the sex drive reaches a notable degree—the psychological life of the child is already richly developed.

Defiance, and Valuation of Masculinity

Freud mentions the view of older authors, who were later joined by Czerny,[17] that children who are stubborn on the toilet often become nervous. In contrast to other authors, Freud traces this defiance to their having sexual pleasure feelings during retention of feces. Although I have seen no incontestable case of this sort, I agree that children who do have such sensations when they retain feces will prefer precisely this kind of resistance when they become defiant. The decisive factor is the defiance, while the inferior organ determines the localization and selection of the symptoms.

I have much more frequently observed that such defiant children produce the feces before or after they have been brought to the toilet, or right next to the toilet; the same is true of the urination of such children. It is the same with eating and drinking; we need only to curb the drinking of certain children, and their "libido" increases into infinity. We need only to tell them that eating regularly is important, and their libido drops to zero. Can we take such "libido quantities" seriously, let alone energetically, and use them for comparisons? I have seen a thirteen-month-old boy who had

[17] Adalbert Czerny (1863–1941), German pediatrician.

barely learned to stand and to walk. If we sat him down, he got up; if we told him, "Sit down," he remained standing and looked mischievous. His six-year-old sister said on one such occasion, "Keep standing," and the child sat down. These are the beginnings of the masculine protest. The sexuality that is meanwhile budding is continuously exposed to its impacts and urges.

The valuation of masculinity also begins remarkably early. I have seen one-year-old boys and girls who evidently preferred male persons. Perhaps it is the sound of the voice, the assured appearance, the size, the strength, the calm that make the difference. I have pointed to this valuation critically in a review (A1910m) of Jung's "On Conflicts of the Soul of the Child," and as I see presently, with some success (see Hitschmann, and Jung, 1913). It regularly gives rise to the wish to become a man.

The other day I heard a little boy of two years say: "Mamma dumb, Nanny dumb, Toni [the cook] dumb, Usi [the sister] dumb, Gramma dumb!" When asked if Grampa was also dumb, he said: "Grampa big." Everybody noted that he had excepted his father. This was taken as a sign of respect. But one could easily understand that he wanted to declare all female members of his surroundings as stupid, himself and the male members as intelligent. He identified stupid with feminine, intelligent with masculine. This equation gave him importance.

I have pointed out in several papers that especially children who have a noticeable organ inferiority, who suffer from defects, who are insecure, and who fear humiliation and punishment the most, develop the craving and haste that ultimately dispose to neurosis. At an early age they will avoid tests of their worth or evade injuries to their sensitivity. They are bashful, blush easily, evade any test of their ability, and lose at an early age their spontaneity. This uncomfortable condition strongly urges toward safeguards. They want to be petted or want to do everything alone, are afraid of any kind of work, or read incessantly. As a rule they are precocious. Their thirst for knowledge is a compensatory product of their insecurity and reaches at an early age toward questions about

54

birth and sex differences. This strained and continuous fantasy activity must be understood as a stimulus for the sex drive as soon as a primitive knowledge of sex processes has been achieved. Here, as well, their goal is to prove their masculinity.

When birth fantasies, thoughts of castration, or analogous thoughts of being below, shortness of breath, being run over, etc., arise in the neurosis, these are neither wishes, nor repressed fantasies, but symbolically expressed fears of succumbing, against which the neurotic endeavors to safeguard himself, or which he calls to mind as a warning.

Fear of Female Dominance

A frequent type which, however, I have considered only rarely, are sons of strong-willed, masculine mothers. They are deeply imbued with a fear of the female. In their fantasies, the masculine woman—that is, the woman who wants to be on top, wants to be a man—often plays a part. Or else they have the symbolic fantasy of the *penis captivus* [vaginismus] —that is, the fear not to be able to come free from the female, borrowing the image from the intercourse of dogs. To be very careful, they exaggerate enormously. Their own sensuality appears to them gigantic, the female becomes a demon, and thus their distrust grows to the point where they become sexually incompetent. They must scrupulously test and spy on every girl (Griselda!).[18]

Again the question arises: Is what the neurotic shows us as libido, genuine? We would say, "No." His sexual prematurity is forced. His compulsion to masturbate serves his defiance and as a safeguard against the demon woman, and his love-passion only aims at victory. His love-bondage is a game that aims at not submitting to the "right" partner, and his deviating fantasies, even his active deviations, serve only to keep him away from love. They serve him, of course, as a

[18] Griselda, legendary heroine of a novel in *Decameron*, by Boccaccio (1313–75), is a poor peasant girl whose obedience and humility are most severely tested by her princely husband.

substitute, but only because he wants to play a hero role and is afraid of getting caught under the wheels if he goes the normal way. The "core problem" of the neurosis, the incest fantasy, usually has the function of nourishing the belief in one's own overpowering libido and therefore avoiding as much as possible any "real" danger.

A CASE OF SEXUALITY AS MEANS
OF PERSONAL STRIVING[19]

I shall now present a case who is still in treatment. But the structure of his neurosis is clear enough that I may give excerpts as illustrations of my assertions.

The patient is a twenty-two-year-old draftsman who complained about frequent trembling of his hands for the past year and a half, and frequent nocturnal pollutions. At the age of five years he lost his father, who had become blind, and who during his last three years was hardly able to walk or even stand by himself. Not until he was seventeen years old did the patient learn that his father had died of spinal consumption, a disease supposedly caused by excessive sexual intercourse. At that time the patient had been masturbating heavily and now became very frightened about his future.

The patient had frequent occasion to fear for his future. As a little boy he was weaker and smaller than his siblings and playmates, and always sought protection from his mother, who conspicuously pampered him as the youngest child. He was always timid and shy. However, he soon insisted on having the last word and on being the first among his playmates, so that he never made friends. Soon he wanted to know everything, in sexual matters as well as in school. His ambition was to become a great man, and he was the only one of his siblings to go to high school.

The following early recollection reflects the masculine protest of his childhood. He was lying on his back in the grass

[19] Translated from A1911a as published in A1914a, 1928 ed., pp. 95–100.

and saw above, in the clouds, the picture of his father—he, the feminine weakling, in the feminine position, with his father above, in the position of the man.

Until recent years he had some feminine traits, and as a child he was often asked to take a girl's part in plays, dressed as a girl. For a long time he shared a bed with his two-years-older sister, where he satisfied his sexual curiosity. In his dreams he had occasional fantasies of incest, relating to his mother and sister.

His mother was very moralistic, and he could observe her harsh discipline toward his older brothers when they had love affairs. Regarding the marriages of her children, she was primarily concerned with material matters, and she harassed one of her daughters-in-law for many years because the daughter was poor. All in all, his mother dominated him in every respect.

Our patient had erections and masturbated from his ninth year on. Later he frequently had erections when he was in the company of girls. At the age of fourteen he began to masturbate more regularly. This spoiled any company of girls so much for him that he preferred to be alone. He became convinced that his sexual libido was immense and hardly to be coped with.

When he learned of his father's disease and had to assume that his father was as sensuous as he himself, this gave him a powerful shock, and he stopped masturbating! Frequently he let himself be carried away to kiss a girl despite his fear of an erection, but afterward avoided for a long while any place where he might meet girls.

Was his libido really as great as he assumed? Especially was it so great that he had to safeguard himself by the fear of being with girls? Certain things would speak strictly against this. He had grown up in rural circumstances and later alone at a high school where ample occasions for sexual intercourse could be found. Some girls had made sufficient advances. As mentioned, when he learned of his father's illness and its cause, he immediately stopped masturbating. Soon after, he took up normal intercourse, but not frequently, and was easily detained from it by the thought of the expense. Girls willing to accommodate him, he left after he had conquered them, for fear of not being able to get rid of them later. He imagined every woman as a demon, extremely sensuous, wanting to dominate him, and toward whom he might be weak. But he remained strong. At the same time he looked down on women, considered them inferior, distrusted them, and always attributed egotistical motives to them.

Two years ago he met a beautiful but poor girl who at first attracted him. When they were contemplating marriage he began to suffer from profuse pollutions and, with prostitutes, from premature ejaculation or impotence. At that time he also began to tremble at work, so that he could draw only with great difficulty, and to hesitate in his speech. But these symptoms occurred only after intercourse or pollution the night before.

The most obvious assumption, that he had seen his father trembling and now imitated him to scare himself, was not confirmed by the patient. But he remembered an old high school teacher who trembled and hesitated in his speech. Then our patient interpreted this as a sign of old age in people who in their youth had had too much sexual intercourse. He had also read a pamphlet that ascribed trembling and hesitating speech to pollutions.

Further information came from his thoughts about the imminent marriage. His mother would be dissatisfied; his rich relatives would look down on him; the girl would marry him only for material reasons; she was sensuous and would draw him into the ecstasy of her lust; he was sensuous himself, and the consequences of his masturbation, pollutions, and sexual relations already set in. On the basis of these arrangements he withdrew from the girl, without really knowing how he could get rid of her completely. This hesitation is the equivalent of a "No" and at the same time safeguards him from other girls.

He trembles today to remind himself of what will threaten him someday. He trembles in order to escape his basic fear of again being under the power of a woman, as he had been with his mother. He trembles in order to avoid the fate of his father or that of the old teacher. He trembles to escape the demon woman, as well as his own sensuality and that of the

58

girl. And he trembles in order to satisfy his mother's wish, contrary to his own, not to marry this girl, and thus, in the last analysis, prove again his dependency on a woman.

This is the reason for the notion of his own excessive sensuality as well as that of the woman, for his frequent erections and pollutions. The latter happen largely because he wants and needs them, and because he continuously thinks of sexual matters in order to engineer them.

I am asking again: How should one appraise the libido of this neurotic where everything has become contrived, arranged, magnified, distorted, a purposive unnatural product, an asset and a liability at the same time?

The following dream reflects all these traits and emphasizes the most important dream tendency, that of safeguarding. "A buxom young woman sits in the nude on a sofa. I don't know what she says." He thinks of a prostitute and his senses leave him when he sees the naked woman. "She tries to seduce me." The demon woman. "I wanted to go along, but at the last moment realized that I was about to have a pollution and held myself back from her." The attempt to take a course in life without a woman. The dream as a whole is a warning against pollutions and intercourse as the exogenous factors of tabes.

The simple explanation that tabes was the result of syphilis had no effect. Only the understanding for his exaggerated safeguarding tendencies stopped the trembling.

What then is the core problem of this neurosis? The incest fantasy served only the purpose to guarantee his belief in his exaggerated, criminal fantasy. The repression of his inclination to masturbate, which was easy, was followed by an equivalent or better safeguard, the pollutions. Only when he was facing marriage and feared to be underneath again as formerly, not like the man, the father, on top, to come under the influence of a woman, and thus to be forced to admit his inferiority before everybody, did he become "sick."

Incidentally, he could tolerate as little to be subordinated to a man, be it one of his colleagues, whom he continuously depreciated and with whom he was constantly on bad terms; teachers who appeared to him in frequent examination dreams; or his superior, before whom he had on certain days his attacks of trembling.

How, then, does sexuality come into the neurosis, and what part does it play there? It is awakened early and stimulated when inferiority and a strong masculine protest exist; it is regarded and felt as gigantic so that the patient may safeguard himself in good time; or it is devaluated and eliminated as a factor if this serves the tendency of the patient. In general one cannot take the sexual impulses of the neurotic or of civilized man as genuine and count on them, let alone continue to represent them, no matter how they are viewed, as the fundamental factor of the healthy or diseased mental life. They are never causes, but always worked-over material and means of personal striving.

The true attitude toward life can be clearly seen already in the first dreams and recollections of a person. This is evidence that the recollection is construed in the sense of a planful procedure.

Our patient's earliest dream, approximately from his fifth year, was: "A bull follows me and wants to gore me." The patient believes that he had this dream shortly after the death of his father, who had been bedridden for a long time. When we establish a connection to the fantasy of the father in the clouds (God?), the thought of the boy's fear of death occurs. The later "reconstruction" (Birstein, 1913) probably took the tabes of the father and his death, which had so shocked the patient, into consideration. The bull must, further, have represented masculinity to the boy, who had grown up in the country, which showed him as the pursued one in an unmanly—that is, female—role. Even if one does not want to go that far in the interpretation, one gets the feeling that the child is filled with dark premonitions.

The second dream continues the bad expectations. He felt as if he had fallen off and landed on a hard surface. Dreams of falling always point toward a pessimistic carefulness of the dreamer, which frightens with bad possibilities, with "being underneath."

His earliest recollection was, he believes, that on the first day of school he went very fast into the girls' school and

60

cried when he was sent off to the boys' school. We may take this as a metaphor of his desire not to be sick, miserable, dead, "underneath," like his father, but to seek the future healthy, strong, and alive, corresponding to a female role as he found it in his strong mother who, according to everyone, conducted her affairs like a man.

The hesitation [*later added:* from a lack of preparation] in his masculine role with all the pertaining, including neurotic phenomena, had become the axis of his psychological life. His sex life necessarily corresponded to this.

CRITIQUE OF REPRESSION[20]

Repression—Culture Circularity

I may presuppose in this circle a knowledge of "repression" as this has been conceived and described by Freud. The causes of repression, however, and the path from repression to neurosis are by no means as clear as is generally assumed in the Freudian school. Attempts at explanation created a very large number of auxiliary constructs, often unproven or even unprovable, not to mention those constructs that in the most obvious manner resort to analogies from physics or chemistry, such as "damming up," "increased pressure," "fixation," "flowing back into infantile paths," "projections," and "regression."

The causes of repression are conceived too summarily in the papers of this school, as dogmatically used stereotypes, but also as intuitions the bases of which are always worth determining. Regarding successful and unsuccessful repression, this problem becomes all the more mysterious if we trace it to "sexual constitution." The simple statement of repression, however, shows lack of psychological insight. The causes of "sublimation" and "substitute formation" are likewise not explained; instead, the same idea is repeated in different words.

[20] Translated from A1911b as published in A1914a, 1928 ed., pp. 100–6, with parts having appeared in A1956b, pp. 60–67.

"Organic repression" appears as merely an emergency exit, showing that changes in the modes of operation are possible; it has hardly any bearing on the theory of the neuroses. Thus the following are considered: repressed drives and drive complexes, repressed complexes, repressed fantasies, repressed experiences, and repressed wishes.

And above all this, there hovers as *deus ex machina* one magic formula—pleasure, of which Nietzsche says so well: "All pleasure wants eternity, wants deep, deep eternity" (*Zarathustra,* iii, 15). And Freud says: "Man cannot forego any pleasure he has ever experienced."

Under this assumption those drastic forms arise that every work of a disciple of Freud must show: the boy who is compelled to suckle at his mother's breast; the neurotic who seeks again and again the enjoyment of being bathed in wine or amniotic fluid; on up to the purer sphere where the man who is seeking the right girl will never find her because he is seeking the irreplaceable mother.

This way of observing represented an important methodological advance. But it lent itself to reification and freezing of the psyche which, in reality, is constantly at work and mindful of the future. The acceptance of the concept of complex was a further step toward priority of the topological over the dynamic view. Naturally, this was not carried so far that the principle of energetics, the *panta rhei* [everything is in a state of flux], could not have been brought in as an afterthought.

The real question is this: Is the driving factor in the neurosis the repression, or is it, as I should like to state it in neutral terms for the time being, the deviating, irritated psyche, in the examination of which repression can also be found?

And now I beg you to note: Repression takes place under the pressure of culture, under the pressure of the "ego drives," with the aid of thoughts of an abnormal sexual constitution, of sexual precocity.

QUESTION: Where does our culture come from?
ANSWER: From the repression.

Efforts and Attitudes Toward the Environment

And what about the "ego drives," a concept as redundant and empty as few others? Do they not have the same "libidinous" character as the sex drive? The ego drives are not rigidified and separate, but [later added: according to the observations of Individual Psychology] efforts and attitudes toward the environment, wanting to be significant, striving for power, for dominance, toward being above. With this understanding we must focus theoretically and practically on two possibilities: Wanting to be significant (a) may inhibit, repress, or modify certain drives, (b) must primarily have the effect of stimulating.

For us the constant factor is the culture, the society, and its institutions. The drives, whose satisfaction is actually considered as a purpose, must be relegated to the function of direction-giving means to initiate satisfactions usually in the distant future. The eye, the ear, and also the skin have acquired the peculiar ability of extending our radius of effectiveness beyond the bodily spatial sphere. Through presensitivity, our psyche steps beyond the present—that is, temporally beyond the limits of primitive drive satisfaction. Here increased efforts are as urgent as repressions, and these relationships include the necessity for an extensive safeguarding system, of which the neurosis is a small part. [Later added: This means that the neurosis is first of all a safeguarding device.]

These efforts begin on the first day of infancy and change all bodily and psychological tendencies to such an extent that, for example, what we see never represents anything original or primary, anything that has not been influenced, or anything that has become changed only at a later time. Instead, the adaptation of the child directs and modifies his drives until he has adapted himself in some way to the environment. In this first stage of life one cannot speak of a permanent model nor of identification when the child orients himself by a model, for this is often the only way for immediate drive satisfaction.

63

If we consider the varied manner and tempo in which drives have been satisfied everywhere and at all times, and how much this has depended on social institutions and economic conditions, we arrive at a conclusion that is analogous to the above, namely that drive satisfaction, and consequently the quality and strength of the drive, are at all times variable and therefore not measurable.

As noted before, from observations of the sex drive in neurotics I have come to the conclusion that the apparently libidinous and sexual tendencies of the neurotic as well as those of the normal individual in no way permit inferences regarding the strength or composition of their sex drives.

Adaptation, Obedience, and Defiance

How does the child adapt himself to a given family environment? Let us recall how diversely child organisms express themselves, even during the first months of life, when one can still gain an over-all view. Some children can never get enough to eat, others are quite moderate; some refuse changes in diet, others want to eat everything. The same is true with regard to seeing, hearing, excretion, bathing, and relations to other persons of the environment. Yet already during the first days the child feels reassured if we take him into our arms. Educational influences that smooth the way for the child are of far-reaching significance here.

Already these first adaptations contain affective values in relation to the persons of the environment. The child is reassured, feels secure, loves, obeys, etc.; or he becomes insecure, timid, defiant, and disobedient. If one intervenes early with intelligent tactics, a condition results that might be described as one of carefree cheerfulness [*later added:* forgivingness], and the child will hardly feel the coercion that is contained in every education. Mistakes in education, on the other hand, especially when the organs are insufficiently developed, lead to such frequent disadvantages and feelings of displeasure that the child seeks safeguards. By and large, two chief trends remain from this situation: oversubmissiveness, or rebellion and tendency toward independence. Obedience or defiance—the human psyche is capable of operating in either direction [see A1910d].

These direction-giving tendencies modify, change, inhibit, or excite every drive impulse to such an extent that any manifestly innate drive can be understood only from this point of view. "Fair is foul, and foul is fair," as the witches chant in *Macbeth*. Grief becomes joy, pain changes into pleasure, life is thrown away, death appears desirable—as soon as defiance interferes strongly. What the opponent loves will be hated, and what others discard will be highly valued. What culture prohibits, what parents and educators disadvise, precisely that will be chosen as the most ardently desired goal. An object or a person will attain value only if others will thereby suffer. Defiant individuals will always persecute others, yet will always consider themselves persecuted. Thus a certain greed or hasty desire arises that has one analogy only, namely the murderous struggle of all against all, the kindling of envy, avarice, vanity, and ambition in our modern society.

The tension from person to person is too great in the neurotic; his drive desire is so intensified that in restless expectation he continuously chases after his triumph. The clinging to old childhood disorders, such as thumb sucking, enuresis, nail biting, and stuttering, is to be explained in this way. In cases where these tendencies, which are only apparently libidinous, have been permanently retained, we can confidently speak of defiance.

The same holds for so-called early masturbation, sexual precocity, and premature sexual intercourse. I knew a seventeen-year-old girl from a good family who had frequent sexual intercourse from her fourteenth year on. Even so she was frigid. Whenever she quarreled with her mother, which happened regularly at brief intervals, the girl always knew how to secure sexual intercourse for herself. Another girl wet the bed after each depreciation on the part of her mother, and soiled it with feces.

Poor progress in school, forgetfulness, lack of occupational satisfaction, and sleeping compulsion are likewise phenomena

65

of protest in the neurotic. In the fight against an opponent they are retained as valuable, I do not say, as pleasurable.

A part of this kind of psyche is described by Siegmund in Wagner's *Walkyrie:* "How many I met, wherever I found them, whether I courted a friend or a brother, I was always ostracized. Misfortune rested on me. What I considered right, others considered bad. Whatever appeared bad to me, others favored it. I got into a fight wherever I was. I met with anger wherever I moved. When I longed for bliss, I aroused but pain."

Thus develops the character of the neurotic that I have described most explicitly in "On Neurotic Disposition" (A1909a) and *The Neurotic Constitution* (A1912a).

Neurotic Striving for Significance, with Two Case Examples

Whence comes this craving for significance, the pleasure in the perverted (*Lust am Verkehrten*), this defiant clinging to errors, and these safeguarding measures against too much and too little, in which latter the patient takes recourse to self-depreciation, only to assert himself afterward, or elsewhere? (See my deliberations on pseudomasochism, A1910f.)

As you know, I have made two foci of psychological development responsible for this, which I shall mention here only briefly. The one rests in the emergence of an increased inferiority feeling, which I have always observed in connection with inferior organs. The other is a more or less distinct hint of an earlier fear of playing a feminine role. Both support the need of rebellion and the attitude of defiance to such an extent that neurotic traits will always develop, whether the individual concerned is considered well, is being treated for neurosis, or makes a name for himself as a genius or a criminal.

From this point on, feelings are falsified. We are no longer dealing with simple, natural relationships but with chasing after and grabbing presumed triumphs that seem to lie tempting in the future and that permanently fixate a diseased attitude. The neurotic lives and thinks much farther into the

66

future than the normal individual and usually evades the present test situations. Very frequently the character traits of the neurotic are hidden. This explains why when I described them, they were considered to be rare, the peculiarities of the eccentric.

What does the neurotic say to these traits of his? Some are aware of them even if they do not recognize their extent or consequences. Many have known them once and then forgotten them out of ambition and vanity. They then safeguard themselves from this undignified egotism by a sort of opposite action. We see in such cases egotistic drive impulses of an undignified kind—for example, avarice, revenge, malice, cruelty —replaced by others, of an ethical content. Thus "the passion to be significant" must be inside, must have taken the lead!

Case 1. A good example of such drive repression is a case of stuttering that I reported in a lecture before the Philosophical Society in Vienna (see A1908e).

Stuttering is a disorder that in every point is constituted by the mechanism of the masculine protest. The patient had delivered a donation of two hundred kronen for charity purposes in the seventh district in Vienna. He was supposed to be at a distinguished restaurant in the inner city punctually, and was already very hungry. Yet he walked the whole way, ill-humored and tired as he was. He wanted to save the carfare, as it turned out during the analysis. As is the case in all neuroses, he wanted to have everything, all the money, all women, all souls, and continuously attempted to depreciate others.

He paid avid attention to his evaluation by others. He could lead an ascetic life when it would bring him recognition; he could be exceedingly studious when it was a matter of excelling others; he could be charitable when people would see it; but he was a miser in small matters when he believed nobody noticed him. When someone accomplished something, he was in bad humor; when someone was liked, he attacked. He was incessantly at odds with his father and not afraid to threaten suicide when he wanted to have his will. His stuttering was directed against his father, upset all his father's plans,

67

and secured for our patient greater freedom of movement. At the same time, he safeguarded himself from marriage. He broke off any relationship to a girl after a while, with the explanation that as long as he stuttered he could not get married. This example of the "long love series," as Freud calls it [*later added:* and erroneously refers to the Oedipus complex], came about in reality because the patient wanted all women, like Don Juan, and was afraid of two things from which he wanted to safeguard himself: (1) that he would be dominated by a woman, be subservient to her, and would have to give up others; (2) that with his egotism (of which he was conscious, however, only in his feelings, not in his thoughts), he would be a bad husband and father, and would therefore be deceived by his wife and children as punishment.

The uncovering of these protest traits is generally the first part of analysis and is usually followed by improvement, but regularly by strong resistance, which manifests itself in attempts to depreciate the therapist.

Case 2. Another of my patients came from Hungary to be treated because, as it turned out in the analysis, he could not bear that his sister, whom I had cured, spoke well of me. You will say, he was in love with his sister. Correct! But only when she thought well of a man. At first the patient was polite, almost humble and modest, and was full of integrity and truthfulness. When I proved to him his revengefulness, malice, dishonesty, and envy, he was for a long time furious, but in the end admitted everything. But he also declared that now he would have to remain with me until he would be well, even if that would take several years. When I replied that he would remain as long as I would approve, he sat for a while in thought. Then he asked with a smile: "Has anyone yet in treatment with you committed suicide?" I replied: "Not yet, but I am prepared for it at any time." "To knock the weapon from his hand"—that is, to make the neurotic's pathological means appear ineffective—is the goal of any psychotherapeutic tactic.

This patient suffered among other things also from sleeplessness. He urged me to discuss this symptom, saying that he would be satisfied if he only could get his sleep back. The explanation went smoothly, and he fully regained his sleep. But he did not tell me about it until quite some time later.

Has then the patient repressed his character traits? Not at all. His entire masculine protest became apparent, however, in a way that he felt was not very offensive, innerly nor outwardly. But Freud describes in similar terms the result of unsuccessful repression. The traces of the repressed drive impulses can always be clearly recognized in the neurosis, an insight to which Freud himself has contributed. They can be seen not only in the fantasies of the neurotic and in his dreams, but especially through psychological analysis, which teaches us to recognize the small and great disharmonies and incongruencies in the life of the patient and permits their resolution.

Inferiority-feeling-Masculine-protest Dynamics and Onset of Neurosis

Of course, this work is still quite incomplete when we have only uncovered the neurotic character. But it is important especially because this knowledge is a warning to the patient. The more difficult part of the treatment leads then in my experience regularly to the two points of psychological development of the neurotic, to the sources of neuroses: the feeling of inferiority and the masculine protest.

But now to the main question: Through what does the neurotic become ill? When does his neurosis become manifest? Freud has paid less attention to this point. But we know that he assumes the cause to lie in an incident through which the repression is strengthened and the old psychological conflict is renewed. This certainly lacks clarity. Perhaps the present discussion will help solve the problem.

According to my experience, the neurotically disposed individual, who in fact always suffers, responds to any feeling of disparagement or even its expectation with an acute or chronic attack. This marks the time of the onset of the neurosis. New drive-repressions are only incidental phenomena that form under the accentuated pressure of the masculine protest, the urge for significance, and the safeguarding tendencies.

CASE OF SEXUALITY CONTINUED[21]

Fear of Female Superiority

I want to demonstrate the above with the first-mentioned case. Our patient remembered that he trembled for the first time while playing the violin at a time when he should have promised marriage to Albertine, the girl whom he apparently loved so much. On account of the trembling he stopped playing the violin. Now we learn the following: Albertine was an excellent pianist, so that he often thought he would like to accompany her on the violin if only he could play better. And if he married her, there might even have been a concert, in which his wife would have been definitely ahead of him. This had been the fear all his life: a wife who would be superior to him.

I have never met a neurotic who would not at least secretly have been afraid of this. From the literature I only would like to mention the case of Ganghofer, reported by Alexander Witt (1911), furthermore a quite analogous case from the memoirs of Stendhal.[22] In both cases we find childhood recollections of a woman stepping over the child. Fantasies of giant women, Walkyries, women who tie or beat boys, who at times do this in pseudomasochism; fairy tales of witches, nymphs, women with masculine genitals, with a fish tail, or similar to the childhood recollection of Leonardo da Vinci are frequent and find their equivalent and similar counterparts in the equally frequent birth fantasies, castration thoughts, and wishes for the role of a girl. This latter often appears in very mild form in the question: "What would be the feelings of a girl?"

Our patient had a similar childhood recollection, namely

[21] Translated from A1911b as published in A1914a, 1928 ed., pp. 106–9, with parts having appeared in A1956b, pp. 67–69.
[22] Pseudonym of Marie Henri Beyle (1783–1842), French novelist.

that a servant girl was above him. That means: "The woman is stronger than the man!" Early childhood recollections, like fantasies of vocational choice, always contain the person's effective outlook on life, regardless of whether the recollections are genuine, fantasied, or reconstructed (Birstein, 1913). (See A1913d.)

This early recollection of our patient was not repressed nor forgotten, but apparently completely disconnected from his present or former psychological state and thus denuded of all its significance. Had it been a causative factor? No one can assume that. From his early history, recollections appear of an energetic mother who as a widow administered her large estate, got along without a husband, and of whom people said she was like a man. This mother who pampered him, yet also punished him, was definitely superior to him.

When subsequently his yearning awakened that he, as a weakly child with feminine habitus who wet his bed and for this was often ridiculed and punished, should become a man, and when he expressed his masculine protest in thoughts, dreams, and defiant bedwetting, such recollections came to his help as that he often play-acted in feminine clothes and that on his first school day he went with his older sisters to the girls' school and refused with tears to go to the boys'. And still there were aggravations that drove him farther into the masculine protest. His pubic hair grew late, and his penis appeared shorter than those of his peers. He established his goal all the higher, wanted to accomplish extraordinary things, wanted to be the first in school, at the office, until he found Albertine, of whose superiority he was afraid.

Depreciation Tendency

Our patient had depreciated all girls and women, including his mother, in the usual way, out of fear. They were not intelligent, not independent, and were frivolous. As Hamlet says: "You jig, you amble, and you lisp, and nickname God's creatures, and make your wantonness your ignorance. Go to, I'll no more on't; it hath made me mad." Our patient additionally claimed that women smelled bad.

Olfactory component. Incidentally, Freud has repeatedly attributed to the "olfactory component" special significance as a libidinous component; but it appears more and more as a neurotic fraud. A fifty-four-year-old patient who from fear of childbirth became seriously neurotic, had toward the end of her treatment the following unambiguous dream: "I am unpacking eggs, and they all stink. I say: Phew, how they stink." The following day her husband was supposed to arrive. She had already depreciated all medical authorities in Germany and Austria.

A neurotic actress in talking about love affairs said: "I am not at all afraid of such affairs. I am actually completely amoral. There is only one thing: I have found that all men smell bad, and that violates my aesthetic sense." We will understand: With such an attitude one can well afford to be amoral without incurring any danger. (For several such cases, see A1911d.) Masculine neurotics do likewise; it is their revenge on the female.

Europeans and Chinese, Americans and Negroes, Jews and Aryans mutually reproach one another for their smell. A four-year-old boy says each time he passes by the kitchen, "It stinks." The cook is his enemy. We wish to call this phenomenon the depreciation tendency, a tendency that finds an analogy in the fable of the fox and the sour grapes.

Sexual relations. From what does the depreciation tendency originate? It originates from the fear of an injury to one's own sensitivity. It is likewise a safeguarding tendency, initiated by the urge toward significance, and is psychologically of the same rank as the wish to be above, to celebrate sexual triumphs, to fly, or to stand on a ladder, staircase, or the gable of a house (Solness in Ibsen's *The Master Builder*). One quite regularly finds in the neurotic that the tendencies to depreciate a woman and to have intercourse with her go closely together. The feelings of the neurotic express plainly: "I wish to depreciate the woman by sexual intercourse." Afterward he is likely to leave her and to turn to others. I have called this the Don Juan characteristic of the neurotic. It corresponds to Freud's "love series" (*Liebesreihe*), which he interprets in a fantastic manner.

The depreciation of women, the mother as well as all other women, causes many a neurotic to seek refuge with prostitutes (A1913g), where he spares himself the bother of depreciation, and beyond this, sees his relatives burst with fury. The boy sees or suspects that it is masculine to be on top. Usually the mother is the woman from whom he tries to establish distance. He wants to play the man toward her, to depreciate her, and to elevate himself. He may even call her names, beat or ridicule her, become disobedient and obstreperous toward her, try to boss her, etc.

Oedipus Complex or Masculine Protest?

Whether and how much libido are involved here are totally indifferent. The neurotic's masculine protest also may turn against other girls and women, usually on the path of least resistance, toward servants and governesses. Later he becomes habituated to masturbation and pollutions, combining with these safeguarding tendencies against the demon woman.

This applied also to our patient. When he could not reach his goal with his mother—namely, to be the master—he turned toward the servant girl with whom, at the age of six to seven, he had more success. He sees her in the nude and reaches under her skirts. Until the present this form of aggression was his chief sexual activity. He could have intercourse only with prostitutes—until he had to prove to himself that he could not marry. Then the pollutions and the impotence began and the fear of his enormous sexuality together with the presumed dangers of paralysis and trembling in old age. Or better: Trembling and stammering set in like pollution and impotence, because they could safeguard him from marriage.

Probably he would have broken off the relationship with Albertine in time and have been spared from neurosis if a third party had not appeared on the scene. This was too much for his pride. Now he could not give way, and yet he did not want to grasp. His "libidinous" strivings, the desire to possess Albertine, filled his consciousness completely. But the unconscious spoke a firm "No" and detained him from courtship by arranging symptoms that argued against marriage. Quite equivalent is his conscious thought: "I can marry only when I have a good job." But at the same time, symptoms developed that made a promotion impossible.

What has our patient "repressed"? Perhaps his sex drive, his libido? Of this he is so conscious that he thinks continuously of how to protect himself from it. A fantasy? His fantasy is in brief that the female is above him, is the stronger. I needed all my preparations to show him the connection between this and similar fantasies, and his neurosis. But then it turns out that this fantasy itself is only a warning, erected by the patient to obtain himself significance, even by devious paths.

Had he repressed libidinal urges toward his mother—that is, does he suffer from an Oedipus complex? I have seen many patients who have come to know their "Oedipus complex" very well, without feeling any improvement. Once one appreciates the masculine protest in the Oedipus complex, one is no longer justified in speaking of a complex of fantasies and wishes. One will then learn to understand that the apparent "Oedipus complex" is only a small part of the overpowering neurotic dynamic, a stage of the masculine protest, which in itself insignificant is, however, instructive in its context. It is a situation that must be taken symbolically and that yields the more important insights into the characterology of the neurotic, as other situations also do.

PART II

Sexuality and the Individual

3

SEXUALITY

DEVELOPMENT OF THE SEXUAL FUNCTION[1]

Because of the existing confusing, unverifiable, and misleading interpretations of the sexual function, we must start with the fundamental physiological and psychological facts. These give no reason for accepting such far-fetched views as an omnipotent sexual libido dominating the human mind and psyche. Such a distorted theory as that of Freud and, with some variations, of Jung, finds acceptance because of (a) the novelty, (b) the many troubles of the numerous persons with neurotic tendencies, (c) the open or hidden feeling of unsatisfied wishes in persons for whom wish fulfillment is the main problem of life.

Humanity—individuals and groups—have always wanted to find a universal power behind all phenomena and experiences of life. Individual Psychology, in a much broader and deeper sense, accepts instead the fact of life itself, in its explainable and unexplainable aspects. One of the first of these aspects is that all strivings, thoughts, feelings, characteristics, expressions, and symptoms aim toward a successful solution of social tasks.

The large number of failures in love and marriage are like all other failures due to lack of preparation. We do not recog-

[1] Reprinted with some editing from A1945b, except for the last section. Original date of paper unknown. A1945b has also been reprinted as A1964a, pp. 219–23.

nize a sexual object. Love and marriage are a task of two equal human beings forming a unit, which can be rightly solved only if these persons are trained for sufficient social interest.

Individual Psychology rejects the view that individual wishes, or the bad results of their repression, are the main problems of life. Such a concept betrays the self-centered nature of a person, as it is often seen in pampered children. It is equally unconstructive to hold to the heritage of our ancestors, who in some ways had not reached the present, still not sufficient, degree of social interest. These authors probably turn their glances to heredity and ancestors because they are satisfied to indulge in some inherited possessions rather than making an effort to use these possessions for new contributions to the welfare of humanity, for an increase in social interest.

Social Adaptation of Functions

So far as we can see, a human being is human, and is rightly called so, because he possesses by heredity all the potentialities needed for coping with social problems. But in order to cope he must develop himself physically and mentally as much as possible. The main question that arises now is: For what? For what goal must the individual strive and develop his inherited human potentialities? Individuals and humanity as a whole use their potentialities, gifts of our ancestors, for increasing these gifts in a world changed by human beings for the benefit of the whole human family. This has been done, of course, only so far as the level of social interest allowed. In addition, we must understand that all problems of life can be solved adequately only by a sufficient degree of social interest.

All human functions—brought into the world by the newborn child as potentialities for development in a social environment—must be adapted to the demands of the outside world. Eating, looking, hearing, making sounds, and moving become more and more adapted to the achievement of this goal.

All human functions are in the beginning of life in a state of confusion and automatic, and are only slowly directed toward interplay with others and with the environment. Gradually the creative power of the child accepts the challenge of the outside world, absorbs experiences, and responds to them in a way that he deems successful for taking part in the surrounding social life. His way of eating becomes proper; his ways of looking, hearing, touching, and moving prove his willingness to co-operate more or less. His thinking and talking contain more and more common values and common sense. His functions of excretion are, or should be, in agreement with the social form of his environment. Thumb sucking, nail biting, etc., being unsocial actions and sources of infections, will cease if the child accepts the social rules of the game of his environment. If they do not, the reason is always that the child has not found the way toward social culture and is striving for a personal goal of superiority.

Primary Sexual Phase

The sexual function is certainly inherited and shows itself, in the beginning, in a higher degree of the tickling sensation. Expanding, along with all the others, it leads to turgescence, erections, and concomitant feelings through automatic impulses. Touching and the resulting pleasurable tickling sensation lead to early repetition of the act, the more so if the child, as a whole, likes to go his own way and is more inclined toward wish fulfillment than toward co-operating, as is the case with the pampered child.

In that way the right co-operation is deferred until a much later time, and the child is compelled to remain at the primary phase of the sexual function. Until he has reached the right age for making the sexual function a task for two persons of different sexes—the secondary, social phase of the sexual function—only autoeroticism in its many forms is available.

79

In the primary phase, the usual course is masturbation. The social feeling of humanity has been and always will be opposed to this because in its hidden thinking and knowing humanity wants the secondary phase to be developed. But there is a discrepancy between the gradual development of the secondary phase, and the strong opposition toward letting children perform it on account of the dangers involved and the necessity to permit it only to physically and mentally mature boys and girls. This creates for younger children an insoluble situation. Not only parents and teachers and dangerous, stupid books and remarks increase the conflicts in the mind of the child, but his social interest, gained in the first three years, also counteracts autoeroticism. Physicians and clergymen agree more and more that the primary phase cannot be entirely avoided, that it is a natural development and should not be treated harshly, and that it does not harm the child physically or mentally.

During this primary phase one can see the power of the social interest. Remorse and diversions are common and willingly accepted. Also the frequency diminishes. But the pampered and greedy child, not able to resist any temptation, is in a worse state and often uses autoeroticism for other purposes —to abuse the attention of the parents, to entice other children, or as an alibi for defeats in school or later life.

Varieties of Autoeroticism

Later, in their distress, children often turn to other varieties of masturbation, such as indulging in erotic fantasies, using erotic pictures and other means of incitement, and sometimes another child. This opens the way to so-called homosexuality, which is only one of the many varieties of masturbation, often found among egocentric, vain adults who cling to the primary, autoerotic phase of the sexual function.

The problem of the so-called natural development of sexuality is not as simple as, for example, psychoanalysis teaches; for whatever might be assumed as the normal, natural development of sexuality cannot take place when the external circumstances stipulate a compulsory development. Keep in mind that no childhood offense is considered as serious and punished as severely as development toward the sexual norm. To be sure, when children behave in any childish, unnatural sexual way, one is not disposed in a friendly way toward them, and they are usually punished. But there is immeasurable horror when a child behaves in the normal sexual way. Thus what we observe in children again and again must be regarded as influenced by external circumstances. We do not know what development sexuality would take if we would not, and would not have to, set up barriers against it.[2]

Certain types who show sexual stimulation when irritated or fearful (as others respond with heart palpitations or intestinal or bladder troubles) indulge in sadistic or masochistic daydreams and night dreams. This type may later become a complete failure in his sexual function by developing the deviation of sadism or masochism.

All the other deviations—fetishism, sodomy, necrophilia, etc.—are varieties of the primary sexual phase. They probably always betray the misconception and the style of life of a pampered or neglected child who has not grown up to a degree of social interest sufficient for full co-operation with others. This is also true of persons who are promiscuous, masturbators, or exclusive frequenters of prostitutes.

The neurotic symptoms of sexual dysfunction, impotence, frigidity or vaginismus, and premature ejaculation also betray the primary phase of sexuality. This phase has not been overcome because of lack of social interest.

Secondary Sexual Phase

Love as a task of two equal persons of different sexes calls for physical and mental attraction, exclusiveness, and a total and final surrender. The right solution of this task of two persons is the blessing of socially interested (adjusted) persons

[2] This paragraph translated from A1928c, pp. 5–6.

who have proved their right attitude by having friends, being prepared for a useful job, and showing mutual devotion.

Expression of the Life Style[3]

Many psychologists believe that the development of sexuality is the basis for the development of the whole mind and psyche, as well as for all the physical movements. In the view of the present writer, this is not true. Rather, the entire form and development of sexuality depend on the personality—the style of life and the prototype.[4]

In childhood, matters are complicated by the psychological relations with the parents. Poor sexual training is incidental to psychological conflict between child and parent. A fighting child, especially during adolescence, may abuse sexuality with the deliberate intention to hurt the parents. Boys and girls have been known to have sex relations just after a fight with their parents. Children take these means of revenging themselves on their parents, particularly when they see that the parents are sensitive in this regard.

The sexual drive should be harnessed to a useful goal in which all of our activities are expressed. If the goal is properly chosen, neither sexuality nor any other manifestation of life will be overstressed. . . . In a normal style of life, sex will find its proper expression. This does not mean that we can overcome neuroses, the marks of an erroneous style of life, merely by free sexual expression. The belief, so widely propagated, that repressed libido is the cause of neurosis is false. Rather . . . neurotic persons do not find their proper sexual expression.

One meets persons who have been advised to give more free expression to their sex instincts and who have followed this advice, only to make their condition worse. The reason . . . is that such persons fail to harness their sexual life with

[3] Reprinted from A1929d, pp. 125–26, 128, 129–30.

[4] By "prototype" Adler (A1929d) means the rudimentary, formative precursor of the adult life style, the "model of a matured personality" (pp. xvii–xviii).

a socially useful goal, which alone can change their neurotic condition. The expression of the sex instinct by itself does not cure the neurosis, for it is a disease in the life style, if we may use the term, and it can be cured only by ministering to the style of life.

WOMAN'S ATTITUDE TOWARD SEXUALITY[5, 6]

There is no firm basis for studying woman's attitude toward sexuality. According to present-day scientific trends, one should study blood composition, draw conclusions from the endocrine glands and their correlates, and assume that the proper physical conditions would result in ideal sexual behavior.

But by what ideal do we judge? Does the goal of woman's sexual development depend solely on the adequacy of her procreative glands? How do we judge good or bad? Are we looking for the greatest happiness, the largest progeny, or full satisfaction of the drives? Do we demand equal value of the two sexes, or the subordination of one to the other? As many questions, as many goals of women's development, so many demands for sexual forms of life! The literature on this most human problem is vast.

More illuminating than the scientific writings, followed by a flood of pseudoscientific absurdities, are the works of poets, novelists, painters, and sculptors. We find that beginning with the Bible and myths and fairy tales, up to modern short stories and plays and the lyrical poetry of men and women, the erotic problem is dealt with and elaborated on. But since art, like science, has so far been almost exclusively the work of men, it reflects primarily man's knowledge of the female soul. Often important problems remain unsolved, reminding us of

[5] Translation of A1926e, as reprinted in A1930d, pp. 89–97.
[6] General references: G. Heymans (1910), Otto Weininger (1918), Vaerting (1923), J. S. Mill (1869), Schirmacher (1905), Ellen Key (n.d.), Paul Moebius (1903), Johann Bachofen (1861), Bernhard Aschner (1924), Wilhelm Liepmann (1922), Hugo Sellheim (1924), Helene Deutsch (1925). [Author's note.]

the confession of old and new riddle guessers that "woman is a riddle."

The masculine preponderance among these opinions is certainly an evil, often reducing woman to an object for male or female drives. Woman's task is generally seen as to be beautiful and to bear children. Moreover, striking deficiencies in character, intellectual freedom, objective striving, and aptitude for vocation and public life are so emphasized that woman's existence is justified almost entirely by love and the care of progeny. This judgment strongly influences women. They usually accept it and appear to submit to the role assigned to them by men. In exaggerated revolt, George Sand lacerates this system with the words: "The virtue of women —that is a good invention of men!"

This suggests that, besides the physical foundations, other factors affect woman's sexual attitude that modify the course of eroticism much more. Among these are the attitude of the culture, the relative number of women, and the great influence of the man due to his prerogative of active courting, his firmer economic basis, and his better schooling and training. As far as we can see, the education of girls for the role of a woman takes these factors always into account and tries to attain an adjustment to them. An attitude toward sexuality based exclusively on physique, a sexuality isolated from all other factors, can be found, if at all, only among the feeble-minded. In all other cases every form of sexuality is based on a preconceived, preparatory attitude toward the love problem.

Individual Perspective

One thing is certain: Female sexuality is by no means uniform and depends on various factors. Granted, a certain uniformity can be noted at different times and locations, with different peoples and ages, similar to fashions. Yet all semblance of uniformity notwithstanding—"Their everlasting aches and groans, in thousand tones, have all one source, one mode of healing" [as the Devil says in Goethe's *Faust*][7]—it is nevertheless evident that each individual case is quite different; for example, from the general wish to find a husband one may not conclude that there is a desirable, because socially necessary, sexual readiness. The restriction of woman's action circle, tradition, personal pride, and economic reasons urge the choice of a partner as much as do sexual impulses. Despite their organic foundation, sexual impulses are guided and changeable according to the individual's form of life and her true ultimate intentions, and can be trained in the most diverse directions. The traces of the sex drive from early childhood are modeled by the surrounding culture, and are like all other drives tamed or incited by individually comprehended experiences that are not limited to the field of sexuality. When a girl's education as a whole leads her to a definitely passive attitude toward life, her erotic behavior will also be passive.

Only in the individual case are we able to determine all these influences that have affected the sexual expression of a woman. In psychological forms of expression, such as a woman's attitude toward sexuality, one cannot expect a real causality. All organic feelings and impulses, as well as all experiences, pass through the filter of the personality and are comprehended from an individual perspective. From the viewpoint of an ideal type, every utilization of the above factors, every self-evaluation and its effect, are developed in a more or less mistaken manner. A woman will experience and evaluate the approach, courtship, inward and outward habitus of a partner according to her goal for her way of life.

All so-called "feminine" traits are extremely subject to the social balance of forces between men and women, owe their origin to it, and may be shaped and destroyed by it. Even apparently innate traits, such as waiting for a suitor, passivity, reserve, feminine modesty, motherliness, and monogamy are subject much more than is realized to the trend of the times, and are directed by the final goal [of the individual]. Hints at

[7] Part 1, Scene IV, Bayard Taylor translation of the original, *"Es ist ihr ewig Weh und Ach aus einem Punkte zu kurieren."*

exhibitionism, usually justified by fashion, must be evaluated as neutral; while more explicit forms probably disclose a more active character.

In connection with this and the depreciation of the partner one frequently finds a fetishistic overestimation of unimportant matters. This often limits the love choice as severely as an ideal picture of the partner. Against both of these demands and still others, any perfection may fail. Often they are only poorly understood pretenses to preclude any choice. Otherwise the love choice, always corresponding to a self-limitation of the sexual drive and its superstructure, may follow the most varied motives. The impressions of early childhood, the image of the father, a brother, or one's own people are often highly codetermining. The choice of the love partner, as long as it is free, will always correspond wholly to the peculiarities, defects, and advantages of the personal attitude. A straightforward feeling of strength, rarely found, will give preference to similar men. Girls secretly seeking superiority often feel attracted to weaklings, or cripples, or choose below their status. Similarly, the choice of someone close at hand, or a relative, points to a feeling of weakness, as does the preference for much older or much younger men. Often a motherly trend is strengthened in a most unfruitful manner, aiming at the salvation or elevation of a fallen partner and attempting to repress the regularities of normal sexuality.[8]

Favorable and Unfavorable Factors

Eroticism is never mere animal sex drive, never, as Schopenhauer believed, merely an allurement of nature for the purpose of procreation of the human race. It is rather a highly qualified part of the human social feeling that reflects the entire personality and thus also the degree of the connectedness with the social life and the preparation for a life for two.

The development of the ability to love is advanced by cer-

[8] This and the preceding paragraph are inserted from pp. 95–96.

86

tain conditions, threatened by others. The situation in childhood is decisive, as well as the early decision by the girl regarding her future role as a woman.

Belief in her own strength, an optimistic view of the future, the ability to make contact with people, the inclination to spread joy, an uncritical feeling of belonging to the female sex, and respect for the feminine role are always favorable elements.

Ignorance of her own feminine role or hesitation during several years of childhood, strong attachment to one single person in the family, general feelings of weakness and inferiority, being raised without love, lack of confidence in herself and others, ugliness but also beauty, and especially contempt of womanhood can under any circumstances disturb the preparation for love.

Unfavorable Development

The situation of a girl in childhood is of the greatest importance. A bad marriage of the parents, rudeness, drunkenness and recklessness of the father, or open unfaithfulness cause daughters to fear for the rest of their lives that they may meet the fate of their miserable and deeply humiliated mother. Even when they have the best sexual constitution, their attitude toward men will never be free from distrust, scruples, and inhibitions. Their goal and final purpose will be to avoid the degradation that they presume to be a certainty in the feminine role, and will force them to exclude that role. This brings into their whole life and attitude toward men a system of safeguards in the form of inhibitions, nervous symptoms, and sexual deviations.

In line with this, their view of the world, their logic, habits, and training of the sex drive—in fact, their entire course of life—are forced into a direction away from men. Depending on the personality, which begins to develop in the first years of childhood, the experiences, and the more or less mistaken perspective, the natural, ultimate goal of eroticism changes into a substitute goal (*Ersatzziel*). This substitute goal (A1917a, p. 281) always lies in the field of secondary matters (sexual deviations of all kinds and accentuation of some sexual details), or it fulfills only a part of sexuality (frigidity), brings fear of men, indifference, or aversion, or a masculine tendency, and leads to a masculine role in sexual life, as well as in the woman's whole *modus vivendi*.

Such partial or total turning away from the feminine role has characteristic expressions. Frequently we find aversion to having children and nursing them; but then again, in milder cases, the child may become the exclusive ultimate purpose, in contrast to the husband. In most cases nervous symptoms of all kinds prevent a harmonious development of eroticism. Inclination toward prostitution and exaggerated polygamous tendencies are also manifestations of the aversion to the feminine role. Vaginismus is also a telling expression of this rejection.

All these manifestations that detract from the feminine role have in common girls' dissatisfaction with their social position in the culture. This is nurtured by the real or apparent preponderance of men, and the resulting belligerent attitudes of women, which may range from open revolt to dull submission. The urge to change this situation causes all ideals of government by women and emancipation, and degenerates in personal life into a hundred forms of the "masculine protest." Kant (1798), in his *Anthropologie*, points to the same experience. And Herder,[9] in his collection of bride songs of all times and peoples, found generally only sad songs.

Also, the commonly held superstition of women's inferiority, the almost complete exclusion of women from highest achievements in science and art—due partly to inadequate preparation, partly to masculine development of artistic forms of expression—generally result in embitterment and early discouragement, while only in dancing and acting women often reach the highest peaks. No wonder that the dissatisfaction with the feminine role frequently leads to an imitation of men —in fashion, wishes and fantasies, conduct of life, and erot-

[9] Johann G. von Herder (1744–1803), German philosopher, poet, and critic.

icism. No wonder that, according to the estimates of experienced physicians, approximately 70 per cent of women are frigid in spite of perfect sexual constitutions.

Along with all these reasons against free development of sexuality in the direction of a social, cultural form of expression, and usually inseparably connected with them, there is an inadequate or poor preparation for love, a serious obstacle to sexual harmony. The prevailing mutual distrust, the exaggerated self-seeking, the urge to outdo one's partner, and the fear of being inferior to him hinder spontaneous devotion and poison the love relationship. Girls who are not so pretty fear a quick cooling-off of the husband, while beautiful women feel oppressed, believing themselves merely sexual objects, and find their human dignity insulted. This is often aggravated by the partner's bachelor habits, poor handling of intercourse, or a misunderstanding of male sexuality. Awkwardness, brutality, or injuries to psychological sensitivity during the first relations may lead to permanent upset. Jealous limitations of freedom of movement at the beginning of the marriage, and impregnation contrary to agreement or against the wish of the wife may have the same effect. Fear-arousing experiences in childhood, and prejudices regarding pain and the dangers of being a woman further increase the inferiority feeling.

Sexual Disorders

The development of the sex drive urges the individual, in the course of awakened impulses, toward autoerotic masturbatory actions. Thus, sooner or later, through seduction or on her own, partly inhibited and partly encouraged by the environment and the culture, the child will happen upon masturbatory satisfactions. Harmless in themselves, they may give rise to a training toward autoeroticism that impedes the development of normal eroticism and its effects, and considerably strengthens the arguments against it because, like an ever-ready valve, it can reduce sexual tension at any time.

This view is in sharp contrast to that of the "somaticists." For us, cultural difficulties and errors, poor guidance and inadequate preparation are in the foreground, whereas those who emphasize the constitution either attribute little importance to these factors or look at them as reactions to glandular deficiencies. Against this we would stress:

1. Even the best-endowed organism may go wrong through errors and mistakes.

2. In some respect, the inferiority of organs, including the endocrine glands, appears sufficiently taken into account in our view, although always within a more important context than the purely organic. This context consists in the relationship of the inferiority to the requirements of the respective culture, and how it influences the self-esteem, leading to a low self-evaluation.

3. The physical and psychological training that ensues from woman's antisocial sexual attitude brings out still other valuations and interests, and always also changes secondarily the organic basis of the sexual function. From this curtailment further difficulties arise. The stimuli from the external world that encourage the function are warded off, impulses from the organ are stopped or postponed, and the organ is artificially put at rest and may be injured still further by the forced change in the way of life. In the "hunger strike" [anorexia nervosa] of girls, for example, which is perhaps always initiated by the "masculine protest" in rejection of the feminine role, the substances of the procreative and other endocrine glands dwindle in the course of the extreme emaciation. But even before this, sex is psychologically excluded, in that the psychological apparatus is filled with interests in nourishment and evacuation.

Lesbian love, persistence in sexual fantasies, masturbation, and pollutions are signs of masculine protest and disclose a fear of men and their rejection. Homosexual dreams are not proof of homosexuality, as is generally and prejudicially assumed, but signs of a training in a wrong direction. Desire for polygamy, exaggerated flirting, passion to compromise oneself, fantasies of being a kept woman, and exaggerated and repulsive clamoring for a man all point beyond themselves to an attempt to exclude marriage. Adultery is always the sign of a revolt against the husband, an act of revenge that is always disguised through purposefully incited eroticism.

The first menstruation often gives the signal for the outbreak of the fight against the feminine role, when there is inadequate preparation. Frequently the resistance flames up anew each time. Pain without organic causes seems to be produced by arbitrary contractions, by slowing up the blood discharge, and to arise from dissatisfaction with and rejection of the event. This view is supported by the fact that often after marriage, when there is a far-reaching reconciliation with the feminine role, the pain disappears. The widely held opinion that the menses imply impurity or sickness, often also advanced by physicians, lowers the self-confidence of women and often produces strong feelings of depression. Heightened sexual feelings (perhaps also because they are not dangerous then) are frequent during this period.

The approach of the menopause and the menopause itself become extremely difficult times for women who see in youth and beauty almost the only value of a woman. They lose the last remainder of belief in their own value. Depressed and desperate, they often try to regain a feeling of worth by increasing demands on their environment. Others plunge into destructive conflicts through their eroticism, which does not disappear at that time but is everywhere rejected, ridiculed, and not taken seriously.

Conclusion

An erroneous attitude toward life works against men and women. While we do take the organic foundations of eroticism fully into account, we must assert that the individual attitude is decisive for the erotic direction and shortcomings.

If we should name the preconditions for a woman's healthy attitude toward sex (*Sexualleben*) that are usually not met sufficiently, they would be:

1. Early enlightenment regarding the unalterability of the sexual role and reconciliation to it.

2. Educational preparation for love in accordance with social interest.

3. Respect for the feminine role.

4. Affirmation of life and of human society.

MAN'S PSYCHOSEXUAL ATTITUDE[10, 11]

Man's psychosexual attitude essentially coincides with that of women. We always measure against an ideal type of man that we envision, and ultimately sense the differences from it in terms of fitness for human living together, and for a man and a woman living together. Also, our evaluation of the uniqueness of a man depends absolutely on these presuppositions.

The difference between the sexes is that our culture has conceded to men, tacitly or openly, privileges in love life that it seeks to deny to women. Man's greater sphere of activity in love life is primarily determined by his greater sphere of activity in life altogether, but is made much easier for him because he remains free from pregnancy as a consequence of sexuality, because of his role of active courting, and because of tradition, an enormous force. In a certain accord with this there is additionally the easy master morality of men to whom the commonly accepted sexual morality does not set such narrow limits as it does to women.

Early Development

The male sexual impulse manifests itself in various intensities, usually long before puberty, and can veer into various wrong directions during boyhood, puberty, or later. Thus the attitude of a man toward the problems of life will always

[10] Original translation of A1926f, as reprinted in A1930d, pp. 98–102, 105.

[11] General references: Wilhelm Fliess (1906), Tandler and Gross (1913), Otto Weininger (1918), Magnus Hirschfeld (n.d.), Robert Müller (1907), Havelock Ellis (1912a), Hermann Rohleder (n.d.), Sigmund Freud (1923), Alfred Adler (A1912a). [Author's note.]

influence his sexual development as well. This is all the more understandable since there is no fixed measure of the sex drive, and its expressions can be increased or reduced through various influences.

Already during boyhood, these influences and the psychological direction assert themselves most clearly. The sexual preparation consists first of all in the strengthening of an adequate boy's role, in a growing understanding of the sexual problem, and in a courageous goal-setting in the direction of love and marriage. Our culture and its institutions take over a part of the work from those who are responsible for the child's upbringing. Different dress, different games, and different educational measures attempt to steer the course of development correctly. The surrounding life, analogies from animals, educational measures, and usually enlightenment by peers advance the insight into the sexual secret; reading, theater, motion pictures, and often also seduction complete this enlightenment. Since furthermore everywhere in his life a boy comes across the facts of love and marriage, since all educational measures also envision a social solution of the love and marriage problem in the future, and since the growing sexual drive seeks such a solution, the boy's world picture of the future develops in this sense.

A boy's attitude toward the other sex is at first usually one of hostility and superiority. Furious aversion against feminine dress, let alone the insinuation of being a girl, are often to be taken as an exaggerated sign of finding one's sexual role. Also, in the later boyhood years, the feeling of superiority usually comes to light, even in coeducation, and equality is denied to the girls, as if it were an obligation to do so. "The boy proudly tears himself away from the girl."[12] In the midst of this critical gesture, we often find traits of affection and being in love. Often already in the fourth, fifth, and sixth year, friendly tendencies—or those of a critical and malicious nature—appear. An inclination to tease, also to attack, is not infrequent.

[12] From Schiller's poem *Die Glocke: "Vom Mädchen reisst sich stolz der Knabe."*

The sex drive may give occasion for masturbation during the very first years. Through seduction we find sometimes in early childhood mutual masturbation or, especially in slums, normal sexual intercourse. It is also noteworthy that for boys during their development it is much easier to turn through mutual masturbation to homosexuality than to turn to normal sexual behavior.

Puberty

The fourteenth year usually brings in boys the decisive turn toward masturbation, from which they sooner or later free themselves. In puberty, the throttled sexual drive vents itself in more or less frequent pollutions. Fatigue and looking badly during this period come almost always from fear of sickness or from some disturbances in development. Masturbation and pollutions of this period can be completely overcome. If they persist for many years, they must be taken as attempts to exclude women.

During puberty and shortly thereafter, an image of the ideal girl is usually formed that is likely to show the traits of a close person. This ideal image is often subject to change later, as other ideals also often dissolve. Often there is fear of sullying this image, or a girl who embodies it, through sensual thoughts. At the same time, the most extravagant fantasy images may occur. Frequently masturbation represents the temptation to transpose sensual desire into reality.

Alongside this purity of sentiment, one often finds the desire for coarse sensuality, or the engaging in sexual relations, following the line of least resistance, usually with prostitutes or servant girls. Both are ready outlets that permit bypassing the way to love and marriage, sometimes permanently. Toward both these erroneous ways young men are often encouraged by trained and untrained educators. To close these paths will be possible only for those who do not defend the absolute necessity of early sexual relations, but are also not afraid to grant full rights to a true love where both partners are prepared to stand up for each other.

Customs and practices of society, gatherings, dances, and projects in which both sexes take part, promote and encourage the inclination toward girls that has by now developed. The training for union is a continuous, ongoing process. In thoughts, on the street, in the theater, in pictorial representations there are constant stimulations that help the inclination toward love and marriage to prevail. Marriage is, of course, to a high degree connected with economic and vocational problems. Up to that point, there is a relatively long period during which all too many youths lapse into sexual waywardness or venereal diseases.

Marriage

When a man enters marriage, he is not only faced with the categorical demands of marriage (A1925b), almost always he brings into marriage his individual requirements as well, which many times have no place there and disturb the relationship. The new situation will be a touchstone of his preparation for marriage. His preparation will always reflect his world philosophy and his attitude toward women. His choice of a mate has already been guided by his ideal requirements of a woman and of marriage.

Depending on whether a man was satisfied with his mother and sister, or could assert himself against them, the girl of his choice will be mentally and physically similar to them, or different. If he is a man who longs for warmth, he will associate with girls from whom he expects to be pampered. If he loves to prevail in a contest, he will seek girls who appear strong to him; or else he will prefer those who by their nature, stature, and strength appear easily guidable to him. Naturally, this will lead to many mistakes, primarily because no girl will tolerate permanent subjugation.

If one is properly trained for marriage, the further course of the marriage and of his sexual attitude will depend entirely on the partner. If she also knows how to create harmony, the two will be the picture of harmonious sexuality until the end of their lives. This may be a rare case, proof of the inadequate education of our progeny for marriage. Closely connected with sexuality, in such cases the feeling of unconditional comradeship will develop, so that disagreeable differences are out of the question or are easily overcome. There will also be enough room in such marriages for the new generation, who will be accepted into the same comradeship. The sexual problem will find a common solution, will not be felt as the dictation of the other, and neither party will feel like an object. The sexual belongingness (*Zugehörigkeit*) will not be troubled by anything until it slowly expires in late years, often beyond the sixtieth year. Sexual intercourse will evidence no shortcomings, nor give cause for bad humor, exhaustion, or sadness.

It is different with those who are ill prepared. In the new situation following puberty, the time of the possible and even desired sexuality, their inadequate preparation will make itself painfully felt under all circumstances, without they themselves being able to give an account. A feeling of insecurity, or inadequate self-confidence, leads one to see in sexuality, and thus in woman and in devotion to her, greater or lesser threats to one's own sphere of significance. Such individuals will lack the straightforwardness that is a main requirement for healthy eroticism. In their behavior they will show detours and deviations, the strongest of which are homosexuality and autoeroticism. Similarly, all other displacements of the sexual role, such as fetishism, sadism, masochism, and perverted mannerisms, reveal to us the old insecurity and the attempt to put private satisfaction of desires in place of those offered by society, in order thus to avoid a test of one's own worth. The choice of prostitutes and the preference for easily dissolved attachments without consequences reveal the same weakness. When we understand this dynamic correctly, we can readily appraise in a Don Juan and in cases of polygamy the lack of courage that characterizes those who do not want to see anything through and prefer to reach for cheap successes. Sexuality is "twosomeness" (Nietzsche), the achievement of two equal partners. There is no place in love for the striving of one partner to stand out at the expense of the other, to satisfy his vanity. This is an abuse, a rudeness; it blasts the structure of eroticism because it does not reckon with the laws of love.

Conclusion

Thus we come to the conclusion that the kind and degree of sexual behavior in man, as in woman, are derived from his personality, generally reflect his activity, and, as long as his sexual organs are approximately intact, are a result of his preparation and training.

SEX EDUCATION AND PUBERTY

Sex Education[13]

The subject of sex education has been frightfully exaggerated in recent times. Many people are, if we may say so, insane on the subject. They want it at any and all ages, and play up the dangers of sexual ignorance. But if we look back on our own past and that of others, we do not find such great difficulties and dangers as they imagine.

The biological difference. A child should be told at the age of two that he or she is a boy or a girl. It should also be explained at that time that one's sex can never be changed, and that boys grow up to be men and girls grow up to be women. If this is done, then the lack of other knowledge is not so dangerous. If it is brought home to the child that a girl will not be brought up like a boy nor a boy like a girl, then the sex role will be fixed in the mind, and the child will be sure to develop and to prepare for his or her role in a normal manner. If the child believes, however, that through a certain trick he or she can change sex, then trouble will result.

Trouble will also result if the parents are always expressing a desire to change the sex of a child. In *The Well of Loneliness* (Radcliffe Hall) we find an excellent literary presen-

[13] Reprinted in slightly edited form from A1930a, pp. 221–26.

tation of this situation. Parents too often like to bring up a girl like a boy or vice versa. They will photograph their children dressed in the clothes of the opposite sex. It sometimes happens, too, that a girl looks like a boy, and then people begin calling the child by the wrong sex. This may start a great confusion, which can very well be avoided.

Equal worth of the sexes. Any discussion about the sexes that tends to undervalue the female sex, and to regard boys as superior, should be avoided. Children should be made to understand that both sexes are of equal worth. This is important not merely to prevent an inferiority complex among the members of the undervalued sex, but also to prevent bad effects among the male children. If boys were not taught to think that they are the superior sex, they would not look upon girls as mere objects of desire. Nor would they look upon the relationship of the sexes in an ugly light if they knew their future tasks.

In other words, the real problem of sex education is not merely explaining to children the physiology of sexual relationships; it also involves the proper preparation of the whole attitude toward love and marriage. This is closely related to the question of social interest. If a person is not socially interested, he will make a joke of the question of sex and look at things entirely from the point of view of self-indulgence. This happens, of course, all too often, and is a reflection of the defects of our culture. Women have to suffer because in our culture it is much easier for a man to play the leading role. But the man also suffers because by this fictitious [spurious] superiority he loses touch with the underlying values.

The physical phase. As regards the physical phase of sex education, it is not necessary that children receive this education very early in life. One can wait until the child becomes curious, until he wants to find out certain things. A mother and father who are interested in their child will also know when it is proper for them to take the lead if the child is too shy to ask questions. If the child feels that his father or mother are comrades, he will ask questions, and then the answers must be given in a manner proper to his understanding.

98

One must avoid giving answers that stimulate the sex drive.

In this connection it may be said that one need not always be alarmed by apparently premature manifestations of the sex instinct. Sex development begins very early—in fact, in the first weeks of life. It is wholly certain that an infant experiences erogenous pleasures, and that he sometimes seeks to stimulate the erogenous zones artificially. We should not be frightened if we see signs of the beginnings of certain nuisances, but we should do our best to put a stop to these practices without seeming to attach too much importance to them. If a child finds out that we are worried over these matters, he will continue his habits deliberately in order to gain attention. It is such actions that make us think he is a victim of the sex drive, when he is really exploiting a habit as a tool for showing off. Generally little children try to gain attention by playing with their genital organs because they know that their parents are afraid of this practice. It is much the same psychology as when children play sick because they have noticed that when they are sick they are more pampered and more appreciated.

If one avoids all forms of premature stimulation, one need not have any fears. One needs only to speak at the right time in a few simple words, never irritating the child and always giving answers in a true and simple manner. Above all, one must never lie to a child, if one wants to retain his trust. If the child trusts the parent, he will discount the explanations he hears from his peers—perhaps 90 per cent of mankind get their sexual knowledge from peers—and will believe what the parent says. Such co-operation, such camaraderie is much more important than the various subterfuges that are used in the belief that they answer the situation.

Summary. These remarks sum up the most important items in the matter of sex education. We see here, as in all other phases of education, the dominant importance of the sense of co-operation and friendliness within the family. With this co-operation present, and with an early knowledge of the sex role and of the equality of man and woman, the child is well prepared for carrying on his work in a healthy manner.

Phenomena of Puberty[14, 15]

Puberty is so striking due to its physical as well as the psychological maturation processes. These begin and end in girls somewhat earlier than in boys. Physical maturation concerns all organs and takes place even when the sex glands are impaired or lost, only that then the secondary sex characteristics are inadequately developed. Psychological maturation can be temporarily or permanently hindered through inappropriate or inadequate education.

Dual aspect of puberty. Poets, researchers, and common sense have been impressed primarily by two forms of expression that permit a dual point of view. On the one hand we note increased capability, which points to qualitatively and quantitatively increased powers. These include social and occupational integration, the ability of abstract thinking, the tendency to seek a complement, the impulse toward social and sexual union, discovery or strengthening of the self, formation of a life plan, and entrance into occupational areas. Also, the tendency toward idealism, development of a life philosophy, conquest of the inner world, idealization and spiritualization of sexuality, and taking an attitude toward the values of life are often noted. All these manifestations stand out palpably when the criteria of childhood are applied to the maturing youth of thirteen to twenty-one years.

On the other hand, if one applies the criteria of the adult to this period, its shortcomings become more striking. Awkwardness and clumsiness, caused by inadequate familiarity with the organs of movement, which have now become larger and stronger; occasional timidity and shyness in unaccustomed situations; defiance, and critical and skeptical behavior; often also exaggerated striving for significance; ecstasy, fasci-

[14] Original translation of A1926g, as reprinted in A1930d, pp. 85–89.

[15] General references: Charlotte Bühler (1923), G. Stanley Hall (1918), Eduard Spranger (1925), Otto Tumlirz (1924), Alfred Adler (A1920a). [Author's note.]

nation, exuberance, an intoxication with phrases and slogans, as if thereby one would succeed in solving the riddles of life; a disparaging attitude toward previously accepted values; opposition and resistance on principle against compulsion and directed also against cultural values—all these characterize this phase. It also includes deviations and excesses of all sorts, which break through as protest and open or secret revolt against the inferiority feeling from childhood.

Thus life during puberty seems to delineate itself from that of the rest of society, often so sharply that many people believe youth quite naturally obeys a law of its own and has a form of life of its own. During the past decades, male youth organizations have become prominent, especially on German soil. They have, to be sure, the positive value of fellowship. But they also bear a certain hostility to culture, which on occasion becomes evident in isolation, a belligerent attitude toward "the parents," and escape from the female sex.

Continuity with childhood. Unbiased observation will discover no essentially new forces during the period of puberty. All its phenomena can easily be recognized as advanced stages of development that were prepared in childhood. The time of puberty, with its approach to the front of life, its maturation of organs, and its complex of increased physical and psychological sexual demands, faces the expectations of the future as in an experiment. The maturing child now takes up these attitudes toward life and its present and future demands, which are in accordance with its previous training. In the social question and the question of the relationship to one's fellow man, of the I to the thou, comradely, friendly world-philosophical traits will appear—or their opposites, depending on the development of the social feeling during childhood.

In the direction of occupational choice, one notices movements of approach or escape, both varying in degree with the strength of the belief in one's own powers. The evaluation and views of sexuality and the sexual goal of earlier years become very much clearer in the movements of the young man and girl during this stage of greater independence and freedom, and greater tolerance on the part of the adults. All these and other questions of puberty are answered as they were

101

approached long ago, showing the person's social interest developed so far, his striving for significance, and inferiority feelings.

Inadequate maturation. The inadequate preparations from childhood consist mostly in incomplete training for life, be it in the social, occupational, or sexual direction, and in the neglect to develop a self-reliant and self-confident, courageous character. Life in our culture requires schooling and an optimistic, resolved attitude, or else conflicts and contradictions are inescapable, which appear already in childhood, in school, in the family, and in relation to comrades. Their effect is harmful, particularly in dependent individuals, due to their greater sensitivity and indecision, which persistently press toward supposedly less resistance. Thus one frequently finds during puberty, near the front line of life where decisions must be made, secret or open deviations from cultural ways, the meaning of which is plainly directed toward evading a test.

Once one understands the disagreeable fermentations of puberty as attempts at compensation arising from a feeling of weakness, then much of what has been regarded as the phenomenon and effect of puberty resolves itself into the result of a progressive but inadequate maturation. Since children are almost generally inadequately prepared, the test of the puberty period gives rise to conflicts. Youth is almost generally discouraged, the main blame for which rests with the lack of courage of large sections of the population, education for cowardliness, pampering or lack of love, and the burden of all-too-great expectations for the future. Consequently there is widespread inclination to subterfuges, excuses, and evasion of pressing demands.

The frequent attempts to arrange pretenses for a flight from social, occupational, and love problems through an escalation of conflicts deserve special attention. Not from strength, but from weakness, forms of life are then often arrived at that are a mimicry, supposed to create the illusion of strength. Often a senseless fight bursts out in the family; worthless battles against real or imagined authorities attract all available strength; hatred, aversion, and lack of interest

102

for one's occupational activity arise mostly out of fear of defeat; and the normal capacity for love is artificially interfered with through a continuous training in the direction of perversions that seem to guarantee more securely one's own superiority. A tendentiously ignited ego cult represents a disturbing throttling of the social feeling, leads to harmful isolation, and is always connected with oversensitivity and boundless ambition that again and again occasion conflicts and further isolation.

In this critical situation, numerous symptoms appear as signs of a retreating movement, such as compulsion neurosis, hysteria, neurasthenia, anxiety neuroses, and as a picture of complete breakdown, dementia praecox. The path to waywardness and to crime in the more active young people is also an expression of discouragement with regard to the normal role, as is prostitution.

Suicide figures begin to rise during puberty when the tendency toward discouraged but revengeful solutions of conflicts easily gains the upper hand in this kind of individual.

The positive side. Alongside these troublesome puberty phenomena one always finds also heightened values. Further developments are seen in all possible performances and abilities. Independence, reliability, and the feeling of solidarity (*Zusammengehörigkeitsgefühl*) become more prominent. Long-practiced preparations and skills express themselves also as heightened interests, and the permanent acquisition of skills and their further development give the life of the more mature person a more definite direction with regard to activity and vocation. While apparent aptitudes for art and science often disappear during this time, in other cases, the creative ability rises to surprising originality. The forms of life previously gained become more clearly outlined with increasing powers and in their struggle for independence. Guiding ideals, usually still in connection with what has been seen, heard, or read, point to the meaning of the future life that is developing at this point.

4

LOVE AND MARRIAGE

LOVE AS A LIFE TASK[1]

To get to know a person completely, we must understand him also in his love relationships. We must be able to tell whether in matters of love he behaves correctly or incorrectly; and why in one case he may be suited, while in another case he would be unsuited. Quite naturally, the further problem arises: What can we do to prevent errors in love relationships? If we consider that human happiness depends perhaps to the largest part on the solution of the love and marriage problem, we will appreciate that these are most important questions.

One difficulty is brought up by most people right at the start. They say that people are not all alike and that two persons could perhaps have been happier, had each found a different partner. Granted this possibility, this consideration tells us only that the persons in question made a bad choice. But we do not know whether the foundering on the problem of love is due to the erroneous choice, or whether he or she would have foundered on this problem in any case, for deeper reasons. An understanding of the human soul and its moving forces can often spare us from failures.

[1] Original translation of A1926a, pp. 3–9.

The Three Life Tasks

The problem of love relationships is a part of the problem of human life. Its understanding is possible only if we regard the coherence with all other problems of life. Life poses three great task complexes (*Aufgabenkomplexe*), from the solution of which our future, our happiness depend.

Social task. The first life task is the social task in the broadest sense. Life demands of everybody a certain behavior and a very far-reaching ability for contact (*Kontaktfähigkeit*) with our fellow men, a certain behavior within the family, and a formulation of his social attitude. It does matter for the fate of a person what kind of social order he sets as his direction-giving goal, to what extent he thinks in his actions of his own welfare, and to what extent of the welfare of others. His inner choice is often difficult to discern from his outward decisions; often he cannot decide at all in questions of social attitude, and often his viewpoint must be understood in another sense than its outward appearance. This is similar to a person's political attitude. People seldom are satisfied with their political party, and very often one would like to assign them to another party. What counts is always a person's behavior toward the human community, his fellow men in the widest sense, not what he or others think about it.

Occupation. A second life task is that of occupation—that is, the manner in which a person wants to make his abilities serve the general public. The solution of this question illuminates most clearly the essence of a person. For example, when a young man finds every occupation loathsome, we shall provisionally consider him not a suitable fellow man, because either he is not yet sufficiently mature for society, or he may never mature on his own. In most cases by far occupational choice is based on unconscious connections. They are unconscious in that at the time of choice nobody considers

105

that he has taken a step for the benefit of the general public, that he has selected for himself a place in the general division of labor. Of course, what he does in his occupation also counts. One may reach an occupational choice but fail within the occupation, or recognize after a while that one really should have become something else. Frequent change of occupation permits the conclusion that the person in fact would prefer no occupation at all, or perhaps considers himself too good for any occupation—actually, not good enough—and only pretends to go along with it.

Love and Marriage. The third life task that every person must solve is the problem of love and marriage, to which we want to give here our special consideration. The child grows into this problem gradually. His entire surrounding is filled with love and marriage relationships. Unmistakably, the child, already in the very first years of life, attempts to take a stand and to give himself a direction toward this problem. What we hear about this in words is not decisive, because as soon as the child touches upon problems of love an enormous shyness often overcomes him. Some children express quite clearly that they cannot speak about this topic. Others are very devoted to their parents yet are not capable of being affectionate with them. A four-year-old boy returned proffered kisses with slaps in the face because the feeling of an affectionate impulse was uncanny to him, seemed to him frightening—one may even say, humiliating.

Also in looking back on our own lives we notice that every affectionate impulse is accompanied by a sort of sense of shame and the impression that thereby one would become weaker or lose in value. This is very remarkable and requires an explanation. Our culture being generally orientated toward a masculine ideal, we grow up in the frame of mind that an affectionate impulse is a disgrace. Accordingly, in school, literature, and any environment, the children are continuously trained to see in love a kind of unmanliness. Sometimes they express this quite clearly, and some go so far that one may say they evade emotion.

106

The Logic of Social Living

The child's first impulses of affection appear very early. As they develop, one can very easily note that they are all impulses of the social feeling. This is evidently innate, since it appears quite regularly. From the degree of its development we can appraise an individual's attitude to life.

The very concept of "human being" includes our entire understanding of social feeling. We cannot imagine that a human being could be designated as such after having lost it. Likewise, throughout history we find no human beings living in isolation. They always lived in groups, unless separated from one another artificially or through insanity. Darwin showed that animals with a less favorable position with regard to nature live in groups. Their vitality becomes effective by forming groups, unconsciously following a principle of self-preservation. Those that lived singly, in whose stepmotherly development social feeling was lacking, perished, victims of natural selection. The principle of natural selection is also dangerous for man, since, in facing nature, his physical equipment is most stepmotherly of all.

The situation of the inferiority and inadequacy of the human race develops in the whole race and in the individual a continuous drive and coercion that drive us on, until an approximate condition of rest is reached and some form of existence appears assured.

We are still on this path, and today it is perhaps the best consolation for man to realize that our present situation is only a point of transition, a momentary phase of human development. He will naturally best pass through this phase, in reference to all problems of life, who is in accord with the actual conditions and does justice to the logic of the facts, whereas those who resist this logic, naturally will meet a merciless destiny. In the deepest sense, the feeling for the logic of human living together is social feeling.

The entire development of the child demands his embeddedness in a situation in which social feeling is present. His life and health are assured only if there are persons at hand who take his part. A newly born calf, for example, can very soon discriminate poisonous plants from others. The newly born human, however, due to the inferiority of his organism, depends on the social feeling of the adult. The child must for a long time be taken care of, taught, and trained until he can look after himself.

When we consider the abilities of which we are particularly proud, which assure us priority above other creatures—such as reason, logic, language, our understanding and preference for everything that is beautiful and good—we can see that the single human being could never have produced them. They are, so to speak, born only of the group mind (*Massenseele*). Thereby further needs have arisen that never could have burdened the single individual—and are satisfied. For a single human being, without coherence with a community, conscious, deliberate logic would be totally indifferent. He would not need to talk, it would not matter whether he were good or bad. Without a relationship to a human community or to a fellow man, these concepts would lose all meaning, as in the case of single animals. All human qualities, all achievements of the human mind, are conceivable only in the coherence (*Zusammenhang*) of men among each other.

Love, Part of Social Feeling

The coherence of men among each other is necessitated not only by the pressing needs of the day, but also by our sexual organization. The division of humanity into two sexes, far from creating a separation, means an eternal compulsion toward one another. It creates the feeling of being mutually related, because in the veins of each a common blood flows, because each one is flesh from the flesh of another.

The marriage laws of the various peoples can be understood only from the viewpoint of love as a common bond of the entire group. Marriage and sexual relations among members of the same family were interdicted because this would have led to an isolation of the families. Poetry, religions, the holy commandments are directed against incest and intended to eradicate it. While scholars have puzzled over the reason for the natural aversion of family members toward one another, we understand it quite easily on the basis of the social feeling that develops in each child and that eliminates all possibilities that could lead to an isolation of man.

Now we can understand that love in its essential meaning, the relationship of the sexes, is always connected with social feeling and cannot be separated from it. Love, as a relationship of two, has, as a part of social feeling, its own laws and is a necessary component of the preservation of human society. One cannot think of a community without it. He who affirms the community necessarily also affirms love. He who has community feeling must favor marriage or a form of love of equal or higher value. On the other hand, a person whose social feeling is throttled, who has not arrived at a free development of his nature within humanity, will also show a strange form of love relationships.

Now we can draw a few conclusions that will facilitate an overview of this large area of love relationships and suddenly shed some light on it. A person whose social development is impaired, who has no friends, has not become a real fellow man, whose world view contradicts social feeling, and who perhaps has also not solved his occupational problem well— that is, one who is more or less completely lost to the community, is bound to have difficulties in his love relationships. Such persons will hardly be in a position to solve the erotic problem. They will take strange ways, will create difficulties, and will, where they actually find difficulties, reach for them as for a safeguarding excuse.

DISTURBANCES OF LOVE RELATIONSHIPS[2]

Let us consider more closely the difficulties people create in their love relationships, and thereby gain a deeper insight into

[2] Original translation of A1926a, pp. 9–18, with some paragraphs rearranged.

the entire problem. In a person's love relationships his entire personality is involved. We can understand his personality from his love relationships, as well as guess at his particular sexual aspirations from an understanding of his personality as a whole.[3]

Seeking Power over the Partner

Obligating through love. Most frequently we find within the sexual relationship the erroneous assumption that love is an obligation for the other party. When we look around, and also observe ourselves, we will see that very often we commit the error of believing that the beloved person, by the mere fact of being loved, is obligated to us. This error seems somehow to be contained in our entire form of looking at things (*Anschauungsform*). It originates in childhood and the relationships with the family, where indeed the love of one is almost equal to the obligation of the other. In the adult, it is a remnant from childhood. The resulting excesses center around the thought: "Because I love you, you must do such and such." Thereby a much more severe tone is often introduced in the relationships of persons who are really devoted to each other. The need for power of the one who, on the strength of his own love, wants to draw the other into his schema, demands that the other's steps, expressions, achievements, etc., take place according to his wishes, "because he loves this person." This can easily turn into tyranny. A trace of this is found perhaps in every love relationship.

Thus we see the same factor permeating human love life that also otherwise leads always to disturbances of fellowship: the striving for power and personal superiority.

In a human community, one must respect the freedom of the personal individuality to the extent of leaving the other

[3] In the year in which this essay was published, Adler introduced the term "life style" into his writings. Thus we find here still the terms "entire personality," "personality," and "personality as a whole," which Adler subsequently equated with life style, while a few pages below he actually uses the term "life style" (p. 113).

person free choices. He who strives for personal superiority prevents his connection with a community. He does not want to fit into the whole, but wants the subordination of the others. Thereby he naturally disturbs the harmony in life, in society, among his fellow men. Since by nature no one wants permanently to have a yoke placed on him, those persons who, even in their love relationships are striving for power over the other, must meet with oversized difficulties. If they continue their inclination for presumption and superiority into their sex lives, they must seek a partner who appears to submit, or struggle with one who seeks superiority or victory on his own or in response to the situation. In the case of submission, love is transformed into slavery; in the second case, there will be a continuous, mutually destructive power struggle by which no harmony will ever be reached.

Selecting a subordinate partner. The ways of doing so vary greatly. Some domineering persons tremble so much for their ambition, their power, that they look only for a partner in whom there is no danger of superiority, who always appears to subordinate himself. These are by no means always worthless persons with high ambition. To be possessed by this striving for power is in our culture a generally prevalent trait causing immeasurable harm to the development of humanity.

In this light we can understand the relatively frequent strange phenomenon that people will in their love choice descend into a much lower and unsuitable social milieu. For example, a study of Goethe's love life would show that this ambitious man was extremely insecure in his love affairs. Concerned with the highest problem of humanity, he surprised his fellow men (*Mitwelt*) by marrying his cook. Emphasizing the equal worth of men, as we do, we are of course not indignant about this. But we regard such action as out of keeping and want to understand it from that individual's viewpoint by examining his ultimate intention.

By our norm those persons will find each other who are socially and by their education and preparation for life best suited for each other. Suitors whose choices deviate from the general expectation are mostly persons who face the love problem with extreme hesitation and prejudices, are afraid of

111

their sexual partner and, therefore, are looking for a partner in whom they suspect less power and strength. It is of course possible that someone may deviate from the norm through a feeling of strength. But mostly it is done through weakness.

Such a choice appears to some of these careful individuals as an extremely happy solution, not understanding that their ultimate intention is to conceal their deeper motives through love and sexuality, and convinced that only Cupid is involved here. But as a rule such a relationship turns out poorly and has many disadvantages—not that the intellectually or socially "superior" partner would be disappointed, or that difficulties of a social nature would occur when the "inferior" partner would not satisfy certain requirements of family and social life. These and other external factors could be eliminated and bridged, if the ultimate intention of the "superior" partner could be realized. But strangely it is the "inferior" partner who does not tolerate for long seeing his weakness abused. Even if he does not understand what goes on, he nevertheless cannot get rid of the feeling that his shortcomings are being abused. From this feeling he takes to a kind of revenge; he will try to show that he is not less than the other.

There are many conspicuous cases of this kind. Often a young, cultured, outstandingly intelligent girl throws herself into the arms of an insignificant, often even immoral person, perhaps sometimes with the idea of saving a man whom she appears to love from the clutches of alcoholism, gambling, or indolence. Never yet have such people been saved through love. This action fails almost regularly. The "inferior" partner feels under all circumstances oppressed by his inferior classification. He does not let himself be loved and be saved, because the moving forces of his attitude to life are quite different and not recognizable by ordinary intelligence, the "common sense."[4] He has perhaps long ago given up hope ever to amount to anything and sees in every situation that makes on him requirements as a fellow man a new danger that his presumed inferiority could become clearly apparent.

Many persons also are interested only in physically

[4] The English phrase "common sense" is used in the German original.

deficient or much older love partners. These cases rightfully attract our attention and call for an explanation. Sometimes we find a natural explanation arising from a particular situation. But even then this inclination always corresponds to a life style of taking the line of least resistance.

Predatory desire. Other persons fall in love almost only with partners who are already engaged. This strange fact may reveal various intentions. It may mean, "No," regarding the demands of love, striving for the impossible, or an unfulfillable ideal. But it may also mean, "wanting to take something away from another," a trait carried over into sexuality from the life style.

The biographies of famous persons show that in our complex culture people grow up with an extraordinary eagerness to rob, to take away. The longing for a married woman always results in further actions—namely, to seize the love object—although this is often disguised in the most noble form. Richard Wagner was apparently of this kind. Almost all his poetic creations contain the meaning, the complication, that the hero desires a woman who already belongs to another. Wagner's own life also shows this characteristic.[5]

Evading Marriage

Many people are not quite sufficiently mature for society, see in love and marriage relationships a danger zone, and express their immature views in various ways that are, on the surface, often unintelligible. Regarding these questions, which continuously bother them, they speak in generalities that, in some context, could be true and would not necessarily be a deception. For example, when somebody who is also otherwise timid believes he does not marry "because life these days is so difficult," each word is true enough. But it is also true for those who do marry. Such truths are expressed only by those who would have said "No" even without these truths. In that event they would have reached for another "truth." It

[5] This paragraph has been moved from p. 16 of the original.

would be undiplomatic to support a preconceived intention with a bad argument when good ones are available everywhere. Alarmingly, many people try to escape from the solution of the life problems, and this also takes the guise of sex.

Unrequited love. This is the case in most instances of repeatedly unrequited love. It is a means for realizing, with a pretense of justification, the life goal of turning away from life, from the world. In such cases an unhappy love cannot be unhappy enough to fulfill its purpose. It strikes persons with a readiness to run away from the problems of life, especially those of love, which sometimes receives welcome reinforcement by a trick, a device. This is not always completely invented but is attached to some actual life relationship. Then it does not look like a device but resembles the obvious result of an experience.

We can also "make" a person unattainable. Often the suitor has, from the start, the impression that he will not be received well, but makes this an occasion for greater action. He believes he cannot live without the beloved person and courts her, although any objective observer would consider it improbable that his love would ever be requited. He even says so to himself. Often such courting takes a form apt to provoke resistance—for example, by being extremely vehement, or occurring at a time before any guarantees for living together are given. Such courtships are aimed at unrequited love. A surprisingly large number of persons steer toward this goal.

Some people have been infatuated even without knowing whether that person exists. This clearly expresses their ultimate intention not to have anything to do with love and marriage. Their infatuation can in all probability never be realized.

One should think, from the outside, that such behavior was not part of human nature. But such a person is an "escapist" throughout, and unrequited love provides him with an excellent hiding place. When he carries his unrequited love with him for five or ten years, he is during this entire time safe from all other solutions of this problem. Of course, he has suffered, paid the expenses for the realization of his intention.

But his goal—which has remained unconscious to himself, which he himself did not understand—to stay away from the solution of the love and marriage problem, has thereby been reached with a good conscience and justification. Such a goal and solution are not compatible with the conditions of this earth and the logic of human living together. They are actually the deepest tragedy rather than a solution. Only by this ultimate deepest insight is corrective intervention possible.

High ideals. For the escapist, one frequently tested device is especially recommended. Let him create a new idea, a special ideal. Let him measure by this ideal all persons who cross his path in life. The consequence is that no one will prove suitable; they all deviate from the ideal. When he refuses and eliminates them, his action looks reasonable and well founded. But when we examine an individual case, we find that such a reasonably choosing person, even without his ideal, is willing from the start to say "No." The ideal contains desirable goals of frankness, honesty, courage, etc. But these concepts can be extended and stretched at will until they exceed any human measure. Thus we have at our disposal the love of something that we have previously "made" unattainable.

This device has various possibilities of concretization. We can love a person who was present once for a short time, made an impression, disappeared, and can now no longer be found. One would have to look all over the world to find him. At first we are touched by such fond and faithful love. However, the condition for the realization of such love on earth is superhuman and raises our suspicion.[6]

Fear and Lack of Reserve

Generally, the feeling of insecurity determines many forms of sexuality. There are young men who like only older women [as mentioned earlier], somehow in the erroneous

[6] These two paragraphs have been moved here from pp. 14–15 of the original.

opinion that in this case living together would be less difficult. They disclose their feelings of weakness also through a certain need for motherly care. They are usually pampered persons who very much want to lean on somebody, who "still need a nursemaid." They can never have enough safeguards against the other sex, and become extremely disquieted when facing it.

There are in our culture alarmingly many such insecure persons with a strong blemish of our phase of development—the fear of love and marriage. It is a general trait of the times. Our society is full of escapists. Through some unhappy and erroneous attitude, they are always as if in flight, always chased and persecuted. Some men isolate themselves and hide. Some girls don't even dare to go on the street, convinced that all men are courting them and that they would always be only the object of attacks. This is pure vanity, capable of completely spoiling the life of a person.

Experiences and knowledge can be put to good use and to bad use. Among the bad uses is the exaggerated reversal of an error, which is equally an error. The opposite of keeping back and being taciturn is openness, and thus we find people who make errors by being open. They always offer themselves to others. Although it is very nice openly to confess one's love, we are firmly convinced that in our complex culture this is a serious mistake. The reason is that there is nobody who could simply tolerate this offer, and the one who made it so hastily will not only have to bear the pain of regret and the burden of resulting inhibitions, but will also disturb the partner in the spontaneous development of his love impulses. Because of the generally prevailing abuse of love and the existing tension and struggle between the sexes, the partner will never be quite sure whether the offer was genuine and true, or whether perhaps bad intentions were hidden behind it. There are no fixed rules—we must take the particularity of the partner into account and go by the given conditions of our culture. Today it appears rather advisable to hold back one's inclinations somewhat.

116

THE SPECIAL SITUATION OF THE ARTIST[7]

Love plays a special part in the lives of artists—happy love as well as, more often, unhappy love. Unrequited love is today so general that almost everybody has at one time become the victim of it and its hardships. Among persons who face life with particular sensitivity, the artist plays a prominent role. He stands out by the very fact that he seeks in his art a life "aside from life," does not work in actual reality, but seeks a substitute world (*Ersatzwelt*), and is almost repulsed by reality. However, he becomes an artist only when he forms his creations so that they advance the real world. A creation becomes a work of art only by having the most general value, in that the artist found in it the way back to reality and the community.

In deviating from real life, one is inclined to experience the institution of love and marriage, with its emphasis on the reality of life as hostile and disturbing. Many artists take the ties of life literally as ties, shackles, or obstacles. They even develop them in their fantasy beyond bounds. Once they sense them as boundless obstacles, they can hardly overcome them. They find themselves in their love relationships before an insoluble task, and herein show not only the movements of a lover, but at the same time and to a much stronger degree the movements of a person fleeing from love. This is expressed in their thoughts and creations, which mirror the human problems in intensified form. The partner of the other sex is felt as somehow overpowering, and soon the field of love assumes the character of a danger.

This thought is found almost literally in communications from poets and writers. All problematical people have this tendency because they are all extremely ambitious and sensitive and take any impairment of their power as a serious insult or danger.

Art is today a predominantly masculine art. It contains the

7 Original translation of A1926a, pp. 18–21.

masculine tradition, presents predominantly masculine problems, and raises the female to a magic or frightening figure, which she is in the eyes of many men. Women cannot keep step with this masculine ideal of the times. They find the practice of art difficult not because they would not be capable, but because they cannot serve the exaggerated masculine ideal.

Regarding the female as danger, the poet Baudelaire[8] says: "I have never been able to think of a beautiful woman without having, at the same time, the sense of an immense danger."

A person who has entered this presumed "danger zone" will display a sequence of defensive and safeguarding movements. Hebbel,[9] as a youth, in a letter to his friend, describes his feelings approximately as follows: "Of course, I live here again opposite the most beautiful girl in town and am over my ears in love. But I hope that here too the antidote will soon be found alongside the poison. . . . And if today I should still see her lover climbing through her window, I would be through with her." From the first sentence we would really have expected a different ending.

The female as danger is an enduring guiding ideal in art; for example, the paintings of Rops[10] represent the female as danger, terror, or at least as an enormous power. In the Preface to *A Thousand and One Nights* the author, particularly frightened, points to the cunning and slyness of a woman who, through incredible inventiveness, saved her life from a man.

Also one of the oldest forms of art, the Bible, whose particular mood grips everybody from earliest childhood on, is permeated by the constant thought that the female represents danger. Thus a child will grow up in shyness, imbalance, and timidity toward the female. Also, Homer's *Iliad* paints with great precision the misfortune caused by a woman. In all works of poetry, in all works of art resounds the problem of

[8] Charles Baudelaire (1821–67), French lyrical poet.
[9] Friedrich Hebbel (1813–63), German poet and dramatist.
[10] Félicien Rops (1833–98), Belgian painter and etcher.

the day: woman the danger. Grillparzer[11] says of himself: "I have rescued myself from love into art."

How unrequited love will work itself out in a given person depends on his total attitude toward life, his life line.[12] If in the face of difficulties one loses his courage and calls off his activity, foundering in love may mean foundering in life. But this is then not a consequence of unrequited love itself. One who goes by the plan of being stimulated by difficulties will pull himself together after unrequited love and arrive at great achievements. A courageous person will draw a different conclusion than a defeated person. Popular psychology frequently points to the great achievements after unrequited love and sometimes recommends it like a medicine. But we know of people who have achieved great things without unrequited love. The kernel of truth is that artists are particularly seized and captivated by the problem of love.

The life of Goethe is, in this respect, particularly informative. He always saw danger in the female and always took flight before her and love. The guiding line of Faust is an eternal seeking for a solution of the love problem. With his own tensions, impulses, and strivings, Goethe built his world, dissatisfied with the facts of life, and conjured generally human concerns before our eyes. It is the greatness of his art that all strings in us resonate when he sounds the eternally new song of the tension between the sexes. Entangled in this tension, men fear that devotion is synonymous with loss of personality, with bondage or slavery.

Here Schleiermacher[13] is also to be mentioned who, in a wonderful essay, tries to prove that love is not such a simple matter, and that it would be foolish to believe that when a man entered adulthood he already knew something about love. Actually, everyone should go through a certain preparation, a preparatory school of an easier sort. This pure idealist,

[11] Franz Grillparzer (1791–1872), Austrian dramatist.

[12] Life line and guiding line are further earlier equivalents of life style.

[13] Friedrich Schleiermacher (1768–1834), German theologian and philosopher.

who is greatly venerated by the most religious people, is also convinced that in love, men do not find one another easily.

MEETING DIFFICULTIES[14]

In my lectures "Understanding Human Nature," which are regularly attended by about five hundred persons, the questions directed to me are largely on love—a sign that people find their way less easily in this question than perhaps that of occupation.[15]

Why are there so few happy love relationships? Because we are still not the real human beings, not yet mature for love, in arrears with being fellow men. We fight against it with all our means because we are afraid. Think of the opposition to coeducation, which only wants the sexes early in life to lose their shyness and fear, and have an opportunity to know each other better.

There is no fixed rule for meeting difficulties in love relationships. The peculiarity of a person's eroticism is a flourish of his total personality, which must be comprehended in each single case. To change a person's erroneous eroticism we must comprehend all his expressions in their coherence, and change his personality and its relationships to the surrounding world. A person's line of movement, which will assert itself also in love, may force him to seek an unrequited love and to persist in it, or it may let him take such an experience more lightly and lead him upward. If a person saturated with personal ambition cannot bear any kind of denial, it may suggest suicide. This is an error, which can be explained from the total context. In our society, which demands subordination, it will offer the opportunity for a highly tragic situation—connecting with the escape from life revenge against society and individual persons.

[14] Original translation of A1926a, pp. 21–23.
[15] Adler refers here to the popular lecture series he gave for several years at the Volksheim, Vienna's most important adult education institute at the time (Furtmüller, 1964, p. 374). These lectures, subsequently published under the same title, became the most widely read and translated book of Adler (A1927a, A1957a).

Love is cultivated and love relationships become beautified and refined through the cultivation and development of the all-encompassing social feeling. Love relationships are not formed suddenly but show a long preparation. The erotic tie is always present among human beings, but certain requirements must be met to make it felt and visible as love.

The beginning of love impulses goes back to those distant childhood days when they were not yet erotic, not yet sexually tinged—the days when the broad stream of social feeling still took the form of attachment and affection. Only that general human relationship was visible that, as between mother and child, connects human beings immediately. The enduring tie between single individuals that serves eternity and the preservation of humanity, which we call love, was not yet formed. It is a tie and perpetuation at the same time. One cannot shape these relationships at will, but rather must permit them to develop.

Knowledge of these matters has not yet matured because man is capable of self-deception regarding the processes of his own soul. Both sexes are easily caught in the whirlpool of prestige politics (*Prestigepolitik*). Then they are forced to play a role with which neither can cope, which leads to disturbing the harmlessness and spontaneity of their lives, and saturates them with prejudices against which every trace of true joy and happiness must of course disappear.[16]

A person who has absorbed these thoughts will naturally not move on earth free from mistakes, but he will at least remain aware of the right way and be able, instead of increasing his errors, steadily to diminish them.

UNDERSTANDING THE TASK OF MARRIAGE[17]

In a certain district of Germany there is an old custom for testing whether an engaged couple are suited for married life

[16] This paragraph is very similar to one on p. 25.

[17] Reprinted from A1931b, pp. 263–68. In accordance with today's usage, in all sections reprinted from A1931b (that is, the rest of this chapter), "mankind" has been replaced by "humanity."

together. Before the wedding ceremony, the bride and bridegroom are brought to a clearing, where a tree trunk has been cut down. Here they are given a two-handed saw and set to work to saw the trunk across. This is a test of how far they are willing to co-operate with each other. It is a task for two people. If there is no trust between them, they will tug against each other and accomplish nothing. If one of them wishes to take the lead and do everything by himself, then, even if the other gives way, the task will take twice as long. They must both have initiative, but their initiatives must combine together. These German villagers have recognized that co-operation is the chief prerequisite for marriage.

Co-operation for the General Welfare

If I were asked to say what love and marriage mean, I should give the following definition, incomplete as it may be:

"Love, with its fulfillment, marriage, is the most intimate devotion toward a partner of the other sex, expressed in physical attraction, in comradeship, and in the decision to have children. It can easily be shown that love and marriage are one side of co-operation—not a co-operation for the welfare of two persons only, but a co-operation also for the welfare of humanity."

This standpoint, that love and marriage are a co-operation for the welfare of humanity, throws light on every aspect of the problem. Even physical attraction, the most important of all human strivings, has been a most necessary development for humanity. As I have explained so often, humanity, suffering from imperfect organs, has been none too well equipped for life on the crust of this poor planet, earth. The chief way to preserve human life was to propagate it; hence our fertility and the continual striving of physical attraction.

In our own days, we find difficulties and dissensions arising over all the problems of love. Married couples are confronted with these difficulties, parents are concerned with them, the whole of society is involved in them. If we are trying, therefore, to come to a right conclusion, our approach must be

122

quite without prejudice. We must forget what we have learned and try to investigate, as far as we can, without letting other considerations interfere with a full and free discussion.

I do not mean that we can judge the problem of love and marriage as if it were an entirely isolated problem. A human being can never be wholly free in this way: He can never reach solutions for his problems purely along the line of his private ideas. Every human being is bound by definite ties; his development takes place within a definite framework, and he must conform his decisions to this framework. These three main ties are set by the facts that we are living in one particular place in the universe and must develop with the limits and possibilities that our circumstances set us; that we are living among others of our own kind to whom we must learn to adapt ourselves; and that we are living in two sexes, with the future of our race dependent on the relations of these two sexes.

If an individual is interested in his fellows and in the welfare of humanity, everything he does will be guided by the interests of his fellows. He will try to solve the problem of love and marriage as if the welfare of others were involved. He does not need to know that he is trying to solve it in this way. If you ask him, he will perhaps be unable to give a scientific account of his aims. But he will spontaneously seek the welfare and improvement of humanity, and this interest will be visible in all his activities.

There are other human beings who are not so much concerned with the welfare of humanity. Instead of taking as their underlying view of life "What can I contribute to my fellows?" "How can I fit in as part of the whole?" they ask rather, "What is the use of life?" "What can I get out of it?" "What does it pay?" "Are other people considering me enough?" "Am I properly appreciated?" If this attitude is behind an individual's approach to life, he will try to solve the problem of love and marriage in the same way. He will ask always: "What can I get out of it?"

Love is not a purely natural task, as some psychologists believe. Sex is a drive or instinct; but the question of love and

123

marriage is not quite simply how we are to satisfy this drive. Wherever we look, we find that our drives and instincts are developed, cultivated, refined. We have repressed some of our desires and inclinations. On behalf of our fellow beings, we have learned how not to annoy each other. We have learned how to dress ourselves and how to be clean. Even our hunger does not have a merely natural outlet; we have cultivated tastes and manners in eating. Our drives have all been adapted to our common culture; they all reflect the efforts we have learned to make for the welfare of humanity and for our life in association.

If we apply this understanding to the problem of love and marriage, we shall see, here again, that the interest of the whole, the interest in humanity, must always be involved. This interest is primary. There is no advantage in discussing any of the aspects of love and marriage, in proposing reliefs, changes, new regulations, or new institutions, before we have seen that the problem can be solved only in its whole coherence, only by considering human welfare as a whole. Perhaps we shall improve; perhaps we shall find more complete answers to the problem. If we do, they will be better answers because they take fuller account of the fact that we are living in two sexes, on the crust of this earth, where association is necessary. Insofar as our answers already take account of these conditions, the truth in them can stand forever.

Task for Two Equal Partners

When we use this approach, our first finding in the love problem is that it is a task for two individuals. For many people this is bound to be a new task. To some degree we have been educated to work alone; to some degree, to work in a team or a group. We have generally had little experience of working two by two. These new conditions, therefore, raise a difficulty; but it is a difficulty easier to solve if these two people have been interested in their fellows, for then they can learn more easily to be interested in each other.

We could even say that for a full solution of this co-operation of two, each partner must be more interested in the other than in himself. This is the only basis on which love and marriage can be successful. We shall already be able to see in what way many opinions of marriage and many proposals for its reform are mistaken.

If each partner is to be more interested in the other partner than in himself, there must be equality. If there is to be so intimate a devotion, neither partner can feel subdued nor overshadowed. Equality is only possible if both partners have this attitude. It should be the effort of each to ease and enrich the life of the other. In this way each is safe. Each feels that he is worthwhile; each feels that he is needed.

Here we find the fundamental guarantee of marriage, the fundamental meaning of happiness in this relation. It is the feeling that you are worthwhile, that you cannot be replaced, that your partner needs you, that you are acting well, that you are a fellow man and a true friend.

It is not possible for a partner in a co-operative task to accept a position of subservience. Two people cannot live together fruitfully if one wishes to rule and force the other to obey. In our present conditions many men and, indeed, many women are convinced that it is the man's part to rule and dictate, to play the leading role, to be the master. This is the reason why we have so many unhappy marriages. Nobody can bear a position of inferiority without anger and disgust.

Comrades must be equal, and when people are equal, they will always find a way to settle their difficulties. They will agree, for example, in questions of having children. They know that a decision for sterility involves their own part in giving a pledge for the future of humanity. They will agree in questions of education; and they will be stimulated to solve their problems as they occur, because they know that the children of unhappy marriages are penalized and cannot develop well.

In our present-day civilization people are not often well prepared for co-operation. Our training has been too much toward individual success, toward considering what we can get out of life rather than what we can give to it. It will be easily understood that where we get two people living together in the intimate way that marriage demands, any failure in co-operation, in the ability to be interested in somebody else, will have the gravest results. Most people are experiencing this close relationship for the first time. They are unaccustomed to consulting another human being's interests and aims, desires, hopes, and ambitions. They are not prepared for the problems of a common task. We need not be surprised at the many mistakes we see around us; but we can examine the facts and learn how to avoid mistakes in the future.

EDUCATION AND TRAINING[18]

No crisis of adult life is met without previous training. We always respond in conformity with our style of living. The preparation for marriage is not overnight. In a child's characteristic behavior, in his attitudes, thoughts, and actions, we can see how he is training himself for adult situations. In its main features his approach to love is already established by the fifth or sixth year.

Early Sex Education

Early in the development of a child we can see that he is already forming his outlook on love and marriage. We should not imagine that he is showing sexual promptings in our adult sense of the term. He is making up his mind about one aspect of the general social life of which he feels himself a part. Love and marriage are factors of his environment: They enter into his conception of his own future. He must have some comprehension of them, take up some stand about these problems.

When children give such early evidence of their interest in the other sex and choose for themselves the partners whom they like, we should never interpret it as a mistake, or a nuisance, or a precocious sex influence. Still less should we

[18] Reprinted from A1931b, pp. 268–72.

deride it or make a joke of it. We should take it as a step forward in their preparation for love and marriage. Instead of making a trifle out of it, we should rather agree with the child that love is a marvelous task, a task for which he should be prepared, a task on behalf of the whole of humanity. Thus we can implant an ideal in the child's mind, and later in life children will be able to meet each other as very well-prepared comrades and as friends in an intimate devotion. It is revealing to observe that children are spontaneous and wholehearted adherents of monogamy—and this often in spite of the fact that the marriages of their parents are not always harmonious and happy.

I should never encourage parents to explain the physical relations of sex too early in life or to explain more than their children wish to learn. You can understand that the way in which a child looks on the problems of marriage is of the greatest importance. If he is taught in a mistaken way, he can see them as a danger or as something altogether beyond him. In my own experience children who were introduced to the facts of adult relations in early life—at four, five or six years of age, and children who had precocious experiences—are always more scared of love in later life. Bodily attraction suggests to them also the idea of danger. If a child is more grown-up when he has his first explanations and experiences, he is not nearly so frightened: There is so much less opportunity for him to make mistakes in understanding the right relations. The key to helpfulness is never to lie to a child, never to evade his questions, to understand what is behind his questions, to explain only as much as we are sure he can understand. Officious and intrusive information can cause great harm.

In this problem of life, as in all others, it is better for a child to be independent and learn what he wants to know by his own efforts. If there is trust between himself and his parents, he can suffer no injury. He will always ask what he needs to know. There is a common superstition that children can be misled by the explanations of their comrades. I have never seen a child, otherwise healthy, who suffered harm in this way. Children do not swallow everything that their

127

schoolmates tell them; for the most part children are very critical, and, if they are not certain that what they have been told is true, they will ask their parents or their brothers and sisters. I must confess, too, that I have often found children more delicate and tactful in these affairs than their elders.

Impressions from Immediate Surroundings

Even the physical attraction of adult life is already being trained in childhood. The impressions the child gains with regard to sympathy and attraction, the impressions given by the members of the other sex in his immediate surroundings —these are the beginnings of physical attraction. When a boy gains these impressions from his mother, his sisters, or the girls around him, his selection of physically attractive types in later life will be influenced by their similarity to these members of his earlier environment. Sometimes he is influenced also by the creations of art: Everybody is drawn in this way by an ideal of personal beauty. Thus in later life the individual has no longer a *free choice* in the broadest sense but a choice only along the lines of his training.

This search for beauty is not a meaningless search. Our aesthetic emotions are always based on a feeling for health and for the improvement and future of humanity; the symbols of the way in which we wish our children to develop. This is the beauty that is always drawing us.

Sometimes if a boy experiences difficulties with his mother, and a girl with her father (as happens often if the co-operation in marriage is not firm), they look for an antithetic type. If, for example, the boy's mother has nagged him and bullied him, if he is weak and afraid of being dominated, he may find sexually attractive only those women who appear not to be dominating. It is easy for him to make mistakes: He can look for a partner whom he can subdue, and a happy marriage is never possible without equality. Sometimes, if he wants to prove himself powerful and strong, he looks for a partner who also seems to be strong, either because he prefers strength or because he finds in her more of a challenge to prove his own strength.

If his disagreement with his mother is very great, his preparation for love and marriage may be hindered, and even physical attraction to the other sex may be blocked. There are many degrees of this obstruction; where it is complete, he will exclude the other sex entirely and become perverted.

We are always better prepared if the marriage of our parents has been harmonious. Children gain their earliest impressions of what marriage is like from the life of their parents, and it is not astonishing that the greatest number of failures in life are among the children of broken marriages and unhappy family life. If the parents are not able themselves to co-operate, it will be impossible for them to teach co-operation to their children.

We can often best consider the fitness of an individual for marriage by learning whether he was trained in the right kind of family life and by observing his attitude toward his parents, sisters, and brothers. The important factor is where he gained his preparation for love and marriage.

We must be careful on this point, however. We know that a man is not determined by his environment but by the estimate he makes of his environment. His estimate can be useful. It is possible that he had very unhappy experiences of family life in his parents' home, but this may only stimulate him to do better in his own family life. He may be striving to prepare himself well for marriage. We must never judge or exclude a human being because he has an unfortunate family life behind him.

PROPER AND IMPROPER PREPARATION[19]

The worst preparation is when an individual is always looking for his own interest. If he has been trained in this way he will be thinking all the while what pleasure or excitement he can get out of life. He will always be demanding freedom and re-

[19] Reprinted from A1931b, pp. 272–78.

liefs, never considering how he can ease and enrich the life of his partner. This is a disastrous approach. I should compare him to a man who tries to put a horse's collar on from the tail end. It is not a sin, but it is a mistaken method.

Proper and Improper Concepts of Marriage

In preparing our attitude to love, therefore, we should not always be looking for mitigations and ways of avoiding responsibility. The comradeship of love could not be firm if there were hesitation and doubt. Co-operation demands a decision for eternity; and we only regard those unions as real examples of love and real marriages in which a fixed and unalterable decision has been taken. In this decision we include the decision to have children, to educate them and train them in co-operation, and to make them, as far as we can, real fellow men, real equal and responsible members of the human race.

A good marriage is the best means we have for bringing up the future generation of humanity; and marriage should always have this in view. Marriage is really a task; it has its own rules and laws; we cannot select one part and evade the others without infringing the eternal law of this earth crust, co-operation.

It is impossible to have the real intimate devotion of love if we limit our responsibility to five years or regard the marriage as a trial period.[20] If men or women contemplate such an escape, they do not collect all their powers for the task. In none of the serious and important tasks of life do we arrange such a "getaway." We cannot love and be limited.

All those very well-meaning and good-hearted people who are trying to find a relief for marriage are on the wrong path. The reliefs they propose would damage and restrict the efforts of couples who were entering marriage; they would make it

[20] This is an allusion to the writings of Judge Benjamin Lindsey (1927), who proposed a companionate marriage which, in many ways similar to earlier ideas of trial marriage, was widely discussed in the late 1920s and early 1930s.

easier for them to find a way out and to omit the work they should do in the task on which they have decided. I know that there are many difficulties in our social life and that they hinder many people from solving the problem of love and marriage in the right way, even though they would like to solve it. It is not love and marriage, however, that I want to sacrifice; I want to sacrifice the difficulties of our social life.

We know what characteristics are necessary for a love partnership—to be faithful and true and trustworthy, not to be reserved, not to be self-seeking. . . . If a person believes that unfaithfulness is all in the day's work, he is not properly prepared for marriage. It is not even possible to carry through a true comradeship if both partners have agreed to preserve their freedom. This is not comradeship. In comradeship we are not free in every direction. We have bound ourselves to our co-operation.

A Case Example

Let me give an example of how such a private agreement, not adapted to the success of the marriage or the welfare of humanity, can harm both partners. I remember a case where a divorced man and a divorced woman married. They were cultivated and intelligent people and hoped very much that their new venture in marriage would be better than the last. They did not know, however, how their first marriages had come to ruin; they were looking for a right way without having seen their lack of social interest. They professed themselves free-thinkers, and they wished to have an easy marriage in which they would never run the risk of being bored by each other. They proposed, therefore, that each of them should be perfectly free in every direction; they should do whatever they wanted to do, but they should trust each other enough to tell everything that happened. On this point the husband seemed to be more courageous. Whenever he came home he had many adventures to tell his wife, and she seemed to enjoy them vastly and to be very proud of her husband's successes. She was always intending to begin a flirtation or a love relation herself; but before she had taken the first step, she began to suffer from agoraphobia. She could no longer go out alone; her neurosis kept her to her room; if she took a step beyond the door she was so scared that she was compelled to return. This agoraphobia was a protection against the decision she had made; but there was more to it than this. At last, since she was unable to go out alone, her husband was compelled to stay by her side. You see how the logic of marriage broke through their decision. The husband could no longer be a free-thinker because he must remain with his wife. She herself could make no use of her freedom because she was afraid to go out alone. If this woman were cured, she would be forced to reach a better understanding of marriage, and the husband, too, would have to regard it as a co-operative task.

Various Improper Preparations

Other mistakes are made at the very beginning of the marriage. A child who has been pampered at home often feels neglected in marriage. He has not been trained to adapt himself to social life. A pampered child may develop into a great tyrant in marriage; the other partner feels victimized, feels himself in a cage, and begins to resist. It is interesting to observe what happens when two pampered children marry each other. Each of them is claiming interest and attention, and neither can be satisfied. The next step is to look for an escape; one partner begins a flirtation with someone else in the hope of gaining more attention.

Some people are incapable of falling in love with one person; they fall in love with two at the same time. They thus feel free; they can escape from one to the other, and never undertake the full responsibilities of love. Both means neither.

There are other people who invent a romantic, ideal, or unattainable love; they can thus luxuriate in their feelings without the necessity of approaching a partner in reality. A high ideal of love can also be used to exclude all possibilities, because no one will be found who can live up to it.

Many men, and especially many women, through mistakes in their development, have trained themselves to dislike and reject their sexual role. They have hindered their natural functions and are physically not capable, without treatment, of accomplishing a successful marriage. This is what I have called the masculine protest, and it is very much provoked by the overvaluation of men in our present culture.

If children are left in doubt of their sexual role, they are very apt to feel insecure. So long as the masculine role is taken to be the dominant role, it is natural that they should feel, whether they are boys or girls, that the masculine role is enviable. They will doubt their own ability to fulfill this role, will overstress the importance of being manly, and will try to avoid being put to the test.

This dissatisfaction with the sexual role is very frequent in our culture. We can suspect it in all cases of frigidity in women and psychic impotence in men. In these cases there is a resistance to love and marriage and a resistance in the right place. It is impossible to avoid these failures unless we truly have the feeling that men and women are equal. So long as one half of the human race has reason to be dissatisfied with the position accorded to it, we shall have a very great obstacle to the success of marriage. The remedy here is training for equality; and we should never permit children to remain ambiguous about their own future role.

I believe that the intimate devotion of love and marriage is best secured if there have not been sexual relations before the marriage. I have found that secretly most men do not really like it if their sweetheart is able to give herself before marriage. Sometimes they regard it as a sign of easy virtue and are shocked by it. Moreover, in this state of our culture, if there are intimate relations before marriage the burden is heavier for the girl.

It is also a great mistake if a marriage is contracted out of fear and not out of courage. We can understand that courage is one side of co-operation and if men and women choose their partners out of fear it is a sign that they do not wish for a real co-operation. This also holds good when they choose partners who are drunkards or very far below them in social status or in education. They are afraid of love and marriage and wish to establish a situation in which their partner will look up to them.

Friendship and Occupation

One of the ways in which social interest can be trained is through friendship. We learn in friendship to look with the eyes of another person, to listen with his ears, and to feel with his heart. If a child is frustrated, if he is always watched and guarded, if he grows up isolated, without comrades and friends, he does not develop this ability to identify himself with another person. He always thinks himself the most important being in the world and is always anxious to secure his own welfare. Training in friendship is a preparation for marriage. Games might be useful if they were regarded as a training in co-operation; but in children's games we find too often competition and the desire to excel. It is very useful to establish situations in which two children work together, study together, and learn together. I believe that we should not undervalue dancing. Dancing is a type of activity in which two people have to accomplish a common task, and I think it is good for children to be trained in dancing. I do not exactly mean the dancing we have today, where we have more of a show than of a common task. If, however, we had simple and easy dances for children, it would be a great help for their development.

Another problem that also helps to show us the preparation for marriage is the problem of occupation. Today the solution of this problem is put before the solution of love and marriage. One partner, or both, must be occupied so that they can earn their living and support a family, and we can understand that the right preparation for marriage includes also the right preparation for work.

134

COURTSHIP AND SEXUAL ATTRACTION[21]

We can always find the degree of courage and the degree of capacity to co-operate in the approach to the other sex. Every individual has his characteristic approach, his characteristic gait and temperament in wooing; and this is always congruous with his style of life. In this amative temperament we can see whether he says "Yes" to the future of mankind, is confident and co-operative, or whether he is interested only in his own person, suffers from stage fright, and tortures himself with the questions, "What sort of a show am I making?" "What do they think of me?" A man may be slow and cautious in wooing, or rash and precipitate; in any case, his amative temperament fits in with his goal and his style of life, and is only one expression of it. We cannot judge a man's fitness for marriage entirely by his courtship, for there he has a direct goal before him, and in other ways he may be indecisive. Nevertheless, we can gather from it sure indications of his personality.

In our own cultural conditions (and only in these conditions) it is generally expected that the man should be the first to express attraction, that the man should make the first approach. So long as this cultural demand exists, therefore, it is necessary to train boys in the masculine attitude—to take the initiative, not to hesitate or look for an escape. They can be trained, however, only if they feel themselves to be a part of the whole social life and accept its advantages and disadvantages as their own. Of course, girls and women are also engaged in wooing, they also take the initiative; but in our prevailing cultural conditions, they feel obliged to be more reserved, and their wooing is expressed in their whole gait and person, in the way they dress, the way they look, speak, and listen. A man's approach, therefore, may be called simpler and shallower, a woman's deeper and more complicated.

The sexual attraction toward the other partner is necessary, but it should always be molded along the line of a desire for

[21] Reprinted from A1931b, pp. 278–80.

human welfare. If the partners are really interested in each other, there will never be the difficulty of sexual attraction coming to an end. This stop implies always a lack of interest; it tells us that the individual no longer feels equal, friendly, and co-operative toward his partner, no longer wishes to enrich the life of his partner.

People may think, sometimes, that the interest continues but the attraction has ceased. This is never true. Sometimes the mouth lies or the head does not understand; but the functions of the body always speak the truth. If the functions are deficient, it follows that there is no true agreement between these two people. They have lost interest in each other. One of them, at least, no longer wishes to solve the task of love and marriage but is looking for an evasion and escape.

In one other way the sex drive in human beings is different from that among other beings. It is continuous. This is another way in which the welfare and continuance of humanity is guaranteed; it is a way by which humanity can increase, become numerous, and secure its welfare and survival by the greatness of its numbers. In other creatures life has taken other means to ensure this survival: In many, for example, we find that the females produce a very great number of eggs that never come to maturity. Many of them get lost or destroyed, but the great number insures that some of them always survive.

With human beings also, one method of surviving is to have children. We shall find, therefore, that in this problem of love and marriage, those people who are most spontaneously interested in the welfare of humanity are the most likely to have children, and those who are not interested, consciously or unconsciously, in their fellow beings, refuse the burden of procreation. If they are always demanding and expecting, never giving, they do not like children. They are interested in only their own persons, and they regard children as bothers, troubles, nuisances, things that will prevent them from keeping their interest in themselves. We can say, therefore, that for a full solution of the problem of love and marriage a decision to have children is necessary. A good marriage is the best means we know for bringing up the future generation of humanity, and marriage should always have this in view.

THE CASE FOR MONOGAMY[22]

The solution of the problem of love and marriage in our practical and social life is monogamy. Anyone who starts the relation that demands such an intimate devotion, such an interest in another person, cannot shake the fundamental basis of this relation, and search for an escape.

Task Orientation

We know that there is the possibility that there will be a break in the relation. Unfortunately, we cannot always avoid it. But it is easiest to avoid if we regard marriage and love as a social task that confronts us, a task that we are expected to solve. We shall then try every means to solve the problem. Breaks generally happen because the partners are not collecting all their powers. They are not creating the marriage; they are only waiting to receive something. If they face the problem in this way, of course they will fail before it. It is a mistake to regard love and marriage as if they were a paradise; and it is a mistake, too, to regard marriage as if it were the end of a story. When two people are married, the possibilities of their relationship begin; during marriage they are faced with the real tasks of life and the real opportunity to create for the sake of society.

The other point of view of marriage as an end, as a final goal, is much too prominent in our culture. We can see it, for example, in thousands of novels, in which we are left with a man and a woman, just married and really at the beginning of their life together. Yet the situation is often treated as if marriage itself had solved everything satisfactorily, as if they were at the end of their task.

[22] Reprinted from A1931b, pp. 280–86.

Another point important to realize is that love by itself does not settle everything. There are all kinds of love, and it is better to rely upon work, interest, and co-operation to solve the problems of marriage.

There is nothing at all miraculous in this whole relationship. The attitude of every individual toward marriage is one of the expressions of his style of life: we can understand it if we understand the whole individual, not unless. It is coherent with all his efforts and aims. We shall be able to find out, therefore, why so many people are always looking for a relief or escape. I can tell exactly how many people have this attitude: all the people who remain pampered children.

This is a dangerous type in our social life—these grown-up pampered children who, as part of their style of life, fixed in the first four or five years, always have the schema of apperception: "Can I get all I want?" If they can't get everything they want, they think life is purposeless. "What is the use of living," they ask, "if I cannot have what I want?" They become pessimistic: They conceive a "death wish." They make themselves sick and neurotic, and out of their mistaken style of life construct a philosophy. They feel that their mistaken ideas are of unique and tremendous importance. They feel that it is a piece of spite on the part of the universe if they have to repress their drives and emotions. They are trained in this way.

Once they experienced a favorable time in which they obtained everything they wanted. Some of them, perhaps, still feel that if they cry long enough, if they protest enough, if they refuse co-operation, they will obtain their own desires. They do not look to the coherence of life but to their own personal interests.

The result is, they do not want to contribute, they always wish to have things easy, they want to be refused nothing; and therefore they wish to have marriage itself on trial or return, they want companionate marriages, trial marriages, easier divorces: at the very beginning of marriage they demand freedom and a right to unfaithfulness. Now, if one human being is really interested in another, he must have all the characteristics belonging to that interest; he must be true, a

138

good friend; he must feel responsible, he must make himself faithful and trustworthy. I believe that at the least a human being who has not succeeded in accomplishing such a love life or such a marriage should understand that on this point his life has been a mistake.

It is necessary, too, to be interested in the welfare of the children; and if a marriage is based upon different outlooks from the one I have supported, there are great difficulties for the bringing up of children. If the parents quarrel and look on their marriage as a trifle, if they do not see it as if its problems could be solved and the relationship could be continued successfully, it is not a very favorable situation for helping the children to be sociable.

Inappropriate Aims and Approaches

Probably there are reasons why people should not live together; probably there are cases where it would be better that they should be apart. Who should decide the case? Are we going to put it in the hands of people who themselves are not rightly taught, who themselves do not understand that marriage is a task, who themselves are interested only in their own persons? They would look at divorce in the same way as they look at marriage: "What can be gotten out of it?" These are obviously not the people to decide.

You will see very often that people divorce and remarry again and again and always make the same mistake. Then who ought to decide? Perhaps we might imagine that if something is wrong with a marriage, a psychiatrist should decide whether or not it should be broken. There is difficulty there. I do not know whether it holds true of America, but in Europe I have found that psychiatrists for the most part think that personal welfare is the most important point. Generally, therefore, if they are consulted in such a case, they recommend a sweetheart or a lover and think that this might be the way to solve the problem. I am sure that in time they will change their minds and cease to give such advice. They can only propose such a solution if they have not been rightly trained in the whole coherence of the problem, the way it hangs together with the other tasks of our life on this earth; and it is this coherence that I have been wishing to offer for your consideration.

A similar mistake is made when people look upon marriage as a solution for a personal problem. Here again I cannot speak of America, but I know that in Europe, if a boy or girl becomes neurotic, psychiatrists often advise them to have sweethearts and to begin sex relations. They advise adults, also, in the same way. This is really making love and marriage into a mere patent medicine, and these individuals are bound to lose very greatly.

The right solution of the problem of love and marriage belongs to the highest fulfillment of the whole personality. There is no problem more closely involved with happiness and a true and useful expression in life. We cannot treat it as a trifle.

We cannot look on love and marriage as a remedy for a criminal career, for drunkenness or neurosis. A neurotic needs to have the right treatment before he is fitted for love and marriage; and if he enters them before he is capable of approaching them rightly, he is bound to run into new dangers and misfortunes. Marriage is too high an ideal, and the solution of the task demands too much of our effort and creative activity for us to load it with such additional burdens.

In other ways, also, marriage is entered into with inappropriate aims. Some people marry for the sake of economic security; they marry because they pity someone; or they marry to secure a servant. There is no place for such jokes in marriage. I have even known cases where people have married to increase their difficulties. A young man, perhaps, is in difficulties about his examinations or his future career. He feels that he may very easily fail, and if he fails he wishes to be able to excuse himself. He takes on the additional task of marriage, therefore, in order to have an alibi.

I am sure we should not try to depreciate or diminish this problem but to set it on a higher level. In all the reliefs I have heard proposed, it is always the women really who bear the disadvantage. There is no question but that men in our cul-

140

ture already have an easier time. This is a mistake in our common approach. It cannot be overcome by a personal revolt. Especially in marriage itself, a personal revolt would disturb the social relationship and the interest of the partner. It can only be overcome by recognizing and changing the whole attitude of our culture.

A pupil of mine, Professor Rasey of Detroit, made a study and found that 42 per cent of the girls she questioned would like to have been boys; this means that they were disappointed with their own sex.[23] Can it be easy to solve the problems of love and marriage while nearly half of mankind is disappointed and discouraged, does not agree with its position, and objects to the greater freedom of the other half? Can it be easy to solve them if women are always expecting to be slighted and believe themselves to be only sexual objects for men, or believe it is natural for men to be polygamous and unfaithful?

Conclusion

From all we have said we can draw a simple, obvious, and helpful conclusion. Human beings are neither polygamous nor monogamous. But to realize that we live on this planet, in association with human beings equal to ourselves, and di-

[23] Marie I. Rasey (1887–1957), professor of educational psychology, Wayne University, Detroit, studied with Adler in Vienna during the summers of 1928 and 1929 (Rasey, 1953, pp. 160–63). Rasey (1947) reports: "Data were secured from responses to the question: 'If you had the wishing ring and could be what you liked, would you stay what you are or would you change your sex?'" (pp. 117–18). The findings were as shown in the following table. Note the girls' decreasing dissatisfaction with their sex, over the years.

	1924 N=6,000		June 1939 N=2,000		Nov. 1939 N=2,000	
	boys	girls	boys	girls	boys	girls
Stay what I am	100%	62%	99%	72%	95%	75%
Would change sex	0%	38%	1%	28%	5%	25%

vided into two sexes, and that we must solve the three problems of life that our circumstances set us in a sufficient way, will help us to see that the fullest and highest development of the individual in love and marriage can best be secured by monogamy.

PART III

Sexual Disorders

5

HOMOSEXUALITY

GENERAL CONSIDERATIONS

Like a ghost or bogey, the problem of homosexuality arises in society. Despite all condemnation, religious and legal anathema, the number of sexual deviates appears to be on the increase, in rural districts and large cities alike. Children, adults, older people, men and women share alike in this evil. It is of concern to the educator, the sociologist, the psychiatrist, and the jurist. All possible measures are continuously taken against it, without appreciable results. Severe penalties, leniency, conciliatory attitudes, even concealment—nothing seems to have any effect on the spread of this anomaly.

There are a vast number of theories and conceptions of homosexuality, including also some that advocate it. Together they testify to the great impression made by the one fact, namely, that large sections of the population are not true to their sexual role, deviating from it in ways which, to be sure, have been taken for a long time.

Incomplete Knowledge[1]

Is homosexuality a throwback, an atavism? Good observers point out that only domesticated animals engage in or permit

[1] Including preceding two paragraphs, translated from A1917b as reprinted in A1930d, pp. 1 and 2.

homosexual attacks. [*Later added:* The latter was observed by Pfungst in a dominant anthropoid ape, which he had spanked to test this idea.]

Neither does the theory of degeneracy yield a useful result, since those working with this model cannot answer the one important question: Who among the degenerates will resort to homosexuality?

Nor can Hirschfeld, Fliess, Freud, etc., answer the question: Who among the many or few who carry simultaneously procreative cells of their own and the other sex will become homosexuals? Krafft-Ebing's "constitutional disposition" and its continuation, Freud's "sexual constitution," are but theoretical postulates of a prejudiced system.

"Fixating experiences,"[2] which presumably point the way to the child's sexuality, as emphasized by Binet, Janet, Schrenck-Notzing, Bloch, Moll, and others, always point again to the already existing inclination toward deviation. Our theoretical opponents and the patients themselves begin their case histories with the words: "Already in early childhood, at the following experience, traces of the innate deviation appeared. . . ."

Our esteem of the above-mentioned studies is by no means diminished when we now assert that our knowledge of the nature of sexual deviations is incomplete and therefore does not permit a firmly founded standpoint toward the social significance of sexual deviation. Although one finds among adversaries as well as defenders of homosexuality many well-trained minds and intelligent arguments, it would be a serious mistake to overlook that our state of knowledge is incomplete.

[2] What Adler here refers to as "fixating experiences" (*fixierende Erlebnisse*) is generally referred to as "subconscious fixed ideas" caused usually by "a traumatic or frightening event that had become subconscious" (Ellenberger, 1970, pp. 372–73).

Critique of Previous Theories[3, 4]

Until recent decades it was assumed that homosexuality was caused by immorality, wantonness, and surfeit. Only lately have physicians realized that a large number of homosexuals actually fight against their inclination and want to be cured of it. The result was that one began to believe in innate factors. Since probably no unequivocal cures from homosexuality have become known to wider circles, this view has gained ground. The far more frequent cases in which persons had simply "gotten over" their homosexuality were forgotten. When cures did occur later and were published, a broader assumption was arrived at.

Krafft-Ebing was perhaps the first to differentiate between acquired and innate homosexuality. He also happened on the idea of a feminine part of the brain in male homosexuals. Binet and Schrenck-Notzing assumed, as did Freud later, a sexual trauma or experience in childhood, the fixation of which was supposed to determine the subsequent direction of the sexual drive. Freud, in the course of his studies, arrived at the view that homosexuality was a part of the libido that was originally repressed and later revived, and existed as inclination and fantasy perhaps in all neurotics.

The views and treatments of Steinach are close to the assumptions of Krafft-Ebing, Hirschfeld, and Weininger, shifting the cause of homosexuality to the inadequacy of the corresponding glands. Today the best known of such theories is Hirschfeld's "intermediates theory" (*Zwischenstufentheorie*), which holds that physical and psychological expressions in men and women depend on the interaction of the androgen and estrogen hormones from which hermaphroditism and homosexuality originate.

[3] General references: Krafft-Ebing (1893), Magnus Hirschfeld (n.d., 1922), Iwan Bloch (1902), Sigmund Freud (1923), Arthur Kronfeld (1922), Oswald Schwarz (1925), Max Marcuse (1923). [Author's note (A1930d, p. 56).]

[4] Translated from A1926h as reprinted in A1930d, pp. 58–59.

I was able to state in 1914 [see A1914i], from numerous original and follow-up studies, that homosexuality is psychological in origin, although physical peculiarities may be facilitating. Kraepelin is also of the opinion that homosexuality is determined by exogenous factors. Moll admits endogenous causes in some cases, but considers psychotherapy necessary. Older authors, such as Naecke, Kiernan, Havelock Ellis, and others, assume bisexuality, as does Hirschfeld, and blame incomplete sexual differentiation.

It was a turning point in the conception of homosexuality when, as mentioned, so many deviates were encountered who considered their deviation a serious, even unbearable torture from which they wanted to be freed at any price. But the homosexuals who complain about their "unfortunate disposition" generally do very little about it. They rather conclude from their futile efforts that they cannot be saved, and by a display of good intentions secure for themselves extenuating circumstances and justifications.

On the other hand, those who pride themselves on being "different" thereby—taking the personality as a whole—regularly compensate for deep feelings of inferiority and weakness toward women. Contempt for women also is a compensation, securing a fictitious satisfaction.

Regarding the assumption of "fixated experiences," my doubt proved completely justified. In such cases I ask: What are the circumstances that bring about the fixation?

Public Opinion[5]

The contributions of Krafft-Ebing, Moll, Hirschfeld, Bloch, and others will always retain their place as extensive preliminary work and valuable collections of data. Yet they

[5] Paragraphs 1–4 translated from A1917b as reprinted in A1930d, pp. 2–3. Paragraphs 5 and 6 translated from A1926h as reprinted in A1930d, pp. 59–60.

were not able even to influence public opinion, let alone the legislative process.[6]

Public opinion is an important factor in the theory of deviation. Surely no theory will ever influence society or social morals in favor of homosexuality. The greatest concession to be expected would be concealment and nonintervention, which is as far as the guardians of the law have occasionally gone already. Many suits have been ruled out of court, and some lists of homosexuals known to the police were never prosecuted, testifying to a more lenient practice. However, the barriers of society against equal rights for sexual deviation remain unshaken by any theory. They are based on the necessary safeguards and the socially developed aversions of the normally feeling individuals. These safeguards are, in the main, socially necessary—incidentally, they also imply a semblance of superiority over the deviates.

Rejection of homosexuality is easily misinterpreted as betraying a struggle against one's own homosexual tendencies. Thereby the attempt was indeed made to increase the number of homosexuals by exactly those who are opposed to it. The attribution of particularly high value to homosexuality, as homosexual circles do to justify their deviation, appears to have equally little validity.

The opinion that homosexuals will die out from their deviation is most plausible. But it assumes an innate quality that we consider a myth. Any "proof" of heredity only weakens the argument, because in mixed cases the heterosexual component would impede natural selection.

Why do most people take an actually hostile attitude toward homosexuality? Why do they consider it a sin, a vice, or a crime, and why is it treated in most civilized countries as a

[6] The penal code committee of the German Reichstag, in October 1929, after a lengthy debate, defeated the general penal ruling regarding homosexual intercourse among men, paragraph 296 of the bill, the equivalent of paragraph 175 of the existing code. Wilhelm Kahl, chairman of the committee, explained, "All in all, the law and the penal process have proven to be unsuitable or quite inadequate means for fighting this vice. Therefore, in accordance with the generally sound tendency of the reform, it is better to rescind this law than to face unavoidable bankruptcy." [Author's note.]

149

punishable offense? Freud and his followers are satisfied with the answer: because they have repressed their own homosexuality or have sublimated it. This explanation is not only improbable, it also can certainly not be verified. It is derived not from facts but from psychoanalytic theory. Alone the logic of man's living together, the urge to preserve the human race—in short, the inherent communal feeling in man—is what compels people toward the energetic rejection of homosexuality.

Of course, the belief that this could be suitably achieved through a prison sentence, which is a further removal from the community, is a mistake of our culture. Nevertheless, homosexuality cannot count on permanent recognition, as is often sought for it, no more than can incest or offenses against the public. We expect from the future first of all a more correct attitude toward this problem, a voluntary decision of the offender to be treated.

CRITIQUE OF EVIDENCE FOR INNATENESS[7]

There are seven main arguments in favor of homosexuality being innate, referring to: general physique, behavior, abnormalities of the sex organs, low regard for the other sex, homosexual dreams and fantasies, early signs in childhood, and incidence in the family. We shall show that each one is untenable.

Physique

The physique of homosexual men is often described as feminine, that of homosexual women as masculine. Primarily involved here are the complexion, the pelvis, the forehead, the breast, facial hair and pubic hair, the voice, the hands, and the feet. Such abnormalities frequently occur together

[7] Translated from A1926h as reprinted in A1930d, pp. 58 and 60–65.

with homosexuality, and more often in passively homosexual men and actively homosexual women. As secondary sex characteristics these signs indicate innate or early acquired disturbances of the sex glands.

But the same phenomena are quite frequently found among completely normal persons. This shows that physical characteristics cannot be considered decisive for homosexual development but that it is a matter of how the individual understands these and what he expects from them. I have seen several men with a feminine, often really childlike physique, whose external genital organs were quite stunted and useless, without homosexual impulses ever having appeared. But these men could undoubtedly have been seduced, just as children and prison inmates can be seduced.

Most homosexuals are of average, normal physique. Others again are outstanding specimens of their own sex, with nothing pointing to abnormality of the sex glands. Obviously, they do not let their physical makeup act as a counterindication. Opposite-sex appearance, due to physical peculiarity, achieves a new meaning and value only when used for a homosexual final goal (see Schwarz, 1922).

Behavior

In opposite-sex appearance due to behavior, the decisive factors are well-rehearsed and long-trained movements, fashioned after the model of the other sex, which are afterward taken as evidence. And again, not really the majority of homosexuals have these means at their disposal. Probably there are just as many with a manner proper to their own sex. But where one finds different behavior, it has been acquired for a definite purpose: dramatic representations, affectation, longing glances, pretended timidity and need for support, coquettishness—in men; boyish attitude, cynicism, daredevilishness, and commandeering—in women. Thus it is not really surprising that one can recognize homosexuals by their behavior as they recognize one another: They make it known.

Sex Organ Abnormality

Abnormalities of the sex organs are frequently recorded in the literature. But they are just as prevalent in normal individuals. In my study on organ inferiority (A1907a) I came to the conclusion that probably all organ inferiorities are accompanied by signs of inferiority of the sexual organs. Likewise, when there are abnormalities of the sexual organs, other organ systems are also inferior, so that the whole biological position of the individual can easily cause a feeling of weakness. This is usually expressed in increased safeguarding tendency and caution toward the problems of life. In special cases, it leads to the exclusion of any solution or to attempts at solutions that appear to be more favorable.

In connection with all other critical facts, the conclusion now emerges that homosexuality is the attempt by faint-hearted persons to solve the sex problem who actually want to avoid it. This is also true regarding genital abnormalities: A phimosis or an enlarged clitoris are never decisive for the turn to homosexuality. What can be important is the misapprehension of the individual that he is inadequately equipped for normality.

Early Disparagement of the Other Sex

The interpretation of early disparagement of the other sex as indication of innate homosexuality is based on superficial observation. Such disparagement turns out to be a biased safeguard against normalcy, constructed from any of the child's most varied experiences that could support it. The exaggerated respect for and fear of the opposite-sex parent may be generalized and create a permanent turning away. But much pampering and one-sided attachment also may become the occasion for avoidance, from fear never again to achieve similar warmth. Insecure boys are often influenced by the

152

usually disparaging description of the female and her almost hostile representation in all literature, beginning with the Bible; girls, by the often-heard exaggeration of the pains and dangers of sexuality, of child bearing, of the magic power of love and of the male, of the difficulties of marriage, and of the unreliability of men in the sense of support.

The insecure child will more readily take all these perceptions as occasions to make only evasive preparations for love. In the course of a prolonged training, the child finally gets to see only the dark sides of the other sex.

Homosexual Dreams and Fantasies

Homosexual dreams and fantasies are regarded by some authors as evidence that homosexual development is innate or unavoidable. This is a daring but incorrect assumption, the pronouncement of which in speech and writing contributes greatly to a general strengthening of homosexuality, as other assumptions also do.

Since dreams and fantasies have for some time been scientifically recognized as pictorial expressions of psychological movement forms, one should attempt to comprehend the movement in them. Dreams and fantasies indicate an arrangement of the individual and not established facts—a demand, not a condition (*ein Sollen und nicht ein Sein*).

Freud, whose dream interpretation was an important advance, has not taken this circumstance sufficiently into account. His undaunted inclination to find in all dreams sexual symbols, and behind these, sexual desires, prevented him from seeing in sexual dream images their more general line of movement.

The dream is a working hypothesis, as I was able to determine (see A1924m, A1927g), and has the function of a training. Thus homosexual dreams and fantasies, insofar as they do not represent other relationships of life in terms of sexual dialect, are to be understood at the most as attempts to support presumed homosexuality—from which one can infer that the dreamer is not very sure of it.

153

A further important training by the homosexual while he is awake, which furnishes a main support for this deviation but is usually mistaken as evidence, is: He diverts his attention continually from the other sex toward his own sex. This is the most important way toward a schematization or mechanization of homosexuality.

Early Habits of Other Sex, and Homosexuality

Homosexuals often report that since earliest childhood they have shown a quite one-sided inclination toward their own sex, or that they have strikingly preferred the habits and games of the other sex. Such preferences can often be understood from the situation of the child. For example, with a weakly or perhaps only boy, many mistakes in upbringing might be made that bring him close to a girl's role. This inappropriate role can be considerably strengthened if the child remains for a long time unaware of his proper sexual role, or if, due to pampering, a passivity is cultivated in him from which he hopes to find satisfaction more easily in the role of a girl.

In the case of girls, the parents' wish to have a boy often influences the upbringing so much that the girls are virtually forced into the role of a boy.

Early affection for the same sex, also of a sexually alerted kind, is extremely frequent. It is also more easily attained and satisfied than early normal sexual intercourse. Normal intercourse is much more strictly forbidden and is usually so severely punished that in view of the dangers connected with it the early-maturing youngsters are deterred from the other sex. Obviously these early signs are inadequate evidence of innate homosexuality.

Familial Incidence

Some authors find further proof for inherited homosexuality in its familial incidence. On closer look one finds that through weakness and insecurity similarly disposed family

154

members were led the same way, or that a consistent, erroneous family tradition in upbringing has led to similar results, especially if pathological pampering or great severity have been passed on for some time. I have often found sexually deviating children among the offspring of sisters who as mothers were equally strict and lusting for power.

Conclusion

From this it amply follows that homosexuality means a failure in education to become a fellow man. Inadequate preparation for one's usual sexual role, erroneous foundations of upbringing, and incorrect interpretation of physical deficiencies become clearly evident from the individual psychological examination of the patient. Pointing decisively beyond itself, homosexuality signifies the exclusion of the other sex and thereby of the preservation of the human race. Therefore it is justly considered to be countercultural (*kulturwidrig*).

Homosexuality is an expression of great discouragement and hopeless pessimism, states in which one is satisfied with life in a small circle, far from the other sex. Thus any general aggravation of the difficulties of life and of the insecurity in human relationships increases the number of homosexuals and makes homosexuality a mass phenomenon. In times when women step more vigorously into the foreground of public life, a large number of men prefer to increase the distance from the female sex and resort among other safeguards also to homosexuality.

SOCIAL FACTORS[8]

Historically, homosexuality can be traced to the beginnings of culture. Records of pederastic acts have been preserved from

[8] Paragraphs 1–5 translated from A1926h as reprinted in A1930d, pp. 56–58. Paragraphs 6–10 translated from A1917b as reprinted in A1930d, pp. 3–5.

the most ancient times. At some times, and with various peoples, this deviation became a mass phenomenon. Its prevalence in many areas of the Orient and in ancient Greece at the time of the "Greek eros" is well known. In our time one finds in all cities, in rural areas, in upper and lower classes, in men and women of all ages and countries occasional homosexuals who are almost always inclined to become social phenomena who are significantly supported by their association and organization.

The prevalence of homosexuality in all countries and at all times has supported the belief that it is unalterable. Many investigators and homosexuals tend to believe that culture has led to a weakening of the sex instinct. Reference to animals, where supposedly only among domesticated animals homosexual acts can be noted, also supports this view. Freud assumed general innate homosexual components of the sex drive in attempting to explain the frequency of homosexual inclinations that prevail under otherwise favorable circumstances as soon as normal sexuality is repressed. His argument that culture leads to repression of sexuality while, on the other hand, culture originates in repressed sexuality, has become widely known.

Situational Factors

Occasional and partial homosexuality are very widespread among both sexes. This came to light in the course of deeper psychological study of individual life histories and of children. Homosexual activities or fantasies and caresses often occur side by side with masturbation and heterosexuality.

Homosexual relations are almost regularly furthered on the one hand by opportunity and strict supervision in prisons, institutions, boarding schools, military barracks, or at home, and, on the other hand, by the seduction of children through adults, etc. But also in married couples and other heterosexuals, one finds the simultaneous practice of this deviation. All possible variations—fellatio, pederasty, mutual masturbation

156

—occur together or separately. Mutual masturbation is the preferred practice. Frequently homosexuality does not go beyond exhibitionism, caresses, and fantasies.

Frequently other sexual deviations are observed simultaneously, such as sadism, masochism, and fetishism. Neurotic and psychotic syndromes have often been described as additions or as the foundation. I have always found a trace of neurosis—compulsion or anxiety neurosis—to be present (see A1912a). Homosexuality is also sometimes connected with drug addiction (morphinism and cocainism).

Cultural Factors: Ancient Greece

Greek eros and its compatibility with a highly developed culture cannot be simply carried over into the present. As far as we know, Greek love of boys arose in a period when women had rapidly gained in esteem and influence. The satires of Aristophanes [c. 450–380 B.C.] on "The Parliament of Women" and on the love of boys probably belong together. At such a time of increasing emancipation of women, which raised their self-esteem, men were more easily brought to doubt their privileged position. From a feeling of insecurity, the conquest of the female appeared a daring undertaking. In such a case, the human mind has two main devices available to establish the fiction of security and superiority: it may depreciate, or it may idealize—that is, elevate the object and thereby move the decision into the distance.

Man's masculine-protest-type answer to woman's growing self-confidence urged first of all a reduction of woman's value. Such depreciation became clearly evident in the Greek love of boys and its psychological expressions, directed as they are against the female. This homosexual trend was strengthened by permitting the adult male to present himself —in Greece!—as teacher, protector, and inspirer of the youth. Thus the masculine privileges could continue unhindered, at least toward boys.

157

The fear of the female (see A1912a, A1914a, A1920a, A1927a), instigated by woman's striving for significance, forced the male to stronger preparations in the sense of his expansion tendency, and to essential and careful evasions. While the love of a boy was for the man an attempt to interpose a greater distance between himself and the woman, it was—taken socially—for the boy a preparation for heterosexual love and for comradeship which, to be sure, in our opinion, deviates from the correct line of approach in about the same way as masturbation does. At any rate, certainly most of the youths returned to heterosexuality.

Homosexuality in our time probably shows the same psychological basic reasons and thus discloses itself as a phenomenon that follows quite naturally when one is in flight from the female. But in contrast to the Greek eros, today the regulating limits are missing. The Greek people were a more homogeneous body than perhaps any other nation. The Greek concept of the state overtowered all other aims of the people so much that even excesses and mistakes, as they became evident in the difficulty of development, were redirected to the benefit of the community. Thus the movement of homosexuality was through the power of the community concept almost transformed into an educative, beneficial trend. These aspects are undoubtedly missing in modern homosexuality. At best, such a relationship degenerates into an unsuitable favoritism; or the young man becomes the tormentor and tyrant of his older friend; or the peers consume themselves in petty jealousies and ridiculous quarrels.

In short: Greek love of boys occurred in a period of mutual benevolence among the citizens, and the communal spirit (*Gemeinsinn*) elicited from it all the values it could yield. The result of psychological factors, homosexuality shares with these a characteristic that is much too little appreciated: It is in itself ambiguous and can be comprehended in its significance only in reference to its time and the particular individual.

ACTIVE CREATION[9]

Expression of Life Line

All sexual deviations—homosexuality, sadism, masochism, masturbation, fetishism, etc.—may, according to Individual Psychology,[10] be summarized in the following points, which they have in common:

1. Every sexual deviation is the expression of an increased psychological distance between man and woman.

2. At the same time it indicates a more or less profound revolt against fitting into the normal sexual role and expresses itself as a planful though unconscious device toward enhancing one's own lowered self-esteem.

3. In this the tendency to depreciate the normally to be expected partner is never lacking, so that, if one looks carefully, traits of hostility and fighting against him or her stand out as essential in the posture of the deviate.

4. Inclinations toward sexual deviation in men prove to be compensatory efforts initiated and tested to alleviate a feeling of inferiority in relation to the overrated power of the female. In women, they are compensatory attempts to make up for the feeling of feminine inferiority in relation to the male, who is felt to be the stronger.

5. Sexual deviation occurs always in persons who are generally oversensitive, overambitious, and defiant. They are deficient in deeper comradeship, mutual benevolence, and common efforts. Egocentric impulses, suspicion, and craving for power are prevalent. There is little inclination to "play the game" toward men as well as women. Consequently, we also find a strong limitation of social interest (*gesellschaftliches Interesse*).

[9] Translated from A1917b, as reprinted in A1930d, pp. 5–14.
[10] General references: Adler (A1912a, A1914a, A1920a, A1927a, A1928a, A1929c, A1929d), Wexberg (1926a, 1928, 1930). [Author's note.]

Anyone who, like a physician, is in a position to feel the vibrations of the social organism, will notice that the relations of the sexes are seriously impaired by all kinds of difficulties. This is statistically expressed in later marriages, fewer marriages, more divorces, and fewer children. The regrets about this condition are well known, as are a number of causes, which various studies have shown. All these discussions, however, suffer from the same mistake: They indict one ultimate cause—generally, the increased difficulty of life.

This is, of course, an important factor. But here, as whenever Individual Psychology becomes concerned with a problem, another problem arises that is therapeutically and in principle more important:

Who will certainly be crushed by such general difficulties?

They are those individuals who are overcautious and doubtful, lacking in self-confidence, and whose activity and preparation for life have thus been impaired. Among the first willing to give up the game when a difficulty arises, to desert, are always those who from childhood on have carried within themselves an inferiority feeling. They have lost faith in themselves and remain for the time being the "nervously disposed persons."

This view will be criticized on two counts: (1) that everybody is cautious at times and needs to be so; (2) that one finds often among nervous persons—this includes for us also the homosexuals—a great deal of self-esteem. The first objection reassures me that our finding is not forced, but expresses a common human attitude, which in the case of neurosis is only more rigid, one-sided, dogmatic, and exaggerated. The second objection rests on an inadequate understanding of the essence of neurosis, takes appearance and consequence for original essence, and misunderstands one of the core points of the nervous dynamics: the heroism of the feeling of weakness.

A digression into the social field shows currently a tendency of the distance between the sexes to increase. This is reflected in the life of the individual, the basic component of this social phenomenon, especially the nervously disposed individual. Such a person cannot maintain a straight line of ac-

160

tivity even during calm periods and conditions, and will with each change in his situation show the hesitating attitude (*zögernde Attitüde*), as I have pointed out [A1912h, p. 169; A1956b, pp. 273, 275, 321]. Any increase in difficulty, apparent or real, will arouse in him further anxiety, further hesitation, and further attempts at detours. There is little difference, psychologically speaking, whether the neurotic, when faced with the problem of marriage and love, points to the difficulty of earning a living, the responsibility of regarding children, the unfitness of the other sex, his own inferiority; or whether he interposes between himself and his partner a proof of illness, hysteria, a compulsion neurosis, a phobia, impotence, compulsory masturbation, a psychosis, or a sexual deviation.

Since according to his unconscious life plan, the neurotic aspires to love and marriage only conditionally or not at all, and must arrange individually prepared detours, he is committed to create a distance that safeguards him from the feared decision. Like someone afraid of high places or of water, he must create the distance that protects him from the anticipated defeat. When the nervous person approaches a goal which, although socially average, has long ago been rejected by him, a feeling of inferiority prevails and forces an arrangement that results in a halt, a retreat, or a detour.[11]

From this we conclude: It is their neurotic disposition that causes a large number of persons, when faced with difficult times and situations, not to want to "play the game," but to work on detours to salvage their ambitious personality ideal. From taking such a detour, moving at a psychologically constant distance around the normal, yet dreaded goal, there follows the unconscious and therefore uncorrectable necessity to complete the arrangement that alone safeguards the distance. Detour and arrangement mean in the present context the

[11] In the first edition of this study (A1917b), which appeared during the World War, I noted at this point that the increasing understanding of war neurosis has strikingly shown the validity of the Individual Psychology view. Since then, these fundamental thoughts of Individual Psychology have become common knowledge. [Author's note.]

safeguarding construction of the sexual deviation to fixate the distance from the sexual partner.

Thus homosexuality, exactly like neurosis, becomes a means of the abnormal individual.

Origin of the Homosexual Life Plan

What previous theories of homosexuality have considered an innate factor or an early fixation through a sexually toned event, is seen by Individual Psychology as a path taken at an early age, according to the life plan (*Lebensplan*), which asserts itself early in childhood.

Striving for significance and response schema. Parallel with the child's physical growth tendencies, psychological strivings toward power and significance develop. In these, the child takes the strongest figure in his environment, usually the father or the mother, as a guiding image. The child compares his own ability with that of these figures and appraises his expectation of the future according to them. Through defiance or submission he seeks space for his own development, while his natural distance from his guiding figures increases his inferiority feeling.

The compensatory life plan of the child results from many trials and preliminary attempts to eliminate this distance and thereby his feeling of weakness. By means of a childhood experience that always contains the natural traces of his physical and psychological weakness and a reflection of his milieu, the child seeks his way to eventual superiority. The continuous testing of this individual way is enforced by the direction-giving goal of superiority, by the expansion tendency of the child. Whether he will someday try to conquer through hatefulness, or through benevolence and love, emerges in this development.

All readinesses for the difficulties of the future, as the child understands these, originate during this period; his attitudes toward life and society are practiced, and his perspective of the world is fashioned. Thus the individually different attitudes arise: direct aggression, straightforward attack, flattering or suspicious avoidance of a person or a problem, delay and hesitation before decisions, an independent attitude, or a gesture of reaching for help. From his own experiences and the imitation of other persons the child gathers all the techniques of his conduct of life and fits these as permanent forms into his bodily posture. All answers a person gives to the questions of life are essentially influenced by a schema from his childhood. He needs only forcefully to imagine the problems and persons he meets later in life according to the schematic figures and experiences of his childhood.

Authoritarian father. We have irrefutable evidence that a child will develop the more one-sidedly and his attitude toward the demands of society will be the more abnormal, the stronger his inferiority feeling. Usually physical and mental inferiorities that can, however, be compensated for, give the most important occasion for this (see A1917c). Almost equally strong is the effect of errors in upbringing that make the child regard the distance between himself and the adult as unbridgeable.

One such error is the stupidity of absolute authority within the family. The father, for example, by being too strict may take away the child's courage for advancement so that he will never trust himself to accomplish what he sees his father doing. Or under other circumstances, if there is bragging about the father's superiority, the child may later be afraid of those life problems that the father appears to have solved. The child may not even have enough self-confidence for any solution. But some day he will make a virtue of necessity, and in secret defiance of his father's dominance disappoint the latter's reasonable expectations and destroy them. Thus the child finally succeeds after all in being triumphant over the paternal "tyrant." Presumably this kind of father becomes more prevalent in difficult times when the world denies a person almost any significance. Then there is the temptation to show off one's superiority, at least within one's own family.

Domineering mother. Quite similarly, the son of a strong, unyielding mother will not be able to muster any real self-confidence, especially toward women. Like the discouraged youth just described, he will evade competition with men, consider his position toward women unpromising, or more likely hostile, and usually be inclined to evade the problem of love and marriage. At least he will make severe conditions, dogmatic demands, and use neurotic devices (evidence of illness) as safeguards. "Moral insanity" arises frequently on the same basis. The greater competition and hateful struggle for existence naturally carry over to the female sex also and create more difficult living conditions.

The domineering mother who pushes her husband and children to the wall is usually herself the individual product of difficult relationships between the sexes. As a rule such women seek their harmonious development in "being like a man," in an increased masculine protest against the woman's role, which enormously increases their craving to dominate and distorts their love relationships. Even a cursory examination of their lives shows such signs as dysmenorrhea, vaginismus, frigidity, few children, sometimes late marriage, a weakly husband, and nervous disorders frequently connected with the menstrual period, pregnancy, birth, and the menopause (see A1916, A1926a).

Distance from the Other Sex

Three quite different groups of feelings and thoughts of male homosexuals clearly appear to have the common core of actively keeping a distance from women.

Contradicting the life of society. The first and probably the most important group concerns the general attitude of the homosexual regarding the present, which always includes also a directive for the future. Obviously the sexual deviate is as little adapted to the life of our society—with regard to all relationships of his own life—as he is to his own sex role. Our social structure is truly all-embracing; it is the basis for the inner conflicts, the contradictions, and the struggles of human society, and for its sexual activity.

This is also why the problem of homosexuality becomes particularly acute when compared with the will of the people

(*Volkswille*). Homosexuality is a veritable denial of the latter in the most decisive point, the ideal of an everlasting continuation. This alone is enough to make some enforce heterosexuality as the norm and to make any sexual deviation, including masturbation, a crime, an aberration, a sin. The self-consistency of a cultural ideal defends itself with just and unjust means, with laws, penalties, and moral condemnation against the emergence of seemingly dangerous resistances and contradictions.

Such general condemnation can, of course, be overdone. Someone may swing the sword of judgment because he considers himself free from guilt and blemish, and wants to prove this to the world; or because he believes he is in the right and must protect the public. Further grounds for caution regarding penalties for homosexuality are that sexual deviation is part of a total illness of the individual, and that the danger of punishment, because of the very psychological peculiarity of the illness, is often experienced as provocation and temptation, but very rarely as deterrent.

The full-fledged homosexual always refers to his own historically self-consistent individuality. All his childhood recollections appear to him to justify his position. It was this unity of development which made the false thesis of an "innate homosexuality" plausible to other writers. Schrecker (1913) and I have pointed out the tendency of childhood recollections to falsify events in favor of the life plan. Thus a main piece of evidence for innate homosexuality is wholly eliminated from the discussion.

Wherever we look, we see the homosexual actively intervening to claim freedom from responsibility for his behavior. Actually he has an actively hostile attitude toward society, which can be reduced to the formula: The goals of the homosexual are in contradiction to the prerequisites of the life of a society, and the patient shows little communal spirit (*Gemeinsinn*), hardly the kind of goodwill toward others through which the bond of unity among men can be tied. Nor does he seek peaceful adjustment and harmony. Rather his cautious but exaggerated expansion tendency leads him to continuous hostile comparisons and contests in support of which he also

165

enters his sex drive. In short, he has not developed into a partner of society.

Opposing female attraction. The second state of affairs revealing homosexuality as an active creation consists of the peculiar psychological pointers, schematic impulses, and mementos that are expressed as the temperament, general attitude, and activity of a person. The "principle" of the homosexual bears with uncanny rigidity the character of distance from the female, a backward movement. This acts like an automatic brake, unconsciously, and removed from deliberation. The significance and purpose of such a psychological mechanism is that, like an organ of attack and defense, it will become active by itself, in this case as soon as the patient has an urge to advance. Although this artificial role is full of activity, it supports the direction of "not playing the game." In homosexuality, as in any sexual deviation, we find regularly voices warning of the other sex and inciting toward deviation— "insufficient attraction of women" [see pp. 151–52], "the beauty of the male body," etc.

Low self-esteem. The third state also points to the arbitrariness of the homosexual's attitude, although less clearly. It is his low self-esteem, which robs him of all initiative toward living *with* others. Often he does not know the full extent of his inferiority feeling. But all his actions and his whole attitude reveal that it exists within him as a precondition, and establishes itself at any time in the deviation. The physician can judge the importance of this factor only if he has completely comprehended this tragic fate of the homosexual, his cowardliness toward normal life. Sometimes this understanding is difficult to achieve, since the cowardliness is largely hidden from the patient himself.

Special Forms of Homosexuality

In conclusion, I want to mention that many special forms of homosexuality are really compatible only with our conception. I am referring to cases of mixed homosexuality and heterosexuality, of which there are quite a few: adolescent homosexuality; senile homosexuality; and the occasional form homosexuality takes in boarding schools, prisons, or on long sea voyages. Our view places into the proper light the free-choice factor in this behavior, which, to be sure, appears to be mitigated by the individual's apparent freedom from responsibility for it. These cases too can be explained by an increased expansion tendency, which uses the always available sex drive.

PSYCHOTHERAPY[12]

Cure and improvement are possible through psychotherapy. In older cases this is not easy. The task is like bringing someone who is trying to escape, to the point where he will take the demands of life fully upon himself. Therapy with hormones, implantation of glands, etc., does not seem to have brought encouraging results. I have seen several such cases of failure. Milder cases often get well by themselves, and under the encouraging influence of whatever procedure, cures can come about. The simplest and most comprehensive formula for understanding homosexuality may be stated as: Homosexuality is a miscarried and misunderstood substitute (*Notbehelf*).

In general, the chances of success of treatment are today as unfavorable as possible. This may seem to contradict the certainty with which we dealt above with the causes of homosexuality. The difficulty of treatment will, however, be appreciated when we formulate the problem into the simple question: How confident of success can one be when one attempts to change an adult coward into a courageous human being? This is essentially what the therapy of homosexuality, as well as psychoneurosis, comes down to, only that in the case of homosexuality, the cowardliness is at times well cov-

[12] Paragraph 1, translated from A1926h, as reprinted in A1930d, p. 65. The remainder, translated from A1917b as reprinted in A1930d, pp. 14–15.

167

ered up, or is limited primarily to the love and marital relationship.

At this point I do not want to discuss therapy in detail; I only want to mention that therapy must:

1. uproot the firmly rooted childish conception of the danger of heterosexuality;
2. show very clearly the distance of the patient from his sexual partner;
3. point out the antisocial line of the patient;
4. uncover his goal of superiority and destroy it as a firmly established utopia.

This is an educative process that requires the greatest tactfulness and most subtle means.

The elimination of homosexuality, and I am sure one will agree with me on this, is a problem of the education of children. In the nursery the most important demands will be not to deprive the child of his courage, not to keep him in the dark regarding the problems of his future life, and to establish from the start his sexual role as fixed and unalterable. Especially on this last point errors are frequently made. It cannot be an accident that in all my cases, not only in those I have reported, I found a striking uncertainty regarding their sexual role in the patients' childhoods. This childhood uncertainty seems to me virtually the main condition in the prehistory of the homosexual.

SUMMARY[13]

With these expositions, which are consistent with the Individual Psychology theory of neuroses, we believe to have sufficiently clarified the problem of homosexuality. A summary of the traits and motives of homosexuality from all the cases with which we have become better acquainted yields the following reliable findings:

[13] Translated from A1917b as reprinted in A1930d, pp. 65–66.

1. No physiopathological substratum, such as feminine form, endocrine variation, acquired or innate eunuchoidism [defective state of the testicles], etc., obligates an individual to seek sexual stimulation or satisfaction from the same sex. On the other hand, in such cases a temptation of the intellect as logical error is easy to understand.

2. The notions of the compelling causes of homosexuality, its innate character and its immutability, can easily be unmasked as scientific myths.

3. The driving and fixating factor is the biased (*tendenziöse*) homosexual perspective. This may arise early in children filled with self-love and pathological ambition as a safeguard insofar as it originates from a fear of the partner.

4. Homosexuality appears as an abortive attempt at compensation by persons with a clear inferiority feeling, and corresponds in its disturbed social activity completely to the attitude of the patient toward the problem of community (*Problem der Gemeinschaft*).

5. Thus homosexuality is also a revolt of the presumed feeling of weakness in the face of demands that are quite natural outcomes of communal life, and aims at a fictitious, subjectively founded triumph of one's own superiority. If, in considering the character of a homosexual man or woman, one disregards the actual sexual manifestations, one finds that his or her personal attitude is also the expression of a life line that aims from an inferiority feeling through a trick, improper conduct, a gesture of revolt, toward the fictitious feeling of superiority. This revolt originates from a belligerent, hostile position of the child within the family.

6. Rejection of homosexuality is spontaneously founded in the social feeling[14] and grows or diminishes in accordance with the strength of the social coherence. Consequently, the homosexual will always meet with the difficulties of social ostracism, legal measures, the reproach of sin.

7. The qualification of homosexuality as a crime must be

[14] In the 1917 edition the German term was *Gemeinschaftsgefühle* —that is, the plural rather than the singular—whereas in the 1930 edition it was the singular without the *e* at the end, indicating that in 1917 Adler's usage of the term had not yet reached its final form.

opposed, because the homosexual has been misguided through general societal weaknesses of thought, his argumentation is advanced by a frequent scientific myth, and he cannot be punished for acts of inner self-defense that originate from a situation that, up to now, has been misunderstood by him and by science. As for many other ailments, so also for the neurosis of homosexuality, treatment should be mandatory.

6

OTHER DEVIATIONS, DYSFUNCTIONS, AND PROSTITUTION

SADISM AND MASOCHISM[1, 2]

The term "sadism" is connected with the ill-famed Marquis de Sade [1740–1814], whose atrocities during the French Revolution led to his arrest by the Jacobins. His books, such as *Justine,* contain the most repulsive descriptions of sexually cruel misdeeds. The concept of "masochism" was coined by Krafft-Ebing after the writer Leopold Sacher-Masoch [1836–95], whose life and short stories showed character traits that correspond to male bondage and voluntary submission to the strong female.

Such phenomena have frequently occupied the public during the past decades and caused the courts and court physicians to become concerned with them. The term "passive and active algolagnia" chosen by Schrenck-Notzing completely coincides with the above concepts. We find one or the other of these deviations in the cults of antiquity, in secret circles of the present, as well as in individual cases.

[1] Translated from A1926i as reprinted in A1930d, pp. 67–74.
[2] General references: Krafft-Ebing (1893), Havelock Ellis (1912b), Schrenck-Notzing (1892), Marquis de Sade (1791), Sigmund Freud (1923, 1924), Rudolf Allers (1922), Iwan Bloch (1902), Albert Eulenburg (1911). [Author's note.]

Like the homosexuals, sadists and masochists tend to meet in secret to satisfy their inclinations through mutual help. Here prostitution plays a large part because prostitutes, voluntarily or against their will, adapt themselves to the wishes of the sado-masochist, alternately to play the role of the sadistic or the masochistic partner. Usually they have in stock an assortment of whips, straps, chains, etc. Henchmen also offer their services, frequently under the guise of "massage" or "severe tutelage."

Perhaps the most frequent forms of algolagnia are sadistic and masochistic fantasies. They usually begin in childhood, at six or seven years. At times sexual feelings become clearly noticeable while the child listens to cruel fairy tales and stories. Often sexual feelings are aroused through spanking, which fills the fantasy with images of beating or being beaten. In such cases, signs of sexuality, erotic pleasure, erections, and masturbation go pretty far back into childhood.

It is, of course, a matter of terminology whether one wants to designate extreme obedience and subservience without sexual feelings also as masochistic. It is likewise an arbitrary action to count the female form of life in general as masochism, and the male form, with its more evident activity during courtship and in the love relationship, as sadistic. Likewise, we regard as justified the Freudian view that all acts of cruelty, such as Caesarean madness, mass murder, and incendiarism, whether of individuals or of entire peoples, are forms of sadism, and cases of stigma and hypnosis, forms of masochism.

However, where the sexual drive joins with aggressive or submissive attitudes, it creates an enormous reinforcement. It is easy to infer the compulsion neurosis of algolagnia from fantasies and actual sexually connected beatings, being beaten, being tied, or violence or murder preceded by rape. But it is difficult to draw such a conclusion from dreams, bad habits and traditions, or the inclination to wrestle and to fight, when feelings of pleasure are absent. The inclination of children and adults to witness horror scenes, torture animals, or listen to ghastly stories frequently originates exclusively from a tendency to train against a softness that is considered weak-

172

ness. In such cases a valid conclusion can always be reached by a psychologically conducted investigation of the total personality.

The excesses of sado-masochism belong probably to the most awful aberrations. Only the physician's sense of duty enables him to overcome the disgust and to remain fair and objective when he listens often to the most repulsive situations the human mind could invent. Soiling in all variations, urination and defecation into all possible parts of the body of the masochist and the victim of sadism, in fantasy and in reality, are frequent occurrences. In light of such choice refinements of these patients, it is difficult to discuss seriously the view that innate factors or a disturbance of glandular functions could be directly the reason for such expressions. They shatter any attempt at a biological, sexual-constitutional, causal, and natural-science theory. The psychological determination of such extravagances is so obvious that the following pieces of evidence become virtually superfluous.

Total Personality

Any theory of sexual deviation will have to deal with observations that originate from psychological investigations, primarily the fact that sexual peculiarities are in accord with the uniqueness of the total personality. There is probably not a single real fellow man among this type. Rather, beyond the sexual problem, also the two other great life problems, those of the community and of occupation, appear precariously far from solved. The development of the whole personality is based on a certain degree of discouragement and a pessimistic world view, so that all achievements derive from a feeling of weakness rather than one of strength. Deficiencies in compatibility, comradeship, friendship, and sociability can always be found and can be traced back into childhood.

The reduced contact with people is of such far-reaching psychological significance that all the insights of a "depth psychology" or an "understanding psychology" cannot ex-

173

haust it. One must also not be deceived by outward successes of such a patient, which often derive from sources of strength other than his own. Occasionally one also finds exaggerated family loyalty, or exclusive devotion to one of the parents as the consequence of an anxious, cautious elimination of the rest of human society.

Training

In accordance with this "distance from the front of life," the normal sexual partner and normal sexual intercourse are excluded. Autobiographical accounts of patients, which always go back to childhood, do not disclose innate drive components, as was usually assumed, but a long history of erroneous training. It is the same as the normal attitude, which also develops only through a continuous training in which experiences are continuously sought and fantasy is required.

The development toward sadism and masochism always has an understandable history and is subject to many fluctuations. Only the goal remains constant: the careful elimination and depreciation of the normal. Closely connected with this is the continuous attempt to harden oneself against initial inhibitions, and to learn to love abnormalities or horrors and to elaborate on them. Thus in the course of time a firmly founded safeguard, support, and rescue device against the norm is developed, which appears to go beyond all measure. "Beaten into flight, he believes he is chasing." Toward this end the deviation develops in line with the total personality.

This has little to do with causality, let alone innate abnormality of drives, as evidenced by the frequent fluid transitions from sadism to masochism, and from homosexuality into masochism or sadism. In every person are traits of defiance and obedience, cravings for domination and submission, that serve the striving for significance. The simultaneous occurrence of sadism and masochism in the flight of the deviate from the front of life is to be explained on this basis.

174

Cowardliness

Furthermore, one finds in such cases early sexual excitations during experiences and fantasies that arouse anxiety. I am convinced that anxiety can excite not only the nervous pathways of the heart, the intestines, the bladder, the sweat glands, etc., but also of the sexual apparatus. Apparently this connection is found or clearly developed only in a certain type. Perhaps this is a sign of inferiority, as I have described in my study on organ inferiority (A1907a). A connection between anxiety and libido will, of course, be more plausible to persons of this type than to others.

This mind-body connection holds a strong temptation to get oneself into threatening, prohibited situations, to provoke them in reality or fantasy, or to empathize with the anxiety situation of someone else. Such thought processes are found particularly in young girls who are likely to imagine the female sexual role as one of being beaten, to retain this fantasy, but to evade its realization with all sorts of excuses. Through diligent practice the sex drive can become connected with all kinds of external situations and goals, once the normal goal has been eliminated through fear of defeat.

The cowardliness of the sexual deviate, which we have emphasized here, will readily find credence as far as masochists are concerned. But we insist that it is also true for sadists: Their victims are always children or defenseless people, and their sexual wish is always in the direction of least resistance.

The Freudian school and its forerunners are, as noted above, inclined to regard sadism biologically, as a constitutional drive component, related and belonging to the male sex drive, and masochism as coupled with the female sex drive. Ever since the Romantics (for example, Baader[3]) and even earlier, science—as the common people have always done—has frequently attributed power tendencies or sexual

[3] Franz Xavier von Baader (1765–1841), professor of philosophy in Munich, in the tradition of German Romantic philosophy, with a mystic-Catholic orientation.

relations to a neutral event. It was not understood that one's own prejudices, one's "unconscious" presuppositions, like all human expressions, exist within a social context, and somehow express the striving for power, significance, and security.

People answer in their sexual lives the ever-pressing problem of what attitude to take to human society and the opposite sex, and the problem of their own significance. One's sexual behavior always reflects clearly how one attempts to arrive at adjustment, significance, recognition, superiority, and security, and attempts to increase one's feeling of worth within society and *sub specie aeternitatis* [under the aspect of eternity].

A real comprehension of these facts yields the understanding: Sadists, like masochists (like all sexual deviates), move along the line of the cowardly. The former seek at least the semblance of power, of a secret, often unconscious supermanliness in a situation of uncontested superiority. The masochist overconfesses his weakness.

Compensation

The confession of weakness can never be a final result, a place of rest. Thus the masochist always points beyond himself, presses toward the elimination of the norm, or continues in sadism. He confounds sexuality with a feeling of humiliation, falsifying the value and meaning of sexuality, thus creating the reassurance of excluding more serious sexual ties. It is the desire for "freedom from conflict" (Seif, 1923–24) that drives these individuals on their false way, while their lowered "self-esteem and its disturbances" (Weinmann, 1926) appear in their sexual deviation.

Yet even in this weakest manifestation of psychological life, in masochism, there is always a compensatory line upward, as when in flagellation the individual seeks a ridiculous justification in thoughts of penance. There is an actively deviating attitude toward the partner, stigmatizing him as oppressor, torturer, soiler. Also, complaints and condemnation of oppression in childhood, nature, and human society, which

176

permit such deficiency and pain, become openly apparent. Critical, depreciating behavior toward others and a tendency toward isolation are also regularly found. The compensation thus takes the direction of a certain hostility.

A further compensation can be seen in masochism as a position of power, as which it becomes "fixated": The partner falls under the dictates of the masochist, and shares with him the asocial and often repulsive role.

Critique of Other Theories

Among other views, the best known is that which originated in the French school, on "the fixation of sexual childhood experiences." As enticing as this appears, it falters before the question why just this one experience was fixated and not others. Or, as Wexberg [1926b] says: "A child who fixates such experiences and elaborates on them is already neurotic and shows beyond this only the further development of his neurosis."

Freud's hypothesis is that all nervous phenomena, including neuroses, are regressions to an earlier biological stage of the sexual libido. This hypothesis draws its strength from a historical and physical comparison: the flowing back of a force (libido) before an obstacle (actual conflict). Thereby, as Freud finds, early stages of libido development or their sexual constitutional components are revived. He considers sadism and masochism to be such components. Against this the following objections may be permitted:

1. Since any development in any phase reflects the present and the future, one can never speak of a regression in the sense of Freud. Otherwise any psychological act would be a regression, since it always draws on experiences from the past.

2. A mixture of activity and passivity is found at all times in the human psyche, and in all periods of history. Wanting to suffer in order to gain a later advantage is very natural for man, endowed as he is with foresight. The strong develop-

ment of this latter inclination is possible only through the feeling of inferiority.

3. The "stages" of libido development are so entirely dependent on the external circumstances that one may say that any sexual bond and search for pleasure correspond to the external circumstances and an underdeveloped sex drive. Thus the question, How does a child arrive at a deviation? may be answered with, Through the circumstances. More important for the psychology of the neuroses is the question, Why does a person remain attached to his deviation? Could it not be because in a normal solution he fears a defeat? Because he fears not to be loved?

Summary

Algolagnia is an expression of a strong inferiority feeling and its misdirected compensations. The sadist is the "triumphant vanquished," the masochist is the "vanquished conqueror." The external situation of algolagnia is always connected with anxious excitement, shuddering, and fear. The sadist helps this along by identifying with his victim. In my patients I always found that anxiety and excitement were connected with sexual excitement differently, or certainly to a greater extent, than in other persons. The patients are the type who when greatly discouraged avoid the normal solution of the sexual problem and enforce their sexual excitement under extenuating circumstances, in situations actually or seemingly free of danger, avoiding real dangers through an arrangement of anxiety in fantasy or as in play. Sadism is more likely in children who have grown up under strong pressure and cannot tolerate other children having a better lot. Thus we too have advanced to an organic substratum, although in a different meaning.

In sadism we find strong aggressiveness that does not lead to the solution of the problem, and a special form of hesitancy, of exclusion, in which sexual excitement leads to the oppression of the other person. It is a vigorous assault that results in a defective—that is, one-sided—solution of a problem. This applies also to masochism, though here the goal of superiority lies in two directions. The masochist gives his partner orders and thus feels in command of the other despite his sense of weakness. At the same time he excludes the possibility of defeat in the normal approach. He overcomes the anxious tension through a trick.[4]

Therapy

The therapy of algolagnia is a difficult task. To be brief, it must take into account the individual schema of inferiority feelings and its compensations in order to destroy these. But it must also make a strong effort to remove the unique hypnosis by which the patient trains increasingly the connection of anxiety arousal with sexual excitement. This permits him to consider his peculiarity as natural and therefore unalterable, whereas our culture is constantly enforcing successfully the transformation of "natural" forms of expression into social forms. Success, however, depends entirely on encouragement of the patient.

The courts of law will also have to do justice to these views and, in the case of guilt, plead for humane custody and treatment.

OTHER DEVIATIONS[5]

Fetishism[6]

After the preceding observations regarding sexual deviations, we can be brief. The characteristic feature of fetishism was always sought in the overvaluation of an object or a part

[4] This paragraph is from A1938a, p. 190, translation modified after the original, A1933b.

[5] Translated from A1926i as reprinted in A1930d, pp. 74–78.

[6] General references: Krafft-Ebing (1893), Havelock Ellis (1912b), Iwan Bloch (1902), Rudolf Allers (1922), Sigmund Freud (1923, 1924). [Author's note.]

of the body, which in normal sexuality plays a minor role. With this inclination, anything and everything can be magically turned into a love object. Most frequently the objects of veneration are pieces of clothing and objects of daily use. But overemphasis of parts of the body, the foot, the hand, the eyes, the legs, the line of the bosom, etc., is also rather frequent and evidently not very alien to the human love relationship. Perhaps every lover has some fetish (eyes, ears, figure). This does not strike one as strange only because it is so prevalent and usually does not disturb the norm of sexuality but may rather increase it, as, for example, the fetishisms of coarse words, mirrors, a perfume, etc. In some cases deformities, persons of a foreign race, or immoral or subordinated persons have this effect.

The usual explanations end where the social significance of fetishism begins. They mostly emphasize that the persons are arrested at a stage preparatory to or accompanying the normal stage. Additionally, psychopathy, degeneration, or, as psychoanalysis does, a sexual constitution together with conflicts are noted.

We believe it is more important to consider what happens to the sexual partner in the case of fetishism. We find that through the displacement of the sexual accent onto the fetish, the sexual partner experiences disparagement, becomes devalued. No longer the person, but often a quite unimportant detail, is given sexual rank and dignity.

The battle of the sexes for superiority also shows its cunning traits in fetishism, makes the deviate more dependent on incidentals and less dependent on his partner, and ends with an alleviation of his fear and feeling of weakness toward the other sex. Fetishism, like all other deviations, is an expression of an inferiority feeling and the attempt to compensate in an erroneous direction, guided by personal experiences and training.

A connection of fetishism with all other sexual deviations, with neuroses and criminal tendencies, can easily be understood from this viewpoint. Likewise, we are not surprised to find fetishism primarily in visual types.

180

Exhibitionism and Voyeurism[7]

The same observations as in fetishism can be made in exhibitionism and its passive variation, voyeurism, a still stronger expression of discouragement.

The concept of exhibitionism was introduced by Lasègue (1877). It means that sexual satisfaction is sought and found in exposures that violate the sense of modesty. Both the exhibitionist and the voyeur, are visual types who in respect to sexuality do not get beyond showing and looking, or at any rate overemphasize this inclination as compared to the norm. The cowardliness and low degree of activity of these persons can be readily observed also in their other life relationships. But this does not rule out that against weaker persons they may often act as tyrants. Exhibitionism also always contains a battle against the norms of society. Furthermore, the urge to frighten and corrupt children through exposure of oneself, and to depreciate others by exposing them, places this deviation close to sadism.

Children who are rebelling against their mentors, while at the stage of seeking their sexual role and later, often manifest far-reaching exhibitionistic behavior. But one should not call this a tendency toward sexual deviation, because normal adult sexual behavior is quite inaccessible to a child or subject to serious threat and punishment. Consequently the sexual activity that remains available to a child will always appear to the unsophisticated observer as a sexual deviation.

The exhibitionistic desires of feeble-minded persons seem to be of a similar nature, while such a trait, well integrated into the sexual experience, would appear normal.

In mania, schizophrenia, progressive paralysis, alcoholism, and senile dementia, often because of loss of the inhibition of modesty, and also because of cowardliness, which is generally the basis of human error, exhibitionism is the prevalent and

[7] General references: Albert Moll (1908), August Cramer (1897), Boissier and Lachaux (1893), Krafft-Ebing (1893), Reimann (1898). [Author's note.]

ultimate achievement of sexuality. Correspondingly, we find increased expressions of the desires to look and to show also in people who are nearly normal and within normal sexuality, due to a lack of self-confidence.

Therapy of this deviation must, in addition to training in the normal direction, always aim at a transformation of the whole personality toward a more courageous approach to life and society. A suggestive influence in this sense through other kinds of therapy is possible, especially in lighter cases.

Sodomy and Necrophilia[8]

Sodomy, the commission of the sexual act with animals, is an extreme form of discouragement and despair regarding sexual possibilities. The exclusion of the human partner is carried to the point of devaluating him in the form of an animal. Lack of choice and isolation as well as exclusive companionship with certain animals may facilitate this deviation when preceded by training of thinking and feeling toward deviation—that is, after a hardening process. Feeble-mindedness, with its lack of human communal feeling, may facilitate such inclinations.

In necrophilia, a man's sexual intercourse with a dead woman, the motive is the desire for complete defenselessness of the partner. The precondition is loss of belief in one's own sexual effectiveness while the sex drive is intact, and far-reaching renunciation of mutuality in sexual enjoyment. In these cowardly men, such behavior is promoted also by the reassuring feeling of no obligations and consequences. The attraction of this deviation lies in the easily attained feeling of unrestrained domination over the dead partner.

From here one gets an insight into the psychology of the sex murderer. His sexual satisfaction depends on his enjoyment of the defenselessness of his victim, as master over life and death, as a god in caricature. The psychological proximity to sadism is striking.

8 General references: Albin Haberda (1905–7), Josef Maschka (1881–82), Albert Moll (1908), Epaulard (1902). [Author's note.]

SEXUAL DYSFUNCTIONS[9, 10]

General[11]

The name and definition of neurasthenia were originated by G. M. Beard.[12] The prevailing definition of sexual neurasthenia, found also in Krafft-Ebing, is: "weakness of sensitivity of the nervous function in the sexual area." Other authors when delineating sexual neurasthenia as an independent disease did not go beyond this definition.

Regarding etiology, the older literature is not very satisfactory. The assumption of a neuropathic disposition at least points to a consideration of the context (*Zusammenhangsbetrachtung*) in that it takes other psychological phenomena also into account. However, the problem is obscured by the assumption of a general human degeneracy.

Still less convincing are assertions regarding masturbation, excesses, abnormal intercourse, coitus interruptus, sexual abstinence, previous gonorrhea, and emotional excitements as causal factors. All these factors are at best significant as symptoms or as attendant phenomena, because anyone who acquires sexual neurasthenia in connection with these phenomena was already neurotic before.

Sexual neurasthenia refers, in men, to weakness of erection, omission of ejaculation, frequent pollutions during sleep, pollutions long or shortly before cohabitation, premature ejaculation, impotence, spermatorrhea, prolonged erection, painful sensitivity of the glans, and pain in the urinary tract. In women it refers to pollutions in waking and sleeping, frigid-

---

[9] Adler's term was "sexual neurasthenia," which we have replaced by "sexual dysfunction," the term in current usage. However, in the text itself it was generally more appropriate to retain Adler's term.

[10] General references: Rudolf Allers (1922), Havelock Ellis (1912b), Sigmund Freud (1924), Leopold Löwenfeld (1911), Hermann Rohleder (n.d.). [Author's note.]

[11] Translated from A1926j as reprinted in A1930d, pp. 78–80.

[12] George Miller Beard (1839–83), American physician.

ity, and vaginismus. In both men and women it includes compulsion to masturbate. Some authors are inclined to regard all sexual deviations as sexual neurasthenia.

The course of all these disorders, which appear soon or late after puberty, is usually quite protracted, aside from some occasional occurrences. The disorder usually resists all medicinal, hydropathic, and glandular treatment, but is under all circumstances accessible to psychological influences.

All these disorders have in common: The history of those afflicted shows a conspicuously unsuitable attitude toward life through which they are inadequately prepared for love. This deficiency becomes evident also in the other life relationships, sometimes of course less clearly.

Sexual neurasthenics have from childhood on always been noted for psychological oversensitivity. They are described primarily as ambitious, vain, impatient, cautious, and timid. They are inclined to be critical, to be basically pessimistic, greatly to limit their life sphere, and to live in isolation. Moodiness points to their weakness, their inability to retain good humor and zest for life. From time to time (some authors call this "periodically") their joy in life breaks through; but this is always forced and must be understood as an attempt to compensate for an inferiority feeling. The attempt of Kretschmer[18] to categorize individuals with such conduct as "pyknics" and "schizoids" is insufficient, since he overlooks or takes too lightly their common ground, the common inferiority feeling, and the nervous character that emerges from it. Incidentally, in life it never matters what one brings along, but what one makes of it.

In this very frequent type of person, confidence in their own strength is diminished or has disappeared. The resulting mood and its consequences cannot be explained materially, but can be comprehended psychologically. This becomes the more evident since successful treatment is possible with all kinds of means, but especially with insight into the deeper context (*Zusammenhang*) and encouragement, the great advantage of individual-psychological treatment. This would

[18] Ernst Kretschmer (1888–1964), German psychiatrist.

confirm that these disorders are not causally founded but rooted in an erroneous attitude toward life.

Pollution and Premature Ejaculation[14]

The understanding of any sexual abnormality is derived from an understanding of the whole person, not vice versa, as Freudian psychoanalysis teaches.

Even so, one must recognize that some of these disorders arise from deep-rooted technicalities for which the facilitating foundation was created from fantasy, as, for example, in pollutions and premature ejaculation. Other, related disorders, especially paresthesia [burning, prickling], hyperesthesia, painful sensations, and spermatorrhea, seem to be connected with frustrated excitations, protracted coitus, and protracted masturbation. In several cases bleeding from the urinary tract has suggested an irritation of the further urinary tract. This may also be suspected in cases of frequent and long-lasting erections and has been considered by some authors as the explanation for premature ejaculation.

In these cases one should also always think of the supportive or basic psychological coherences, as in premature ejaculation, where I have always found indications of nervous impatience and fear of a more intensive commitment. The latter, together with fear of progeny, is also found in cases of lack of orgasm and ejaculation.

Frequent pollutions and compulsory masturbation after puberty point primarily to a fear of women and are the sexual form of expression of the isolate. Occasionally it is assumed that the ultimate cause of such phenomena is being in love with one's own body, narcissism (Naecke).[15] Actually, such self-love is secondary, a result of necessity, brought about by the exclusion of other sexual objects.

When such a patient worries about his sex life, this may be a hint to the physician to put an end to the patient's hesitation

---

[14] Translated from A1926j as reprinted in A1930d, pp. 80–81.
[15] Paul Naecke (1851–1913), German psychiatrist.

by ordering him to have sexual intercourse: Then the patient's intention becomes evident—to evade responsibility.

Incidentally, we advise against relationships with prostitutes. The patient must be educated for honorable female companionship and for love. Escape into prostitution is cheap and cowardly, makes the correct solution more difficult, and advances the inferiority feeling.

Vaginismus and Frigidity[16]

Vaginismus, the painful cramps of the vaginal muscles, is the bodily expression of "No!" Examination of such cases shows tendencies toward isolation, aversion against the feminine role that did not develop beyond the preparatory stage, and fear of loss of one's own value, of depreciation, and of disappointment. Rude behavior of the male partner and pain during cohabitation, as well as slight injuries at the entrance of the vagina, may instigate or increase cramps in women who are psychologically so disposed. Occasionally an unusual firmness of the hymen may be the instigating factor. In vaginismus as well as in frigidity, sensitivity of the clitoris may be preserved, usually as a remnant of masturbatory responsiveness.

Sexual coolness is always a sign of absence of passion toward either a particular man or men in general. Frigid women "don't go along" with the partner. The psychological reasons are the same as in vaginismus, except that the latter represents a passive resistance. "Cold women" will in other life relationships display an outward submissiveness, a laissez-faire. The coldness may exist from the beginning; but it may also follow a period of normal sexual enjoyment, when disappointments set in. Satisfaction in the relationship with another man is greatly promoted through the passionate intention to prove the inadequacy of the former partner.

[16] Translated from A1926j as reprinted in A1930d, pp. 81–82.

Impotence: Rationale[17]

The observations of Individual Psychology (A1920a, A1930j), especially its demonstrations of nervous symptoms as forms of expression, have contributed much to an understanding of psychoneurosis. Thus today no neurological school or practicing physician could approach neurological problems without having taken a stand toward the views of Individual Psychology.

It is an irreparable mistake to tear symptoms from their natural context (*Zusammenhang*) and to consider them by themselves. Such procedure, presently still generally practiced in the psychology of the neuroses, is like taking one note from a melody and regarding it by itself. To understand nervous phenomena we must keep firmly in view their socially given and socially effective context.

Therefore, the most important question in all nervous symptoms—that is, symptoms lacking organic foundation—is: What happens when the symptom occurs? In the case of psychological impotence, the answer is: Sexual commitment is excluded. If one asks the patient about his intentions, one will hear what every living creature has in mind. But if one asks for counterarguments, one will hear more than one would expect: fear of venereal disease, the bad "present" general conditions, compunctions about seducing an innocent girl or about becoming the prey of a seductress. These and hundreds of other reasons, which by themselves are plausible enough, represent the front line of the patient's safeguards. Against these, the dialectics (*Dialektik*) of the physician prove powerless unless he accepts our viewpoint: Love is the only safe means against venereal diseases and also prevents the other harmful consequences; sexual intercourse without love is misconduct (*Unart*). It cannot be the physician's task to educate for misconduct, even if presently he cannot remove it from the world.

[17] Translated from A1926j as reprinted in A1930d, pp. 82–84.

After this is settled, one arrives at the second line of safeguards: the fear of disgracing oneself (*Blamage*). According to the usual principles of a simplified understanding of human nature ("he who proves too much, proves too little," etc.), one puts the situation correctly: This fear of a defeat represents a much more significant motive than those previously mentioned. It is actually the provocation of the other safeguards. As long as it exists, sexual élan is excluded to such an extent that wishes, feelings, and words are of no significance.

The understanding of Individual Psychology that impotence is based on inferiority feelings has become an unquestioned explanatory principle, especially because it also offers an incomparably safe standpoint for therapy. Our conviction becomes unshakable when we observe, cautiously following our suspicion, that this illness occurs altogether only in persons who also otherwise in their lives show the hesitating attitude. They live with throttled activity but, at the same time, set themselves the highest goals. Thus they arrive at the synthesis: to evade every decision, since it could turn out against them.

Such a form of life shows itself in the simplest way in that many different things are started, but nothing is ever finished; the contact with people is inadequate and takes place only with difficulty; and the person's love relationships never develop properly.

Regarding all impediments, paralyses, inhibitions, and other symptoms of neuroses that prevent or aggravate the solution of the problems of life, I have shown: If one completely disregards these, one can find—once one has correctly recognized the personality of the patient—a whole series of thoughts, attitudes, and forms of expression that could equally serve as excuses, only that these psychological processes lack consequences and do not lead to a decisive attitude and movement. But instead of the expected consequence, the symptom occurs—in this case, the impotence. It is as if, through the psychological hindrances that were mentioned, the necessary élan were weakened; as if the much-desired goal of sexual satisfaction met with a number of counterarguments.

These counterarguments and the symptom that corresponds to their strength, are, however, not at all chance occurrences, acts of thoughtlessness, or groundless weaknesses. Rather they have arisen from the faint-heartedness of the whole personality whose final intention is a frictionless superiority, at least a condition of "absolute freedom from conflict" (Seif, 1923–24). In sexual impotence the patient's faint-heartedness is materialized in a main line of life. He evades the very aggression that he longingly desires. While his words, his thoughts, and his desires express his longing, his body, his sexual organ, speaks another language, expressing his cowardliness.

In this way also the frequent variation in impotence can be explained. Under certain favorable conditions, sexual intercourse succeeds, as when there is loving and helpful accommodation; when all consequences have been eliminated; with subordinated persons of lower status, youths, or older women; with the aid of physical or psychological stimulants; after friendly and patient encouragement by the partner; until contracting a venereal disease; until any disappointment; after encouragement by the physician; after taking some alcohol or medicine, or after applying an external stimulant, etc.

Much depends on the suggestibility and credulity of the patient; therefore these ameliorating conditions fail as often as they help. This also explains why the most varied interventions are occasionally successful and mislead the physician to believe in the correctness of his view, as well as the patient. Actually, the success is to be attributed to the temporary or permanent increase in courage, with or without the knowledge of the physician.

These patients have generally little success in contact with other persons. They are not real fellow men; their interest in the present and the future society is rather limited. It seems the natural consequence of their world philosophy that "their seed shall be wiped out"—unless they change their attitude.

189

Impotence: Therapy[18]

The élan of the sexual drive is subject to change, and certainly not a fixed constitutional formula. It may flare up where it previously acted quite moderately, and vice versa. Sexual ideas, pictures, reading, or conversation may call forth sexual excitement, as justified or unjustified inhibitions may thereby be removed. Also abstinence practiced within certain limits generally causes an increase. Both measures have often brought therapeutic results, in a superficial manner. That deprivation of sexual satisfaction and denial will increase desire, and all-too-willing permissiveness will create apathy, are well-known facts.

Man's sexual behavior thus depends on various factors. We can neither observe a possible primary, uninfluenced, sexual impulse, nor measure its strength, because strong influences are always acting upon it. Not even a complete turning away from love and marriage in men indicates weakness of the sexual drive. It is usually a matter of training, of inhibitions that are due to the generally neurotic peculiarity of the individual.

But there is one exception. In cases of eunuchoid habitus and severely stunted or infantile genitals, unsuitable for intercourse, as they are found in disorders of the hypophysis, after early castration, in certain diseases such as diabetes, serious kidney malfunctioning, and locomotor ataxia (tabes dorsalis), etc., we may infer organically determined impotence and lack of sexual drive. The sexual drive of course also diminishes with age, and becomes extinguished approximately around the seventieth year.

Most forms of impotence by far, however, as well as premature ejaculation and absence of ejaculation, are evoked by psychological, always erroneously created, inhibitions and can be removed by appropriate cessation of these inhibitions. The supreme remedy is change of the personality into a coura-

[18] Translated from A1926f as reprinted in A1930d, pp. 102–5; last five paragraphs directly from A1930d, pp. 105–6.

geous, self-confident fellow man. Such a transformation should be carried out in a clear, deliberate manner, preferably according to the principles of Individual Psychology.

But [as mentioned above] we must admit that the change happens sometimes in response to some word or action of the physician, without either he or the patient noticing that the courage of the patient increases. The same effect is occasionally undoubtedly obtained with medicines, the so-called aphrodisiacs, despite their unreliability. In such cases very often the visit to the physician itself signifies resurgent strength, which only seeks the further encouragement by the physician, so that any therapy may meet with success.

Since time immemorial, scholars and nonscholars have tried to discover remedies to strengthen the sexual impulse. Prayers, charms, magic potions, sexual pictures, animal testicles, and later, extracts of the latter following the council of the famous Brown-Sequard[19] were supposed to boost dwindling virility. In recent times Steinach[20] and his adherents, Voronoff[21] and others, have tried to achieve this goal, partly through one-sided elimination of the testicles, partly through the implantation of testicles. According to the preceding discussions, the failures are more decisive than possible successes. Steinach's view on the "puberty gland" is probably still open to dispute, but meets increasingly firm opponents.

More as an assumption than an observation, one finds, as we shall explain below, the view that the sexual position of man toward woman depends primarily or solely on the quality of the male sex glands, or on a female component in the physical organization of the man (Schopenhauer, Moebius, Fliess, Weininger, Hirschfeld). The experimental studies of Steinach which, to many, signify definite proof—making female rats male and male rats female through corresponding changes of the sexual glands—show only gross differences, but not the fine nuances that we encounter in man. In any event, it is questionable if even in the most extreme artificial

[19] Charles Edouard Brown-Sequard (1818–94), French physiologist.
[20] Eugen Steinach (1861–1944), Austrian physician.
[21] Serge Voronoff (1866–1951), Russian physician in Paris.

effemination of man, as through castration or implantation of ovaries with all the conceivable physical consequences, a psychological change would necessarily follow, as in rats. Numerous cases of pseudohermaphrodites have in accordance with their education and preparation taken on feminine development without showing discernible changes in their sexual glands, and eunuchs and eunuchoids have undoubtedly shown masculine behavior. Such cases attest that psychological preparation plays an incomparably greater role in man than in animals.

The significance of inhibitions or their cessation for man's sexual attitude toward woman is evident from numerous phenomena of love life. A depressed mood may cause the élan to disappear in relation to one woman, as it may kindle it toward other women. Especially thoughts of revenge against one woman are easily able to ignite love for another. Likewise, sexuality frequently collapses when a bachelor who is disinclined to marry is threatened by the proximity of a marriage. Satyriasis, a continuing excitation of the genitals, can be observed (besides in cases of leukemia) occasionally when there has been continued prevention of sexual intercourse. In psychotics, it is the absence of inhibitions that is responsible for sexual excitation. In cases of paralysis, senile dementia, and alcoholism, one finds stronger as often as weaker sexual desire.

Undoubtedly a person continuously trains for the sexual role and the sexual ideal he has before him. The sum of this training cannot be overestimated: It includes his gait as he walks on the street, his association with the other sex, the comparison of himself with others of his own sex, etc. Consequently, in the case of faulty development of a person, once we have uncovered the errors in the development, we are still faced with a difficulty. It is somewhat like making a left-handed person sensitive to his deficiency when he had not been aware before that nature had endowed him like a stepchild, with an awkward right hand. This awareness alone does not enable him to achieve parity in his performance.

The difficult task is one of training, to have those who, in their sexual development have gone outside the normal range, catch up with the training that in normal persons plays such an enormously important role. The difficulty of such retraining can be appreciated if we remember that we have described sexual intercourse without love as misconduct, the education for which cannot be the task of the physician, even though he is not able at present to remove it from the world [same sentence as p. 187]. I should not like to put anyone in touch with prostitutes or suggest any love adventures.

Whether there is a solution for this problem, I do not know yet. It is the same difficulty that we find in all problems of education, where others speak of a "lack of aptitude," but where we are actually faced only with a lack of the correct method. We obviously need some invention to raise poorly trained persons to a better level of training without doing harm to them and to society. Undoubtedly the method plays the decisive role here. Whether one will perhaps someday be able to find through biology a substitute for the social training —this training of feelings and logic that is necessary for the development of a normal love life—I should like to leave to your judgment.[22]

The most important component of the Individual-Psychological method to make up for, and to substitute for such inadequate social training consists in encouragement—in the sense of a communal feeling (*Gemeinschaftsgefühl*) aware of responsibility and capable of co-operation, a better adaptation to the logic of human living together of which love life is a part, a better understanding of the meaning of life.

PROSTITUTION[23]

Premises and Standpoints[24]

In daily life as in research the discussion of simple or important issues is often stymied because of preconceived and

---

[22] This paragraph translated from an earlier version (A1928c, p. 7), because we found it more poignant than the corresponding later paragraph.

[23] New translation of A1920c, as in A1930p, pp. 230–38.

[24] Subheadings as found in the original, while otherwise in this volume generally supplied by the editors.

usually unexamined premises. Thus it is often less the opponent's acumen than his differently oriented attention by which he succeeds to raise or invalidate objections, to introduce and evaluate data and statistics, or to advance new viewpoints. No matter how objective we believe or hope to be, we must consciously and critically emphasize our personal standpoint and its derivatives to qualify for scientific investigation and discussion and to be able systematically to develop our premises. Without such clarification the inquiring spirit becomes circular and believes in the end to know as certain what at the beginning of the investigation had been only tentative assumptions. All methods lend themselves to such abuse, as has often been demonstrated regarding statistics. [*Added in later editions:* This also applies to any psychological trend that is not discriminating in its methods.]

We define a prostitute as a person, usually a female, who permits sexual intercourse to earn a living. From the standpoint of the societal coherence of human beings, prostitution is an occupational institution based on replacing various great responsibilities of a sexual union by demanding a monetary equivalent, as in a trade.

This [*later added:* rejecting] view leads unmistakably to the further premise: Society has, at least for some time to come, given certain forms to the relationship of the sexes and furnished it with responsibilities found suitable, necessary, and tested for the continuation of that society. Many of these forms, such as the duration and the phenomenon of courtship in love, appear to be firmly established. In addition, there are the voluntary commitments to comradeship and the founding of a family and the demand for mutual dignity. These consequences of sexual relations are also the self-evident demands of this society, which seeks to secure its existence by these methods.

This is not only in full accord with historical, legal, and sociological considerations, but is also the only view by which we can completely comprehend the ethical problem of prostitution—the old unsolved question, why society continuously marks as shameful, or even makes illegal, an institution that it brings forth itself and tolerates. Our view leads us to conclude that society has created in prostitution a malformation that serves as an emergency exit, a way out in the face of difficulties, to which numerous comrades see themselves condemned. The same society, however, on account of its different goals, must morally condemn this way out.

The Public and Prostitution

The social structure of prostitution is then a compromise of the worst order, between two opposing social tendencies—condemnation and support. An individual's stand on this issue will be importantly influenced by his stand on another issue: whether he affirms or denies the immanent demands of our present social life. A person's attitude toward prostitution will inform us better about his attitude toward the demands of the community and his social adaptation than he could as a rule do himself.

The satiated, satisfied citizen will generally have incorporated the social ideal of legal marriage mitigated by prostitution as a self-evident premise of his world philosophy. The one with conservative views, who strives toward preservation of the family as the cell of the state, especially who desires a strengthening and increase of the population, will logically focus on the disadvantages of prostitution. On the other hand, the new tendency toward a dissolution of the family may regard the nature and significance of prostitution more mildly, and may possibly even demand its cultivation.

These types cannot be sharply and dogmatically distinguished, and one easily loses the social coherence the less they consciously emphasize their own position toward the problem of society. In such investigations we must usually appraise the attitude of persons toward the community independently of their own assertions. This is perhaps even more necessary regarding the attitude toward the other sex, on which the attitude toward the problem of prostitution depends directly.

Our investigation of the falsifying premises of all commentators on prostitution shows us generally three groups of prejudices leading to worthless, barren, or harmful attitudes as far as practical consequences are concerned.

Misanthropic bias. The first group consists roughly of authors, commentators, and lay people who, having turned their backs upon the world and become misanthropical, have ceased to work seriously toward cultural progress. From their stand toward life—never logically conceptualized, but expressed in their feelings—they see in prostitution but another confirmation that everything that exists is reprehensible. Their personal attitude will emphasize the evil side of this "necessary evil," as they usually count on innate shortcomings of human nature, and stress in a hostile manner the uselessness of all human endeavor. This barren, superstitious standpoint may be replaced by vehement condemnation, disguised as moral, ethical, or religious criticism.

But from our standpoint—that one's attitude toward the intriguing problem of prostitution depends on one's attitude toward society—we find that all this pathos serves only a prejudicial standpoint, and that all such moralizing has so far remained ineffective. Neither could the use of force do away with prostitution. To understand the uselessness of all countermeasures so far we must realize that society needs exactly a form of prostitution and produces it, in which some individuals exert a supporting influence and others suppress or condemn it. The legal measures and the average social morality correspond to this compromise position.

Feminist bias. No matter how objectively we regard prostitution, we will find that it can arise only from human conditions that accept the female as a means to sexual lust and an object or property of man. In other words, prostitution is possible only in a society whose goal is the need satisfaction of the male. Consequently, the feminists find prostitution an insult to womanhood and fight against it. While we are quite in sympathy with this viewpoint, it is also based on an unconscious premise, namely, the intent to revolt, to overthrow the existing social order, with its masculine privileges.

Hygienic and patriotic bias. Finally, the inseparable connection of two human problems—prostitution and venereal

196

disease—brings about the strong attacks against prostitution by hygienists, friends of the people, and nationalists. We see such efforts especially in small, endangered nations that still muster enough energy to secure a sufficient birth rate to guarantee their continued existence. Their attitude toward existing conditions reveals moderate tendencies, often toward a radical change of social life.

If we now ask which strata of society are quite in accord with prostitution, we shall find it in those circles who consider the present stage of human culture as suitable and unalterable. One stratum is the large, compact one of the so-called average citizen. Since he constitutes the majority of the urban and rural population, this view is also shared by the authorities. Consequently, they take prostitution as an unalterable institution, and conduct the fight against venereal disease only halfheartedly at best. They are augmented by a relatively large number of physicians and fathers who in the hope of preventing stronger emotions among their wards advocate in a kind of fetishistic conviction regular sexual intercourse of the young people—that is, visits to prostitutes. We consider such referral of young people to the line of least resistance as barren as the attempts by young men to prove the prerogatives of their fomenting manhood without effort on prostitutes. Yet these groups of advocates also despise prostitution. They are even capable of feeling inhuman contempt of the prostitute as a person and at the same time recommending her for sexual intercourse. They thus reflect most faithfully the psychology of a culture that cannot do without degraded prostitution as a supplement to its system—aggravated procreation of society.

The Circle of Prostitution

Three groups of people are so closely related to prostitution that in order to understand the psychological problem of prostitution we must understand the individual psychology of these persons.

197

Those who need prostitution. To this group belong the very large number of people of a certain nervous type whom I have described in detail in *The Nervous Character* (A1912a) and "The Homosexual Problem" (A1914i). A schematic description follows.

Outwardly these persons appear often quite dissimilar. They include men prone to temper tantrums and a tyrannical lust for domination, who have armed themselves with great intolerance and oversensitivity against relations with society, up to a certain degree. They are conspicuously careful, generally choose occupations that offer security, are very distrustful, and have never been real friends. They are pathologically ambitious and jealous. When they feel obliged to take on public offices, they usually meet their tasks with much cunning, intrigue, and prestige politics. Sometimes they achieve marriage, as if by mistake. But then they treat wife and children with inconsiderate strictness and constant nagging, and often find their way back to prostitutes. Or they may treat their wives like prostitutes. They timidly avoid any difficulty or try to make a cunning detour around it. [*Added in later editions:* They fear commitment to one person as subjugation; polygamous tendencies dominate.] Their whole life and striving are aimed at cheap triumphs; they are guided by innumerable principles that always put the other in the wrong. They are always accusing and judging, and border on the type described above which, however, is more consistent in its rejection of human society by also rejecting prostitution. Their dissatisfaction extends to women, whom they consider altogether a lower kind of human being. Thus they reduce the female to a means, as do the strict antifeminists; they use her where her lack of resistance seems to support unconditionally the myth of male superiority.

This type of man creates and maintains the need for prostitution. Corresponding to his line, he is also convinced of the absolute dominance of the sex drive, often disguised in an extremely bizarre and scientific fashion. The real motive of his world view—unknown to him—the precondition of his thinking and acting, his masculine paroxysm, is to sneak around the great difficulties of life in order to harvest cheap triumphs over those who are without will or have been rendered irresolute. Bordering on this type are certain chastity fanatics who, out of fear of women, make difficult, often unfulfillable conditions for sexual intercourse, thereby, however, also escaping the real difficulties.

Another definite type of adherents to prostitution are sons from good families who are superficially described as "morally insane" and considered incurable. However, in our experience as described above, they are evading the demands of life because of their insecurity. In view of their latent sensitive ambition they prefer to accept moral condemnation rather than expose themselves to a presumed defeat in the course of honest striving. Such persons are very much like prostitutes toward whom they feel driven, as shall become clear later on.

A strong tendency toward prostitutes can also be observed among persons who easily succumb to alcohol, because they too, like the entire group discussed here, are inclined toward a cheap compromise in life, seek excuses for their shortcomings, and are masters in the art of rejecting serious responsibilities. Men with criminal tendencies also are often inclined to prostitution. Their criminal tendency too is founded in their predilection to evade individualistically attempts at a more difficult solution by breaking a social convention.

There is also a particularly close relationship between certain forms of neurosis and psychosis, and prostitution. As evidenced by their complaint, such persons suffer from inferiority feelings, lack of self-confidence, a pathological drive for significance, inclination toward irresponsibility, and a predilection for psychological devices and practices that flatter their self-esteem, such as the paid conquest of a woman. Psychologically related are those who seek spouses of a lower cultural level, or even prostitutes, in order to silence their fear of the female and at the same time satisfy permanently a hesitating lust for dominance.

Certainly the stream of visitors of prostitution goes beyond these clearly outlined types. Occasional or passing situations may bring also persons of a different kind into similar relationships, when an increased inferiority feeling reaches for a quick, effortless satisfaction. In the same way an unsuited girl

199

may occasionally fall to the rank of prostitution. In such cases the effort to establish other social relationships can be clearly seen. However, not they, but the large, inexhaustible number of "those who need prostitution" are the pillars of prostitution as an institution.

The procurer. We understand procurers as persons in whom inadequate social interest, an inclination toward cheap successes, conception of the female as a means to an end, and a tendency toward effortless satisfaction of their lust for dominance, also establish again and again the connection with prostitution as a mass phenomenon. Prostitution is greatly advanced by this category. The procurer or the white slaver function as a pacemaker, directing the novice prostitute toward public prostitution. They support secret inclinations and remove the last remnant of a feeling of responsibility from girls who, if left alone, might still waver and hesitate. The psychological kinship with "those who need prostitution" is unmistakable. The line of the procurer's personality is oriented toward an effortless livelihood; the distance from the criminal is usually minimal; the tendency toward alcoholism and brutality are paroxysms of a considerable feeling of weakness, compensating acts of an unsatisfied drive for significance. The attitude of the procurer toward society includes visibly a critical, fighting, revolting note. His officiously prominent postures as savior and protector of the prostitute are eloquent hints at his grandiosity. He bears legal fines like a duelist bears his wounds, and finds reward and consoling satisfaction for these in the increased respect and admiration from his like-minded circles. Thus he, too, has constructed or found a subjective world that complies with his pathological drive for significance in a fictitious manner, far removed from hard reality. I hope we shall not be misunderstood if we emphasize his relationship also with the "nervous character." This investigation finally also clearly illuminates the psychological condition of those persons who, when confronted with difficulties in life, seek an emergency exit by paying with the surrender of their wives to others the price for their own advancement.

The prostitute. The customary views about the motives toward prostitution have yielded little psychologically useful

200

data. The view that need and misery are decisive is untenable. First of all, it ignores that those who may become victims of prostitution are a selection of poor girls. To maintain that whether one becomes a prostitute depends on the extent of deprivation is to underestimate the aversion against the social humiliation that is generally connected with the concept of prostitute—not to speak of morality and character.

The mistaken view may be influenced by quite different deplorable social phenomena, such as the frequent fact that girls under the pressure of great worries or misery may sell the "property" of their femininity permanently or temporarily to the first one who comes along, without considering their inclination, or even against all inclination. Such girls differ, however, from real prostitutes in that they do not show the continuous occupational zeal of the latter, which causes prostitutes who have become rich still to keep on pursuing their profession with the zeal of a professional. What holds these persons with such iron force to their occupation? It is the same satisfaction that a businessman obtains from fulfilling his tasks, the same need for significance, the same "expansion tendency" that we find in all human beings, but particularly developed in all those whom we generally designate as "nervous characters."

Above, we have described the paroxysmic attempts by which certain persons become clients of prostitution or procurers—and have recognized these deceitful exaltations as escapes, as borrowed semblance of strength. These asocial phenomena reflect fear of the normal demands of society that are consistently rejected—that is, inadequate confidence in one's own competence regarding the expectations of social life. They are a device to gain through the sexual relationship in an easy and compliant manner the feeling, the subjective impression of a heightened self-esteem. That the latter self-enrichment is based on the increased semblance of perfect manliness was already indicated. What if the same motives were found in the psychological structure of the prostitute? What if it were these motives that alone would make a girl suitable for prostitution and would show her the way?

Before discussing these questions and the answers by

others, we want to mention still another very prevalent misconception regarding the psychological constitution of the prostitute, namely that she is an abyss of sensuality, a creature who is always aroused. This view of the prostitute is pardonable for ignorant lay people who must condemn her profession if they want to remain faithful to their societal obligation. But when scholarly specialists arrive at such a view, they must be thoughtless or blind. Yet this view is found quite frequently in scientific papers, at times adorned with Lombroso's untenable assertion of the innate prostitute character.

Against this we must emphasize that in practicing her profession the prostitute lacks any sensual excitement. It is different, of course, when she enters a love relationship, or toward her procurer, or in homosexual relationships, which she favors surprisingly often. One may say that only in these relationships does her sexuality assert itself, often in form of a deviation that points to the aversion of the prostitute against the feminine role. In her profession she only acts as a female for the gullible partner. For her own sensitivity, however, she is far removed from the female role, is only the salesperson, and remains frigid. And whereas the client believes he feels his male superiority over a woman, she is aware only of her ability to solicit and her fee—that is, her worth. She degrades the man to the dependent means of her livelihood. Thus both, by way of a fiction, arrive at the deceptive feeling of their personal pre-eminence.

With this observation we have come closer to the core of the above questions. The daring device to translate sexual intercourse into a monetary equivalent characterizes prostitutes as it does the other two groups described above. As in the men involved in prostitution, the fiction of a satisfactory triumph, of an ever newly gained significance, causes this institution to prevail and endure. This fiction is also the chief temptation of all participants in prostitution.

The ability to exchange an inalienable function of the female, of her body and her soul, for money can be achieved only by one in whom the premise of woman's inferiority is firmly anchored. This shows up also in the pertinent customs and in the history of every prostitute. Usually corrupted early in life, these girls consider themselves the victim of the "superior" male, who remains the respected attacker while the girl is condemned. No wonder then that the female waiting for a male is considered a weakness, the enemy, a fatal deception. In the same sense, it becomes plausible to the untrained mind to act like a man, to court as he does, and to dispense with female attitude and morality, all the more so as a deepening of the feminine role, marriage and motherhood, and the expectations of society become inaccessible through the girl's previous history as well as through her feeling of futility vis-à-vis men. The career of the prostitute is regularly characterized by seeking in prostitution a way out and by securing for herself the significance that is elsewhere denied. This way out is generally taken after futile, or apparently futile, efforts—after having been fired as a maid, governess, or factory worker. Always, however, she follows thereby the model of the "active" man, not of the "passive" woman.

In this development the widespread poison of a supermanly world philosophy is decisive. It permeates the family home of the future prostitute, where it allows the father to be a tyrannical despot, and makes the wife and mother into a frightening model of a future feminine role. It raises the brothers to an envied rank and makes the girl feel her femininity as a blemish and accusation. The belief in her own power vanishes, and the seducer, who is often himself still immature, finds a nonresisting, cowardly creature. She has grown up in the fear of men, or is in contained rage against her feminine fate, and also often for the same reasons in rebellion against the rules of her parents. Thus she cannot find her normal development, and the successful seduction takes her still farther away from it.

The further consequences of the seduction are also notable: The girl does not draw conclusions in the sense of a correction; instead, the inferiority feeling, the disbelief in her own strength, and her revulsion against the feminine role are deepened. The broad path of prostitution now opens before her in an intoxication of activity, as a revolt against the demands of society, as a way out from goals that are more

203

difficult to attain. This way seems closer to soliciting and earning masculinity, promises significance, and redeems her from the feeling of total nothingness. This calculation may not strike us as correct. But ask the prostitutes and their procurers!

Prostitution and Society

Thus the circle closes. On the one hand, we have the human society, which today is still not capable of making its own demands more firm to enable their realization. Added to this are the human beings who are afraid of the adversities of life and seek cheap escapes. Furthermore, we have a culture that increasingly co-ordinates its ideals with the way of thinking of the marketplace. Finally, we have its victims, who attempt to make a virtue out of necessity, and in doing so fill a gap in our normal social life, only, while being tolerated and despised at the same time, to perish [*added in later editions:* to become exterminated].

7

CASES OF HOMOSEXUALITY

In the following few case histories I want to demonstrate the basic principles. From these I hope an understanding of the homosexual psyche will result, as well as the validity of the dynamics described above.

DEVELOPMENT OF DISTANCE FROM THE FEMALE (CASES 1 AND 2)[1]

Case 1. Being "Milked" by Older Sisters

From an autobiography written before therapy: "I grew up with my older sisters, who used me in their games just like a toy. I remember especially painfully one of the games, in which I was a cow and was milked by the girls on my penis. Only when I finally complained to our governess was this torment ended.

"We children also liked to ride on the knees of our governess, but preferred to ride on those of male friends of the family, and expressed our pleasure in happy screams. But, in contrast to my sisters, I found that my penis got in the way. I thought up a more comfortable horsie: I stuck a cushion between my legs and rode on it around the room by the hour.

[1] New translation from A1917b as reprinted in A1930d, pp. 14, 15–20.

My sisters also gladly participated in this game, and we were quite in love with our cushions. Later, the cushion became a baby that we let drink at our breasts. We also liked to suck on the corners of the cushion, which led to continuous fights with the members of the household. When, for reasons of health, my hobby horse was taken away from me, I came through reflection to see the connection of this measure with the sexual organ, and made the strange discovery that I could make my testicles disappear into the abdomen. Thereupon I attempted also to make my penis disappear, in which I succeeded, however only temporarily, and by compressing it very much. As a grown-up youth my keenest desire was to be bisexual. Then I could as a man move unnoticed among men, and as a girl dominate them.

"I was not cut out to play a subordinate role. I was extremely ambitious and stubborn. When going on rides with my sisters, I was always the one who decided on the direction, and I even forced the girls to look only in the direction that I told them.[2]

"As a boy of twelve, I liked best to be in the stable with the coachman and the stable boy. There I often had the opportunity to see their sexual parts which, in comparison to mine, seemed gigantic. One day I saw the stable boy introducing his arm into the sexual part of a mare. All these dimensions confused me so much that I was afraid of my future.

"Another time I reached for the penis of the stable boy, who gave me still further instructions—and thus my first homosexual action came about, which filled me with enormous pride. Until today, it has remained that way; the power that I exert on men fills me with ecstasy. Recently, I seduced an older staff officer, who had always been heterosexual, to have homosexual intercourse. I almost had a satisfaction when I saw him afterward quite exhausted before me, and I asked him not to hold the attack against me. He misunderstood me as he replied: *'Tout comprendre, c'est tout pardonner!'*"

In this autobiography of a patient the basic schema that I

[2] This and the following paragraph reversed from the original.

have outlined [in Chapter 5] becomes clearly evident: the preponderance of the female part of the family, the inconvenience of the differentiating sex organ, the uncertainty as a child regarding his sexual role, the hope to be able to alter it, and the directive line of ambition that seeks its triumph by detours.

Case 2. Feeling Degraded by One's Mother

A twenty-six-year-old man, looking somewhat dreamy and bashful, introduced himself as a homosexual. His question was whether I would allow him to get married. Such a question addressed to a psychiatrist (*Nervenarzt*) is always only a pretense. He would never have asked me, if he really had wanted to. The very next inquiries showed that he considered homosexuality as something unalterable, and supported his view with a whole series of citations from well-known authorities. I would not say that this very prevalent incorrect view causes tangible damage. But in the case of sexual deviation, which is constructed on a mass of errors and thus keeps the patient bound in myth, such authoritative assertions as the "incurability of homosexuality" are very well suited to support the deception of the patient. It is therefore recommended, in accordance with our viewpoint, to go easy with this assertion.

Asked about his life, the patient told that he was the illegitimate child of a peasant girl and did not know his father. Subsequently, his mother gave birth to a second illegitimate child. Then she got married and had two girls, whom the patient had to look after, day and night. He greatly disliked this job and remembered very well how he regarded not only the two little girls, but also girls and women in general, as hostile creatures who were to blame for his despised fate. Besides, certain comments of his grandmother, disgracing his mother quite openly before the boy, contributed to this opinion. Along with this attack and his own sad experience of having his mother herself degrade him by assigning him to the service of the two little girls, he heard continuously, especially from his grandmother, how despicable love relationships were altogether. Like other boys and men he understood this to mean: Be very careful of women. For that, he had surely had the proper preparation through his own fate.

His way of reacting to feelings of disparagement can perhaps be best understood when we learn that he, the boy who was despised by all, firmly decided to become a priest. This meant nothing less than to be the first man in the village. This childhood fantasy of vocational choice also shows that already early in life he sought his goal (as a Catholic) far from wife and love. In grade school he was the most diligent and gifted, and after much effort he succeeded in being admitted to high school (*Gymnasium*). But after he had successfully finished the second year, his guardian took him out of school and used him as a gooseherd.

The fate of this boy was then not at all suited to make him a good partner of society. For two years he looked after the geese, until some strangers took an interest in him and prevailed upon his guardian to guide this gifted boy toward another occupation. He wanted to become a mechanic, but his guardian forced him to become a weaver's apprentice.

After a three-year apprenticeship, at the age of seventeen, he gave up weaving, as he had decided long ago, and became an apprentice in a technical factory. At the same time, he started to study intensively at a vocational school and obtained, after much effort, the good position that he had at the time of the interview.

Already as a weaver's apprentice, he had found a friend in whom he could trust completely, in contrast to other people. At the same time, he was not able to extend his self-esteem so far that he, who had up to now been oppressed by all, gained an influence over somebody. We are not surprised that when his sexual drive awakened it took the same direction as his firmly established attitude toward life: distance and fearful aversion from women, and particularly close devotion to his friend as the first human being who came to meet him lovingly. At the same time, under the whip of his sexual drive, he succumbed to the temptation to gain a dominating position over another person through a sexual bond. Thus he, the despised, everywhere slighted, but longing for triumph, became the seducer of his friend and an active homosexual.

He succeeded in occasional heterosexual attempts in his later life, but always found a way to record them as unsuccessful. For example, after normal intercourse with a prostitute, he found this action "disgusting." One finds this reaction not exactly only in homosexuals. But our patient takes his disgust as proof of his "innate perverse orientation"—and feels himself further committed to it.

Some time ago, he had been talked into getting married, and he became engaged to a girl who was introduced to him. But he acted so repulsively and awkwardly that he was gladly given an opportunity to withdraw. No sooner had he become engaged than he came to see me to introduce himself with his "innate homosexuality." Surely this was less to seek a cure than to acquire a sanctioning of his illness and thereby the obligation to step back from the marriage.

When he had submitted to the compelling reasons of the above view, he fell in love with a fourteen-year-old girl—that is, an unsuitable object—again only in order to gain time, while breaking his engagement. But our treatment did not succeed in having him overcome his old fear and aversion of women. Unfortunately these had grown in him through the strange events of his life, but certainly did not need to remain unalterable.

Summary

Far be it from me to talk in these two cases of a cure of homosexuality. But we succeeded in both in reducing considerably the distance between the patient and the female sex. Especially the second case seems to be in a favorable position and may well, after a while, undergo an essential reconstruction toward normality. But I should like to warn against underestimating the difficulties.

Altogether, our findings give us much more grounds for advocating the prophylaxis of homosexuality than its therapy, which is so exceedingly difficult. On the other hand, let us point out that therapy must not stop even at the greatest difficulties.

In the above cases, of which the first tended more toward a feminine, the second more toward a masculine role, the apparent fixation in homosexuality was soon shaken, and both patients engaged in heterosexual activities, although of a scanty kind. But the normally oriented young man also often needs quite some time of preparation to do justice to his sexual function without complaints. One should allow the improved patients also ample time.

With many homosexuals, however, there will be a second reason for treatment, one by which it will become absolutely necessary. These are cases in which the neurosis that regularly accompanies homosexuality has become so prominent that treatment must be requested to enable the patient to go on with life. The present cases also had numerous nervous symptoms—such as hypochondriasis in the first, and insomnia, blushing, and bashfulness in the second—which also originated in fear of social demands.

The necessity of treatment becomes particularly evident in the following case, which also shows the many-sidedness of the deviation, which is frequently emphasized in the literature.

A HOMOSEXUAL NEUROTIC LIFE LINE (CASE 3)[3]

Introduction

From the study of neuroses and the psychologically similar sexual deviations I gained an understanding of the uncanny and often well-hidden defiance of the patient, trained in childhood against a stronger person, and later against the social demands that were experienced as too overwhelming. This can be clearly seen from our introductory presentations.

[3] New translation from A1917b as reprinted in A1930d, pp. 20–41.

Childhood defiance is the regrettable result of false upbringing.

A special yet frequent case is the following: The best of boys may become strangely defiant and negativistic—only to be rid of his inferiority feelings and to grow beyond his father. This may happen in a false understanding of the justified desire to become a real man. In this way the child may point his entire willing and acting primarily in one direction—to spoil things for his father, with two possibilities for further development. If the father is loving, the child will hide his defiance from himself and others; but in his actions, and especially with the consequences of his actions, the child operates contrary to the expectations of his father, perhaps through clumsiness or with the semblance of a persistent inability. Or, if the father is strict, his domination may favor and strengthen open defiance to the point where the child loses faith in himself, the belief that he will be equal to the others in the future. In this case, he will need and construct a strong safeguard against losing his feeling of personal worth through defeats and detractions in comparison with his father. A. Hoche and M. Lewandowsky have come upon similar facts of "safeguarding" ("*Sicherung*").

This line of caution will also always lead to a detour exactly when [*added later:* one of the three problems of life (A1927a)] the most important social problem, the relationship to the female sex, enters a decisive stage. Then only the path to neurosis and, under favorable conditions, sexual deviation is open. In summary, we may say that in the prehistory of the homosexual one will always find a conscious or unconscious hostile attitude toward the father, the guardian, or the mother, in addition to the traits we have described previously: uncertainty about the sexual role, fear of making decisions, construction of a future life without a woman, and the consuming desire for triumphs.

Delicate Physique and Feeling of Weakness

The patient introduced himself as a homosexual suffering from terrible obsessions. The latter very much interfered with his job as an office employee (*Privatbeamter*). His further

211

education, his study of economics and business, was also jeopardized by these obsessions. He had begun his studies after the recent death of his father, to advance more rapidly in his career. He had to provide for himself and his mother.

For his age (twenty-five years) he was weakly, with a delicate, pale complexion and Hutchinson's teeth.[4] When asked about his father, he told that he had died from a stroke during a paralysis. The patient was an only child, born late in the life of his mother, who was five years older than his father.

The detrimental effects of syphilis on the procreative cells has been amply described by pathologists and pediatricians—for example, Hochsinger (1910). In view of these numerous injuries to development, which may affect any organ, we may expect in children of syphilitic parents a sickly childhood and in its course the appearance of inferiority feelings. The worry of such parents about their weakly child usually aggravates the situation. In other cases, the father, humiliated by his syphilis, establishes a regime of terror or develops hypochondriasis. In any event, feelings of weakness and insecurity will dominate the mind of the child.

The family life of our patient was ideal. His parents were intelligent and friendly people, and his mother, who hardly let her only son out of sight, knew how to make any temporary moods and depression of her husband disappear quickly through friendly submissiveness.

Some things stand out firmly in the patient's memory: He was weakly, was always carefully watched, and had a speech impediment, which his relatives ridiculed. He speaks of his development without concern, while we slowly see the pointers emerging from which we infer his life line.

Domination over the Mother

There are pronounced ideas of grandeur. The patient reports about his mother that she devoted herself completely to

---

[4] Hutchinson's teeth are notched and narrow-edged front teeth, considered a sign of congenital syphilis, but not always of such origin.

his care. During his third and fourth years he counted already so much on her devotion and tried to increase it that later he still felt a terrible wrong was done to him when his mother was not with him. We see here the error in upbringing that, above all, undermines the independence of the child and makes him cowardly for life. Quite in keeping with this attitude, the mother was, until recently, extremely suspicious of the maidservants. She gave her son no opportunity to be alone with girls and even explicitly discouraged him. And so it happened that he who exercised complete dominance over his mother soon came to renounce any advance in a social direction, a main reason being that he did not believe he could dominate elsewhere as completely as he thought it was necessary.

Another memory points to defiance and rivalry toward his father, and shows that he was not at all satisfied with the dominance he had gained over his mother. He slept in a room adjoining the bedroom of his parents. One evening, when he may have been six years old, after his parents had gone to rest, he jumped out of bed in a temper tantrum such as he had never had before, reached for a cane, and beat on the stove until his mother came to quiet him. He also remembers how he had often called for his mother before going to sleep and asked her for all kinds of services.

This tendency to take possession of his mother, to place her in his service and thus secure a feeling of dominance in a cheap way, is very prominent and could easily tempt one to discover an incestuous tendency, to transform all expressions of the patient into a sexual jargon and thereby gain what one has put in—the sexual etiology of homosexuality.

But our patient reports that until his twelfth year he lacked any knowledge of sex differences, any sexual interest or impulse, probably due to his mother's strict watch. Toward the admonitions of his father to act like a boy, he was without understanding, awkward, and probably also defiant. One can easily understand that this child, in his feeling of inferiority, looked for support, found it in his mother, and did not reach for his father because he did not lend himself to this.

I readily leave it to anyone with experience with children to

213

decide how much more tenable this explanation is, as to why this child had to lean on his mother, than the arbitrary claims of Freud, which derive the psychological development of a boy, with all its ramifications, from an incestuous inclination determined by the sex drive.

Defiance of the Father

The atmosphere in which this pampered boy was to develop was not only the reason for his continuously expanding desire to dominate his mother, to achieve recognition from her through love and sometimes through rage, but also sharpened his antagonism toward his father.

In the present case, where the father carefully avoided exerting pressure, the boy's antagonism did not develop into open defiance and hostility. Still, it was unavoidable that the father's superiority, in the nature of things, occasionally forced the son into the background, as, for example, when he asked his father for help with his arithmetic homework. For this he always took revenge by getting the father furious and excited through an unconsciously contrived lack of understanding.

The patient's physical weakness mentioned above likewise created a situational antagonism to his father, who was strikingly tall and strong. This antagonism was increased through the father's incessant urging the boy not to behave "like a girl," not always to cling to his mother, but to roughhouse like a boy, to go around with other boys, and to get into mischief. Since a feeling of antagonism had taken root, the father could not be the proper leader but rather always met with resistance from the boy.

The father had to fail also for a second reason, which again and again threatens treatment with failure, unless one can remove it: Our patient, as an insecure child, had developed his compensating ambition so far that he could only take ways in which his own superiority would come to light, not that of his father or, later, his physician. Furthermore, the patient would hardly have cut a good figure in the games and pranks of boys.

The boy could have fallen into a compensatory negativism, into an openly defiant, annoying, sadistic attitude, as one finds otherwise in nervously disposed children. But this way was closed through the amiable, friendly relationship of the father, who preferred the hidden path of persuasion and pedagogical affection. In the face of this method, only one countermove was left for the boy: to maintain and increase his father's love by similar hidden paths, in order to insure dominance over him too. At the same time, with the quickly learned schema of a passive attitude and incompetent weakness, he obviated the persistent demands of his father for manly conduct.

Devious Methods of Domination

In this psychological state in which the exclusive dominance over his mother and her subordination appeared to the patient as the only proof of his superiority to her and his father, each movement and each attitude were determined by his fictive goal: to satisfy his will to power despite his weakness of physical condition and age, through detours and secret tricks (*Schliche*), but never through straightforward aggression and provocation of a fight.

Some of these fencing positions can be accurately reconstructed, and show facts and preparatory actions that later became reality, or reveal the early direction of his fantasy. For instance, as a child he would disarrange his pillow or covers as a reason for calling his mother away from the side of her husband; later, as an adult, he wanted to tear her away from his father by trying to make her suspect her husband of marital infidelity.

Apparently contradictory traits. The cunning and sly secretiveness of the patient's method was the natural result of his lack of self-confidence for open action. This is the reason for apparently contradictory traits which, however, point equally to proving his superiority—the misunderstood "split personality" of some authors. For example, he had to muster enough love and be sufficiently diligent and industrious not to forfeit his importance for his father and mother. Consequently, he was capable of all this.

On the other hand, he had to carry on his secret defiance toward both, so that they would be continuously occupied with him. Consequently, he was defiant and incapable, as other neurotics perhaps manifest enuresis, stammering, or masturbation.

The physician must expect the same model of behavior during treatment and must explain it to the patient, because certainly all apparently contradictory impulses of the neurotic —love and hatred, defiance and obedience, dominance and submission, sadism and masochism, activity and passivity, homosexuality and heterosexuality—are only means to reach the fictive final purpose of over-all superiority. With this explanation, however, their antithetic character disappears!

Continuous patronizing. Another, less important trait that one often finds in homosexuals and also in other neurotics is continuous patronizing. It is to be explained by their secret ambition, and sometimes leads to the familiar forms of false charity and sympathy. Advice, rendering polite assistance, services, warnings, and other patronizing actions come continuously to light. Here a stone is removed from the path, there attention is called to a nail or a piece of glass, the other person is neatly brushed, his necktie is straightened, he will be reminded to leave on time, etc. One gets the impression of a thoughtful person whose officious, altruistic actions can, however, become a nuisance. The thoughtfulness becomes suspicious through its exaggeration. In fact, the patient grabs the reins in everything, and the exclusiveness with which he tries to think and act for everybody, and the way in which he condemns others to passivity, are often experienced as oppression, even without a psychological examination. Upon examination this impression is greatly strengthened when one notices that a tendency to spy and to criticize in a disguised way is part of the patient's behavior. This attitude of lust for superiority while evading straightforward aggression appears snakelike and tortuous. At times I have noticed this essential attitude in homosexuals in a snakelike movement, as a compulsive movement whenever they were faced with an apparently difficult problem that they wanted to get around. The present case also manifested this compulsive movement.[5]

Childhood Dreams, Games, and Sex Role

To verify at this stage of understanding if one has found the right line, one must draw on further childhood recollections—for example, "unforgettable dreams" from childhood —to see if one finds in them, perhaps, the same and only the same line, representing the beginnings of the patient's tactics. One of these dreams, from about his sixth year, was: "I am climbing a mountain, on the top of which my mother is waiting for me. I am walking in serpentines. Behind me a man is following in the same paths. He is dressed like a guard, and I had the feeling he wanted to do something to me." If one lets this dream naïvely act on one, it yields the upward striving, the fight for the mother, the secretiveness of the hidden path, and the hostile attitude of the father.

A second dream, from his seventh year, was: "I am walking with my father in the street. Behind us is a person who acts like mad. He knocks everybody's head off." Although this dream could not be understood completely without recourse to certain assumptions, one can at least see from it with certainty that the patient considered life outside his home, "on the street," as full of danger, and that he assured himself of the protection of his father.

The preparations of this boy clearly pursue a line of safeguarding and advance "from below to above," toward superiority over all others, while nevertheless evading direct attack. We may expect to find this line as far as possible again in all other areas of activity. This should be particularly the case in preferred occupations and play because such activities are especially seized by the child as preparations for life.

[5] This paragraph was originally at the beginning of the case, A1930d, pp. 21–22.

And indeed the patient tells us that he never played with other children, or only when forced, and that since early childhood he preferred to play almost exclusively with trains and was particularly interested in their mechanisms. From other material (see A1909a) I may assume that such curiosity about mechanisms arises from a strong feeling of insecurity regarding knowledge, which seeks and gropes for satisfaction. Such a child is not a fighter, which is confirmed by further information about this man's childhood. Is this not the same impression that may have moved the father to complain that the patient behaved like a girl and not like a boy? When we recall his delicate appearance, his curls, furthermore, that until his fifth year he was dressed like a girl, and that almost until puberty he was not certain about sex differences nor even his own sexual role, we are impressed that his insecurity regarding knowledge includes insecurity regarding his sexual role. Regarding girls, I can state analogously that fighting and wrestling, climbing and running, exaggerated sports performances and dreams of such activities, as Stanley Hall and [Theodate] Smith (1903a, 1903b) have pointed out, indicate dissatisfaction with the feminine role and the "masculine protest." This is a new, reinforcing note in the picture of our patient: Unsure of his future sexual role, he has renounced the masculine striving for power.

From his spontaneous communications we learn further that at about the age of ten the patient had come to the conclusion that children were born by the mother's belly bursting open. At the same time he suffered from the phobia that the boiler on his train would burst. Here we find in the form of a phobia hidden thoughts and impulses that, by necessity, contained a protest against the feminine role.

Another circumstance also made it plausible that he would someday have to play a feminine role. Throughout his childhood he was in contact with a girl cousin six years older than himself whose uncommon energy and courage filled him with respect and fear. Most often the two would play wedding—with our patient having to take the bride's role, dragging a long train, while the girl played the groom (see A1911c). This probably means that it was the boy's organ inferiority that accounted for his being considered a girl and not unquestionably a boy. In time, he tacitly accepted this tacit view, and finally reached the point where he could not decide simply whether to take a masculine or a feminine role.

His neurotic mother had decided only late in life in favor of her feminine role—that is, marriage—and then was afraid of having a second child and overdid her care for the only one. His father, too, on account of his syphilis, was worried about the future of his boy and decided too late to let him run about freely. Thus we see before us the development of an organically inferior child whose uncertainty regarding his sexual role was through isolation extended too long, and whose feeling of deficient masculinity was further supported by the nervous family tradition. The patient finally found a way to gather all these feelings of inferiority and increase them so that they could nevertheless merge into an extremely ambitious goal: the attempt to become superior through the feminine attitude with feminine means!

At the age of sixteen, in a play at school, he played a feminine part, was admired by the other pupils, and flirted quite readily with a strange visitor, who was captivated by this charming creature whom he assumed to be a girl.

Gaining Distance from the Other Sex

But even earlier, in his twelfth year, an event occurred that significantly strengthened his unconscious guiding line to renounce women. From about his eighth year on he was inclined to masturbate. It was thigh masturbation and, as is perhaps always the case in this form of masturbation, no seduction had taken place. Four years later, when he had mutual sexual contact with a schoolmate in a bathhouse, he discovered that he suffered from phimosis [tightness of the skin covering the glans of the penis].

This case then also shows, as I originally described, sexual inferiority, for which phimosis represents the peripheral sign of degeneration, together with other inferiorities (see A1907a). This ambitious boy experienced this affliction as a blemish. Because he now thought that in addition to everything else his sexual powers were impaired, he succeeded in dropping all natural preparations for winning a woman, especially since he was already well along in this direction.

From this time on, women no longer played a part in his life because he believed he was not up to a decision.[6] The patient's way now led ever closer to men, ending one day in open homosexuality.

This decision also was not made suddenly, let alone that he had been surprised by it. A whole series of preparations, in which his active intervention was indispensable, show us his active tendency toward sexual deviation. Yet this was done in a manner that he could escape responsibility—in a manner of self-deception. Among his preparations the most important were: a neurotic, biased grouping and evaluation of facts, the depreciation of women, and "hardening measures."

Our patient had his first homosexual experience at the age of sixteen. He was already initiated into the secrets of sexuality and claims to have remained generally cold toward girls. A closer look, however, proves this assertion incorrect. The patient speaks in fact of virtually ardent affections toward several girls, but he never wanted to seize the chance of even a comradely approach. In accordance with his life plan he needed distance from girls—and consequently created it. By underscoring the difficulties, by purposely emphasizing "feminine" shortcomings, by the observation, which later proved to be incorrect, of their indifference toward him, by deluding himself of special feminine deceitfulness, he always managed to scare himself off and to kill any budding interest. At the same time he also learned the tone that necessarily repulsed girls, and mastered it instinctively.

He stressed all the more the attraction boys exerted on him at outings or while bathing. For a long time this did not go beyond platonic infatuations, occasional kisses and embraces. Twice he remembered mutual touching of the genitals. He

[6] I have traced the same psychological mechanism in cases of fetishism, masturbation, other sexual deviations, and the choice of a partner who is socially markedly inferior (see A1920a, A1929c). [Author's note.]

regarded these experiences, which he had actually staged diplomatically after thorough deliberation and preparation, as signs from heaven, and they, too, fortified his belief in his "innate" homosexuality. Usually his excitations led to thigh masturbation. His father tried to prevent this through veiled insinuations—understandably in vain, because he was the patient's rival for power.

At the time of puberty, when the patient was already homosexually prepared, he associated his sexual excitations always with homosexual fantasies while again overlooking his own influence as the biased judge. In his fantasies he preferred figures of tender boys to whom he was easily superior, or particularly strong, giantlike men who, overwhelmed by his spell, attempted to gain possession of him by violence. His fantasy act represented a situation in which, in full consciousness of the incongruity, he was changed into a female. Interestingly, only later did mutual fellatio take place in his fantasies.

This stage of development needs closer consideration. If we considered our task as solved by having traced homosexuality to a feeling of inadequacy and established it as the attempt to arrive more easily at a fictitious ideal of superiority by renouncing women, then our patient's occasional attraction to pretty girls could confuse us, even as it would confuse adherents of an innate homosexuality. But if we look more closely, we see that our patient systematically depreciated the natural impulses of his masculine role until he was no longer aware of them. With equal zeal, he cut off every inclination to approach the female sex, because this would have endangered his neurotic life plan.

The essential weakening of his activity was so important to him that he advanced it until he was hindered from any initiative, also toward men. He had homosexual relations with three men, but never took the initiative. He never contributed more to the relationship than shy, coquettish behavior. As in childhood, where we saw him incapable of attacking his father, his mother, or comrades, or to get into an open fight, he remained always the object of the conquest, up to the time of therapy. He had found no opportunity to learn to take the offensive, and when he was supposed to develop it into a love relationship, confidence in his strength, along with a readiness for victory had been completely lost.

He believed he lost the last chance to pull himself together through the phimosis, which he evaluated as unmanly. Now he took automatically the emotional turn familiar to him since childhood—to feel himself the stronger by eliminating women, and by conquering men through devious ways and feminine means. No matter how much he dominated his mother, this success could never seem perfect or sufficient for his exaggerated ambition, because his father had stronger rights and greater influence. The scene from his childhood in which he furiously hit the stove shows us his sense of defeat by his father. When now he had an eye for girls, this was only to train himself in denial, in order firmly to establish his distance from the female sex and to learn how to drop relationships quickly after they had barely begun.

Neurotic Valuation and Fantasy as Preparation

This trick of "hardening," part of the preparatory safe-guarding tendency, is of the greatest significance within the mechanism of neurosis. It teaches us impressively how the individual life line of the neurotic, including its goal, once they are established, become decisive. They group the recollections, raise experiences to rank and dignity or plunge them into oblivion, crumble their significance, enhance sensitivities or blot them out, use weaknesses and errors as tricks and devices, whip up the drive life or change it, create "libidinous" impulses, deviations, and fetishistic traits, let them soon submerge again, and are at any time capable to make something out of nothing, or nothing out of something. It is an established fact that the psychological life of the nervous patient, and thereby the neurosis, can be understood only through knowledge of this mechanism. Actually, it is so clearly before our eyes that it is impossible to overlook it.

This mechanism is also found in the luxuriating masturbation of our patient. We may well state that his homosexuality was made possible only by the arranged homosexual preparations of his fantasy, which were also served by his masturbation. The entire attitude of his later homosexuality can be found and traced in his masturbation fantasies, and certainly also in his dreams of that period as preparations. From this it follows necessarily that the neurotic symptom of homosexuality, like all other symptoms of neurosis, is fashioned and arranged, and that after many trials it is made a suitable part of the patient's unconscious life plan.

From this we see regarding the significance of masturbation in neurosis: (1) Originating from real stimulus conditions, it is soon made suitable for the neurotic schema. (2) Accompanying guilt feelings have only the function of putting the "great significance" of masturbation in the proper light or of safeguarding from excess; they also serve as proof of the patient's "everything-surpassing sexuality." (3) The accompanying fantasies must be regarded as preparations that disclose the goal of the nervous patient, before which he still hesitates. (4) All the facts of masturbation show that a feeling of inferiority or the fear of a defeat, both culminating in the fear of the sexual partner, seek to postpone the decision of an ambitious patient.

In respect to the last point, fear of decision, we find in our patient the same large measure of inhibited aggression as otherwise in his life. His reserve toward the partner of the same sex is as great as his distance from life in general—a congruency from which we can see that we have correctly understood the line of the patient. Was not his previously described attitude toward his father, his mother, and people in general unconsciously and therefore unalterably determined by the same feeling of inferiority, by his fear of decision, and by his too-highly tensed goal of domination of his environment? Also his other devices—his ingratiating, snakelike manner; the secret defiance that manifested itself in a passive attitude toward all demands; the partial incapability when faced with any problems; his going along unmanly, generally considered "feminine" ways; but especially his well-prepared seizing of the homosexual direction with all the relevant, successively

223

readied, individual peculiarities—testify that this patient had subjugated his real thinking, feeling, and willing until he had chosen the "proper" neurosis. As against all the miscarried attempts so far to understand the choice of neurosis, I want to point to the following results of my investigations: In the end the patient acquires that neurosis that he feels corresponds best to his fictional goal and corresponding life plan.

Behavioral Incidents

When our patient had come so far with his preparations that he practiced mutual masturbation with a schoolmate in a bathhouse, he had to set up a further arrangement to fortify this position of his homosexual development: He lent homosexuality the most magical charm, praised it as the highest form of love, and devalued the norm further by seeking to feel it as lowly, animal-like, and common. On the strength of his life plan, he actually succeeded in this. "Fair is foul, and foul is fair" sing the witches in *Macbeth*. These acts of sorcery, these falsifications, undervaluations, and overvaluations in the neurotic psychological life, as preparations and arrangements for the purpose of enhancing one's own self-esteem, are described in detail in my book *The Neurotic Constitution* (A1912a).

The homosexual, like every deviate who, after excluding the community-advancing form, enthusiastically pays homage to the shabby remainder, has by this trick escaped the complications of normal love life, has safeguarded himself from it in an intelligent manner, but in doing so, shows neither common sense nor courage nor communal feeling (A1928f).[7]

The patient took many preparatory "hardening" measures to make him suitable for another variation of the homosexual act, mutual fellatio. He wanted to delete the last trace of aversion and resistance and to give homosexuality, through this perversion, so to speak, the higher unction. In the course of this the following incident occurred, which still puzzled the

[7] This paragraph is new in the 1930 edition.

224

patient. He woke up one morning with a dim recollection of having drunk urine from a glass. Some urine was still in the glass. This happened at a time when he still resisted the efforts of a friend to seduce him for fellatio. Soon afterward he was willing.

Between these two homosexual experiences there are two others of which I want to mention one as evidence of the patient's continuing passive role. One day he met in a public lavatory a man who attracted his attention at first through his worn overcoat. The outward scrupulousness and carefully selected clothing of many homosexuals, which is also seen in our patient, points again to the fundamental feeling of weakness that attempts to compensate with superficialities, working through bribery, so to speak. Their glances met—and they understood each other. This circumstance, the mutual recognition of homosexuals, is somewhat puzzling for the uninitiated. It probably would rarely happen that a homosexual would make a mistake in judging a similarly oriented deviate. To my questioning regarding this fact, I have always received only general answers. "The glance lingers," is how the patients commonly express themselves—thereby, however, designating the fact of the recognition rather than its cause.

And yet, in view of the countless preparations of the homosexual, this sure judgment is easy to understand. The act of recognition happens apparently unconsciously but under continual probing and testing of the glances, as a question-and-answer game. The eye takes on the task of expressing the consent and readiness. And the great experience of the homosexual in his field comes into its own.

Although our patient was thus sure of his grounds, he withdrew from the pursuit of the homosexual who now followed him, rejected the plan to have anything to do with him as foolhardy, and went on his way thinking of this as a warning for increased caution. Also, as time went on he was, in his relationships, which naturally were very rare, never the soliciting party, and he approached the other only with the greatest caution.

Shortly afterward he became the victim of an extortioner, who accused him unjustly of illicit propositioning. We can well understand from his previous history that this experience greatly strengthened his passivity.

Vocation and Compulsion Neurosis

He had barely entered the academy when his father died. The patient was now obliged to go to work. Since he wanted to avoid any aggression and insecurity, we are not surprised to hear that he decided on the career of an office employee.

But even this occupation conflicted with his inclination to passivity and with his ambition. The image of his father, who had achieved more in life than he, was continuously before him. And so he arrived imperceptibly at the decision to take up law. His habitual attitude, however, required that he remain not responsible for his entire future. Consequently, he did not decide against his present occupation, but it so happened that it fatigued him, his thoughts wandered, and finally, obsessive thoughts set in, which interfered with his work—the most important purpose of any compulsion neurosis. At the same time, however, the content of these obsessions disclosed his latent, yet effective, ideas of grandeur. He built up in his fantasy the idea of a "higher power," with which he carried on dialogues and which he could call into his service through all kinds of little actions, such as jumping out of bed, not smoking, etc.

In other words, he created in himself the fiction that he was even stronger than the highest power he recognized, and this, through a secret magic trick. The triumphs and achievements that he thus could enjoy came about, to be sure, only through a curious overvaluation. Usually this game went according to the following pattern: When he was supposed to close an account, he thought that his mother would die if he did not finish by a certain time. Then he called on the "higher power," sacrificed a half-smoked cigarette to it, and was able to work on peaceably. In this way, his mother's survival was his own accomplishment! Obviously this compulsion neurosis wasted much time. But was not "time" the greatest danger for this young man who, due to his cowardice in life, felt himself committed to passivity? And is this not also the same line that has led him to homosexuality, just so that he would not have to prove himself toward women?

Thus, psychologically speaking, his homosexuality was the equivalent of his compulsion neurosis. Both were devices, magic tricks of a person who eagerly longed for triumphs but did not trust himself to achieve these by ways of normal aggression! It goes without saying that the studies that he had begun failed on account of his compulsion neurosis. But he retained the fiction of a godlike superiority over everybody, which only through an annoying "innate" or pathological trifle could not gain prevalence. There arises before our eyes the symptom complex of paranoia, on which homosexuality borders in many points. We see the driving factor clearly in the tendency to avoid the expectations and demands of society because of one's own insecurity, and to dismiss one's responsibility in case the measure of superiority that one demanded of oneself would not be reached, through the certification of illness or the emphasis on being "innately" different. (See A1914k, A1914m.)

Crisis Factors

The timing of his compulsion neurosis confirms our view further. A year earlier this patient had entered a homosexual relationship with a colleague who after a while deceived him with a girl. This was such a humiliation for him that he completely severed the relationship. Soon after this his ambition found a compensation in the fiction of the "higher power," which was at his command. But his friend pressed him vehemently.

In this condition of perplexity he came to me unshaken in his belief that his homosexuality was unalterable. One could easily see that he did not really want to turn away from homosexuality but wanted to use a potential failure of my treatment as justification for resuming his homosexual relationship. Of course, this not unusual constellation creates new and increased difficulties for treatment.

Soon it became evident that he wanted to forgive his friend. But he also met a situation that was most highly suitable to make him conciliatory. For some time a distant relative had been living in his house who became a threat to his homosexuality. The very fact that she was a relative, and as such closer to him—nothing whatever threatening about her, nothing but sympathetic traits which soon established a good relationship—forced him to move farther away from her. To make this relationship also correspond to his life plan—that is, to make it fail—he turned again to the trusted means of "hardening measures."

He often "tested" himself in resisting the charms of the girl, and succeeded each time in reassuring himself of this. To us, these proofs mean nothing, for after all, he was a bribed judge. We find striking proof in the following: Whenever a new suitor for the girl appeared, our patient would always have a feeling that he described as something like jealousy, and found no peace until, through sharp criticism and all kinds of little intrigues, he had put the suitor out of the running. But when the girl remained without a suitor for any length of time, then he would have thoughts of how one could get her married as quickly as possible, and would often play Cupid—only to destroy again whatever relationship might ensue. We see his old game, which he also played in his vocation, in order not to move from the spot, because every advance would bring him closer to a decision. It had become the task of his life not to submit to any test because he had lost belief in himself.

When his relative was once more without a suitor for some time and came closer to him, he took for safety's sake a big step, confessing to her that he was homosexual. This disclosure did not have the desired effect on the girl. Indeed, she tried to come still closer to him in order to save him—a frequent fantasy among girls. Only then did he begin to feel the infidelity of his friend more keenly, and tried again, according to his habit, to influence him by being coquettish.

With this patient I was able to check my assertions regarding the nature of homosexuality over quite a period of time. He always approached his friend with homosexual feelings when he felt attracted to the girl in his vicinity. His means to regain his friend were the same as before, all fashioned from the familiar models of female coquettishness.

Treatment and Outcome

The significance of Individual-Psychological treatment also became quite apparent: Whenever he approached his friend, the patient became conscious not only of the reason for his fear of women and lack of confidence in his masculine role, but he also saw in his friend clearly what caused his own homosexuality: lust for triumph, with sexual means in the direction of less apparent resistance, in the direction of men. This antidote was sufficient at the time to limit the patient to sterile coquettishness. There was no further homosexual activity.

At this time and later, the patient made several tests, as other neurotics also always do. The tests are supposed to convince oneself and others, usually also the physician, of the "good intentions" of the patient. Their bad endings must be expected from the start. They are nothing but a last attempt, now that the patient has become more convinced of his recovery, to demonstrate once more the incurability of his affliction. These tests are so designed that even a well person would fail them. Our patient demonstrated with an unattractive, unmannerly prostitute. On this occasion he succeeded in transforming his neurosis into one of impotence, later into masochism. Both forms meant "No!"—the same fear of women, the impotence expressing the arrangement of distance, the masochism being a memento that became an actual scene. The patient easily understood when I pointed out the bias of his "tests," because he had himself been scared. He understood immediately that he could not be the judge, the

229

plaintiff, and the accused all in one person, and that his "evidence" was all froth.

The same line, a very modest "go-ahead!" could naturally be observed in his studies. His obsessions—the time-wasting, purposefully inhibiting occupation with the "higher being," which had up to now functioned as a brake—disappeared under the pressure of the treatment. They had become unsuitable as a means to gain distance from social life because they no longer excluded his responsibility. He began to attend lectures and studied for the examination. But then he noticed in this "test" a dreadful, "irresistible" sleepiness during the lectures, which prevented any further progress. This became much less when we noted that the sleepiness was well prepared by a cleverly arranged sleeplessness at night (see A1914p). Yet his progress here, as in his love problem, remained very limited; his attitude remained hesitating.

After these interpretations I lost sight of the patient for quite some time. I did not see him again until the beginning of the war, in the summer of 1914. My first interest then was his relationship to the war. I ventured the following construction: His ambition would drive him forward; his lack of self-confidence in masculine activities would act as a brake; my treatment and his behavior since then may have reduced his cowardliness. He too immediately spoke of the war. He had at once registered as a volunteer. But the closer the date of his call approached, the greater his fear became, and the desire to get out of it. From this attitude, I could easily guess the present phase of his sexual development. It turned out that he had come closer to women but that the affair usually ended in sexual impotence, at times also in lack of satisfaction, signs that he was still not able to give himself completely. His war experience is noteworthy in that it briefly shows the line of the manic-depressive, which I have pointed out—an impulsive "Forward!" which is followed by a "Back!" In both phases a "No!" is rather obvious.[8]

[8] A similar coherence of deviation with cyclothymia was found by Dr. Max Marcuse (1912) in a case of homosexuality. [Author's note.]

230

COMPULSIVE DESPOTISM (CASE 4)[9]

This report is based on "Specialist Opinion, rendered jointly with Major Sigmund Scharf, M.D., chief, Neurological Unit, Imperial & Royal Garrison Hospital XV (1917), Colonel L. Dabrowski, M.D., commanding officer, concerning Mr. I., age fifty-nine years, farmer, referred to Unit VI for psychiatric examination."[10, 11]

The patient tells that his parents died early, that he grew up in the house of his brother-in-law, and that he, the patient, was later sent to a boarding school. Of ten sisters and brothers, seven died. He was himself weakly and did not do as well in school as his older brother. The patient had no childhood diseases, but for the past twenty years suffered frequently from headaches and insomnia. He left high school (*Gymnasium*) without graduating, and left the military service, which he had chosen, after one year.

At the age of thirty-two he married without being in love, and after five years his wife gave birth to a daughter who, he claimed, was mentally retarded. His marriage turned out badly, since his wife resisted his domineering demands; he beat her at times. Fifteen and ten years ago he contracted gonorrhea from prostitutes. Both times it healed under medical treatment within the normal time span. He never had syphilis, and his drinking habits were moderate.

[9] Translated from A1917b as reprinted in 1930d, pp. 41–45.

[10] I wish to express my gratitude to Dr. Scharf for pointing out that cases such as the present uniformly show traits of debility. [Author's note.]

[11] In explanation of this preamble, Adler was during World War I, in 1916, drafted into the Austrian Army Medical Corps, where he was most of the time assigned to the Neuropsychiatric Unit of Garrison Hospital No. 15 in Cracow (Ellenberger, 1970, p. 587). Cracow, in Galicia, was then part of Austria, close to the Russian border, and is now in Poland.

Domination over Social Inferiors

The patient attributes his abnormal sexual development to seduction to mutual masturbation at the age of thirteen by the manservant at the boarding school. The patient continued this form of sexual activity until very recently, engaged in normal sexual intercourse only occasionally, and even during his marriage only for a short while and seldom. Before marriage he had occasional intercourse with girls, but always only with poor peasant girls or prostitutes. He had never had a love affair nor much inclination for marriage. He finally married on the urging of his relatives.

In his homosexual relations the patient was said to have always been the aggressive partner. His victims were always subservient persons. He had always taken advantage of the surprise and submissiveness of the partners he had chosen.

One of his last victims denounced him after an unsuccessful attempt at extortion. The patient was convicted, but belatedly came to our unit for mental examination.

His physical condition was found to be completely normal. He is slender, flexible, and shows no feminine traits. Asked what bothered him most in his case, he answered: the public disgrace about his misdemeanor and the conviction.

His social behavior can be seen from the following: He never related like a lover to the subservient persons whom he selected for his victims. Rather he demanded their sexual submission, as he otherwise also requested strict obedience. His court files show that he acted in a clearly tyrannical manner against his servants and employees, resorting without hesitation to punishment, illegal detention, immediate dismissal, and lawsuits.

His general behavior thus gives the impression of a despot toward his servants as well as his wife, the same despotic line as in the course of his homosexual attacks.

232

Failure in Work and in Love

This self-consistency of the patient's life conduct, however, disappears when we consider his vocational history and his love relationships to women. Then we find largely failure. His homosexual relationships were only with servants, never with even approximately social equals. Our view that his despotic character demanded the complete submission of others is supported by the finding that also in approaching the other sex he apparently thought only of socially inferior girls or prostitutes. Apparently he sensed womankind as something strange, inaccessible, and unapproachable, and could come closer only when he was encouraged by the privilege of being undoubtedly superior. The defeat by his wife, as well as the subsequent two gonorrhea infections, must have given him, in his condition, the instinctive incentive to give up heterosexual attempts completely for the past ten years, and to limit himself to such homosexual relationships as assured him in his feeling of dominance.

Our attempt to arrive at an understanding of the convict's firmly rooted sexual misconduct receives at this point a remarkable confirmation. Witnesses as well as the examinee frequently pointed out that, quite aside from his love life, he was not a man of persistence and easily gave up when difficulties arose. His farming enterprises were generally described as senseless and planless and never got beyond modest beginnings. Indeed, the examinee tended consistently soon to break off any enterprise he had begun. He left high school without graduating, left military service after one year, dissolved his marriage, and broke off his farming enterprises again and again. Also, his homosexual relationships lack persistence and present the picture of a deviating Don Juan.

We find then a vacillating, easily discouraged person who shrinks back from difficulties and prefers to develop overheated energy and, as we have seen, despotic power, but only where he is not threatened by contradiction or defeat. This

233

picture is directly augmented by his homosexual orientation toward servants, which resulted from his previous history and his inner sexual need. In his sex life also he quickly breaks off his efforts for the female, is thereby driven from the norm, leaves even the female servants and prostitutes on whom he looks down and whom he had found disastrous, and separates from his wife, whom he had tried in vain to humiliate. Even from these alleviated sexual goals, feelings of insurmountable difficulties call him away time after time, toward the cheap sexual triumphs over masculine servants with whom he seeks satisfaction and unshakable significance, simultaneously for his sexual drive and for his craving to dominate.

However, to banish for all time his uneasiness regarding his homosexual activity and to secure it, to appear not responsible for it before himself and others should the conscience of the community (*Gewissen der Gemeinschaft*) awake in him and against him, he equips his deviation with the halo of unalterability and of a mysterious fate, and connects and poisons his sexual impulse with his most outstanding character traits: craving to dominate and cowardice. Through a feeling of inferiority stemming from his childhood, he deviates from the line of masculine aggression. In his craving to dominate, he turns his fear of women into a revolt. To appear victorious in life, he becomes a despot and a homosexual.

Discussion and Conclusion

This psychological development, which can be similarly traced in the life of all homosexuals, takes place not in the sphere of critical thinking and deliberation, but in the field of drivelike volition (*triebhaften Wollens*). It thereby receives a compulsive character because it is uncontrollable, and can no longer be corrected or ended by the deviate through the use of logical arguments. A homosexual perspective develops and the argumentation takes place in a manner favorable to the homosexual direction because the deviation proves itself a desired outcome and a safeguard against the "difficulties" and injuries of the normal love life. Besides, such difficult psychological considerations are practically never accomplished by the neurotic on his own—and the deviate is a neurotic, also, otherwise. Rather, the general and often scientifically disguised myth of the innateness of the deviating tendencies and their unalterability come to the help of the deviate. The change of a deviate into a person with normal feelings can be attained only in rather prolonged psychotherapy, which would give him the suitable means for a cure, and in no other way.

We arrive at the conclusion that the examinee suffered from homosexuality, which has been clearly developed since puberty. It has been necessarily deepened and fixated by his aberrant character, which developed "in the stream of life." His homosexual line, like his entire nature, bears the clear traits of fear of difficulties and despotic lust to dominate his sphere of influence. Like a delusion, it cannot be corrected because the psychological means for a cure are not accessible to the patient. It is characterized from the medical viewpoint as a compulsion neurosis that suspends personal responsibility.

MASCULINE PROTEST (CASE 5)[12, 13]

The patient is a young woman of thirty years from a lower middle-class, very religious background. Her distance from the problem of marriage stands out and must, somehow, lead to the life style (*Lebensstil*) of the patient.[14]

[12] After a talk given at the International Society of Individual Psychology, Vienna Branch, 1926. [Author's note.]

[13] Translation of A1930d, pp. 45–52.

[14] Note that in this case, presented originally in 1926, the term "life style" appears for the first time in this volume, which consists predominantly of older material. Ansbacher (1967) concluded from other sources that Adler introduced the term "life style" in 1926.

Inferiority Feelings and Obsessive Striving

The patient has several siblings, including a slightly older sister who, through charm and spirit, overshadows all the others. This recollection and account, given right at the beginning of the treatment, reveal an important cause for a feeling of inferiority, which is obviously at the bottom of her distance from marriage. Despite her desire, she seems to evade marriage because she is afraid of the long-familiar being left behind for another girl, originally her older sister.

From everyday observation, we may presume that this inferiority feeling was reinforced by her having been for about two years the youngest in the family, exposed to a natural pampering situation from which she was later torn away. This overthrow hits most children more or less severely. Through such a new, unwelcome situation, at the very birth of the personality, the inferiority feeling of incredibly many children becomes aggravated. It urges their life style strongly toward the useful side, most often, however, toward the useless side of childhood behavior problems, or neurosis. This change, which is understandable from the nature of the situation, is very clearly expressed among first-borns. Our patient was closer to being the darling of the family than the other siblings and was therefore particularly affected by their preponderance.

Since early in life, she tended to evade problems. Shyness, reticence, a tendency toward isolation, and depreciation of others together with original respect disclose her inferiority feeling. Since fear of defeat kept her from accomplishing anything, she soon was considered incapable and awkward. She had no close girl friends and avoided company as best she could. Already before puberty she suffered from moral and religious obsessions. She continuously blamed herself for sins and errors, for which she tried to do penance through vows and prayers, and which she tried to change. She believed the vows were forced on her by the fear that otherwise somebody from her surroundings would go to hell.

By separating these obsessions and compulsions from their content, as prescribed by the Individual-Psychological method, we retain a purely formal movement that clearly enough leads from below to above without exactly being of general usefulness and without making the least change in the attitude of man to fellow man. On the way of least resistance, free from any competition, especially from the favored sister, the patient appears to have succeeded in assigning to herself the task of a person completely free from fault or sin, however only for the future, in that she is severely after her smallest, often most ridiculous trespasses. She considers herself the more righteous person who works on her purification more than the others.

The patient does not know that she thereby assigns to herself an exalted position. But she takes this position. It does not enter her mind that she is now superior to her sister, but she is on the way to compensate for her inferior feeling. From the unbearable situation of being inferior to her sister, she has developed an upward striving that, for the time being, can serve her as a consoling substitute for the feeling of her worthlessness, and promises victory for the future. For this substitute she gladly pays all costs, as she is gaining in her own eyes and gradually also in those of the others the certification of a sickness by which she is more easily excused from useful performances, or can at least request easier conditions for herself. She cannot mourn, complain, and suffer enough, since the more she suffers, the more clearly her claim to holiness emerges.

As if in confirmation of this, the second part of her obsessions shows the same formal upward tendency: Whether somebody goes to hell or not is within her power. A small vow from her lips, and he is redeemed. Here one can almost touch the godlikeness that Individual Psychology has asserted. Also, the restlessness and fear that overcame her when she did not use her might, now appear in the proper light. These, like the feeling of being compelled to make a vow, are means to remain in power, to maintain a self-consistent life style that redeems her from her inferiority feeling. The creative power of this girl, who was too cowardly for useful solutions, is sufficient only for this fictional arrangement, the equivalent of a life lie.

Masculine Protest and Homosexual Inclination

At the age of twenty-four she met a new blow. An equally tender-footed young man courted her. But upon the first objection of his sister, he desisted from any further courting before he and the patient had warmed up to each other.

Again she had reaped defeat, on a main line of her life where she could perhaps have attained the feeling of parity with her sister. Her discouragement had progressed farther. In similar cases, we could predict that now a further retreat from the big problem of life, the problem of love, would occur. And indeed, until our treatment, she had lost all interest in men.

But already the approach to the above-mentioned young man could have disclosed the weak position of the girl. She herself described him as a puppet (*Hampelmann*). It is virtually the tragic fate of such discouraged human beings that they, in turn, very easily meet discouraged partners and thus increase their own difficulties, as altogether in this sphere of discouragement the difficulties pile up. The fragility of such relationships becomes quite evident in our case.

Here, I hear again our esteemed critics asking: But how about the "masculine protest"? How about the feeling of feminine inferiority? There are still some writers who, in order quickly to dispose of Individual Psychology, see in the "masculine protest" the beginning and end of our views. They do not understand that the "masculine protest" represents only one, although an important, concretization of the formal striving for superiority, not much different from a boy attempting to realize this striving by choosing to become a coachman, a streetcar conductor, or a general.

Maybe the understanding of these coherences is not quite

simple. Perhaps we come closer to clarification by asking a simple question. Why has this girl developed outside the feminine norm? Because she was not as beautiful as her sister. From this we can conclude that she had the notion that a girl had to be beautiful to play her role. This overvaluation of feminine beauty, a thoroughly masculine device that leads to a damaging, permanent dependency of women on the judgment of men, is a quite common foolishness that rules men as well as women and limits a woman's possibilities in life enormously. Especially among the discouraged, and this includes all nervous women, one always comes across this deeply rooted view. The male privilege in our culture manages to falsify an important principle of natural selection, namely beauty as a guarantee for the health of future generations, into a power factor in favor of the man. Our patient had fallen into this dependency. She found herself automatically urged to evade the feminine role, not to seek in it the concretization of her striving, but to seek it in a fictive power position in which she only pretended to do something, or to participate in the game only conditionally, as when the masculine partner was a puppet, or perhaps not a man at all. It goes without saying that in her youth she often thought how much better it would be to be a man.

Her feminine inferiority feeling thus seems to be beyond a doubt. But where is the masculine protest? Well, her entire neurotic life style is a revolt against her feminine role, is a striving toward masculine powerfulness, toward the development of her life in the direction of the father's, not the mother's, position. But it seems that clearer proofs are necessary. Here they are: One day she discovered unambiguous, active homosexual inclinations.

The psychoanalytic press regularly reproaches us for having forgotten love or eroticism. It is only that we are not trained, nor obligated, to regard all psychological phenomena from this viewpoint. We had more important things to do. We had to show that the sexuality of a person in childhood, as well as later, always takes on the form that belongs to the life style of the individual within a definite situation.

Thus we could have guessed how this girl, after her defeat

on the way toward normal love, had to turn her sexuality, which of course was present, around in accordance with her masculine protest and her evasion of the norm by the exclusion of men. "Driven into flight, he believes he is chasing."

Power Increase Through Symptomatic Suffering

One of her many physicians, caught in sexual-psychological fallacies, thought he could bring about her cure through a sexual advance. The result was a state of confusion, which lasted for weeks and only slowly receded. Perhaps it was only a misunderstanding on the part of the girl. But even this would be sufficient indication to prevent by all means the "transference"—should our discussion not have made it sufficiently clear that the patient was not suited for love relationships, and should anyone still doubt that the inferiority feeling must first be diminished before such a person can wake up to life. Since she had become the victim of the general mistake of men and women, that it is the sole task of a woman to cast a spell over a man, and she did not believe herself capable of this noteworthy achievement, any pressure in the direction of sexuality could only evoke panic. A large number of psychoses and many neuroses originate in this mood of panic, which as a rule is not understood by the psychiatrist. In this state of perplexity all real values are extremely undervalued.

To return to the content of this girl's obsessions, they represent a gross abuse of religious forms, and concretize very strikingly the striving for power, the formally compensating movement, because they presume such powerfulness as could only be ascribed to a god: It is now up to her whether someone is condemned to hell or is to be redeemed, and thus she decides on the fate of men.

A further obsession that tormented her was that she could poison someone through her words or glances, especially while eating. Incidentally, the human psyche seems to be extensively accessible to this foolish idea, because such power

240

has been ascribed to people with the evil eye and to witches. A remnant of this superstition apparently survives in the belief in clairvoyance and the supernatural. On closer look, one finds the root of all this foolishness in the still generally held myth that there are some special innate abilities that are simply never accessible to other people.

Many neurologists and psychologists will object to what appears strange and incredible also to the patients: If, in the case of such symptoms such powerfulness is reached, why is the patient thereby so painfully affected and suffers? Let us assume the patient would enjoy the feeling of his power, as we could notice in women poison-murderers, without any real extension of power having occurred. Then we would be dealing perhaps with a case of depression or schizophrenia—that is, the patient would have separated himself so far from the ties of communal feeling that he would have lost also the power of logic—reason—which ties us all.

But this is not so in the case of a compulsion neurosis; the patient himself recognizes his thoughts as foolish. But foolish as they may be from the viewpoint or the goal of a fellow man, they are completely suited as a means for the neurotic to disengage himself from those tasks that he is afraid to fulfill. Furthermore, he finds himself completely justified in the position he has taken on the useless side of life. He would lose this justification if he were to be happy in his neurotic actions. Therefore, he suffers.

Excessive suffering becomes further necessary because the patient thereby shakes not only the air but also his immediate surroundings and makes them subservient to him. Could he do this if he were happy?

Third, his suffering from these obsessions is closely associated with indications of his magic ability, his magnanimity, his holiness. The more he suffers, the clearer his powerfulness becomes to him. He cannot suffer enough, because his suffering is the only part in the entire compulsion system that attempts to co-ordinate itself to reality, that has reality value. From his suffering, he obtains the certainty of his greatness. But he looks at his suffering just as all other observers of compulsion neurosis have done up to now, and

241

does not permit his power to become apparent. We must teach (*lehren*) him to pay attention to the fictional increase in power on account of which he, in his faint-heartedness toward useful tasks, contrived his neurosis.

Treatment

The task of Individual Psychology is to replace the neurotic frame of reference (*Bezugssystem*) with one of fellowship, and this is tantamount to encouragement. In this way it was possible to restore the social, occupational, and loving abilities of this girl. One may well regret the time that passed uselessly. But thanks to the present state of our knowledge, the neurosis has led the patient to a point where she has a better perspective on life and a better understanding of the necessity of acting in the sense of general usefulness. She has gone through the purgatory of Individual Psychology, and the word of the Bible applies to her: In heaven, there is more joy over one repentant sinner than over ninety-nine righteous persons.

DISAPPOINTMENT IN WOMEN (CASE 6)[15]

A case of agoraphobia, a man of fifty-three years of age could not breathe properly when he was in company with others. He lived with his sister, and had a son whose characteristics were very much like his own. When I investigated the cause of this man's unusual concentration of interest upon himself, I found that he had been orphaned at the age of ten, and there were two older brothers in the family. The patient had his first attack when the brothers quarreled. This indicates the tendency to meet a difficult situation with a breakdown. The man was the youngest of eight siblings and was raised by his grandfather. A grandparent is invariably a spoil-

[15] This appeared originally in A1929c, pp. 92–95, and was modified after A1930d, pp. 52–55.

ing foster parent. The patient's father and mother had been happily married; the father was superior and the mother rather cold, so that the boy became more devoted to his father.

Mother and Wife

A child's first friendship is always with his mother if she is present, so that if the child inclines more toward the father we may assume that the mother does not give the child sufficient attention. She is probably unloving, otherwise occupied, or more loving to a younger child. In such circumstances the child turns to the father if possible, and in this case, the resistance to the mother was very marked.

People often cannot correctly remember their earliest situations; but our experience enables us to reconstruct their circumstances from relatively slight indications. One man said he could remember only three incidents from his early childhood that had deeply impressed his memory. The first occurred at the age of three, when his brother died. He was with his grandfather on the day of the funeral when his mother returned from the cemetery, sorrowful and sobbing; and when the grandfather kissed her, whispering some words of kindness and consolation, the boy saw that his mother smiled a little. He was very much upset by this, and for long afterward resented his mother's smile on the day that her child was buried. The second memory that he had preserved was of a friendly reproof from his uncle, who had asked him, "Why are you always so rough toward your mother?" A third remembrance from the same period of his life related to a quarrel between his parents, after which he turned to his father, saying, "You were brave, Daddy, like a soldier!" He was very attached to his father, and pampered by him; and he always admired his father more than his mother, although he realized that his mother's character was of a better kind.

All these memories, from his third or fourth year, showed the fighting attitude toward his mother. The first and the third

243

memories were clearly ruled by his goal, which was to criticize his mother and to justify himself in turning toward the father. His reason for turning away from the mother is easy to see. He had been too much spoiled by her to be able to put up with the younger brother's appearance upon the scene—that same younger brother who figures in an apparently so innocent manner in the first recollection.

[To return to our patient], this patient had married at the age of twenty-four. The marriage was a disappointment because of his wife's demands upon him. A marriage between two pampered children is always unhappy, because both remain in an expectant attitude and neither begins to give. The patient went through varied experiences and tried different occupations without success. His wife was not sympathetic, and complained that she would rather be the mistress of a rich man than the wife of a poor one. The marriage ended in a divorce. Although the man was in fact not poor, he was very stingy toward his wife, and she divorced him by way of revenge.

Homosexual Tendencies and Agoraphobia

After the divorce he became a woman hater and developed homosexual tendencies. He had no actual relationships with men, but a desire to embrace men. This homosexual trend was, as usual, a kind of cowardliness. He had been twice defeated and disappointed by women—first by his mother and afterward by his wife—and was now trying to divert his sexuality toward men so as to evade women and further possibilities of humiliation. To strengthen in oneself such a tendency, one can easily falsify the past by recollecting and magnifying the importance of certain common experiences, which are then taken as evidence of inborn homosexual tendencies. Thus our patient remembered that he had been in love with a schoolmaster and had been seduced by a boyhood friend into mutual masturbation.

The decisive factor in this man's behavior was that he was

a spoiled child who wanted everything for nothing. His agoraphobia resulted from the fear of meeting women on the one hand, and on the other hand it was also dangerous to meet men because of a possible erotic inclination toward them. In this tension of feelings about going out of doors or not he developed stomach and respiratory troubles. Many nervous people begin to swallow air when they get into a state of tension, which causes flatulence, stomach trouble, anxiety, and palpitation, besides affecting the breathing.

When I made him realize that this was his condition, he asked the usual question: "What shall I do not to swallow air?" Often I reply: "I can tell you how to mount a horse, but I can't tell you how *not* to mount a horse." Or I often advise: "If you want to go out and feel in a conflict about it, swallow some air quickly." This man, like some other patients, swallowed air even in his sleep, but after my advice he began to control himself, and he discontinued the habit. Air-swallowing during sleep and vomiting upon waking occur in patients who suffer from stomach trouble and anxiety when they are bothered by a difficulty that they must meet the following day.

Outcome

The patient began to improve once he came to understand that, as a pampered child, he expected continually to take without giving. He now realized that he had first stopped his normal sexual life, looking for something easier, and afterward adopted a fictitious homosexuality in which he also stopped short of danger. The whole process was merely a well-prepared way of coming to a standstill. The last obstacle to a complete standstill was removed by his fear of mixing with strangers who paid no attention to him, such as the people in the street. To exclude all situations in which one is not the center of attention is the deeper motive of agoraphobia.

245

WANTING TO BE A GIRL (CASE 7)[16]

A fourteen-year-old boy with a strong expectant attitude toward life had great difficulties in learning how to swim, as he was altogether disinclined to learn, especially mathematics. With this type of children, mathematics is often the main difficulty, probably because it requires a particularly independent ability to devote oneself to work.

He admitted to his mother, who was his best friend, that for a while he had had sexual excitation when he saw the muscles of men in a swimming pool or elsewhere. His earliest recollection was to have taken a walk with his mother, when people often commented when they saw his light curly hair: "What a pretty girl!" Early memories often give us illuminating hints of the way in which the sexual attitude was constructed.

When asked if he would like to be a girl, he emphatically denied it. In his consciousness, it was better to be a man than a woman. But since in reality he wanted to attain everything as easily as possible, he instinctively evaded the necessary preparation for the masculine role, and his goal consisted of wanting to be courted and receive tokens of attention, as if he were a girl. This seemed possible since he was pretty to look at, whereas success in any other ways seemed difficult and questionable. Thus he fled into laziness and inability. Such a life style—this we must always keep in mind—gives the patient occasionally the feeling of power and domination. Such a style is connected with violent aversion to any situation that one cannot dominate, so that we are not at all surprised to learn that the boy has an excessive fear of thunderstorms. A thunderstorm, after all, is the most extreme example of something one can neither arrange nor control.

Having the high-flying ambition of a second and youngest

[16] This appeared originally in A1929c, pp. 141–42; it was modified after A1930d, pp. 55–56.

child, this boy was, through his obvious defeats, rendered unable to have the self-confidence required for a corresponding success as a man: hence the striving to form a homosexual goal and to dominate passively by being loved and adored.

ESSAY:
ADLER'S SEX THEORIES

by Heinz L. Ansbacher

I. BASIC ASSUMPTIONS AND TERMS

This essay, a commentary on the preceding writings of Alfred Adler on women, love, and sexuality, is intended to fill the gap of well over fifty years between their composition and the present, and to facilitate their understanding and evaluation. As stated in the Preface, this attempt provides some historical and biographical background, refers to Adler's subsequent works, and examines his contributions in light of present developments. The essay follows the general order of the preceding presentation of Adler's writings.

To establish an appropriate frame of reference, it seems necessary to give a brief account of some of Adler's basic assumptions and corresponding terms. This is all the more needed since these are often different from those of other personality theorists. Other theorists often leave their basic assumptions implicit, while Adler recognized the importance of stating them explicitly. In fact, the first selection in this book begins with an assumptive statement on human dynamics: "The two factors that dominate all psychological processes are social interest and striving for significance. . . . for power, and for superiority." They will determine the manner in which the individual meets "the three main tasks of life—love, occupation, society."

The present section includes an expansion of this brief statement into (1) five basic Adlerian assumptions and (2) the corresponding terms he devised for them. The former remained quite constant throughout the years, while some of the latter were developed to higher levels of theoretical sophistication.

Unity of the Organism: Life Style

1. For Adler the unity of the individual is the most important basic assumption, from which all the others are derived. It is the foundation of his holistic social theory of personality, psychopathology, and psychotherapy, which he named Individual Psychology. "Individual" is to be understood not only as indivisible, but also as the actual irreducible unit in the higher biological forms (see Ansbacher, 1974b). The individual is an active, living organism. Life is active movement.

2. The term "life style" was chosen by Adler eventually, to express the totality of the human individual's functioning. "The . . . mind remains pressed into the path of the . . . style of life, as does everything that has a name in the various schools of psychology, such as instincts, impulses, feeling, thinking, acting, attitude to pleasure and displeasure, and finally self-love and social interest. The style of life commands all forms of expression; the whole commands the parts" (A1956b, pp. 174–75). This of course also includes the sex drive and all behaviors connected with it.

The term "life style" was introduced by Adler around 1926 (see Ansbacher, 1967). But the concept was there from the start, expressed variously as "guiding image," "life form," "life line," "life plan," "line of movement," "personality," "psyche," "total person," "whole individual," "whole personality"—all to be found in the present volume. For these the reader may well substitute "life style." As we noted, "life style" is used relatively infrequently in this volume because most of the material was written before 1926.

Unitary Dynamics: Striving for a Plus Situation

1. A concept of man as a unitary organism requires a unitary dynamic principle. Adler derived the corresponding assumption from life in general. All forms of life are characterized by a movement in the direction of growth and expansion. Man, with his capacity to anticipate the future and his necessity to make choices, creates ideals and goals toward which he wants to develop and that provide him with criteria for making choices. Man is decisively directed not by objective causes, but by subjective goals and ideals. "The most important question . . . is not Whence? but Whither?" (A1956b, p. 91).

2. It is difficult to name this unitary dynamic principle. In his first attempt Adler termed it "wanting to be a man," in the sense of the sexist stereotype of the male role in the culture of his day: privileged, strong, powerful. This would be the ultimate goal of both sexes. In more pronounced form and especially in the neurotic it would be the "masculine protest," a term found frequently in the early writings included in this volume.

This was soon replaced in part by the "will to power," in the sense of being powerful, not necessarily of lording over others (see Ansbacher, 1972). Later terms were: "striving from a feeling of inferiority to superiority," "perfection," "completion," "a goal of success as subjectively perceived, from a felt minus to a felt plus situation," or simply "overcoming difficulties." "In comparison with unattainable ideal perfection, the individual is continuously filled by an inferiority feeling and motivated by it" (A1956b, p. 117).

Relative Self-determination: Creative Power

1. While Adler fully recognized the influence of heredity, including the sex drive and other drives, as well as the impor-

tance of general environmental and cultural influences, he did not hold that these determine behavior directly. Instead, once man has been brought into existence, he develops the capability of influencing and creating events, as witnessed by the cultural products all around us, beginning with language. To the extent that man is not fully determined by heredity nor by environment, Adler assumed relative self-determination. He compared man to an artist in creating his style of life from the available material and circumstances.

2. This assumed "third force," in addition to heredity and environment, which is ultimately the determining factor, was named by Adler the "creative power" (*schöpferische Kraft*) or simply the "creativity" of the individual. This is not something with which only a few "gifted" persons are endowed, but is common to all, with the exception of the truly feeble-minded. In recent years this has in the general psychological literature been frequently referred to as the "creative self," a term less dynamic and more conducive to elementaristic, reified thinking than Adler's term (see Ansbacher, 1971b, 1971c).

Social Context: Social Interest

1. The human being is an indivisible whole composed of many co-ordinated, interacting parts, a system. But he is also a part of larger wholes or systems—his family, the community, all of humanity, our planet, the cosmos. He has by nature the aptitude to live in harmony with the systems network into which he is born. If we find him frequently in conflict with the world, this is not due to human nature as such, but due to mistakes resulting from inadequate training and misunderstanding of his place in the world.

2. Adler assumed a natural aptitude for living in harmony with the conditions into which we are born as part of a social system. He called this in the end "the aptitude or potentiality for social feeling or social interest" (*Gemeinschaftsgefühl*). Previously he had understood this as an innate behavior or

dynamic force on an equal level with and opposed to the striving for superiority and power. In Chapter 4, Adler writes: "The beginning of love impulses goes back to . . . childhood . . . when the broad stream of social feeling still took the form of attachment and affection." A year later, in our initial quotation, dated 1927, we still find, "two guiding lines . . . : social interest and striving for significance." But this would be dynamic dualism, quite incompatible with a holistic theory. Dynamic unity was assured when Adler (A1929c) made the correction: "Social feeling is *not inborn;* but it is an innate potentiality that *has to be consciously developed"* (p. 31, italics added). It is then like any aptitude, such as that for reading, cooking, skiing, etc., only more important, leaving the upward striving as the sole innate dynamic force shared with all of life.

Once developed, however, social interest, again like any other aptitude, is likely to acquire secondary motivational attributes. Human beings like to do what they are capable of doing well. Such interests become part of one's self-concept and goal orientation, part of one's striving.

Social interest differs from conformity and superego in that it implies spontaneous "socially affirmative action" (A1929c, p. 35), leaving room for social innovation, even through rebellion.

Life as Problem-solving: Three Life Tasks

1. If one assumes man to be essentially a part of larger systems, then his difficulties are seen not so much in how he gets along with himself, his drives, his inner nature, but on how he functions within his systems. His problems are always seen as problems of social relations (as Harry S. Sullivan later also saw them). And even the solution of apparently personal problems is assumed to be facilitated by seeking the solution not within the person, but from the setting of the problem within the larger order of things, and by seeing it in its proper proportion.

252

2. The term in which Adler encompassed these assumptions is the "three life tasks," or "life problems," by which he meant the social problem, the problem of occupation, and the problem of sex and marriage, the last being of course the problem with which the present volume is primarily concerned. Since all three problems are in the end social problems, their satisfactory solution requires a sufficiently developed social interest. Mental health is related to the satisfactory solution of the three life problems, or better, problem complexes.

Mental Health: Social Usefulness

From the preceding follows Adler's conception of mental health and mental disorder. In mental health we find self-confidence and a highly developed social interest, which assures identification and empathy with the surroundings, especially the social, and facilitates a successful solution of the life tasks. It is the life style of the fellow human being whose goal of achievement represents a general socially useful contribution.

Mental disorder is characterized by strong inferiority feelings, which may be hidden behind a façade of superiority, together with underdeveloped social interest. This leads to difficulty in solving the life tasks. Adler generically characterizes all forms of mental disorder as "failures in life." They share the life style of a pampered child whose goal is one of self-centered expectation rather than self-transcending contribution, and represent a socially useless striving.

As Adler conceived of mental health as social usefulness, so he wanted his psychology to be of greatest use to the largest number—a psychology of and for all. Adler (A1925g) expressed his creed in the words: "Individual Psychology aims at serving the community rather than forging new arms for a caste of scholars. As it intends to reinforce the contact among fellow men, it must become common property. As it intends to eradicate neurosis and raise the self-esteem of the

253

individual and society, it must hand over all its knowledge and skills to the community. . . . It will never do to permit less knowledge to the teacher, the parents, the patient, than to the physician or the philosopher" (pp. 222–23).

Antithesis to Freud

These five assumptions all refer to traditional basic issues in psychology that invite possible opposite assumptions (see Michael Wertheimer, 1972). In fact, the opposite assumption on each of these issues was made by Freud. This difference is the result of Adler's understanding of psychology as an organismic, socially oriented discipline, whereas Freud's ideal was a physicalistic discipline (see Ansbacher, 1974a). In contrast to Adler's assumptions, Freud asserted: (1) The human organism is divided into different regions, and conscious and unconscious parts. (2) There are two groups of opposing instincts, the life and the death instincts. (3) Man is subject to forces beyond his control; he is not master in his own house. (4) Social living is possible only through repression. (5) The solution of social life tasks is but a devious way of primitive primary gratification.

In sum, Adler's assumptions are optimistic regarding human nature and the possibility of psychotherapy, Freud's assumptions are pessimistic.

II. PSYCHOLOGIST OF WOMEN'S EQUALITY

Chapter 1, "The Myth of Women's Inferiority," is a simple, straightforward account of Adler's position on the "woman question." It is as much a sociological and educational as a psychological statement, and refers more to life situations and educational action than to individual cases. Our comments will refer largely to Adler's life circle and action circle, and can be considered a small biographical study.

Interest in Socialism

Theoretically. In his student days and probably earlier, Adler became interested in the emerging socialist movement. Furtmüller (1964), Adler's early intimate friend and co-worker, described the socialist student group and Adler's relationship to it. "They studied the books of Karl Marx. . . . There was an intense intellectual life among the members of this circle, and an enthusiasm to prepare the world for a better future. . . . Adler stood rather aloof in his student days, and only personal friendship connected him with members of the socialist group. As a young doctor [he obtained his M.D. degree in 1895] he joined the group, and appeared in their debating meetings . . . [as] a listener, not a speaker and debater. Nor did all sides of the Marxist theories . . . stir him with equal interest. I think that the economic theories of Marx never got much of Adler's attention" (pp. 332–33).

But, Furtmüller continues, "It was quite a different thing with the sociological conception on which Marxism is based. This had a decisive influence on the whole development of Adler's thinking" (p. 333). Manès Sperber (1974) agrees, predicting: "It will become increasingly apparent how much Adler's Individual Psychology is dialectical in spirit and in form, as well as in content." Two of Marx's "challenging formulations that are certain to have impressed and influenced young Adler" are: (1) "The human essence is no abstraction inherent in each single individual. In its reality it is the ensemble of the social relations," and (2) "The individual is not only the product but also the producer of his condition" (p. 18). (These formulations are reflected in the third and fourth Adlerian assumptions given earlier.) Henri Ellenberger (1970) concurs: "The influence of Marxism can be recognized in several basic concepts of Individual Psychology" (p. 629).

In his writings Adler mentioned his interest in Marx and socialism only rarely, although, according to Sperber

(1974), "In our early conversations . . . Adler quoted both Marx and his disciples quite often" (p. 18). A paper "On the psychology of Marxism" was never published and has been presented only in abbreviated form through the Minutes of the Vienna Psychoanalytic Society, where Adler (A1909d) read the paper. He considered the proletariat to be sensitive "to every kind of degradation," and this sensitivity to be "the affect that lies at the root of class consciousness. . . . Marx's greatest achievement is . . . that he brought this sensitivity into consciousness, the first full-scale analysis of masses" (pp. 173–74). Nine years later, Adler (A1918a) acknowledged that he shared with Marx the basic assumptions of man's goal orientation and aptitude for social interest. In fact, "Karl Marx . . . showed the way toward the final realization of social interest" (p. 598). The occasion was the paper in which Adler drew a sharp line between himself and the terror tactics of the Russian Revolution.

The most explicit and last statement on Marx is found in Adler's reply to a lecture before the Vienna Society of Individual Psychology by Max Adler (1925), no relative of Alfred Adler, in which the philosopher of Austromarxism attempted to set certain limits on Individual Psychology in relation to Marxian socialism. Toward the end of his reply Alfred Adler (A1925g) asserted: "I consider the study of Marx extremely valuable. His work, perhaps like no other, is suited to sharpen the eye for contexts (*Zusammenhänge*). I agree with the speaker that Marx's thoughts are born of the strongest social interest and can lead to the strongest social interest. But I would go farther, stressing that Marx's scientific contribution furnishes in many ways, although in a different field, a wonderful contextual approach (*Zusammenhangsbetrachtung*) that is close to that of Individual Psychology. Like the latter, it takes attitudes and final goals into account in assessing the meaning of overt behavior. But we should not forget that this is also found elsewhere, especially in great literature (*Dichterwerken*) and the various religions" (p. 223).

Practically. Adler contributed articles on psychological matters to socialist newspapers and periodicals (for example, A1923b, A1924a, A1925c), including his first article on sex

256

and education (A1905a), to which we shall refer again later. He also published three papers on general political issues, rejecting the accusation by the Allied victors of the peoples of the defeated countries of collective war guilt (A1919a), decrying the Bolshevist terror (A1918e), as just mentioned, and calling for new methods to combat the striving for power over others among individuals and peoples (A1928m).

While Adler (A1912a, p. 24n) once in an added footnote referred to "My well-known socialist world philosophy (*Weltanschauung*)," his political participation was very limited. According to all accounts he was a member of the Social-Democratic Party, and in the early days of the Austrian Republic was for a short period vice chairman of the Workers Council of his residential district, which had minor administrative functions. As such Adler was primarily interested in educational affairs (Furtmüller, 1964, p. 372). But he soon gave up all political activity, including his party membership, to "give all of his time and energy to the field where he could not be replaced by anyone else" (p. 372). This included the establishment of a system of free child-guidance clinics in Vienna and elsewhere, and innumerable public lectures to carry his psychology directly to the largest number of people.

Adler's relationship to socialism is still being remembered and acknowledged today. Bourdet (1971) included Adler in his Biographical Dictionary of the International Labor Movement. Yet this inclusion seems to be founded only on the fact that the socialist municipal government of Vienna at the time permitted Adler to install his child-guidance clinics in public schools, made other facilities available to him, and made him an honorary citizen, "although he was not a militant social democrat."

Demand for Equal Rights for Women

One of the socialist positions was the demand for equal rights for women. August Bebel (1885), cofounder of the

German Socialist Party, wrote: "One of the most important questions . . . is the woman question" (p. 3). "The subjugation of woman by man was accomplished with the established rule of private property" (p. 33). "The Socialist Party is the only one that has made the full equality of women, their liberation from every form of dependence and oppression, an integral part of its program. . . . For there can be no liberation of mankind without social independence and equality of the sexes" (p. 7).

Adler made this demand largely his own. He referred to the "excessive pre-eminence of maleness" as the "cancerous damage of our culture" (*der Krebsschaden unserer Kultur*) (A1910d, pp. 88–89). Or he spoke of male dominance as "one of the deepest wounds of our social life." But whereas the socialists thought of a political solution, Adler had essentially an educational solution in mind. "Psychological recovery is to be expected from an education that not only talks to the child, but also knows how to awaken the feeling of equal rights of the sexes despite our present situation, which demonstrates the opposite" (A1913f, p. 150).

As early as 1908, Adler expressed himself on this issue in a discussion with Fritz Wittels and Freud. Wittels (Nunberg and Federn, 1962) denounced the feminist movement, stating: "People do not appreciate the perversity and senselessness of these strivings; nor do the women themselves" (p. 350). Adler rebutted: "Wittels . . . being a reactionary, has turned to the most distant past in order to look for shortcomings there" (p. 352). Adler continued that the essential difference between his viewpoint and that of the speaker and of Freud was: "Whereas it is generally assumed that the framework of present relationships between men and women is constant, socialists assume that the framework of the family is already shaky today and will increasingly become so in the future. Woman will not allow motherhood to prevent her from taking up a profession; motherhood may either remain an obstacle for some, or else it will lose its hardship. . . . First of all, the attitude that a woman is a possession must be given up" (p. 352). To this Wittels replied, "One cannot be a Freudian and a Social Democrat at the same time" (p.

353), a statement with which we would agree. In a later discussion the same year Adler (Nunberg and Federn, 1967) added: "We must not forget that woman has only just begun her fight" (p. 91).

This cultural bias against women, Adler noted, is expressed even in our language, a factor of which we have become so much aware today. Adler (1936n) wrote: "Language denies to women the complete equality essential for love. We still say that a man 'takes' a wife. Words and proverbs in which the old prejudices still linger are more potent than most men realize. They keep false traditions alive and subtly corrupt our judgment. There should be no 'taking' in love or marriage, but a mutual 'give and take'" (p. 152). In the selection in Chapter 1 we find more. "Figures of speech, anecdotes, proverbs, and jokes of all peoples are full of depreciating criticism of women. They are accused of quarrelsomeness, unpunctuality, pettiness, and stupidity. . . . For some men the worst insult is, 'just like a woman,' whereas in girls manliness does not mean derogation."

The fullest statement by Adler (A1914f) on the woman question, prior to the selection in Chapter 1, is the following: "Perhaps the most important question in our society is the woman question (*Frauenfrage*). Our life is oriented toward work and earning a living. From this it follows that, expressed in figures, the male demands and obtains a higher value than the female. This economic relation is reflected in most minds in the form of the female existing for the male and for being at his service. This is an unnatural assumption, an artificial division of the natural coherence of the sexes, a myth that is, however, likely to originate from the occasional indispositions of the female. This myth is usually retained throughout life by women as well as men. Such valuation must be sought not in words and conscious thoughts, but in the persons' attitude. . . . [In women] the weapons of the weak, detours to excessively high goals, and traits of submission emerge that at first appear exaggerated but soon turn into the lines of craving for domination. The natural meaning of the body and its organs becomes falsified and all impulses are altered and poisoned by the desired, and at the same time

259

undesired goal, the compulsion of marriage" (pp. 482–83, original translation).

Adler continues, "The reason for this condition is that the traits of natural femaleness have suffered depreciation and can be restored only conditionally. Learned authors believe to have found 'innate feminine' traits—in the bad sense of the word, as feminine in nature—which condemn the individual to permanent inferiority. But such traits are only artificial products brought about by the fact that the little girl has interiorized the masculine myth of the hopelessness of her intellectual striving and now continuously tries to speak with a masculine voice. . . . But the human soul cannot find peace in such self-depreciation. The result is a strange hostility against the apparently privileged male, which is usually hidden but can easily be deciphered. . . . This is the most basic sickness of our social organism" (p. 483, original translation).

Although Adler considered women disadvantaged, he did not become sentimental about them. He believed that on account of their position of inferiority, women tend to be more self-centered than men. "Women now feel inferior. . . . If the reader is not convinced of this, let him look at the strivings of women. . . . They usually want to overcome others and often develop and train more than is necessary. They are more self-centered than men. . . . Women must be taught to develop more social interest and not always to seek benefit for themselves without regard for others. But in order to do this, we must first banish the myth regarding the privileges of men" (A1929d, pp. 120–21).

Regarding the disadvantaged in general, Adler expressed the same lack of sentimentality and developed the frustration-aggression hypothesis, as follows: "Difficulties in earning a livelihood, bad working conditions, inadequate educational and cultural facilities, a joyless existence, and continuous irritation, all these factors increase the feeling of inferiority, produce oversensitivity, and drive the individual to seek 'solutions.' . . . Motives of hatred appear most clearly in the economic disturbances of our time. . . . Destruction means to the masses a release from situations felt intolerable and

260

thus appears to them as a preliminary condition of improvement. . . . Children in poor neighborhoods grow up in fear of a strong father, etc., and carry this fear into adulthood. The average proletarian indeed gives the impression of being less friendly toward the world than the bourgeois who is more courageous" (A1956b, pp. 452–53).

The Right of Abortion

Quite consistently with the preceding, Adler (A1925i) took a stand against existing anti-abortion laws. We have included his paper on this subject as an appendix to the first chapter, since the problem of abortion is one of the social and sociological aspects of the woman question, with which this chapter is concerned.

Interestingly, Adler justified his position not so much by the arguments which we generally hear—namely the benefit to the woman involved, that she has a right to her body, etc.; rather he discussed the problem from the viewpoint of the benefit to the child and the possible self-centeredness of the woman.

This is characteristic for Adler's approach to all problems, including especially those occurring in psychotherapy. The solution will be sought and found not by going "deeper" into the "unconscious" of the individual in question, but by placing the problem into its larger context, where the individual's actions can then be evaluated in terms of their consequences for the other persons involved, for the larger good. By making the individual aware of his responsibilities, Adler would enable him to solve his problem in a way that would be a contribution to the larger whole.

Male Dominance, a Cultural Development

That women are innately inferior was a widely held opinion during the latter part of the nineteenth century, up into

261

the twentieth century. While this was the case, the opposite opinion—that male dominance is a cultural development—received strong support by Johann Jakob Bachofen (1815–87), a Swiss jurist, historian, and anthropologist.

Bachofen (1861) in his book *Das Mutterrecht* (The Mother Right), established the thesis that the monogamous patriarchal family, with the resulting subordinate role of woman, did not always exist. It was not an immutable condition determined by certain innate characteristics of the sexes; rather it was the outcome of a historical development in three broad stages. The original state was one of sexual promiscuity. This was followed by matriarchy, since women were the only parents known with certainty. Then men became dominant and patriarchy was established. According to August Bebel (1885), Bachofen believed that the women vehemently opposed this social transformation and that the many myths of Amazon kingdoms found the world over are "proofs of the struggle . . . of women against the new order" (p. 33).

Shortly after Bachofen, Lewis H. Morgan (1877), an American anthropologist, from his studies of American Indians, arrived independently at the conclusion that matriarchy preceded patriarchy.

The Bachofen-Morgan theory became very important to those standing for equal rights for women. If patriarchy was not the only form of family life but was preceded by matriarchy, then women as well as men would by nature have the capacity to rule and would probably in other capacities also be equal to men. Thus the socialists Friedrich Engels (1884) and August Bebel (1885) referred extensively to Bachofen and Morgan, adding their own interpretation. Bebel, for example, wrote: "The matriarchate implied communism and equality of all. The rise of the patriarchate implied the rule of private property and the subjugation and enslavement of woman" (p. 33). "It is the common lot of woman and workers to be oppressed. . . . But . . . women were slaves before men" (pp. 9–10).

Adler also used the Bachofen-Morgan theory to support his case for the equality of the sexes. We read in Chapter 1, "In

262

the time of *Mutterrecht* it was the mother, the woman, who played the more important role in life. . . . Male predominance has therefore not been a natural state." Since Adler refers in this connection to Bebel, we may safely assume that it was through him that Adler learned about Bachofen's theory. This would have been during Adler's early student days when he first became acquainted with socialistic literature. He would then have been interested in the social problems of equal rights for both sexes long before he became concerned with psychological problems.

Today the Bachofen-Morgan theory is no longer accepted. Only matriliny (establishment of lineage through the female line) has been verified. "No reliable evidence" has been found (*Encyclopaedia Britannica*, 1973) for matriarchy (rule of women). However, what the theory was supposed to demonstrate, namely, that women's subordination is not naturally but culturally determined, has today been accepted.

Overcoming the "Masculine Principle"

In the *Neurotic Constitution*, Adler (A1912a) confessed an "initial overvaluation of an abstract masculine principle" (p. 130) on his part, which is indeed surprising in view of his later strong stand on equal rights for women. This would also seem to be indicated in some of Adler's childhood recollections of antagonism toward his mother. An earlier version of these, found in Chapter 7, does not reveal them as Adler's own, while a later version does (see Bibliographical-historical Commentary).

In the later version Adler (A1930o) tells: "On the day of [my younger brother's] funeral I was taken to my grandfather's. . . . After the service was over, my mother came to bring me home. I can still remember how this good woman . . . clothed all in black and wearing a black veil, went on crying and crying. My grandfather turned to comfort her and whispered a few words, which brought a smile to her face. . . . I was shocked. How could a mother smile on her child's burial day? . . . I understood this antagonism toward my mother all the better since I could establish it also in two other dim remembrances. The first is as follows: After a quarrel between my father and my mother, I turned to him full of admiration and remarked to him: 'You are as brave as a soldier.' At which he put his finger to his lips in alarm and whispered to me: 'You mustn't tell a single soul a word about it.' In the second incident I remember an uncle on my mother's side reproaching me severely for being always so stubborn with my mother. I was rather startled. Till that moment I had never noticed this obvious fact. I decided to be friendlier, and found it all the easier since my mother was exceedingly good-natured. After this event I never again put myself in opposition to my mother, and to this day I consider her one of the greatest of mothers" (p. 7).

Adler considered two factors important, if not determining, in homosexual development: (1) a negative attitude toward the other sex, and (2) doubt as a child about one's own sexual role, which Adler considered basic in neurosis in general. The first factor might be inferred from the above recollections, while the second factor might be considered applicable to Adler (A1912a) as he writes: "I have often asked myself whether in my own childhood development a similar doubt [regarding my future sexual role] did not prevail, although the hermaphroditic problem attracted me only as a critic—that is, apparently as a secondary concern—and very late in life" (p. 130).

Yet Adler had, of course, no homosexual tendencies, nor did he manifest any form of masculine protest. How are we then to understand these reflections of Adler about himself, which seem to contradict his own theories as far as he is personally concerned?

Regarding a negative attitude toward the female sex and adherence to the "masculine principle," we find on closer observation indeed a great difference between the early recollections of actual homosexuals and those of Adler. The homosexuals accuse the other sex of hostility directed against them, while Adler takes the blame upon himself. He accused his mother of nothing worse than a smile, which he considered inappropriate, and described her as "this good woman" who "was exceedingly good-natured," "one of the greatest of mothers," stating in the earlier version also that her "character was of a better kind." Regarding doubt of his sex role, Adler continued: "Still my world view tells me that I must have very well become master of an old childhood disjunctiveness (*Gegensätzlichkeit*) in me, without developing an exaggerated masculine protest. In my life as in my scientific work I have, after initial overvaluation of an abstract masculine principle, rejected with objective calm the flood of arguments supporting the primary inferiority of women" (A1912a, p. 130).

Psychiatrists have often used their own condition and described their own cases in developing their theories, although they have generally not stated this explicitly. Ellenberger (1970) gives numerous examples to that effect. In reference to Adler he points out, as others have done before him, that Adler's affliction at an early age with rickets "would account for his theories of organ inferiority, inferiority complex, and compensation" (p. 889).

To this we may now add that it was probably Adler's own experience of opposition to the other sex, his own experience of uncertainty of his sexual role, and his own "initial overvaluation of an abstract masculine principle" that became important factors in his early theory of neurosis and homosexuality. Furthermore, these experiences, like that of organ inferiority, became equally or even more important in his theory of relative self-determination and psychotherapy: Objective and even subjective factors are not absolute determiners of an outcome. They create only certain probabilities of outcome in that the individual is easily "seduced" by them to go in the wrong direction. However, they can be overcome, and outgrown, and must in any case be understood in their context.

Adler tells us how he changed, how he reconstructed the situations. In the first instance he made the decision to be friendlier to his mother and to recognize her actual good-naturedness. In the second instance he terminated his doubt

265

about his sex role—that is, wondering whether he would be "a real man," or "like a woman," by recognizing the equality of the sexes. Thus he started in both instances to see the situation from the viewpoint of the "opponent," empathizing with him—which amounts to an increase in social interest, the main factor, after encouragement, in Adler's theory of psychotherapy.

The precondition was that Adler saw himself as an active agent, not as a passive victim and sufferer. This active and constructive reaction to adversities and acknowledged misdeeds and shortcomings of his own becomes evident in nearly all his memories. When Adler almost died from pneumonia at the age of four, he "decided to be a doctor, so that I should be able to guard myself in the future against illness and death" (A1930o, p. 7). When at the age of three he found himself suffering from a mild spasm of breathlessness whenever he grew angry, he decided "to give up being angry altogether" (p. 6). When at the age of ten he once happened to hurt another boy, "the injury I had involuntarily inflicted . . . [which] was by no means severe . . . made such an impression on me that . . . I preferred to spend more time indoors, working at home" (p. 6).

This characteristic of overcoming adversities of all kinds, which stands out in Adler's early recollections, became the keynote of his psychology. "Life is always a matter of overcoming. . . . Herein lies the foundation for our view of the striving for superiority" (A1964a, p. 32). "Everything grows 'as if' it were striving to overcome all imperfections and achieve perfection. This urge toward perfection we call the goal of overcoming—that is, the striving to overcome" (p. 86).

Other sources of Adler's early recollections, in addition to the two sources given here, and partly overlapping with them, are Adler (A1920a, pp. 176–81) and Phyllis Bottome (1957, pp. 30–33). Some of Adler's recollections became the points of departure for articles by Brennan (1968), Rayner (1957), and Mosak and Kopp (1973).

Marriage to an Independent Woman

Not only had Adler become interested in the struggle for the equality of the sexes, but he also acted accordingly in that he married in 1897, two years after graduation from medical school, a girl who herself strongly believed in women's rights and equality. This is further support for the view that Adler's social convictions antedated his psychological convictions.

The girl was Raissa Timofeyewna Epstein from Moscow, who had come to Vienna to attend the university, after a year at the University of Zurich. Raissa came from a wealthy Jewish family which was involved with the new Trans-Siberian Railway and had been granted the privilege of living in Moscow, where Jews ordinarily were not permitted to live. Adler's biographer, Phyllis Bottome (1939) described her as a good-looking, petite girl with "a very strong, independent and upright personality" (p. 45), radical ideas, and interested in political change. Raissa and Adler were first seen together at socialist meetings. Their common interest in social betterment must have been a great part of their mutual attraction. Soon after their marriage, Raissa Adler (1899) published a paper on coeducation in medicine, which was then still controversial. The paper summarized a survey by a Dr. Erismann conducted among Swiss professors who have had some thirty years of experience with medical coeducation. They were found to be full of praise for the female medical student. Erismann's results appeared in Moscow in a symposium volume supporting the women's movement.

While in time Alfred Adler increasingly came to advocate change on the individual, psychological level, Raissa continued to think in terms of political action. This difference caused considerable marital strain, according to Bottome (1939). In addition, Raissa felt neglected by her husband who spent all his time with his patients and writings. Furthermore, "Raissa took no pleasure in the details of domesticity; . . . and at this period of her life neglected all interest in dress. . . . She was probably too bent upon what she thought

267

constituted the character and duties of a human being, in a world that she intended to have a good try at changing, than in giving pleasure to an overworked husband" (p. 49).

Bottome describes a photograph from that period, with Adler standing by Raissa's side holding his first-born child in his arms. "The father is looking down at the child . . . while Raissa looks into the distance. . . . Yet she seems to be quite sure that father and child are wholly hers and will behave as she has a right to expect of them" (p. 50). Many years later a photograph very similar to the one just described was published (Scarf, 1971), in which Adler sits down, holding his second-born daughter in his arms and looking at her, while Raissa stands slightly behind him looking straight ahead, and the first-born turned toward her father with her hands resting against his lap stands in front of her mother. The caption of that picture reads, "Adler dandles his daughter Alexandra . . . under the stern overview of Frau Adler . . ." (p. 46). Both pictures seem to illustrate the further comment: "The children [four in all] all vastly preferred their ebullient, outgoing father to their sternly political mother" (p. 45).

Bottome (1962) reports from the time when she was introduced to Mrs. Adler in 1934 and expressed her deep debt to Adler's teaching that Raissa replied: "I do not agree with all that Adler teaches. . . . I think these matters have an economic basis and should be dealt with politically, and my husband does not" (p. 182).

Bottome (1939) had arrived at the conclusion: "Theoretically Adler always believed in the equal status of women . . . he supported it. . . . Nevertheless, fighting for the emancipation of women, and living with a woman who had emancipated herself, are two wholly different things; and it is probable that Adler found them difficult as well as different" (p. 50).

Yet Raissa was actually never as active politically or otherwise as she intended to be. We only know about some political friendships, work as a translator, some book reviews, and an enthusiastic report on education in the Soviet Union (Raissa Adler, 1931), after a visit there.

Bottome (1939) calls the Adlers' four children Raissa's

268

"only tangible fruit of all her dreams" (p. 117). She must have become particularly disillusioned about the developments in Russia under Stalin, which ended for the Adlers in the tragedy of their daughter, Valentine, the oldest of the four children. The others are Alexandra and Kurt, psychiatrists in New York, and Nelly, who also lives in New York.

In contrast to her father, Vali, as she was called, was a devoted supporter of the new order in Russia. In an article in her father's journal, Vali Adler (1925) noted that the polarization of masculine-feminine is much greater in bourgeois than in proletarian circles, where the woman's movement is part of the general struggle for liberation. "In Soviet Russia there is no woman problem" (p. 310). When Hitler came to power she had to leave Berlin, where she had settled, and immigrated with her husband to her mother's country—Russia. Eventually she was imprisoned, as all refugees from Germany were, regardless of their political convictions, and there were no further communications. Years after the Second World War the family finally learned that she had died in 1942. A fellow prisoner, Susanne Leonhard (1968), survived to write a book about her own experiences, a kind of early, personal *Gulag Archipelago* in German. She had known Vali well from Berlin and mentions her throughout the book. She describes her as a fierce fighter who gradually, however, grew weary and came to hate the Stalin system passionately. "If I shall survive this . . . ! If I shall ever get out of this hell and write a book about it . . . !" (p. 344), the author quotes Vali. It is a sad irony that the father immediately denounced the communist revolution for its methods, while the daughter became an enthusiastic follower—and its victim.

To return to Raissa, when toward the end of his life Adler really needed her, her instant positive response changed both their lives. In Bottome's (1939) words, "They were restored to each other" (p. 224). After Adler's death, his "Individual Psychology . . . became Raissa's chief interest, and she gave unflagging help and support to the Adlerian Society in New York, of which she became lifelong honorary president" (Bottome, 1962).

269

Demarcation Line Against Marxism

Since Adler's view on the equality of women brought him in this respect, as in others, close to the Marxist position, it is important to delineate how he differed from Marxism, theoretically and politically.

Theoretically. Adler (A1927a) did not accept the historical determinism that many followers of Marx stressed. He did of course recognize that man is not completely free in that he is always confronted with his biological conditions and "tasks that are inseparably connected with the *logic of human social living* . . . and can only to a certain degree become subjected to his influence." He held that we must take "the immanent rules of the game of a group . . . as an absolute truth. . . . A significant share of these basic facts has been captured in the materialistic conception of history that Marx and Engels have created. According to this theory it is the economic foundation . . . that determines the 'ideological superstructure,' the thinking and behavior of man" (pp. 18–19). Adler, however, continues, "So far reaches the accord with our view of the effective 'logic of human social living,' of the 'absolute truth.' But history, especially our insight into individual lives . . . teaches us that the human psyche is likely to respond with errors to the impulsions of the economic foundations" (p. 19). If man were completely determined by the circumstances, we could not speak of errors.

Adler goes on: "More important than disposition, objective experience, and milieu is *their subjective evaluation.* . . . In group psychology this fundamental fact is difficult to discover because the 'ideological superstructure over the economic foundation' (Marx and Engels) and its effects force a leveling of individual differences" (Adler, A1930p, p. 4). Actually, "In each immediate present the economic conditions are reflected and answered by each individual and each group according to their previously acquired life style" (A1934i, p. 137).

270

A further argument against determinism was that its acceptance as a personal philosophy stifles individual initiative while strengthening the tendency to blame one's circumstances and to remain free from responsibility. "It is the fault of my parents, my fate . . . blaming fate—just as in the Greek tragedies—to save his self-esteem" (A1956a, p. 270).

On the social level, Adler (A1934i) noted: "Maybe the great emphasis on . . . the materialistic interpretation of history strongly diminishes the élan of the adherents of historical materialism, all denials notwithstanding" (p. 137). This stress on determinism applied primarily to the moderates in the Marxist camp. Adler was indeed criticized by the moderate socialists for expecting too much from individual initiative. A Berlin socialist newspaper, while reporting otherwise very favorably on one of Adler's successful lectures there, criticized him for not referring "to the present limitations for the fulfillment of the community ideal, set by the existing class structure" (M.R., 1930).

According to some authorities, the moderate Social-Democratic majority of the Marxists had settled down to the relative apathy of optimistic determinism. They believed that the forces in the social process, quite abstractly conceived, would spontaneously work out all right (Bauer, 1952, pp. 13–20; Lichtheim, 1961, pp. 235–38).

By attributing to the individual some freedom of choice, some responsibility, Adler at the same time raised the patient's self-esteem and encouraged him—most important factors in psychotherapy. Since Adler's focus was on helping the individual to become as free and contributive as possible under the existing circumstances, Adler did not dwell on the social hindrances, although he was well aware of the existing evils of society and the necessity for change.

Politically. While Adler disagreed with the determinism of the moderates, he rejected completely the approval of violence of the less deterministic radicals. As soon as the Bolshevists had ascended to power, Adler (A1918e) took a firm stand against their abuse of power. He wrote: "The most important characteristic of Bolshevism is enforcement of socialism by violence. Many people think of this as a matter of course. But granted that the simplest way to create everything that is good and promising would be through force, where in the life of man or in the history of humanity has such an attempt ever been successful?

"The struggle for power has a psychological aspect. . . . Even where the welfare of the subjugated is obviously intended, the use of even moderate power stimulates opposition everywhere. . . . Human nature generally answers external coercion with a countercoercion. It seeks its satisfaction not in rewards for obedience and docility, but aims to prove that its own means of power are the stronger" (pp. 598–99).

"This party and its friends pursue goals that are also ours. But the intoxication of power has seduced them. . . . We see former friends, old brave fellow travelers, in dizzy heights. Seduced by the power drive, they arouse everywhere the demand for power. . . . If there are means to call them back, it can only be the remembrance of the miracle of social feelings, a miracle that we must perform and that will never succeed through the use of power. For us the way and the tactics result from our highest goal: the cultivation and strengthening of social feelings" (p. 600).

In a paper "The Psychology of Power," which appeared in a *Handbook of Pacifism,* Adler (A1928m) urged that "the typical ideal of our time," which is still the isolated hero for whom his fellow men are mere objects, be replaced by the "ideal of the saint, purified, to be sure, from fantastic clinkers of superstition" (p. 171).

We have mentioned before that in the early 1920s Adler gave up all political activity to give his full time and energy to his psychology. Several years later he severed relations with some of his followers who were communists at that time, including Manès Sperber and Otto and Alice Rühle. Furtmüller (1964) commented on this separation: "We have seen how Marx's sociology influenced . . . the roots from which Adler's psychology developed. Some of his followers . . . tried to make Individual Psychology as such a satellite doctrine of Marxism. . . . Adler was always aware that common ideological indebtedness to Marx could relate Individual Psychology to other movements based on his sociology. But he declined to see Individual Psychology made a partisan affair" (pp. 387–88).

Child-guidance Clinics and Women Coworkers

When Adler gave up his political activities he engaged in his own social action, so to speak, in that he set up free child-guidance clinics in the Vienna public schools, with the consent of the school authorities but on a completely voluntary basis. The most characteristic feature of these clinics was that they were conceived not so much alone for the benefit of the child and the parents than as training seminars for teachers and other interested persons, including parents, physicians, social workers, students, etc. Thus the clinics were generally conducted before audiences of thirty to fifty persons. The clinics were so popular that on some occasions children came on their own.

According to a survey by Sophie Freudenberg (1928), there were by 1927 twenty-two Adlerian clinics in Vienna plus twenty in the rest of Europe, among these five in Munich under the leadership of Leonhard Seif (p. 39). The clinics in Vienna were frequently sponsored by social-democratic parents' or women's groups (p. 35). Thus when the reactionary Schuschnigg government ascended to power in Austria, in 1934, the clinics in Vienna, which by that time numbered over thirty, were closed (A1956b, p. 393; A1964a, p. 380). The German clinics had already been closed by the Nazis a year earlier, or were taken over by them. In accordance with Adler's acceptance of women as equals, a large number of his coworkers at these clinics—as well as his followers—were women.

Relationship to German Social Work

Social work in Germany was closely related to the woman's movement which in turn was related to the socialist labor

273

movement, all three deriving from the humanistic ideas of the era of the Enlightenment. This interrelationship is reflected in the three original demands of the General German Women's Association founded in 1865: demands for women's right to work, social measures to enable them to work, and better education for women (Ottenheimer, 1959, p. 929).

Within this intellectual context the psychology of Adler whose philosophy was also that of the Enlightenment (Ellenberger, 1970, p. 628) found wide acceptance among social workers. A review of social work up to the Hitler period states: "Especially Individual Psychology, founded by Alfred Adler, Vienna, became closely related to social work in Germany. On the other hand, Sigmund Freud's psychoanalysis had not had much influence in the schools, in remedial education, nor in social work in general. Psychoanalysis forces man to come to terms with himself; Individual Psychology demands that he come to terms with the reality of his surrounding world (*Umwelt*). Since in social work we are mostly dealing with persons who have lost their ties to the community [anomie], the Adlerian theory was ready-made to determine remedial measures. Adler's focusing on practical work, which resulted in the foundation of numerous child-guidance centers, is significant. The principle of individualization, which is characteristic for welfare work for the period from 1914 to 1933 . . . was largely oriented by the theory of Alfred Adler" (Ottenheimer, 1959, pp. 849–50). At the Congress of Individual Psychology, in Berlin, 1930, with over two thousand participants, one third of the members of the honorary congress committee were leaders in the field of social work (Kankeleit, 1931). Among them was Alice Salomon (1872–1948), founder of one of the first schools of social work and internationally prominent feminist (Kronfeld and Voigt, 1930).

Among papers by Adlerians in this area is one by Sophie Freudenberg (1926) on social work with adolescents, one by Lene Credner (1926) on delinquency, a review paper by Raoul Simon (1937) on Adler's psychology and the courts, and two papers by Adler (A1921, A1935m) on the prevention of delinquency.

274

Relationship to Woman's Movement

Adler (A1964a) considered his psychology of great relevance to all humanistic progressive social movements, a scientific resource for all of them. Therefore he did not want to become too closely identified with any one movement, be it religious, political, or the woman's movement. "The very foundation of my scientific work resists the norms formulated in the rigid laws of all other movements that are beyond science. . . . Individual Psychology must use only purely scientific methods, must remain a pure science and reach the people in this unalterable form, in the hope of being fruitful also to other scientific movements and currents that stand closer to practical life. . . . I am less inclined to take a hand in religious or political movements, since I have confidence in the strength and effectiveness of Individual Psychology, although . . . I would have to reckon with a long time before this would be felt. Meanwhile, I am satisfied to see how its views keep on gaining ground in the ministry, the schools, criminology, education, and psychiatry—as even in the political parties the idea of the community continues to gain. . . . I consider it the given task of Individual Psychology to maintain a central position and to make its results available to all" (pp. 280–81).

In line with such policy, Adler expressed his support of the woman's movement with reservations on the relatively few occasions that he did so.

In Chapter 1 we read, "We must actively support the present goals of the woman's movement of freedom and equal rights"; but he added the qualification, "because ultimately happiness and joy in the life of all humanity will depend [1] on the creation of conditions that will enable women to become reconciled to their feminine role, and [2] on how men will be able to answer the problem of their relationship to women." And he introduces this passage with the low-key statement, "We have no reason to oppose the present goals of the woman's movement." He also warned, the woman's movement at times does "overdo things in the heat of battle."

As might be expected, numerous women, beginning with Hedwig Schulhof (1914), wrote on the woman question in the light of Individual Psychology. Margarete Minor (1925) compared the woman's movement to the masculine protest, to which Hilde Grünbaum-Sachs (1926) took strong exception. Alice Friedmann (1936) advocated that women take advantage of their new opportunities by outperforming men in work and love. The greatest contribution is a four-hundred-page volume by Alice Rühle-Gerstel (1932) which was reprinted, after forty years, in 1973. The book's primary concern is how women meet each of Adler's three life tasks, of love, work, and society. The author, one of the Marxists eventually rejected by Adler, sees most women in an inferior position on two accounts: as proletarians and as women (p. 399). The ideal woman would be "a comrade and fellow man . . . courageous, cheerful, intelligent, competent" (p. 409). Interestingly, marriage and children are not mentioned.

As writers of today's woman's movement have drawn support from novelists and dramatists (De Beauvoir, 1953, pp. 185 ff; Millett, 1969, pp. 179 ff), so Adlerian writers also dealt with female characters from fiction to show how throughout history women have fought against their disadvantaged situation (Freschl, 1914; Lazarsfeld, 1927; Oppenheim, 1924/25; Plottke, 1947; Schmid, 1914; Schulhof, 1923, 1923/24a, b).

Freud, Psychologist of Women's Inferiority

Adler's stand for woman's social equality was one of the issues on which he was diametrically opposed to Freud. Still, this particular opposition does not become explicit in Adler's writings. His criticism remained focused on Freud's theories of human sexuality. An explanation may be that when Adler offered his "Critique of Freud's Theory of Sexuality" (Chapter 2), Freud had not yet made his important statements devaluating women. Freud did not do so until 1914, with the strongest statements in 1925 and 1933. By that time Adler no longer answered Freud's development in detail.

But one of Adler's followers, Erwin O. Krausz (1934), did. He showed that "The psychoanalytic conceptions of 'femininity' . . . are permeated by a submerged *overvaluation and privileging of man* and thereby a *depreciation and devaluation of women*. . . . Psychoanalysis represents in the end a defense of the usurped right of the male to regard the female as a sex object and to degrade her to this role" (p. 16).

One of the merits of today's feminist writers is that they have fully exposed Freud's views of women's constitutional psychological inferiority to men. Kate Millett (1969) gives an excellently documented account of thirty-four pages of Freud's position, in which she considers him "beyond question the strongest individual counterrevolutionary force in the ideology of sexual politics during the period [1930–60]" (p. 241). Betty Friedan (1963) attacks Freud in a chapter of twenty-one pages, in which she holds: "The old prejudices . . . reappeared in the forties, in Freudian disguise. . . . It is a Freudian idea . . . that has trapped so many American women today" (p. 95).

The Freud quotations used by these two authors are some of the very same that Krausz had used some thirty years earlier. Freud's perhaps most condemning passage about women is quoted in part by all three. It is: "It must be admitted that women have but little sense of justice, and this is no doubt connected with the preponderance of envy in their mental life; for the demands of justice are a modification of envy; they lay down the conditions under which one is willing to part with it. We say also of women that their social interests are weaker than those of men, and that their capacity for the sublimation of their instincts is less" (Freud, 1933, p. 183; Krausz, 1934, p. 30; Friedan, 1963, p. 108; Millett, 1969, p. 253).

The statement with which Freud concludes his lecture "The Psychology of Women" is quoted by Krausz and Mil-

277

lett. It reads: "That is all I had to say to you about the psychology of women. It is admittedly incomplete and fragmentary, and sometimes it does not sound altogether flattering. You must not forget, however, that we have only described women insofar as their natures are determined by their sexual function. The influence of this factor is, of course, very far-reaching, but we must remember that an individual woman may be a human being apart from this" (Freud, 1933, pp. 184–85; Krausz, 1934, p. 31; Millett, 1969, p. 272).

Krausz recommends a very careful reading of this sentence; especially the concession that "an individual woman may be a human being apart from this" deserves not to be forgotten.

From the above it follows quite naturally that Freud would be opposed to feminism. Freud (1925) wrote: "I cannot escape the notion (though I hesitate to give it expression) that for women the level of what is ethically normal is different from what it is in men. . . . Character traits that critics of every epoch have brought up against women . . . would be amply accounted for by the modification in the formation of their super-ego. . . . We must not allow ourselves to be deflected from such conclusions by the denials of the feminists, who are anxious to force us to regard the two sexes as completely equal in position and worth" (pp. 196–97). A few years later, Freud (1931) added: "We should probably not err in saying that it is this difference in the interrelationship of the Oedipus and the castration complexes that gives its special stamp to the character of woman as a member of society. It is to be anticipated that male analysts with feminist sympathies, and our women analysts also, will disagree with what I have said here" (p. 258).

Freud's opposition to feminism was not a development of these later years. It was an established attitude of twenty years or longer. As early as 1908 Freud stated: "Women as a group profit nothing by the modern feminist movement; at best a few individuals profit" (Nunberg and Federn, 1962, p. 351).

278

A Women's Monument for Adler

An anecdote from the biography by Orgler (1963, pp. 192–97) seems a fitting conclusion for this section. The anecdote is related by Danish sculptress Thyra Boldsen (1884–1968), who came to California after 1931 and was known for monumental works in marble such as "The Flood," "Mothers of the World," and "The Melody of Life," as well as busts of such celebrities as actress Eva le Gallienne and Charles Lindbergh. She also took an active interest in philosophy and education (Bodelsen, 1933–44). Thus, while still in Copenhagen when Adler lectured there in January 1931, she was host to him for the group who had invited him. In a letter to Ms. Orgler dated December 28, 1937, Ms. Boldsen reports the following table conversation with Adler:

BOLDSEN: "I, as a woman, must especially thank you for the help you have given women. What you have written to explain the psychology of superiority by men toward women is of great value to women in their striving for self-adjustment to their natural place in society. The patronage of men shall no longer crush us since we know it is from vanity and fear. And your request to women, that they must awaken to their part of the responsibility for the fate of mankind, is just and of great significance."

ADLER (turning toward Boldsen, emphatically): "If women knew what I have done for them they would erect a monument to me."

Five years later, Ms. Boldsen continues, when she was in California and Adler happened to be lecturing there, this became her opportunity to begin such a monument. She was then working on a large monument in memory of women's franchise. One of the figures was to bear Adler's likeness, while the others would all be women who "have proved and exemplified the abilities of women by their important contributions to culture." For one week Adler actually sat as a

279

model several hours a day. "Dr. Adler told stories while he was my model because I wanted his bust smiling. He was the most lively and interesting model I have ever had."

But we do not know what has become of the project.

III. MASCULINE PROTEST

A presentation of Adler's theories of sexuality must come to grips with those of Freud, in opposition to which Adler developed them. The controversy centered around Adler's concept of "masculine protest," which represents the core difference between Freud's and Adler's psychologies altogether. It is the subject matter of the selections of Chapter 2, which were written between 1910 and 1912. The controversy found its forum until February 1911 in the weekly meetings of the Vienna Psychoanalytic Society.

One way of formulating this core difference is to say, as we did at the outset, that Freud's was a physicalistic drive psychology, whereas Adler's was a humanistic value psychology. For Freud, sex or libido was the most important drive, whereas for Adler it was only one important drive among others, all drives being subordinated to man's evaluation and utilization of them for his purposes.

Adler saw man's dominant purpose or goal as the attempt to overcome inferiorities and difficulties, to be strong and powerful, and to be successful according to the individual's own unique definition of what represents success. At first this presented itself to Adler, as he saw it in his patients, as "wanting to be like a man," not a woman, to be "masculine," not "feminine." For this overriding desire Adler coined the term "masculine protest."

Both parts of this term require further explanation. "To protest" as used here is synonymous not only with "to object," as the term is usually used, but also with "to assert." And "masculine" has little to do with the physiological sex characteristics of the male. Rather it refers to the preferred status of the male over the female in the general culture, and

280

how the individual reacts to this. The culture has created entire syndromes of positive and negative traits for "masculine" and "feminine," respectively, and these have become particularly significant to the neurotic.

In a paper entitled "On the Masculine Attitude in Female Neurotics," Adler (1911c) stated in the opening paragraph: "I regard as the main motive force (*Motor*) in neurotic disease—the masculine protest against feminine or apparently feminine stirrings and sensations" (p. 74). Beginning with the second reprinting of this paper in 1924, Adler preceded this by the previously not translated paragraph on the inferiority-superiority dynamics.

"No person can simply tolerate the feeling of a real or apparent inferiority. Wherever we observe inferiority feelings we also find feelings of protest and vice versa. The *will* itself, insofar as it precedes actions . . . always moves in the direction from 'below' to 'above,' which of course at times becomes apparent only through a consideration of the context (*Zusammenhangsbetrachtung*)" (p. 74).

The following passages from Kant, which were introduced in the 1924 edition as preambles, were also not previously translated.

The craving to dominate (*Herrschsucht*) originates in the fear of being dominated by others and aims at gaining in good time the advantage of power over them.

When refined luxury has reached a certain level, a woman will turn out to be modest only by mistake and will not conceal wishing that she would rather be a man: Then she could give greater and more refined scope to her inclinations. But no man would want to be a woman.

—Kant, *Anthropologie*

Importance and Transitoriness of the Term

Importance. When Adler coined the term "masculine protest" it was rather well suited to focus on the main difference between himself and Freud. With Freud sex was the all-important biological phenomenon, represented by libido and its repression. With Adler sex appeared to be such an important factor in neurotics because of the culturally determined status difference between the sexes, with the resulting fear that one may not live up to one's sexual or gender role in the case of a man, and dissatisfaction with one's assigned sexual role in the case of a woman. "Behind what one sees as sexual, there are concealed far more important relationships that merely take on the guise of sexuality—that is, the masculine protest" (A1911i, p. 149).

Adler (A1910n) introduced the term before the Vienna Psychoanalytic Society with the words: "It is a question of what the neurotic understands by 'masculine' and 'feminine.' It turns out that by 'feminine' he understands almost anything that is bad, certainly anything inferior. . . . Everything that is active is regarded as being masculine, everything passive as feminine" (p. 425). "The effort to get rid of these 'feminine' traits is experienced as 'masculine.' . . . In neurotics, the *masculine protest,* this protest of masculinity, can always be shown to be present" (p. 426).

The term is then a metaphor for human value striving in neurosis. Adler (A1911h) designated it as "the *primum movens*" (p. 111) of what he had a few years earlier described as the "aggression drive" (A1908b), by which he had meant not only hostility, but also an inertia-initiative continuum, as aggression was later understood by George Kelly (1955, pp. 508–10; 1963, p. 143), although Adler did not explicitly make this point.

When Adler introduced the masculine protest he thereby replaced the aggression drive, giving, as we read in Chapter 2, the following important explanation: "The conception of the aggression drive . . . suffered from the defect of being a biological one and not suitable to a complete understanding of neurotic phenomena. To this end, one must consider a conception of the neurotic . . . that does not admit of definition in biological terms, but only in psychological terms, or in terms of cultural psychology."

Transitoriness. At first Adler likened "masculine protest" to Nietzsche's "will to power," considering his own concept actually more inclusive. But the term is not really suited to such a broad meaning. The phenomenon is possible only in a social order of male dominance. As Valentine Adler (1925), Adler's daughter, pointed out: "With the destruction of male dominance, the male-female power problem disappears and with it its dialectical transformation, the 'masculine protest'" (p. 307). Thus over the years Adler (A1928k) limited masculine protest to "a frequent special case" of the general "upward striving, the will to power . . . a form of the striving for superiority" (p. 28). About this striving Adler (A1956b) then wrote: "All our functions follow its direction. They strive for conquest, security, increase, either in the right or in the wrong direction. The impetus from minus to plus never ends. The urge from below to above never ceases. Whatever premises all our philosophers and psychologists dream of—self-preservation, pleasure principle, equalization—all these are but vague representations, attempts to express the great upward drive" (p. 103).

The "frequent special case" to which Adler (A1933b) limited masculine protest was the "attitude on the part of woman, of protest against her sexual role, . . . a superiority complex based on the inferiority complex—only a girl" (p. 64). Yet the term remains strongly connected with Adler's intellectual development and some of his most important conceptions.

Adler did not always announce changes in his theory and terminology. Sometimes he even expressed himself as if his earlier views had never existed. The following extreme example of this tendency refers to the masculine protest. Accusing his critics of quite misunderstanding him and doing him injustice, he writes in a selection from Chapter 7, "There are still some writers who, in order quickly to dispose of Individual Psychology, see in the 'masculine protest' the beginning and end of our views. They do not understand that the 'masculine protest' represents only one, although an important, concretization of the formal striving for superiority." In all fairness, Adler could have faulted his critics only for not having kept up with his development since 1911 which included his quiet limitation of the meaning and usage of the term masculine protest, and introduction of additional terms.

"Will to Power" and Its Misunderstandings

The introduction of Nietzsche's "will to power" by Adler in connection with masculine protest immediately led to the misunderstanding—which still exists—that Adler believed that a striving for power over others was the general human dynamic and that he actually advocated such striving. Yet Adler saw such striving for power only in the neurotic and strongly opposed it in favor of co-operation. [Incidentally, according to Walter Kaufmann (1974), for Nietzsche also the will to power "is essentially a striving to transcend and perfect oneself" (p. 248), rather than to dominate over others.]

Adler deplored (A1928m) that "today we have constructed our guiding ideal still too little in accordance with social interest and too much in accordance with personal power. . . . The striving for personal power is a disastrous delusion and poisons man's living together. Whoever desires the human community must renounce the striving for power over others" (pp. 168–69).

Adler made repeated efforts to correct the misunderstanding about his use of "will to power." In the Introduction to the second edition of *The Neurotic Constitution,* seven years after the first, he saw the necessity to counteract "meaningless talk": "The serious reader will, I hope . . . with me . . . regard each human psyche in a self-consistent progression toward a goal of perfection, so that movements, character traits, and symptoms point invariably beyond themselves. These insights will burden him with a life task: to show the way in the reduction of the striving for personal power and in the education toward the community" (A1928k, p. iv).

Three years later, in the Introduction to the third edition, Adler once more asserted: "The views of Individual Psychology demand the unconditional reduction of the striving for

284

power and the development of social interest. The watchword of Individual Psychology is the fellow man and the fellow-man attitude toward the immanent demands of human society" (A1928k, p. vi).

Ten years later we read: "Regarding the striving for power, we find the misunderstanding that Individual Psychology not only regards psychological life as the striving for power, but propagates this idea. This striving for power is not our madness, it is what we find in others" (A1956b, p. 113). "The striving of each actively moving individual is toward overcoming, not toward power. . . . Striving for power —better, for personal power—represents only one of a thousand types, all of which seek perfection, a security-giving plus situation" (A1956b, p. 114).

The development of the concept of power in Adlerian theory has been traced by Kurt Adler (1972).

Psychological Hermaphroditism

Adler (A1910c) introduced the term "masculine protest" in a paper on "psychological hermaphroditism" (see Chapter 2), which thereupon became his most important paper.

Hermaphroditism meant the presence in each individual of biological components of the other sex, in various proportions, and was equated with bisexuality. Psychological hermaphroditism meant a corresponding presence in an individual of character traits of the other sex, depending on his sexual constitution.

Parenthetically, we should like to point out that both "hermaphroditism" and "bisexuality" have today acquired different meanings. Hermaphroditism means "a congenital condition of ambiguity of the reproductive structures so that the sex of the individual is not clearly defined as exclusively male or exclusively female" (Money and Ehrhardt, 1965, p. 285), while bisexuality means to engage in homosexual as well as heterosexual relationships.

Adler removed psychological hermaphroditism from any

285

direct dependence on biological factors. In contrast to Freud (1905), he held that such factors are at best only indirectly connected, and that individuals of either sex have the capacity to be more "masculine" or more "feminine" depending on which they prefer and best serves their purposes. In this view it becomes important that we live in a male-dominated culture that has created more favorable conditions and stereotypes for the male than for the female. Thus members of either sex may prefer to be "like a man" rather than "like a woman." This is the masculine protest, which in a mild form is quite widespread, while in the extreme is neurotic.

When Adler (A1910n) introduced these thoughts before the Vienna Psychoanalytic Society he believed that he was "touching upon the most delicate point in the area of psychoanalytic investigation" (p. 428), and he was right. They were exactly what led to the break with Freud, and the paper by Adler (A1910c) on this topic became the one most often referred to by Freud in his controversy with Adler.

Social Origin of the Term "Masculine Protest"

Adler considered his Individual Psychology in a sense a social psychology (A1956b, p. 157). This relationship is actually so close that he adopted the term "masculine protest" to the dynamics of the individual directly from the social scene and the woman's movement.

Adler (A1911h) explicitly stated: "The valuation of masculine and feminine in neurosis is only a crystallization of the valuation that has also existed all along in our culture and that began at the start of civilization" (p. 109). In a female patient, *"The entire armory of woman's social battle for emancipation will be found again only distorted, altered into something senseless—that is, childish and worthless*. It is an individual battle, so to speak, a private enterprise against male prerogatives. But as an analogy, as precursor, often also as companion of the great surging social battle for equal rights for women, it shows that it originates on the way from inferiority to compensation, from the tendency to be *like a man*" (A1911c, pp. 86–87, author's italics).

Adler (A1911i) also established a connection between masculine protest and ideas of evolution (struggle for existence). In his paper before the Vienna Psychoanalytic Society at its historic meeting of February 1, 1911, he said in the Introduction (included only in the *Minutes* and not in the published full account): "The problem of the origins of protest tendencies in man and woman, and whether they exist, can be answered by referring to the development of human culture and society. It shows that these driving forces have in fact always been alive and active. The fact, among other things, that all of us have become familiar with, the idea of the struggle for existence, is evidence of this. In a similar manner, another point—that woman is devalued by man—is clearly expressed in our culture; indeed, it can even be regarded as being a driving force in our civilization. All that is needed here is to refer to the literary endeavors of the so-called antifeminists" (p. 141).

Two years before he had coined the term "masculine protest," Adler already observed: "Women are only just beginning to lead their own independent lives, apart from their family, and to develop their characters; these tendencies may constitute a certain barrier to complete merging in intercourse. This circumstance may be the reason for the particularly high incidence of [sexual] anesthesia [frigidity], in our time" (Nunberg and Federn, 1962, p. 307). Adler gave an estimate of 70 per cent of women being frigid.

In Chapter 4 we find: "The urge to change [woman's present condition] brings about all ideals of . . . emancipation, and degenerates in personal life into a hundred forms of the 'masculine protest.'" But, Adler warns, the social struggle for woman's equality must not enter her personal relations. Woman's disadvantaged position is a cultural mistake. "It cannot be overcome by a personal revolt. Especially in marriage itself, a personal revolt would disturb the social relationship and the interest of the partner. The mistake can only be overcome by recognizing and changing the whole attitude of our culture."

In the light of all this, the question whether the woman's movement is to be understood as an extension of the masculine protest is to be answered with a definite "No." Rather the masculine protest is a miscarriage from the woman's movement into an individual woman's private life—on the generally useless side of life.

Two Examples of Masculine Protest

In this connection Adler (A1911c, p. 87) refers to Helena Racowitza (1845–1911), whose memoirs had recently been published. Her name was probably meaningful enough for Adler's readers then. But today we are perhaps justified to present her case briefly.

Helena Racowitza was the daughter of a Prussian nobleman, von Dönniges, professor of political science in Berlin, later a diplomat in the service of the King of Bavaria. As a rebellious young girl Helena succeeded through considerable perseverance in having an affair with the brilliant socialist leader Ferdinand Lassalle, twenty years her elder. This led to a duel in which Lassalle died at the hand of a second suitor, the wealthy Romanian nobleman Yanko Racowitza. Helena married the victor "for reasons she could certainly never explain to her friends. . . . She was touched, she said, by his tender devotion, his loyalty and chivalry, in refusing to accept the world's view of her relations with Lassalle" (Bonsal, 1911). A few months later, Yanko died of consumption. Helena then went on the stage, wrote several novels, married twice more, and lived altogether an adventurous life, which she ended by suicide. The affair with Lassalle was so sensational that "about one hundred volumes, including two by the heroine" (Bonsal, 1911) were written on the subject.

In her memoirs, Racowitza (1910) writes of "equality of the sexes" (p. 29) and may give the impression of standing for the emancipation of women. But soon a wanting to be "like a man" becomes apparent. As a twelve-year-old she suggested to a newlywed friend who complained about the

288

sexual escapades of her husband, "Why don't you do the same?" (p. 29), and she remembered distinctly that on this day "the foundation was laid to all my future life" (p. 28). The following passage shows that she was indeed fighting an "individual battle" for personal triumphs and humiliation of the opponent. "I always demanded and obtained from my admirers unequivocal recognition of the superior qualities of their favored rivals. In Yanko's case, when he at first refused to study Lassalle's works with me, I said, 'You must. You owe it to yourself. You ought to know how great is the intellect of the man I prefer to you, for when you recognize the superiority of his mind your pride will no longer suffer'" (p. 79). One sees her lack of compassion, her desire for "childish and worthless" triumphs, her lust to dominate and humiliate.

Adler (A1912a, p. 176) mentioned these memoirs once more, this time together with those of Marie Bashkirtseva (1889), as "mostly refined descriptions of all these attempts of masculine protest" (p. 176). By birth a Russian noblewoman, Bashkirtseva (1860–84) was a brilliant girl with many-sided gifts who by the age of twenty had become a naturalistic painter of some renown in Paris. She died of tuberculosis at the age of twenty-four. Her memoirs show her original great ambition to make something of her talents, and become very moving reading as she faces death. But her case does not seem quite so striking.

Social, Psychological, and Philosophical Origins of Other Concepts

The derivation of "masculine protest" from the social scene was only one aspect of Adler's general position of regarding psychology as a social and cultural science—not primarily a biological science in the mechanistic sense—regardless of his *Study of Organ Inferiority and Its Psychical Compensation* (A1907a). Ironically, Freud held against him exactly: "Instead of psychology, Adler's doctrine presents, in large part, biology" (A1911i, p. 147). Or, earlier, "Adler

289

subjects the psychological material too soon to biological points of view" (Nunberg and Federn, 1967, p. 432).

Adler (A1956b, p. 92) objected to Freud's use of metaphors from physics and mechanics. Since man is not a machine, such metaphors cannot do justice to the subject matter. Instead, Adler borrowed his terms and metaphors from social life and the social sciences. The group is composed of individuals; therefore, what becomes apparent there should also be valid for the individual. The following are some of Adler's concepts that can be traced to social scientists.

Subjective evaluation of objective facts. When Adler (A1920a) stated, "More important than disposition, objective experience, and environment is the subjective evaluation of these. Furthermore, this evaluation stands in a certain, often strange, relation to reality" (p. 4); he compared this to the concept of the "ideological superstructure over the economic foundation" of Marx and Engels. However, in mass psychology the facts created by the ideological superstructure "enforce a leveling of the individual differences" (p. 4). These passages referring to Marx and Engels are, incidentally, not included in the English edition of *Practice and Theory of Individual Psychology.*

Creative power of the individual. The subjective evaluation that is to a considerable extent free from the objective reality is attributed by Adler to the "creative power" (*schöpferische Kraft*) of the individual. This was Adler's answer to any absolute determinism. He credited Heymann Steinthal (1823–99), an early social psychologist, for having "presented the psyche as organic creative power" (A1920a, p. 85), only that Steinthal used *Gestaltungskraft,* a synonym for *schöpferische Kraft.*

Oversensitivity. Oversensitivity (*Ueberempfindlichkeit*) is important in Adler's description of the neurotic disposition. The patient with increased inferiority feelings easily "considers himself neglected, hurt, small, or besmudged" (A1956b, p. 290). Adler credits Karl Lamprecht (1856–1915), cultural historian, for having observed such sensitivity (*Reizsamkeit*) in the psychology of nations (*Völkerpsychologie*).

Life style. This term, which became so prominent in

Adler's later writings—that is, after 1926—was most likely indirectly suggested to him by Max Weber (1864–1920), German sociologist and politician. Weber meant by this term the life style of a group or subculture. Thus when Adler introduced the term, he specified it at first as "individual life style" (see Ansbacher, 1967). Continuing the parallel between culture and individual, Powers (1973) has shown that as myths provide a key to the understanding of a culture or group life style, so an individual's early recollections provide a key to the understanding of his individual life style.

Symptoms as safeguards of self-esteem. With regard to his insight that laziness, for example, and really all inhibiting neurotic symptoms can be understood as devices by the patient to safeguard his self-esteem, Adler (A1920a) refers to German historian Barthold G. Niebuhr (1776–1831). He quotes from Niebuhr's *Roman History,* Vol. 3: "National vanity, like the personal variety, is more ashamed of failure that betrays limitation of power, than of the greatest disgrace that follows from lazy and cowardly omission of any effort. By the former arrogant claims are destroyed, in case of the latter they continue" (p. 71). In Adler's (A1956b) own terms this becomes: "Lazy children are like tight-rope walkers with a net underneath the rope; when they fall, they fall softly. It is less painful to be told that one is lazy than that one is incapable. . . . Laziness serves as a screen to hide the child's lack of faith in himself, prohibiting him from making attempts to cope with the problems confronting him" (p. 391).

Various concepts. As a social psychologist, Adler was also a philosophical psychologist, philosophy being a part of the humanities in contrast to the natural sciences, and he gladly acknowledged his debt to philosophers. (This again is in contrast to Freud who, for example, denied any knowledge of Nietzsche when certain similarities in thinking were pointed out to him [Nunberg and Federn, 1962, pp. 359–60].) Adler took *"Everything depends on one's opinion . . ."*—the motto for his first major book (A1912a)—from the leading Stoic philosopher Seneca. "Will to power" was, of course, borrowed from Nietzsche. The concept of *purposive adaptation* was strengthened in Adler, and the value of *fictions* in this process was suggested to him by the work of German pragmatist philosopher Vaihinger (1911b), who became particularly significant for Adler. *Early recollections* as a diagnostic tool was clarified for Adler by French pragmatist Bergson (Ansbacher, 1973). For the concept of a unified *life plan*, which for many years preceded the concept of life style, Adler acknowledged partial accord with the important teachings of Steinthal, Vaihinger, and Bergson (A1913h; in the later printings Steinthal is omitted). *Common sense* vs. *private intelligence* as descriptive of mental health vs. mental disorder was most likely accepted by Adler from Kant (Ansbacher, 1965). Adler's understanding of the three main conditions of our lives (on this earth, in social interaction, and in sexual dimorphism) as *life tasks* (*Aufgaben*) is in accord with the neo-Kantian Hermann Cohen, who considered that in man everything that is *gegeben* ("given") is really *aufgegeben* ("propounded") like a riddle or a task (Vleeschauwer, 1974). Finally, Adler's concept of *social interest* or social feeling (*Gemeinschaftsgefühl*) had its forerunner in John Stuart Mill's "fellow feeling" and "social feelings of mankind, the desire to be in unity with our fellow creatures" (Ansbacher, 1968, p. 140).

Beyond belonging to the social sciences, Adler's sources share a common ground from which Ellenberger (1970) concluded quite correctly: "Adler definitely belongs to the philosophy of the Enlightenment, with his emphasis that man is a rational and a social being, endowed with free will and the ability to make conscious decisions" (p. 629).

Dialectical Dynamics

As stated above, Adler replaced the concept of "aggression drive" with that of "masculine protest," because he wanted a conception that would not be expressed in biological terms "but only in psychological terms, or in terms of cultural psychology." We may add that he wanted to express himself not in terms of a mechanistic natural science, but in social science terms. Drive is a mechanistic concept; machines neither protest nor strive.

Bipolar conception. Typical for a mechanistic concept, a "drive" is *unipolar*—that is, it is simply a force that is applied, and nothing else. It is a *demonstrative,* positivistic conception. On the other hand, a "protest" is a solemn declaration of opinion, usually of dissent or objection, although it may also be an assertion. "Opinion" implies that different views regarding the same subject matter are possible about which one may dispute. Thus "protest" is a *dialectical* conception and is also *bipolar,* as we shall see. Rychlak (1968) has shown in detail that these two conceptions represent two philosophies of science and that "Dialectical terminology presents us with the *most accurate* picture of the fundamental condition" (p. 255).

A dialectical conception is bipolar in that it includes a thesis and an antithesis. But it includes also a third, uniting factor, namely the common point of reference of the first two, or how their antagonism may be resolved, the synthesis. When Adler (A1910c) introduced the concept of "masculine protest," he specified these three factors as follows: "(A) Traits evaluated as feminine. (B) Hypertrophied masculine protest. (C) Compromise formation between A and B." While Adler soon gave up the terms "feminine," "masculine," and "masculine protest" for his dialectical dynamic conception, he retained its structure and meaning.

Point A was in turn designated as inferiority feelings, normal or intensified; feelings of insecurity, weakness, or being "below"; or a felt "minus position."

Point B received the largest number of successive names: wanting to be a real man, wanting power, or wanting to attain a goal of power, superiority, success, perfection, completion, a "plus situation."

Point C became the movement, the striving toward these goals, a continuous overcoming of difficulties, compensation, or, in mental disorder, a construction of additional difficulties (the symptoms) as excuses for not reaching one's goals out of fear of failure, while still saving a vestige of one's self-esteem.

In the same year, although not so precisely, Adler (A1910f) expressed the dialectical structure in terms of (a) inferiority feelings, (b) psychological compensation tendencies, and (c) corresponding behavior and attitudes. The passage in question reads: "A basic psychological law is the dialectical reversal of organ inferiority via a subjective inferiority feeling into psychological tendencies of compensation and overcompensation. However, this is not a natural law, but a general, plausible seduction of the human mind. The behavior and attitudes of the child who is thus neurotically disposed show clearly the traces of this dialectical reversal, very early in childhood" (p. 54).

The dialectical dynamic is described by Adler (A1929d) particularly well in the following, where it is also tied in with the concepts of the past and the future. "The future is tied up with our striving and with our goal, while the past represents the state of inferiority or inadequacy that we are trying to overcome. This is why . . . we should not be astonished if in the cases where we see an inferiority complex we find a superiority complex more or less hidden. On the other hand, if we inquire into a superiority complex . . . we can always find a more or less hidden inferiority complex. . . . If we look at things this way, it takes away the apparent paradox of two contradictory tendencies . . . existing in the same individual. For it is obvious that as normal sentiments the striving for superiority and the feeling of inferiority are naturally complementary. We should not strive to be superior and to succeed if we did not feel a certain lack in our present condition. . . . The striving for superiority never ceases. It constitutes in fact the mind, the psyche of the individual" (pp. 27–28).

Acknowledgment of Hegel and Nietzsche. As Adler formed dialectical, bipolar conceptions, he also acknowledged Hegel (1770–1831), dialectician and teacher of Marx. When in 1907 he addressed the Philosophical Society at the University of Vienna on organ inferiority and compensation, and explained Freud's concept of repression as a restraint on "unsuitable or immature methods of overcompensation," Adler (A1908e) pointed out: "The fact that in this process [of overcompensation] a character trait, drive, wish, or concept may fall into its opposite—that is, may express itself by its antithesis—is a special case reminding one to some extent of Hegelian dialectics" (p. 31). In 1909 Adler credited Hegel with having "enabled the idea of evolution to make a breakthrough in philosophy" by placing "in the foreground of his philosophy his conception of dialectics—that is, the transformation of one thing into its opposite, of the thesis into the antithesis—matters that occupy us continuously" (Nunberg and Federn, 1967, pp. 333–34). The following year, 1910, Adler introduced his concept of masculine protest—a dialectical construction, as we have seen.

As to "the idea of evolution," Hegel had asserted that "it is possible for something to both be and not be when it is in the process of 'becoming'" (Rychlak, 1968, pp. 286–87). The "becoming" was one of the great concerns of Adler, from the beginning and throughout his life. Thus he quoted on the final page of *The Neurotic Constitution* from the minor German philosopher Rudolph Hildebrand (1824–94): "Through the great *being* that surrounds and deeply penetrates us, there extends a great *becoming* that strives toward the perfect *being*" (A1917a, p. 445; see also Ansbacher, 1962a).

At the time of his first acknowledgment of Hegel—that is, in 1908—Adler expressed also great admiration for Nietzsche (1844–1900). "Among all great philosophers . . . Nietzsche is closest to our way of thinking. . . . In Nietzsche's work, one finds almost on every page observations reminiscent of those we make in therapy" (Nunberg and Federn, 1962, p. 358). This affinity also rested largely on dialectics. According to Walter Kaufmann (1974, p. 84), Nietzsche was more consistently dialectical even than Hegel. Thus Adler could easily make the transition from the masculine protest to Nietzsche's "will to power." " 'I want to be a real man' is the guiding fiction in every neurosis, for which it claims greater reality value than the normal psyche. . . . Nietzsche's 'will to power' . . . includes much of our conception." That "will to power" did not mean essentially power over others but wanting to be strong, able to overcome obstacles, including one's own weaknesses, was discussed earlier.

Teleological principle. Important for both Nietzsche and Adler is the teleological principle—that is, not to look for causes of behavior in the past but for goals in the future. Nietzsche (1884) phrased this principle as "Not whence you come shall henceforth constitute your honor, but whither you are going! . . . Your nobility should not look backward but ahead!" (pp. 315–16). Nietzsche's influence may be seen in Adler's (A1956b) parallel phrase: "The most important question of the healthy and the diseased mental life is not Whence? but Whither? . . . In this whither? the cause is contained" (p. 91).

Questioning attitude. Kaufmann (1974) judged Nietzsche to be "more consistently 'dialectical' " than Hegel, because Nietzsche "was . . . a far more rigorous questioner. . . . All assumptions had to be questioned" (p. 84). This is illustrated by the quotation from Nietzsche, "I am not bigoted enough for a system—and not even for my system" (p. 80). The same questioning attitude is reflected in Adler's (A1956b) statements: "We regard man as if nothing in his life were causally determined and as if every phenomenon could have been different" (p. 91), and "General rules—even those laid down by Individual Psychology, of my own creation—should be regarded as nothing more than an aid to a preliminary illumination of the field of view in which the single individual can be found—or missed" (p. 194). And finally, "Don't blindly believe any 'authority'—not even me!" (A1930e, p. 172).

With all these methodological similarities it is important to recognize that in matters of substance Adler was essentially on the opposite pole from Nietzsche. This is best reflected in their respective model of the ideal man—for Nietzsche it was an elitist "superman"; for Adler, a democratic "fellow man."

Objective reality or thought process?—Vaihinger. Regarding the dialectical method, a main issue is: Do the objective events in the physical world follow the principle of dialectics, or do only our thought processes operate in this manner?

Hegel represented the first position. As Thilly and Wood (1957) formulated it, for Hegel "the dialectical evolution of

296

the concepts in the mind of the philosopher coincides with the objective evolution of the world; the categories of subjective thought are likewise categories of the universe; thought and being are identical" (p. 480). This of course reflects Hegel's idealism. But interestingly, especially the last phrase, "thought and being are identical," can, in reverse order, also be cited as an assertion of pure materialism.

The second alternative, that only our thought processes operate dialectically, is accepted by Nietzsche; most forcefully by Vaihinger, in whom Adler found strong support; and by Adler.

Nietzsche, according to Kaufmann (1974), did not believe "that reality is self-contradictory. Only unqualified judgments about reality involve us in superficial inconsistencies" (p. 80). Thus Nietzsche can be regarded as a "dialectical monist" (p. 235). "The metaphysics of the will to power is a dialectical monism in which the basic force is conceived as essentially creative" (p. 241).

Hans Vaihinger (1852–1933), German pragmatist, is known for his theory of fictions, his philosophy of "as if." Vaihinger's (1911b) basic assumption is that thinking is an activity for the purpose of solving problems in the real world, and that it is well suited for this purpose, while at the same time it differs from the objective processes. "The ways of thought are different from those of reality. . . . The greatest and most important human errors originate through thought processes being taken for copies of reality itself" (p. 8). Vaihinger singles out Hegel for having committed this mistake. "The Hegelian system offers historically the most glaring and typical example of this general error of philosophy: the confusion of thought processes with events, the conversion of subjective thought events into objective world-events. (That the Hegelian dialectic is, however, based on a correct insight into the nature of logical development, we shall have occasion to remark later)" (p. 8).

Vaihinger indicts Hegel for "abuse of abstractions" (p. 204), a phrase that Adler adopted. "Abstractions are a necessary aid to thought and meet a practical need, but they furnish no theoretical knowledge, twist and turn, define and differentiate them as we may. We confuse fact and fiction, means and ends, if we attempt to deduce anything from such linguistic aids" (p. 205). Vaihinger (1911a) holds that Hegel placed the contradictions that he had found in his abstractions "erroneously . . . into reality, after having made the very abstractions into realities first. It is the abuse of the abstractions that creates the disturbances through 'the most grotesque contradictions'" (p. 395).

Adler's general dialectical approach. Adler's dialectical conception extended into the various aspects of his theory and its applications, making it a remarkably integrated and self-consistent system. We shall have occasion to refer to Adler's dialectics in connection with his views on human creativity and self-determination, understanding of marital conflicts, methods of problem-solving and conflict resolution in general, theory of neurosis, understanding of symptoms, and techniques of psychotherapy. At the same time, Adler firmly adhered to the demonstrative unity and spontaneity of the organism rejecting the assumption of objectively, firmly established categories, dichotomies, and contradictions. Thus it seems well warranted to describe Adler's approach philosophically as one of "dialectical monism," the term applied by Kaufmann (1968, p. 241) to Nietzsche.

A survey of Adler's "use of the dialectic" has been published by Robert Dolliver (1974). It is quite good, except for Dolliver's understanding of Adler's development, with which we disagree.

Joseph F. Rychlak (1968), who brought the importance of the dialectical tradition to the attention of contemporary American psychology, quotes as the hallmark of the dialectical approach the Talmudic metaphor, "Every stick has two ends" (p. 328). This metaphor is indeed appropriate for the general approach of Adler, the practitioner, and for present-day Adlerian psychologists. In fact, there is a small paper entitled "Every Stick Has Two Ends" by William Beecher (1946), a no-nonsense Adlerian and pungent writer. The paper is about a boy who after a serious illness had become increasingly dependent on his parents, so that they had actually become his slaves. Beecher reports this case as a re-

298

minder that "Too often we may grasp the wrong end of the stick. We forget that the 'weak' individual is the one who is in the stronger position. It is useless to ask him to give up such a favorable spot—as long as his 'slaves' remain willing or intimidated into his service" (p. 85).

But Rychlak (1968) apparently believes that dialectics is completely associated with dualism. He does not appreciate that one can well be a monist, in the demonstrative tradition, as far as objective reality is concerned, and at the same time a dialectician as far as the subjectivity of human psychological processes is concerned—that is, a dialectical monist. Thus Rychlak (1973) quite erroneously concludes that at heart Adler was as distrustful as Freud of dialectics, "and after he left the Freudian camp he positively opposed any oppositional type of theoretical formulation" (p. 209). Dolliver (1974) sees Adler's development the same way and even ventures the daring explanation "that Adler tried to eradicate the influence of the dialectic from his theorizing because of its association to Freud" (p. 20). It is true that Adler continued perfecting his holistic model of human structure, removing all remnants of dualism. In fact, he declared any theory that accepts dichotomies in a positivistic sense to be unscientific (p. 54). But as far as human subjective functioning is concerned, we hope this essay will furnish ample evidence that a dialectical conception is central in Adler's theory of apperception and cognition, and in his practice of reconstructing these functions.

Freud, Dialectician in Spite of Himself

Freud was strongly opposed to dialectics. To refer to Rychlak (1968) again: "Freud would never have accepted the label of dialectician. Indeed, he would have been riled by the suggestion, for he equated dialectic with sophistry" (p. 323). Although Freud established numerous antithetical concepts such as ego vs. sex instincts, ego vs. id, eros vs. thanatos, conscious vs. unconscious, etc., these were not to be understood dialectically, as two poles of one, more comprehensive reality.

Rather Freud conceived of these as dualisms representing independent conflicting forces, which he virtually reified. He made this particularly clear in a discussion of his concept of ambivalence. Freud (1917b) saw this in melancholia, for example, as "countless single conflicts in which love and hate wrestle together" (p. 168). And, as if to underline this distinctness, Freud (1915) stated that "love and hate . . . did not originate in a cleavage of any common primal element, but sprang from different sources and underwent each its own development" (p. 81).

Another example for Freud's stanch nondialectic yet dualistic position refers to his dream interpretation. Freud (1900) had found in dreams "a particular preference for combining contraries into a unity or for representing them as one and the same thing." Dreams are also likely "to represent any element by its wishful contrary" (p. 318). This would seem a quite obvious instance of human dialectical functioning. Not for Freud. As Freud (1910) commented ten years later, this was "a statement about one of the findings of my analytic work that I did not then understand" (p. 155). The occasion for this comment was that he believed to have reached at that time such an understanding from having read a paper by the philologist Karl Abel on "the antithetical meaning of primal words." Abel elaborated in this paper on the observation that in ancient languages "there are a fair number of words with two meanings, one of which is the exact opposite of the other" (p. 156). The understanding that Freud reached from this was, consistent with his position, "a confirmation of the view we have formed about the regressive, archaic character of the expression of thoughts in dreams. And . . . we should be better at understanding and translating the language of dreams if we knew more about the development of language" (p. 161). Freud did not infer to any kind of dialectics, nor generalize that dream language could be related to human psychological functioning at large. By limiting his understanding to language as such, Freud could leave his conception intact that opposites in dream content, apart from the language used, are traceable to distinct oppositional forces.

300

In the sense that Freud always looked for two theoretically demonstrative opposing forces, he certainly can be called a "dualist." Jones (1955) comments on this point, "Most students of Freud have been struck by what has been called his obstinate dualism; had he been a philosopher he certainly would not have been a monist nor would he have felt at home in William James's pluralistic universe" (p. 422). We would call Freud a positivistic, demonstrative dualist. In contrast to the dialectic metaphor "Every stick has two ends," appropriate for Adler, an appropriate metaphor for Freud's conception of two opposing forces would be the gas pedal vs. the brake pedal on a car, and their respective functions.

And yet, since the human mind does function dialectically, Freud had to do justice to this phenomenon somehow, in spite of his contrary "knowledge." This was recognized by Adler. While he noted that Freud's "way of observing lent itself to reification and freezing of the psyche which, in reality, is constantly at work and mindful of the future," and that Freud's "acceptance of the concept of complex was a further step toward priority of the topological over the dynamic view," Adler acknowledged that Freud did not carry his mechanistic approach "so far that the principle of energetics, the *panta rhei* [everything is in flux], could not have been brought in as an afterthought." Adler's reference to Heraclitus' notion of *panta rhei* implies dialectics. According to Klaus Riegel (1976), "Dialectical psychology is committed to the study of actions and changes. Therefore, both Hegel and Marx have sought their roots in Heraclitus' notion of 'ceaseless flux' rather than in the static abstractions of Eleatic being" (p. 696). The method by which Freud unadmittedly brought dialectics in through a back door so-to-speak was, as Adler stated it, by investing "with unsurpassable grace each of his instincts with human traits" (p. 126). Rychlak (1968) concurs, using almost the same metaphor, when he writes: "Freud made his energies behave dialectically. . . . As is well known, the libido's versatility is limited only by Freud's genius in making it do his theoretical bidding" (p. 314).

The Neurotic's Antithetical Mode of Apperception

The comments in this section refer essentially to Chapter 2. Adler held with Vaihinger that the dialectical, antithetical mode, based as it is on abstractions, applies only to thought processes—that is, to processes dealing with reality, but not to processes of reality itself. In the objective world there are no definite categories, antitheses, and dichotomies, only continua and distributions according to the normal bell-shaped curve. As Kurt Lewin (1935) stated, in a good scientific theory "the places of dichotomies and conceptual antitheses are taken by more and more fluid transitions, by gradations that deprive the dichotomies of their antithetical character, and represent in logical form a transition stage between the class concept and the series concept" (p. 10).

This applies also to psychological processes, when *objectively* approached. Said Adler (A1931b), "People often believe that left and right . . . man and woman, hot and cold, light and heavy, strong and weak are contradictions. From a scientific standpoint they are not contradictions, but varieties. . . . In the same way, good and bad, normal and abnormal are not contradictions but varieties. Any theory that treats sleep and waking, dream thoughts and day thoughts as contradictions is bound to be unscientific" (pp. 95–96). Likewise, consciousness and unconsciousness, remembering and forgetting, truth and imagination are objectively not "two antagonistic halves of an individual's existence" (A1956b, p. 233).

Yet abstractions, categories, dichotomies, and antitheses—all included in Vaihinger's term of fiction—are very useful devices for coping with the real world. Man is continuously forced to make decisions—that is, to choose among alternatives. To facilitate the decision-making process it is convenient to maximize existing differences, to dichotomize, to create opposites.

Reification of fiction. Adler developed this thought further. The normal person generally quite unknowingly uses these abstractions as working hypotheses, as useful fictions in "casting up the accounts of life," and discards them when they no longer serve their purpose. With the neurotic, due to his greater insecurity, it is different. "The neurotically disposed individual has a sharply schematizing, strongly abstracting mode of apperception. Thus he groups inner as well as outer events according to a strictly antithetical schema, something like the debit and credit sides in bookkeeping, and admits no degrees in between."

Such understanding has much later become one of the components of the communication theory of schizophrenia of Bateson et al. (1956), which has become well known for its concept of "double bind." They observed that all human communication involves metaphors, but that "the schizophrenic uses *unlabeled* metaphors" (p. 205), thus giving them reality value. Bateson (1955) had noted that the patient fails "to recognize the metaphoric nature of his fantasies. . . . The phrase 'as if' is omitted, and the metaphor or fantasy is narrated and acted upon in a manner which would be appropriate if the fantasy were a message of the more direct kind" (p. 190). In therapy the patient "is driven to insert an 'as if' clause" (p. 192). "The schizophrenic's error is in treating the metaphors . . . with the full intensity of literal truth" (p. 192).

Primitive orientation. Adler pointed out that the reification of fiction is a primitive way of dealing with the world. "Primitive thought, mythology, legend, cosmogeny, theogeny, primitive art, psychotic productions, and the beginning of philosophy," all proceed in similar fashion. They all mistake for reality what is man's dialectical mode of dealing with reality.

Adler refers here to the categories of Aristotle and the Pythagorean table of opposites. While he merely mentions them, we thought it would be instructive to add a brief account of them.

Aristotle (384–322 B.C.) established ten categories that he considered to be "the most fundamental and universal predicates which can be affirmed of anything" (Thilly and Wood, 1957, p. 103). The categories are: substance, quality, quantity, relation, space, time, position, state, activity, and passivity. "The categories are not mere forms of thought or language, but are also predicates of reality" (p. 103). Aristotle believed they were "basic features of the real" (p. 103).

Pythagoras (c. 580–500 B.C.) left no writings, so that one speaks generally of his school, the Pythagoreans. They believed that "nature itself is a union of opposites" (p. 29), and they offered a table of ten such opposites: limited—unlimited; odd—even; one—many; right—left; male—female; rest—motion; straight—crooked; light—darkness; good—bad; square—rectangle.

It will be noted that the Pythagorean table includes male—female, which as masculine—feminine furnished the basis for Adler's dialectical dynamics. In the neurotic, all of life is oriented according to these opposites, which are at the same time correlated with numerous other opposites in accordance with the false valuations of the culture. Some of these opposites given by Adler (A1928k, p. 56; A1930p, p. 23), as correlated with masculine—feminine, are:

above — below	aggressive — inhibited
powerful — inferior	active — passive
personality ideal — inferiority feelings	competent — incompetent
	defiant — obedient
security — insecurity	brave — cowardly
victory — defeat	rich — poor
triumph — inferiority	cruel — tender

To assume erroneously that life actually corresponds to such constructions leads to "dichotomizing judgments" by which reality is artificially divided.

All-or-nothing attitude. One aspect of such dichotomizing judgment is what Adler (A1930a) called the all-or-nothing approach, expressing high, self-centered ambition. "People who live according to such an antithetic device have a formula that can be expressed by the maxim 'all or nothing.' Of course, it is impossible to realize such an ideal in this world. . . . There are a thousand and one gradations between these two extremes. This formula is to be found principally among those children who have a deep feeling of inferiority and who became inordinately ambitious as a compensation. There are several such characters in history—for example, Caesar, who was murdered by his friends when he sought for the crown" (pp. 145–46).

The all-or-nothing maxim is quite unreasonable. It corresponds to "a private intelligence contrary to common sense" (p. 146). Adler (A1928f) asserts, "We must make a sharp distinction between reason, which has general validity . . . and the isolated intelligence of the neurotic ('all or nothing' . . .)—in short, the intelligence of the failures with whom we are always occupied" (p. 46).

An example of this is seen in Philip Mairet's (1969) Adlerian interpretation of *Hamlet*. The first characteristic of Hamlet is his "all-or-nothing attitude," followed by his "goal of godlikeness," lack of social feeling, depreciation tendency, and pessimism. "Throughout the play we find Hamlet's mind falling back upon this kind of perfectionism combined with pessimism—it takes very varied forms. Hamlet is not satisfied with what merely approaches perfection; when it is not everything, he counts it as nothing . . . the all-or-nothing attitude" (p. 77). The famous statement of the problem, "To be or not to be," was a false antithesis. The real problem was rather to avenge a heinous crime, and Hamlet did not have to take it upon himself to be the avenger. As Mairet explains, "A Renaissance prince in his position . . . would be almost expected (by the political morale of the age) to mount a counterconspiracy—and do so successfully" (p. 73). "Hamlet's right course would be to confide in friends . . . and to gain their co-operation" (p. 80). But for this he was too self-centered and lacking in social feeling.

The Adler-Freud Controversy

The real issue poorly identified. At the time neither Freud nor Adler stated—nor were they probably capable of stating —the deeper issue that was at stake. It was a difference in their respective philosophies of science. Freud stood for a positivistic reductionism, a psychology as a physicalistic natural science. Adler stood for a value-oriented organismic humanism, a psychology as a social science.

Today this difference is far better understood by those in the know. For example, Arndt (1974) sees Freud within the Lockean tradition "that holds man to be inert and devoid of human nature," while Adler is within the Leibnitzian tradition "that assumes man to be an active, unified system endowed with uniquely human potentials" (pp. 463–74). Rychlak (1973) similarly finds that Freud "would have preferred to remain within the Lockean frame of reference," although in fact he worked with Kantian principles, while Adler openly "named Kant as the intellectual forebear" of important concepts in his theory (pp. 202–3). It is the difference between positivism, on the one hand, and "idealist positivism" or "positivistic idealism," on the other, to use the terms of Vaihinger (1911b, p. xli), who provided Adler's philosophical foundation. This philosophy is close to pragmatism, Adler's relationship to which was described in detail by Winetrout (1968).

At the time of the controversy, this difference in philosophy of science was at best only vaguely indicated. Most often the stated differences were limited to more or less surface matters, as they are still today by less-informed authors; for example, Freud's comments were at first that Adler's conceptions are "not psychoanalysis," "they are something else entirely" (Nunberg and Federn, 1974, p. 146), without specifying the difference. The first discussant of Adler's presentation in January 1911, Paul Federn, took a wider perspective when stating that Adler in part was "simply expressing himself from a different point of view" (p. 105).

Some of Freud's criticisms were from his viewpoint well taken. He accused Adler of "antisexual tendency" (p. 146), of presenting "instead of psychology of the unconscious . . . surface ego psychology," and of "a considerable overvaluation of the intellectual factor." Freud's most important objection was that "neurosis is seen from the standpoint of the ego . . . as it appears to the ego" (p. 147). Compared to Freud, Adler was indeed antisexual, although he only reduced sex from being the most important factor entering into all behavior to an important factor among others. He did develop an ego psychology, anticipating the turn that today large sectors of the psychoanalytic movement have taken. And he did emphasize the intellectual factor, as is done today by the cognitive psychologies.

Some other criticisms by Freud were quite strange. He thought Adler's "entire doctrine has a reactionary and retrogressive character" (p. 147). Actually, in general it was Freud who was the conservative (Ansbacher, 1959), and he was well aware of Adler's progressive, socialistic orientation. Freud also accused Adler of being "biological," as mentioned above. Finally, Freud called Adler's psychology a pessimistic, dreary look of life, bare of joy, whereas in fact subsequently Freud invented the death instinct and Adler assumed an innate aptitude of social feeling through which, when developed, a person could live in harmony with the conditions of his life and death.

Adler's more systematic statements regarding the controversy are of a much later date. In 1931 Adler (A1964a) wrote: "The Freudian view is that man, by nature bad, covers this unconsciousness badness through censorship merely to get along better in life. Individual Psychology, on the other hand, states that the development of man . . . is subject to the redeeming influence of social interest" (pp. 210–11). "Freud was wholly confined in a mechanistic conception" (p. 218n). "The main problem in psychology is not to comprehend the causal factors, as in physiology, but the direction-giving, pulling forces and goals that guide all other psychological movements. Thus Individual Psychology arrived at its finalistic conception" (p. 216).

Personal relationship. The relationship between Freud and Adler during the actual controversy was polite and correct. Adler (A1911b) paid considerable tribute to Freud, stating: "The ground for the examination of all these problems . . . was prepared for by Freud's work, which was what made it possible even to discuss them" (p. 104). Adler similarly acknowledged that the seed of his own views "is to be found in Freud's teachings" (p. 111). And finally, Adler is described in Nunberg and Federn (1974) as saying: "His writings have been perceived by Freud and some colleagues as constituting a provocation; but they would not have been possible if Freud had not been his teacher" (p. 174). Yet Adler never considered himself an exclusive disciple of Freud and strongly rejected any statement to the contrary (Ansbacher, 1962b). Adler (A1956b) did, however, admit in his late years: "I profited by Freud's mistakes" (p. 358).

Although Freud's criticisms were sharp and he predicted that "all these teachings of Adler's . . . will, at first, do great harm to psychoanalysis" (Nunberg and Federn, 1974, p. 147), he also paid his respects to Adler. He considered his teachings "not without importance" and the work of a "significant intellect with a great gift for presentation" (p. 147). And while Freud criticized Adler for having committed "scientific errors," he continued, "They are errors that do great credit to their creator. Even though one rejects the contents of Adler's views, one can nevertheless appreciate their consistency and their logic" (p. 172).

Off the record, Freud's tone was different. Around the same time he wrote to Jung, on January 22, 1911: "Recently Adler expressed the opinion that the motivation even of coitus was not exclusively sexual, but also included the individual's desire to *seem* masculine to himself. It's a nice little case of paranoia" (McGuire, 1974, 231F). And in a letter of March 14 of that year he wrote: "Adler represents the paranoic ego. . . . Adler's ego behaves as the ego always behaves, like the clown in the circus who keeps grimacing to assure the audience that he has planned everything that is going on. The poor fool!" (240F).

Freud retained this devastatingly hostile attitude to the very end. When Arnold Zweig wrote to Freud that he was deeply moved by the news of Adler's sudden death in Aberdeen in 1937, Freud gave the by now frequently quoted reply: "I don't understand your sympathy for Adler. For a Jew boy out of a Viennese suburb a death in Aberdeen is an unheard-of career in itself and a proof of how far he had got on. The world really rewarded him richly for his service in having contradicted psychoanalysis" (Jones, 1957, p. 208).

No corresponding off-the-record documents from Adler

exist, but those of us who knew him many years after the event can attest that he did not have kind words for Freud. Maslow (1962) recalled an unusual outburst of Adler on the question of his alleged "discipleship" under Freud, when Adler said "this was a lie and a swindle for which he blamed Freud entirely, whom he then called names like swindler, sly, schemer, as nearly as I can recall. . . . He had made it clear from the beginning that . . . he had his own opinions." Publicly Adler limited himself to carefully guarded statements about Freud. When after a lecture he once was asked for his opinion on certain Freudian theories, Adler (1936p) replied: "That is a very inconvenient question. Freud is this year celebrating his eightieth year. All the world is worshipping him, and I am not going to utter a word of criticism."

The Adler-Freud controversy has often been misstated as essentially a clash of personalities, implying that their scientific differences could have been reconciled. We do not believe this, but agree with Freud and Adler that their differences were unbridgeable, based as they were on different philosophies of science. And yet, had Freud and Adler been able to formulate their differences in such terms, they might have been able to part ways on more amicable terms.

Freud's Reaction

Of the critiques brought forth and new terms introduced by Adler, Freud reacted most strongly and lastingly to "masculine protest."

At first, when Adler introduced "masculine protest" in 1910 before the Vienna Psychoanalytic Society, Freud simply rejected it with the words: "The concepts of 'masculine' and 'feminine' are of no use in psychology and we do better . . . to employ the concepts of libido and repression. Whatever is of the libido has a masculine character, and whatever is repression is of a feminine character. . . . What Adler has described is a change of nomenclature through which we lose clarity" (Nunberg and Federn, 1967, pp. 432–33).

309

Freud's remark is at first somewhat puzzling, yet it directly hits the crucial difference. Libido-repression refers to a presumed basic unconscious *intrapsychic* conflict expressed in highly abstract terms, while masculine-feminine refers to an *interpersonal* transactional conflict expressed more concretely. When Freud then insists that this is merely a matter of semantics, he either did not realize the full significance of his cogent formulation or tried to deny it.

Castration fear and penis envy. But Freud did not let matters rest with this simple denial. Shortly after, he adapted the masculine protest to his own system by subsuming it under the castration complex—that is, castration fear and penis envy. He succeeded with this adaptation so well that he is today often considered the originator of masculine protest. Yet the issue around the masculine protest never came to rest with Freud. For him the masculine protest became quite justly the symbolization of the controversy with Adler and continued in focus throughout his life.

Freud (1911) introduced masculine protest in his well-known paper on the Schreber case in the following: "This feminine phantasy [of Schreber's] . . . was met at once by indignant repudiation—a true 'masculine protest,' to use Adler's expression, but in a sense different from his" (p. 426). What Freud meant by this "different sense" he expressed at a meeting of the Psychoanalytic Society the same year. "In . . . neurotics who set such great store by their masculinity, . . . one can almost always succeed in tracing the neuroses to the castration complex. . . . If the castration complex is taken into consideration, it will be possible to bring a number of Adler's propositions into harmony with our views" (Nunberg and Federn, 1974, p. 275).

A few years later, Freud (1918b) joined masculine protest and castration complex in his paper "The Taboo of Virginity." "Women go through an early phase in which they envy their brothers the token of maleness. . . . This 'penis envy' forms part of the castration complex. If 'masculine' is to include the connotation of 'wishing to be masculine,' the term 'masculine protest' fits this attitude; this term was coined

310

by Alfred Adler for the purpose of proclaiming this factor as the foundation of all neurosis in general" (pp. 230–31).

The clearest statement on the matter is found in one of Freud's last papers. Freud (1937) held: "We must not be misled by the term 'masculine protest' into supposing that what the man repudiates is the *attitude* of passivity, or, as we may say, the social aspect of femininity. . . . What they reject is not passivity in general but passivity in relation to *men*. That is to say, the 'masculine protest' is in fact nothing other than fear of castration" (p. 357n).

Adler's rebuttal to this argument was from the start: "The castration fear is to be taken symbolically: The patient establishes this fear . . . to secure himself against any kind of undertaking whatsoever. . . . The castration complex . . . serves as a safety measure" (Nunberg and Federn, 1974, pp. 277–78). In other words, it becomes an obsessive idea through which the individual excuses himself from attending to socially more important matters for which he feels unprepared.

Narcissism and ego ideal. His reductionistic reinterpretation of masculine protest notwithstanding, Freud tacitly acknowledged the deeper theoretical significance of Adler's concept by introducing three years later some concepts of his own serving similar functions.

The deeper significance of Adler's paper (Chapter 2, Section 1) was, as we have shown, the dialectical structure of masculine protest: (a) a present state of feminine traits, feeling inferior (thesis); (b) a goal in the future of masculine strength and superiority (antithesis); and (c) the striving and movement from (a) to (b). Whereas the end point of Freud's dynamics had been the attainment of an object to satisfy a drive, Adler's "goal" concept was an aspired future condition of the person himself, a self-ideal.

Such a concept involving a future projection of the individual was introduced by Freud (1914b) in his paper "On Narcissism." The concept was "ego ideal," which subsequently became the "super-ego." The editor of the *Standard Edition* of Freud's works, John Strachey, underlines the importance of this paper in his Introduction:

"The paper is among the most important of Freud's writings and may be regarded as one of the pivots in the evolution of his views. . . . It enters into the deeper problems of the relations between the ego and external objects, and it draws the new distinction between 'ego-libido' and 'object-libido.' Furthermore—most important of all, perhaps—it introduces the concepts of the 'ego ideal' . . . the basis of what was ultimately to be described as the 'super-ego' in *The Ego and the Id* (1923). . . . At two points . . . it trenches upon the controversies with Adler and Jung. . . . *One of Freud's motives . . . was, no doubt, to show that the concept of narcissism offers an alternative to Jung's nonsexual 'libido' and to Adler's 'masculine protest'"* (p. 70, italics added).

Summary and conclusion. Freud thought at first that Adler's "masculine protest," based on the masculine-feminine dialectics, could simply be reduced to his own main concepts at that time, "libido" and "repression." But it turned out that Freud had to develop his system further to provide an alternative for the social considerations introduced with the "masculine protest." This took over a decade, after which Freud introduced the concepts of id, ego, and super-ego, which appeared more vital than libido and repression. Yet today they are found wanting, even among psychoanalysts, for being too static.

We have seen, then, that Adler had a profound influence on Freud. Freud was unable "to let Adler go," as Paul Roazen (1975, p. 208) stated it. Roazen also noted that "Adler's ideas were swept up by Freud's pupils even though they may not have been aware of what they were doing" (p. 205). Adler (A1933b) had come to a very similar conclusion when he wrote: "It will appear to many as though I had unfairly anticipated the development of psychoanalysis during the past twenty-five years. I am the prisoner of psychoanalysis who does not let it go" (p. 255; new translation).

Regarding Freud's criticisms of Adler, Roazen (1975) concludes: "Contemporary analysts, if asked to defend Freud's criticism of Adler, would find themselves in an embarrassing position" (p. 204). Roazen supports this by list-

312

ing concepts of Freud that have disappeared from the psycho-analytic literature and concepts of Adler that have silently been taken over.

IV. SEXUALITY, LOVE, AND MARRIAGE

Holistic and Goal-oriented Approach

Adler's approach to sex, love, and marriage (Chapters 3 and 4) is in accord with his holistic and teleological orientation. He sees the human being as a unified whole not only in space but also in time, with relatively constant goal orientation and methods of approaching his goal, resulting in a relatively constant style of life, although the concretization of the goal changes over time. A person's life cycle represents a self-consistent unity. "The psychological life of a person is oriented toward the final act, like that of a character created by a good artist" (A1956b, p. 94).

But not only is the individual seen as a unity in space and time, he is also best understood as a part of larger units to which he belongs and that in turn are also goal-oriented. These units extend in space from the mother to the family to the larger community, eventually encompassing all of humanity; and again also in time, with humanity extending into the past and the far distant future.

Social interest. Successful individual striving is co-ordinated with this projected tendency of humanity, the societal evolution, the ascent of man. Such striving is on the generally useful side, directed by a well-developed social interest or social feeling. In the broadest sense Adler (A1964a) means by this, "feeling with the whole, *sub specie aeternatis* (under the aspect of eternity). It means a striving for a form of community that must be thought of as everlasting, as it could be thought of if humanity had reached the goals of perfection. It is never a present-day community or society, nor a political or religious form. Rather the goal . . . would have to be a goal that signifies the ideal community of all humanity, the ultimate fulfillment of evolution" (pp. 34–35).

Sexual function and its development. Adler's understanding of the sexual function within this framework is given in Chapter 3. It is a late paper, in which he obviously answers Freud's assertion of psychosexual stages of development. A holistic theory emphasizing the unity of the individual not only in space but also over time would logically minimize the importance of developmental stages as artificial abstractions that cannot be very relevant for the individual case. Furthermore, one cannot know anything about natural psychosexual stages because the sexual function, like any other, is immediately influenced by cultural and other environmental factors, as well as the individual's personal attitudes.

All Adler acknowledges is an initial primary phase of autoeroticism and an ultimate secondary phase of heterosexual functioning. Between these is a painful period when the young person is capable of heterosexual relations but is prevented by the culture. "The slow development of the sexual function and a lack of conditions favorable to its growth into a social function—that is, when it is a task for two persons of different sexes—obstruct its right evolutionary development for love and procreation and for the preservation of humanity" (A1938a, p. 201).

Adler has no ready solution for this dilemma except the addition: "The degree of social interest determines the issue" (p. 201). He also speaks against "coarse sensuality," and, in the case of older adolescents, against relations with prostitutes, which was quite general in his day. Instead, Adler favors granting young people "full rights to a true love where both partners are prepared to stand up for each other." This includes that parents would subsidize early marriages of their children.

Adler's comments on homosexuality among children will be discussed below.

The question of purpose. Already in his first paper on sexuality, "The Sexual Problem in Education," Adler's orientation was teleological or purposivistic. Writing three years after having joined Freud's group, Adler referred to Freud's (1905) monograph *Three Essays on the Theory of Sexuality* as his "theoretical foundation" and accepted Freud's basic assertion of infant sexuality and its ubiquity. But beyond this, Adler redefined sexuality as a form of sensuality (*Sinnlichkeit*) connected with the sense organs. Thereby Adler attempted to integrate sexuality with a person's total interaction with his environment.

Adler (A1905a) asked: "What purpose does nature intend when it has equipped the infant with sexuality as he enters the world?" He answers: "The meaning and significance of this fact and furthermore of the spreading of sensuality over the entire body—its conspicuous attribution to all sense organs, including the olfactory organ—are apparently to be sought in the following: Sensuality and the passion for satisfaction, force the individual into entering relations with the outside world with all his organs, to gather impressions and nourishment. Thus the sexual motive, the sensual mechanism of the cell, serves the purpose of leading the child to the things of the outside world and to initiating relations with the culture. In education sexuality must be made to serve the same purpose" (p. 361).

From the very start, Adler was then concerned with the individual's transactions with his cultural environment rather than with intrapsychic phenomena, and he regarded sexuality within this framework. The validity of Adler's answer here is of less importance than the fact that he raised the question, and how he answered it. This shows the fundamental difference from Freud, which eventually led to Adler's separation six years later, in 1911. To follow Watzlawick et al. (1967): "There is a crucial difference between the psychoanalytic [intrapsychic] model . . . and any conceptualization of organism-environment interaction. . . . They stand in a relation of conceptual discontinuity" (p. 29).

The "ultimate" purpose. Some thirty years later, Adler raised again the question of purpose in connection with sexuality. This time he considered sexuality one of the human potentialities, all of which the individual must develop for coping with his problems. The question of purpose is now projected farther, beyond the individual's welfare, to some more ultimate purpose, transcending the individual. Adler's question now is: "For what? For what goal must the individual strive and develop his inherited human potentialities?" And he answers: "Individuals and humanity as a whole use their potentialities, gifts of our ancestors, for increasing these gifts in a world changed by human beings for the benefit of the whole human family." This presupposes a certain degree of social interest as the prerequisite for the satisfactory solution of all important life problems.

The question of purpose or meaning is of course a philosophical question, especially when projected to an "ultimate" meaning. But the question does, explicitly or implicitly, arise in human beings and is therefore of legitimate concern to human psychology. All the problems of life are more easily met when found meaningful—that is, when they seem to involve a greater purpose.

Adler attempted to answer the question "What should life mean to you?," which was also the subject of one of his books, while still remaining on a solid scientific foundation, by taking a pragmatic or idealist-positivistic (Vaihinger, 1911b) position. There is no "ultimate given," "absolute truth," or ultimate purpose or meaning. But one can fill the breach by working hypotheses, as long as these are recognized as such, do not contradict what is given, and are useful.

Thus Adler's "ultimate" meaning became "the ultimate fulfillment of evolution" or "the benefit of the whole human family," requiring self-transcendence in the form of social interest. The justification for this is that human beings (1) are best understood when we regard their actions *as if* they were goal-oriented, even in the absence of a conscious goal, and (2) function more to their own satisfaction as well as that of others when striving for a goal that is also meaningful to others, that is socially useful. All failures in life can be seen as oriented toward goals on the useless side of life concomitant with underdeveloped social interest. "All failures—neurotics, psychotics, criminals, alcoholics, problem children, suicides, perverts, and prostitutes—are failures because they are lacking in social interest" (A1956b, p. 156).

316

Love and Marriage as "Tasks"

For the organismic psychologist the individual does not react passively to stimuli and situations like a mechanism but is an active participant in the situation. Similarly, according to neo-Kantian philosopher Hermann Cohen (1842–1918), the individual is not confronted with cold, absolute facts but with problems of perception and interpretation. "Nothing is *gegeben* ('given'), he urged; all is *aufgegeben* ('propounded,' like a riddle) to thought" (Vleeschauwer, 1974, p. 396). The material given to our senses becomes immediately an *Aufgabe* (a proposition, a problem, or a task to which the mind responds creatively). A perception is already to some extent a production or creation, and a reaction to the situation certainly is. The situation becomes a task or problem because there are various ways of meeting or not meeting it, so that the individual must understand, discriminate, and decide. Thus, according to Cohen, "in various dimensions cognition (*Erkenntnis*) becomes an 'infinite task'" (Landry, 1959, p. 260).

One of three life tasks. It is doubtful whether Adler knew of Cohen. But Adler used a conception and terminology very similar to Cohen's that are quite consistent with Adler's general Kantian and neo-Kantian orientation. Adler (A1924n) grouped the main "givens," or objective facts of our lives, into three relational systems (*Bezugssysteme*): (1) Human being–earth: We find ourselves physically on this earth and must maintain ourselves under these conditions. (2) Individual–community: We live among other human beings and must interact with them. (3) Male–female: We live as members of one of two sexes and must come to terms with our complementarity with the other sex.

These three "givens" Adler called the "three main ties" of our existence. They become our tasks or problems (*Aufgaben*) and are best dealt with if understood as such. They are the problems of work, communal life, and love and marriage. Actually, these are three groups of problems of which

317

Adler spoke originally as task complexes (*Aufgaben-komplexe*).

Beyond formulating these three main problems of human life, Adler (A1956b) recognized them as essentially social problems in that they require co-operation for their successful solution, which in turn is best assured by a well-developed social interest. "All failures approach the problems of occupation, friendship, and sex without the confidence that they can be solved by co-operation. . . . No one else is benefited by the achievement of their aims, and their interest stops short at their own persons" (p. 156).

Broad frame of reference as facilitator. Regarding love and marriage, Adler stressed not only that it is a unique task for two individuals of different sexes but that it is of particular social significance. It is "not a co-operation for the welfare of two persons only, but a co-operation also for the welfare of humanity." Marriage offers "the real opportunity to create for the sake of society." Such a broadened meaning can be argued on various grounds and does facilitate a constructive way of meeting the problem. Psychologically, in the individual case, it is a construction, in Vaihinger's sense a fiction, an "as if" construction.

Indeed, Adler does at times describe it in this way, as for example when he states that a socially interested person will try to solve the problem of love and marriage "*as if* the welfare of others were involved. He does not need to know that he is trying to solve it in this way. . . . He will spontaneously seek the welfare and improvement of humanity." In this case the social orientation would be the inference, or construction, of the psychologist. Another time, when Adler expresses that a break in a marriage is easiest to avoid "*if* we regard marriage *as* a social task that confronts us," the construction would be that of the person involved.

Such constructions are practical or ethical fictions in the sense of Vaihinger (1911b), among which ideals are also included. The ideal, although "in contradiction with reality . . . has an irresistible power" (p. 48). The fiction of the broader social nature of marriage is justified because it facilitates dealing with the problem. The fictional character of marriage

318

as of general social concern, fictional in the sense of an ideal, becomes evident from the following passage from Adler (1931b): "Love and marriage are not private affairs, but common tasks in which the whole of humanity should take part in mind and spirit" (pp. 252–53). The "should" designates this as an ideal. The ideal is symbolized or concretized in the many marriage ceremonies in which the community participates, although one can get married privately—or live together without getting married at all.

Prestige politics as inhibitor. While the universal human dynamics was for Adler an upward striving for overcoming, power, success as subjectively perceived, the actual relationship of the sexes in the culture was one of male dominance, leaving the woman largely dissatisfied with this inequality. The solution of the love and marriage problem is facilitated if the two partners, overcoming the cultural prejudice, would in equality strive for a common goal transcending the selves. Adler's effort was directed at describing and advancing such a solution.

On the other hand, the dynamics of marital discord were almost self-evident. They would be a personal power contest in which the partners engage in "prestige politics." Interestingly, some forty years later Kate Millett (1969) would write a book entitled *Sexual Politics.*

In a love relationship, Adler noted, the need for power "can easily turn into tyranny" toward the beloved. "The same [damaging] factor permeates human love life, which otherwise also generally disturbs fellowship: the striving for power and personal superiority." "Both sexes are easily caught in the whirlpool of prestige politics. Then they are forced to play a role with which neither can cope, which leads to disturbing the harmlessness and spontaneity of their lives, and saturates them with prejudices against which every trace of true joy and happiness must of course disappear."

Freud, with his emphasis on the sex drive, was not interested in concrete male-female interpersonal relations. He was interested in an abstract libido and repression. Lief (1972), thinking of Adler as a psychoanalyst in the broader meaning (see pp. 100–2), points out: "With the exception of Adler,

319

for whom power became a central theme, power has been almost totally neglected in psychoanalytic publications. . . . [This] may be due to a deliberate avoidance because Adler made so much of the issue of power, or to unworked-through conflicts regarding power in Freud himself (. . . perhaps he never altogether gave up his earlier power drive), or to the very nature of psychoanalytic therapy itself . . . in which power is . . . hardly ever discussed in terms of power" (p. 117).

Broderick (1972) concurs: "Adler is the clinical theoretician who has given the most prominence in his work to the concept of power. . . . Even the famous Oedipus complex and its resolution may be evaluated as a power struggle" (p. 150).

Paradoxical power tactics. Broderick (1972) continues: "The late Don Jackson, Jay Haley, and their colleagues at the Mental Research Institute in Palo Alto, California, have more recently taken this concept a step farther. . . . Watzlawick, Beavin, and Jackson (1967) developed this idea farther by analyzing marital communication in terms of the attempt to 'one-up' the spouse in conflicted symmetrical and metacomplementary relationships" (p. 150).

The work of these authors blends very smoothly with Adlerian theory. Haley (1963) finds that in a marital struggle "The tactics . . . are those of any power struggle: threats, violent assault, withdrawal, sabotage, passive resistance, and helplessness or physical inability to do what the other wants" (p. 126). Helplessness and physical inability as power tactics would be "paradoxical communication" (p. 131). Adler focused on such tactics from the start: "The masculine protest . . . in women is usually covered and changed, and seeks to triumph with feminine means." But also in general: "Obedience or defiance—the human psyche is capable of operating in either direction." As specific tactics, Adler (A1956b) enjoyed pointing out: "Tears and complaints—the means that I have called 'water power'—can be extremely useful weapons for disturbing co-operation and reducing others to a condition of slavery" (p. 288). Especially regarding depressive and suicidal patients, Adler (A1964a) wrote: "They always . . .

attempted to influence others through increased complaining, sadness, and suffering. . . . Reduced to the simplest form, the life style of the potential suicide is characterized by the fact that he hurts others by dreaming himself into injuries or administering them to himself" (pp. 251 and 252). Suicide then becomes a form of paradoxical communication (Ansbacher, 1969).

The Ideal Relationship

The problem of the ideal becomes inevitably a part of Adler's goal-oriented pragmatic psychology. The following is a more detailed description of his ideal of love and marriage, with recommendations for approaching it.

Dyad of equal partners. In his last paper on the subject, Adler (A1936n) wrote: "Modern love is based upon mutual physical and spiritual devotion. We are not lovers until we know that *it takes two to make love.* . . . Paradoxical as it may sound, the average person does not realize that *love is a task for two.* . . . Love may have its beginnings in a sudden infatuation, but . . . it does not deserve the name of love, without labor and discipline, sacrifice and co-operation. . . . Love is not an unequal partnership, where one gives all and the other gives little or nothing. *Love is the equal partnership between a man and a woman—where two are merged into one, a human dyad, reconciling the sex urge of this individual with the biological needs of the race and the demands of society*" (pp. 148–49).

The term dyad, according to the first dictionary definition, "two units treated as one," corresponds to Adler's earlier assertion, "The division of humanity into two sexes, far from creating a separation, means an eternal compulsion toward one another." From the start, Adler deplored the "artificial division of the natural coherence of the sexes." This is exactly why Adler considered male domination so damaging to the general welfare.

In earlier writings Adler described the love and marriage

relationship as a "twosomeness" (*Zweisamkeit*), a Nietzschean term created in contrast to "lonesomeness" (*Einsamkeit*). "Sexuality is 'twosomeness,' the achievement of two equal partners."

Ethical implementation: the larger context. Adler's ideal relationship between the sexes is furnished with all the old virtues insofar as they are reconcilable with equality of the partners. This is effected through social interest, which is as necessary here as in the other two life tasks. "In love, so richly endowed with bodily and mental satisfaction, social interest manifests itself as the immediate and unquestionable molder of our destiny" (A1938a, p. 59, modified translation). Adler relates social interest to *agape* (love of one's fellow man), and considers sexual love, parental love, filial love, and love of humanity all derivatives of social interest (Ansbacher, 1966, p. 114). According to Adler (A1933c), "Where there is a strong permeation of social feeling," there will also be "love of one's neighbor, or *agape*" (p. 283).

Obviously there is here a meeting ground between Individual Psychology and religion. Adler acknowledges that they "have things in common, often in thinking, feeling, willing, but always with regard to the goal of perfection of humanity" (p. 281). Furthermore, he sees the function of applied Individual Psychology "to protect and further the sacred good of all-embracing humaneness where the religions have lost their influence" (p. 281).

Adler's ethics spring, however, not from idealism, but from positivistic idealism, as mentioned earlier. This means that the ideals, as fictions, must be justified by their desirable effect in the concrete reality. The individual does in fact experience greater well-being when he becomes interested in the physical and social world beyond himself, identifies with it, and becomes committed to it. Social interest becomes, for Adler, together with self-esteem, the condition of successful living. Adler (A1931b) stated this difference from religion in the following: "The most important task imposed by religion has always been 'Love thy neighbor.' . . . Now from a scientific standpoint we can confirm the value of this striving. The pampered child asks us, 'Why should I love my neighbor?

Does my neighbor love me?' . . . It is the individual who is not interested in his fellow men who has the greatest difficulties in life and provides the greatest injury to others. It is from among such individuals that all human failures spring" (p. 253). It was Freud (1929) who had asked, "Why should we love our neighbor?" (p. 81), and answered, if he is a stranger, "I must confess he has more claim to my hostility, even to my hatred. He does not seem to have the least trace of love for me" (p. 83). Freud believed there was a "primary hostility of men toward one another" (p. 86).

The resolution of personal problems by referring them to their larger social context was Adler's general method. We have met it before with regard to abortion. It may be called a dialectical approach to problem-solving—that is, trying to solve the problem not on the level on which it is presented, but going to the next higher level of abstraction for a solution. It is in fact a reframing of the problem (Watzlawick et al., 1974). Adler called this *Zusammenhangsbetrachtung* (consideration of the context or coherence), the methodology of the "understanding" psychology as established by Wilhelm Dilthey (Seelbach, 1932).

Request of monogamy and fidelity. Adler extols monogamy, fidelity, and chastity, and takes a definite stand against "trifling with love," always emphasizing the effects of such behavior on the well-being of the individual or those affected by his actions, sometimes even in the form of an "as if" construction, as mentioned earlier.

On *monogamy*, Adler asserts that human beings are by nature "neither polygamous nor monogamous," but "the fullest and highest development of the individual in love and marriage can best be secured by monogamy." "The higher psychological values are so much part of monogamous marriage that only the faint-hearted is inclined to evade it. To succeed in this evasion he steers his inclination in another direction. Then, of course, he has feelings that his weakness demands" (A1926q, pp. 22–23). "The solution for the problem of love and marriage *in our practical and social life* is monogamy" (italics added).

In view of the above, Adler's contention that "children are

spontaneous and wholehearted adherents of monogamy" should be modified by "under the prevailing conditions." Such relativity becomes apparent from Adler's designation of "a good marriage" as "the best means we know for bringing up the future generation of humanity, and marriage should always have this in mind."

Regarding *fidelity* we find, "If one human being is really interested in another, he must have all the characteristics belonging to that interest. He must be true, a good friend; he must feel responsible; he must make himself faithful and trustworthy." "Infidelity contradicts the task of marriage" (A1926q, p. 23). "Infidelity is always a revenge. True, persons who are unfaithful always justify themselves by speaking of love and sentiments, but we know the value of feelings and sentiments. Feelings always agree with the goal of superiority, and should not be regarded as arguments" (A1929d, p. 117).

Adler deplored any *trifling with love.* "We cannot treat love and marriage as a trifle." "Such trifling with love (*Bagatellisierung*) as is seen in promiscuity, in prostitution, in perversions, or in the hidden retreat of the cults of nudism, would deprive love of all its grandeur and glory and all its aesthetic charm" (A1933b, p. 61). "Sexual intercourse without love is misbehavior (*eine Unart*)."

"The refusal to enter into a lasting union sows doubt and mistrust between the two partners in a common task and makes them incapable of devoting themselves entirely to one another" (A1933b, p. 61). Thus Adler spoke also against *trial marriages,* or, as it was also called, companionate marriages. *The Companionate Marriage* was the title of a book by Judge Ben B. Lindsey and W. Evans (1927) proposing two kinds of marriage, one for companionship and more easily dissolved, and one for procreation. The book caused much discussion and controversy at the time.

Achieving the dyad. "To achieve the dyad of perfect love," Adler (A1936n) recommends the following rules:

1. Don't look up to your mate, and don't look down: Approach love as an equal.

324

2. Don't expect an impossible perfection in others, of which you yourself are incapable: love a woman, not an angel; a man, not an eidolon [phantom, ideal].

3. Don't think of yourselves as one or as two, but as a twosome.

4. Don't take without giving, nor give without taking, in love.

5. Don't pick out a partner who does not entice you physically, but do not entangle your fate with one who appeals to you only on a physiological basis.

6. Don't fail to co-operate with your mate on every plane—socially, economically, intellectually, spiritually, emotionally, and biologically.

7. Don't lose yourself in bypaths and blind alleys: There is always a way out of emotional labyrinths—potentially all humans are fundamentally normal.

8. Be a slave neither to convention nor to your own idiosyncrasies: Remember you are not merely an individual, but a unit of your social group and the human race [p. 149].

For the selection of the right partner in love and marriage Adler (A1933b) recommended further: "In addition to physical suitability and attraction, primarily the following points are to be considered, as indicators of a sufficient degree of social interest: (1) The partner must have proven that he can maintain friendship; (2) he must be interested in his work; (3) he must show more interest in his partner than in himself" (p. 63, new translation). In other words, he must have given evidence of the right approach to all three life tasks.

For women Adler (A1927a) recommended additionally that they ask their prospective partner, " 'What is your stand toward the overtowering masculine principle in our culture, especially within the framework of the family?' This question usually remains undecided throughout life, with the result that there will be a continuous contest for equal rights, or various degrees of resignation" (p. 101).

Present-day Confirmations

Adler conceived of his psychology as a "cultural psychology" and to be applicable to daily living. Since culture changes over time, one should expect such a psychology to become somewhat dated, especially in the areas of sex, love, and marriage where such revolutionary changes have taken place in recent decades. And indeed, Adler's views on these matters do at times sound somewhat old-fashioned. Yet on closer examination one finds that this is more a matter of style and some particulars than of essentials.

Especially three basic principles have well stood the test of time: rejection of "trifling with love," commendation of monogamous faithfulness, and co-operation between the partners.

Rejection of trifling with love. Nearly forty years after Adler had rejected "trifling with love," while the sexual revolution had been well under way, Rollo May (1969) picked up the thread, so to speak, where Adler had left off. Speaking of "trivializing sex" (p. 38) and "banalization of sex and love" (p. 64), May noted: "Contraception, like all devices and machines, can increase our range of freedom and choice. But the new freedom . . . now expresses itself in the banalization of sex and love. . . . Surely an act that carries as much power as the sexual act, and power in the critical area of passing on one's name and species, cannot be taken as banal and insignificant except by doing violence to our natures, if not to 'nature' itself" (pp. 120–21). Such banalization goes "with a confusion of motives in sex . . . almost every motive being present in the act except the desire to make love." There is a diminution of feeling and passion that "often takes the form of a kind of anesthesia in people who can perform the mechanical aspects of the sexual act very well. We are becoming used to the plaint from the patient's chair that 'We made love, but I didn't feel anything'" (p. 59); or, "in the long run, the lover who is most efficient will also be the one who is impotent" (p. 55).

When Adler considered it "a well-known fact" that "all-too-willing permissiveness will create apathy," May thus gives another confirmation of this fact. Regarding Freud, May observes in this connection that surely Freud "himself had no desire to render sex and love banal" (p. 332). Yet, "When his concepts of 'drive' and 'libido' in the popular sense are taken literally, Freudianism in the popular sense plays directly into the banalization of sex and love, however contrary the real intentions of its author were" (p. 82).

In a more spiritual vein, Adler (A1933b) commented: "Trifling with love . . . would deprive love of all its grandeur and glory and all its aesthetic charm" (p. 61). Today, Masters and Johnson (1975) agree: "To reduce sex to physical exchange is to strip it of richness and subtlety and . . . means robbing it of all emotional value." Similarly, Nikelly (1977), an experienced counselor of college students, notes: "Genuine sexual revolution means . . . sexual equality . . . a sexual freedom that includes the freedom to love and to express tenderness and affection. People who feel that playing 'games' and assuming 'roles' are necessary aspects of their sexual lives are . . . caught in a form of sexual tyranny" (p. 220).

Commendation of monogamous faithfulness. As of late, sex researchers and therapists have pointed out the importance of a real commitment toward the partner as against mere sexual technology; for example, Helen Singer Kaplan (1974), in the last paragraph of her book on sex therapy, says that more important than technical proficiency in lovemaking is love itself, by which she means commitment and true intimacy. "Mutual love can profoundly change the quality of life" (p. 524).

Masters and Johnson, the well-known "sexual engineers," say today that they are and always have been interested not so much in sex per se, as in the extent that it enhances human relationships. As Adler had found that love demands "a decision for eternity," so Masters and Johnson (1975) hold that sex should mean commitment, "developing a long-range relationship rather than concentrating it all on short-term pampering of the individual self" (p. 136).

It is particularly remarkable that Masters and Johnson deplore "pampering of the individual self," since for Adler the "pampered style of life" (A1956b, pp. 241–42) was a central concept of poor adjustment. "When two pampered children marry . . . each of them is claiming interest and attention and neither can be satisfied." "A marriage between two pampered children is always unhappy, because both remain in an expectant attitude and neither begins to give."

In endorsing sexual fidelity and commitment, Masters and Johnson (1975) deplore also that words such as loyalty and faithfulness have come into disuse. "Yet all human association depends on these and other such values, and they cannot be ignored in relation to marriage" (p. 203). Coming especially close to Adler's concept of social interest, they define commitment as "the cement that binds individuals and groups together" (p. 268). In a good relationship both partners "act in each other's best interests" (p. 269). We had previously reached the conclusion that social interest is best defined, in Ralph Barton Perry's words, as an "interest of one person in the interests of a second person" (Ansbacher, 1968, p. 140).

Finally, Masters and Johnson (1975) also find that infidelity is mostly not due to greater attraction to a third party, but to a desire "to settle a score" (p. 145) with one's spouse. Likewise Adler had noted that a woman's "adultery is always . . . an act of revenge," and that in a man it is "thoughts of revenge against one woman [which] can easily ignite love for another."

Co-operation metaphor: old and new. For Adler (A1929d) an old German marriage custom was a metaphorical description of a good marriage as the co-operation of two equal partners. The young couple is given a double-handled saw and is asked to cut a tree trunk. This is a real task for two. "Each one has to be interested in what the other is doing and harmonize his strokes with those of the other. This is thus considered a good test of fitness for marriage" (p. 122).

Adler was very fond of this story and used it frequently, in slightly different versions. In an earlier version the custom signified that "love is not a private matter and that it is important to think of the other, to make things easier for him or her" (A1926o). In the version reprinted in the present volume, the meaning was a test of trust and co-operation. "If there is no trust between them, they will tug against each other and accomplish nothing. . . . Co-operation is the chief prerequisite for marriage."

To this date this custom is practiced in the Harz Mountains, although it is gradually disappearing, according to Adolf Reinecke (1975), historian of the region. He describes the custom, one of several, as meaning that the young couple "should face all matters of life together . . . that they must carry out difficult tasks also, and that there is always work before pleasure."

Today, Masters and Johnson (1975) describe a recent development among truck drivers that may be taken as a modern version of this old custom. They write: "On long-distance hauls, where the drivers must operate in pairs so that one can spell the other at the steering wheel, a small but growing number of husbands and wives have been teaming up . . . striking evidence that the principle of equality of the sexes is spreading. . . . The advantages of such a joint venture . . . seem transparently clear. . . . The husband . . . accepts his wife's co-operation. . . . The wife, no less female for driving a truck, gains the security of a closer relationship with her husband. . . . If an image is needed to characterize the relationship between husband and wife today, perhaps it can be found here: codrivers of a vehicle taking both to the same destination, each trusting the other to help steer in the direction they want to go, traveling together because they do not want to be apart" (p. 91).

Altogether, this book by Masters and Johnson (1975) would be well suited for an Adlerian reading list.

Nondogmatic Stance

As mentioned, one should expect that statements on sex, love, and marriage made during the first third of this century would sound somewhat dated in the last quarter. From his social, psychological, pragmatic, and dialectical positions one would also expect Adler to have been aware of this time factor. And indeed, he (1) limited his claims as being applicable primarily to the culture of his period, and (2) anticipated and accepted changes.

Temporal-cultural limitations. In a paper presenting his ways of understanding human nature to a lay readership, Adler (A1926k) noted: "We take into account that the high point of our understanding certainly coincides with our present-day culture. We do not believe that we have explored the ultimate things, pronounced the last wisdom, but that all this may be only a component of our present-day knowledge and culture. We are looking forward to those who will follow after us" (p. 218).

In his contribution to a large two-volume *Handbook of the Science of Work,* Adler (A1930n) wrote: "Our appreciation of man's relationship to this earth, some community, and sexual dimorphism—as well as our establishment of the unity of the personality within these limits—keep us from a one-sided belief in an eternally unshakable wisdom and understanding. Individual Psychology claims no more for itself than to be taken as a theory that does justice to the present condition of civilization, and to our present knowledge of man and his psychological conditions, and does so better than other contextual theories" (p. 47).

This is of course a partial cultural relativism that must be faced and for which Adler (A1929d) gave an example from sexual behavior. "Besides the influence of childhood environment as reflected in the style of life, political and economic conditions in a country influence sexuality. They give rise to a social style that is very contagious. After the Russo-Japanese War [1904–5] and the collapse of the first revolution in Russia, when all the people had lost their hope and confidence, there was a great movement of sexuality known as Saninism. . . . One finds a similar exaggeration of sexuality during revolution, and it is of course notorious that in wartime there is a great recourse to sexual sensuality because life seems worthless" (pp. 128–29).

330

Anticipation and acceptance of changes. Implicit in all of Adler's psychology is a belief in change, ultimately for the better (see A1937g), which would affect some of his formulations. Regarding the family structure, he did not believe "that the framework of present relationships between men and women is constant" but that "the framework of the family is already shaky and will increasingly become so in the future" (p. 258 above). Several years later he referred to "the new tendency toward a dissolution of the family." This was in connection with prostitution, which he considered very undesirable. This tendency, he continued, "may regard the nature and significance of prostitution more mildly, and may possibly even demand its cultivation."

Adler fully appreciated the extent to which character traits may be culturally determined and are thus subject to change with the culture. "Even apparently innate traits, such as waiting for a suitor, passivity, reserve, feminine modesty, motherliness, and monogamy, are much more than is realized subject to the trend of the times, and are directed by the final goal." Motherhood will become less important as women will achieve greater economic equality. "Women will not allow motherhood to prevent them from taking up a profession; motherhood may either remain an obstacle for some, or else will lose its hardship" (p. 258 above).

Women will also achieve a more active love life. This is implied in Adler's observation that "man's greater sphere of activity in love life is primarily determined by his greater sphere of activity in life altogether." From this it follows that as women participate more actively in life they will also become more active sexually.

Regarding premarital relations, Adler believed that "The intimate devotion of love and marriage is best secured if there have not been sexual relations before the marriage." The ultimate justification of this opinion was, however, that "in the present state of our culture, if there are intimate relations before marriage the burden is heavier for the girl." Adler also rejected "reliefs" of the marriage tie on the grounds that "it is always the women really who bear the disadvantage." Since it was the woman's welfare he had in mind, one may conclude that as better methods of birth control became available, among many additional factors, Adler might well have modified his stand on this issue.

In Adler's considerations of marriage, the propagation of humanity and the willingness to accept the responsibility of raising children were of great importance. But in his last book (A1933b) he acknowledged, "Since humanity has fulfilled the command to multiply . . . the human social feeling has no doubt become less rigorous in its demand for unlimited offspring. . . . Social circumstances offer no inducement for further rapid propagation" (p. 62). Instead, Adler accepted that this and the various technical advances "have helped to assign to love, in addition to its task of providing for the propagation of the species, an almost independent part—a higher level, an enhancement of pleasure—which certainly contributes to the welfare of humanity" (pp. 62–63).

Finally, while Adler's ideal was the permanent marriage, he accepted the occasional desirability of divorce. "Since no rule for life has been found to be absolutely invariable, there are reasons for discussing the dissolution of the ties of love or marriage. . . . This question should be dealt with by experienced psychologists who can be relied upon to give a decision in accordance with social interest" (p. 62).

Sex Education of Children

On the problem of sex education of children, Adler considered it most important that they be taught (1) their sexual identity and its unalterability and (2) the equal worth of the sexes. Instruction in the physical side of sex was of quite secondary importance to him and can be summarized into: "Wait until the child becomes curious." "Answer his questions in a true and simple manner." "Avoid answers that stimulate the sex drive."

Sexual identity. Adler (A1956b) considered uncertainty regarding one's sexual role first among "the typical occasions for the onset of neurosis and psychosis" (pp. 296–97). Therefore it was of the greatest importance to him that a little

332

boy be taught that he will grow up to be a man, and a little girl, that she will be a woman. Any ambiguity in this respect is to be avoided and prevented.

This requirement is quite independent of any sexual stereotypes of the culture. As Money and Ehrhardt (1972) have emphasized: "Nature herself supplies the basic irreducible elements of sex difference, which no culture can eradicate . . . women can menstruate, gestate, and lactate, and men cannot" (p. 13). Men can impregnate. Thus, "despite great variability between cultures in the prescription of gender-dimorphic behavior . . . the options are not limitless . . . if that culture is to . . . survive" (p. 145). The present changes in gender-role definitions are not to be interpreted as affecting basic sex differences but simply "as an accommodation of certain traditional facets of gender role, male and female, to changing times and circumstances" (p. 13).

In recent years a number of research studies have supported Adler's contention of the psychopathological hazard of sex- and gender-role uncertainty. They have been summarized by Biller (1973), one of the main authors of this research, who concluded that sex-role uncertainty is indeed "a very basic determinant of psychopathology."

Equality of the sexes. At the same time, Adler considered it most important to teach children the equal worth of the sexes and to provide equal opportunities for them. Adler (A1929c) wrote: "I should never forbid a girl to play with trains, to climb trees, or to play any boys' games, but I am fully convinced that much trouble would be saved in the later life of children if they were brought up from the first in knowledge and preparation for their right sexual role. This is impossible, of course, if the atmosphere is charged with suggestions of feminine disability and of masculine privilege, as is so often the case" (p. 43).

This is today essentially the viewpoint of the staff of one day-care center run by a women's liberation organization, The Women's Action Alliance, New York (Hammel, 1974). Quoting Jan Galvin: "Children identify first with which sex they are, and we think it's very important this be a positive identity throughout one's life." Another staff member, Barbara

Sprung (1974), writes, "It is possible to bring up girls and boys who understand their biological sex identity . . . yet feel free to choose from all of life's options because they are not forced into only certain roles that are culturally defined."

Primary Prevention

Since equality was certainly not reached in Adler's time, he also saw as a matter of primary prevention the necessity of fortifying girls against injustices to which they would be exposed. Thus Adler (A1925a) wrote: "For preventive and therapeutic reasons, one must first of all impress upon the little girl early in life the unalterability of her organic sexual character. But it is also necessary to teach her that all inflicted wrongs are not insurmountable, and how to understand and fight them like other difficulties of life. Thereby, we believe, the insecurity and resignation will disappear from woman's work, and at the same time also the exaggerated urge for significance, which has made woman so often appear inferior" (p. 72, newly translated).

Additionally, Adler (A1929d) believed, "Our education is certainly too strict in the direction it follows. Instead of preparing boys and girls as if for sin, it would be much wiser to train the girls better in the feminine and the boys in the masculine role of marriage—but train them both in such ways that they would feel equal" (p. 120).

Love and Marriage Counseling

Recognition of need. Adler (A1926o) found that the problem of sexual relations was uppermost on people's minds, with nearly 70 per cent of the questions after his popular lectures referring to this problem. One might conclude from this, he wrote, "that humanity is moved exclusively by the sexual problem, and seriously attempt to reinterpret the other problems also in a sexual sense. In all these problems great insecu-

334

rity reverberates, only that in the sexual problem it is greater than in all the other problems of life" (p. 14). This greater insecurity is due to "ignorance, inadequate preparation, and the resulting tension." Sexuality represents for everyone "a completely new problem—the concrete relations to a person of the other sex—for which no prepared path, no tradition, no appropriate knowledge show the way to the solution. No wonder that so many incorrect answers are given!" (p. 13).

Thus Adler (A1926q) advocated premarital and marital counseling. He believed: "It would be a real blessing for marriage, humanity, and the future generation if before every marriage there were some marriage counseling by experienced Individual Psychologists to supplement inadequate preparations and improve erroneous attitudes" (p. 23).

About marital counseling as such, Adler (A1929d) wrote: "We see so many mistakes made in marriage that the question inevitably arises, 'Is all this necessary?' We know that these mistakes were begun in childhood, and we know, too, that it is possible to change mistaken styles of life by recognizing and uncovering the prototype traits. One wonders, therefore, whether it would not be possible to establish advisory councils that could untangle the mistakes of matrimony by the methods of Individual Psychology. Such councils would be composed of trained persons who would understand how all the events in individuals' lives hang together, and be capable of sympathetic identification with the persons seeking advice" (pp. 118–19).

Incidentally, Adler became interested in every aspect of better adult preparation in matters of sexual relations. For example, he supported a book by Heinrich F. Wolf on the male approach to courtship by writing the Preface for it (A1926o). It is actually from this Preface that the first two quotations of the present section are taken.

Adler (A1936n) also appreciated the merits of literature on sexual techniques. He wrote: "Even the most idealistic lover must realize that love is an art that requires technique. Both the Occident and the Orient have given us manuals of love, textbooks of passion. There is something to be said for *Kamasutra*, for *The Scented Garden*, even for *Lady Chat-*

335

terley's Lover, and there is much to be said for popular scientific books that attempt to give expert knowledge to amateurs. But all knowledge and all artistry are vain unless they are shared by both lovers in a mutual devotion. We should not, with false modesty, close our eyes to the truth that love, even in its physical aspect, is a task involving the harmonious and wholehearted co-operation of both parties" (p. 151). As we have seen, Helen Kaplan and Masters and Johnson would well agree with this (pp. 327–29 above).

Rationale and projected outcome. For Adler marriage is a task for two people of different sexes living and working together. A satisfactory solution is facilitated if the problem is seen in a larger context—two people as part of humanity working on a problem of some social concern and connected with the past and the future. An improvement here, as in all problems, lies in the change from a more self-centered, expecting, immature, narrow-focus, pampered outlook—Adler (A1956b) speaks of "the 'narrow stable' of the neurotic" (p. 278)—to a more task-centered, self-transcending, contributing, mature, co-operative outlook informed by social interest. From this viewpoint education, prevention, counseling, and psychotherapy become similar as efforts of teaching a more satisfactory, less erroneous way of living. Adler's is not a medical but an educational model.

Psychotherapy, of course, requires special techniques of teaching. During the last decades many contributions in this area have come from behavior therapists and family theorists. To the extent that these techniques are actually theoretically neutral, they fit very well into the Adlerian framework in that they stress concrete behavior, behavior change, and a transactional, dialectical systems approach, respectively.

Since Adler's conception is not medical but educational, he also does not speak of solutions or cures. Instead, he promises a less erroneous way of living, where otherwise large errors have been made or might be made. "A person who has absorbed these thoughts will naturally not move on earth free from mistakes, but he will at least remain aware of the right way and be able, instead of increasing his errors, to diminish them continuously."

336

This form of phrasing a claim for the therapeutic effectiveness of his approach was used by Adler on several occasions. In connection with occupational counseling, Adler (A1956b) wrote: "If an individual goes through life with the right attitude, we cannot promise that he meet with immediate success. But we can promise that he will keep his courage and will not lose his self-esteem" (p. 431). With regard to psychotherapy in general, we find: "In practice we attempt to undo the great errors, to substitute smaller errors, and to reduce these further until they are no longer harmful" (p. 187). And finally: "Big mistakes can produce neuroses, but little mistakes a nearly normal person" (Adler, 1929c, p. 62). Psychotherapy will be discussed in greater detail below.

Implementation. While many of Adler's cases involved marital problems, there is no knowledge of him personally having engaged in marriage counseling as such. However, one of Adler's very active associates, Sofie Lazarsfeld, started a marriage- and sex-counseling center in 1926. It had been preceded by a letter-answering column in a Vienna newspaper. Lazarsfeld (1931b) reported that during 1929 and 1930 300 cases were seen, of whom the last 168 showed approximately the following distribution of chief complaints: general extramarital difficulties, 29 per cent; marital difficulties, 24 per cent; loneliness, 18 per cent; sexual matters specifically (masturbation, impotence, frigidity, homosexuality), 29 per cent. Among Lazarsfeld's conclusions was: "Sexuality is not an autonomous area, separate from the rest of psychological life, but influences the entire behavior of a person as the latter influences the sexuality."

Marriage counseling has ever since been a part of Adlerian practice. Danica Deutsch (1956, 1967) describes marital counseling at the Alfred Adler Mental Hygiene Clinic in New York, where she also instituted group therapy with married couples. Her 1967 paper includes a brief questionnaire as a guide for premarital counseling. Helene Papanek (1965) reports on group psychotherapy with married couples. W. L. and Miriam L. Pew (1972), cocounselors, describe conjoint or four-way marital therapy. They often counsel before a group of other couples and students of counseling, which they have found to benefit not only the group but the counseled couple as well.

Adlerian Sex-and-marriage Books

Sofie Lazarsfeld (1931a, 1934), who started Adlerian marriage counseling, is also to be credited with the first Adlerian book on sexuality, addressed to women. Published in German as *How Woman Experiences Man,* it appeared in 1934 in English as *Rhythm of Life: A Guide to Sexual Harmony for Women,* and was within the following twenty years translated into several further languages. It is as pertinent today as when it was written, for its sexology, psychology, and sociology. Strongly advocating the equality of the sexes, Lazarsfeld (1934) writes: "Many nervous and sexual troubles among both sexes will disappear once this senseless coercive attitude, born of the unjustifiable overevaluation of man, has been abandoned. . . . Sex will be able to shake off its unnatural rigidity and will develop into a more beautiful and a richer thing than it has been heretofore" (p. 81). "Once the woman feels herself fully adequate sexually . . . it will not be difficult to educate her to a rational cultivation of this new possession" (pp. 81–82). In reference to sexual dysfunction Lazarsfeld notes: "We create our own sexual type according to . . . our life style . . . in pursuance of our personal prestige. . . . Whatever seems adapted to the enhancing of our personality or prestige will be attractive to us, while we react negatively whenever we fear a disparagement of our own worth" (pp. 209–10).

A second popular Adlerian book on sex and marriage is *The Art of Being a Woman* by Olga Knopf (1932). Presenting all the views of Adler, she likewise stresses the subordination of sex to the personality as a whole, the life style, and hence stresses the use that a woman makes of her sexuality. Knopf lays much marital disharmony to the situation and especially the feeling of inferiority. From this she develops helpful insights into the solution of differences. Marital dis-

338

content frequently arises from a wrong understanding of prestige. In this matter "there is no difference between the sexes. . . . Prestige is often confused with self-respect. Now self-respect or dignity comes from an objective judgment of one's own qualities. Prestige is a subjective judgment influenced by the wish to impress others" (p. 136). Adler had spoken of "the whirlpool of prestige politics" in love and marriage and its devastating effects.

The third book of this order is *The Challenge of Marriage* by Rudolf Dreikurs (1946). It still enjoys a wide circulation today and was also translated into numerous languages. Like the two previous authors, Dreikurs points out the dependence of sexual behavior—as of all behavior—on the individual's life style, including his goals. Beyond this, Dreikurs stresses the unreliability of feelings; these are also in the service of the goals and hence changeable and under the control of the individual.

As in his other works, Dreikurs goes beyond Adler in introducing therapeutic techniques. For one, everybody can improve a social-conflict situation by changing his own behavior and thereby changing indirectly the behavior of the partner. "One of the fundamental prerequisites to a solution [of a marital problem] is the recognition that the only point at which either one can start is with himself" (pp. 145–46). But "If I change my behavior, he cannot continue his" (p. 187). "When we muster our courage and try to think in terms of 'What can I do to improve the situation?'—then we are on the right track" (p. 189).

Like Adler, yet in his own way, Dreikurs also places the marriage situation into the perspective of a larger whole. Our love and sex life and attitudes have "significance for all our contemporaries. We reinforce certain social trends and negate others, while we believe that we are minding our own business. We need to become more aware of the part we play through our opinions in the concerted strivings of humanity toward a more satisfactory way of living. We must learn to evaluate better the social meaning of our personal convictions and preferences," and how to integrate them better "into the one current of actual evolution" (p. 240).

Twenty years later Dreikurs (1968) came to the further conclusion: "One of the crucial factors in bringing about marital discord is the prevailing pessimism in regard to the prospects of a happy, lasting marriage" (p. 98), "this latent pessimism, which increases with the percentage of marital failures" (p. 101). The antidote still is what Adler also would have recommended, "first of all, courage, belief in one's ability to cope with whatever problems may arise. . . . Beyond that, the willingness to contribute, to be useful, instead of the increasingly prevalent concern with pleasure and getting" (p. 101).

Letter to a Daughter on Her Marriage

A letter by Adler congratulating his eldest daughter, Valentine, and her husband on the occasion of their wedding may serve practically as a summary of this section. The letter is taken from the Adler biography by Phyllis Bottome (1957, p. 111). It epitomizes in the first part in a touchingly warm, personal way Adler's recommendations for a successful marriage. The second part shows equal parental concern in dealing with some very practical matters, but was not considered relevant here.

Dear Vali and Dear Georgey:

I send you my fondest greetings and take you in my arms and congratulate you with all my heart! My thoughts are always with you.

Do not forget that married life is a task at which both of you must work, with joy.

Remember that the monogamous form of life means the finest flower of sex culture.

I ask you to fill yourselves with the brave resolve to think more about each other than about yourself, and always try to live in such a way that you make the other's life easier and more beautiful.

Don't allow either of you to become subordinate to the other. No one can stand this attitude. Don't allow

anyone else to gain influence over the shaping of your
marriage relation. Only make friends with people who
have a sincere affection for you both. . . .

Many kisses and greetings,
Papa

V. SEXUAL DISORDERS: GENERAL

The preceding four sections of this essay were intended
mainly to explicate Adler's theories and to fill out the picture
of Adler the man and his time. In some instances we also examined Adler's position with regard to the contemporary
scene. In the present section, on sexual disorders in general,
commenting on Chapters 5 to 7, the emphasis is on compar-
ing Adler's theories with current developments. We shall see
that these largely bear out Adler's positions, although his
name is generally not mentioned.

A Consensual Development

For the sake of convenience and clarity we shall in our
comparisons draw mostly on the writings of a group of psychiatrists involved with theoretical issues whom we consider
representative of developments on a still larger scale. We are
referring to the American Academy of Psychoanalysis, and
the seminal writings of Sandor Rado (1890–1972). The
group is well represented in two volumes edited by Judd Marmor (1965, 1968). Founded in 1956, the Academy had by
1976 attained eight hundred members. They refer to themselves as "modern psychoanalysts" or as "progressive psychoanalysts" and include many of those previously called "neo-
Freudians" or "ego psychologists."

The broader meaning of psychoanalysis. Since this group
identifies itself with "psychoanalysis," this raises the ubiqui-
tous problem of the meaning of that term. Indeed, after his
separation from Freud in 1911, Adler named his own new

341

group Society for Free Psychoanalytic Research. How could Adler do this and later deny that he had been a disciple of Freud? How can an academy of psychoanalysis in fact validate much of Adler? And how, on the other hand, could Ellenberger (1970) make the claim, "When studying Adler, the reader must temporarily put aside all that he learned about psychoanalysis" (p. 571), a claim that we strongly support? The answer is that psychoanalysis has a broader and a narrower meaning.

The broader and earlier meaning of psychoanalysis is that of personality study and psychotherapy, to which Freud made the important methodological contribution of replacing hypnosis with free association. We can cite the following illustrations of this broad usage. The subtitle of the *American Psychoanalytic Review,* founded in 1914, was *A Journal Devoted to an Understanding of Human Conduct.* Furtmüller (1914), Adler's coworker, wrote in a paper "The Psychological Significance of Psychoanalysis": "The two essentially new tasks that psychoanalysis poses and the solution of which it makes possible are the scientific study of the contents of the psyche and exploration of personality" (p. 172). And the Merriam-Webster Dictionary, Pocket Book edition (1974), gives but one definition of psychoanalysis: "A method of dealing with psychic disorders by study of the normally hidden content of the mind, esp. to resolve conflicts." In all three examples nothing particularly Freudian is mentioned. It was such a broader meaning that Adler had in mind when he spoke at first of "Free Psychoanalytic Research."

The narrower meaning of psychoanalysis associates it specifically with Freud's teachings. This usage is illustrated by Chaplin's (1975) dictionary definition: "A system of psychology directed toward the understanding, cure, and prevention of mental disorders, as conceived by Sigmund Freud." This is the general meaning of the term in academic circles today, the meaning we have employed in this book in contrasting Freud's theories with those of Adler, and the meaning Ellenberger had in mind. It was also Freud's (1914a, p. 340) meaning when he berated Adler for having chosen the name "Free Psychoanalysis." Adler soon accepted the narrower meaning of the term, leaving "Psychoanalysis" entirely to Freud, and calling his own orientation "Individual Psychology." For a discussion of the origin and meaning of this term, see Ansbacher (1974b).

The American Academy of Psychoanalysis accepts *de facto* the broader meaning of "psychoanalysis," dismissing much of Freud's theories while, however, paying homage to his name.

Adaptational viewpoint. The theoretical position of the Academy can be characterized by the adaptational psychodynamic viewpoint of Rado, based on the evolutionary biological principle. This is quite in contrast to Freud, who was concerned with intrapsychic unconscious processes and instincts aimed at reinstating a status quo.

An adaptational viewpoint had been taken by Adler from the start and is well expressed by him (A1956b) in the following: "Individual Psychology stands firmly on the ground of *evolution* and, in the light of it, regards all human striving as a striving for perfection. . . . We must connect our thought with a continuous *active adaptation* to the demands of the outer world if we are to understand the direction and movement of life. . . . It has always been a matter of overcoming . . . of establishing a favorable relationship between the individual and the outer world. . . . In speaking of *active adaptation* I am referring to *adaptation* under the aspect of eternity. . . . An *adaptation* to immediate reality would be nothing other than exploitation of the accomplishments of the striving of others" (pp. 106–7, italics added).

But Adler, having left the Freudian circle, remained largely unread by psychiatrists. It remained for Rado, who declared his independence from Freud some twenty to thirty years after Adler, to gain a hearing and a sizable following among psychiatrists for the adaptational viewpoint. Quite parallel to Adler, yet without any reference to him, Rado (1949) stated: "Biology is at present in the process of recognizing the adaptive aspect of life. The adaptational point of view permeates the writings of Charles Darwin. . . . We hold that this frame of reference is fundamental to all biology" (p. 124). Rado (1969) continued: "Adaptational psychodynamics emphasizes the part played by motivation and control in the organism's interaction with its cultural environment . . . in terms of organismic utility" (p. 6). "In the human species it is necessary . . . to extend the meaning of the word 'adaptation' so that it includes all those ecological reactions by which the individual influences the environment for its own purposes" (p. 7).

A breakaway organization. The American Academy of Psychoanalysis was founded, according to Masserman (1958), because "some of Freud's less able followers fostered a doctrinaire, isolated, and narrowly administered cult. . . . To counter this tendency, more broadly oriented and progressive analysts . . . began to form groups dedicated to renewed research . . . and in 1956 . . . united to form the Academy of Psychoanalysis" (p. v), later amended to American Academy of Psychoanalysis. Marmor (1968) stated the purpose of the Academy as "to promote the progressive, scientific development of psychoanalysis by furthering communication among psychoanalysts of all viewpoints and their colleagues in other disciplines in science and in the humanities for the purpose of inquiring into the phenomena of individual motivation and social behavior" (p. ix).

As of today, the Academy has succeeded in gathering under one roof a broad spectrum of dissidents from the narrow psychoanalytic line. Among them are followers of Erich Fromm, Karen Horney, Harry Stack Sullivan, etc., and among its founding members were Nathan Ackerman, Franz Alexander, Silvano Arieti, Irving Bieber, Paul Hoch, Donald D. Jackson, Judd Marmor, Jules H. Masserman, and Lewis R. Wolberg.

In many ways the Academy's purpose is similar to that of Adler's original society: "The Society for Free Psychoanalytic Research was founded in June 1911 by some members of the Vienna Psychoanalytic Society . . . who believed to have noted that the members of the old Society were to be committed to the dogmas and theories of Freud in their entirety. Such procedure seemed to them not only hard to reconcile with the general basic conditions of scientific research, but also particularly dangerous in as young a science as psychoanalysis. In their opinion premature commit-

344

ment to certain formulas and surrender of the possibility of investigating new solutions endangered the achievements to date. Convinced of the critical significance of the psychoanalytic method and approach, they felt a scientific obligation to secure a home for completely independent psychoanalytic research" (Vorstand, 1912).

With such similarity of purpose and basic theoretical position between the Academy and Adler's group, Academy members have taken many of the theoretical steps first taken by Adler. Perhaps a majority have come to reject such basic Freudian concepts as libido, cathexis, primacy of id impulses, significance of bisexuality, latent homosexuality, and many others, and some have come up with such Adlerian concepts as primacy of the personality, future orientation, goal striving, power striving, adaptation, symptoms as coping devices, life style, and many others, as we shall show below. They have thus furnished a broad independent consensual validation for Adler's original position. Yet a substantial minority of Academy members are still strongly committed to basic Freudian concepts. "It is one of the virtues of the Academy," writes Marmor (1977), "that we all live together with these differences and are able to discuss them without rancor."

Under these conditions friendly relations exist between the Academy and present-day Adlerians. Kurt Adler (1972) participated with a paper in the Academy's symposium "The Dynamics of Power." At the Academy's meeting in 1977 in Toronto, Adlerians were invited to present an "Oral-history Portrait of Alfred Adler." Marmor (1972) acknowledged the contributions of Adler with the words: "Alfred Adler is without a doubt the most underestimated figure of the early psychoanalytic movement. . . . Adler truly deserves to be recognized as one of the most original, creative, and progressive thinkers in the history of modern psychiatry. He must be credited with being the first of the ego psychologists, and the first psychoanalyst to conceive of human psychology in holistic terms" (p. 153). Lewis Wolberg (1970) noted: "The full significance of Adler's work has never until recently been fully appreciated. It is a matter of great amazement to discover . . . how many so-called modern trends in mental

345

health parallel Adlerian theories and methods" (p. 16). Leon Salzman (1962) acknowledged: "Adler . . . has been the intellectual prophet for much of the neo-Freudian innovations" (p. 67).

Critique of Freud's Concepts

As mentioned earlier (pp. 285–86), Adler's most important paper in his relation to Freud was that on "psychological hermaphroditism." The term, quite frequently used at the time, meant that either sex may show psychological characteristics of the other sex, leaving the relationship to constitutional or somatic hermaphroditism somewhat unclear.

Psychological hermaphroditism, bisexuality, masculine protest. Freud (1905) rejected the term "psychological hermaphroditism" in favor of "bisexuality" to designate that a person's behavior characteristic of the other sex is constitutionally based. Bisexuality became most important for Freud's interpretation of homosexuality, which he called "inversion." "A bisexual disposition is somehow concerned in inversion, though we do not know in what that disposition consists" (pp. 9–10). And in general, Freud found, "Without taking bisexuality into account I think it would scarcely be possible to arrive at an understanding of the sexual manifestations that are actually to be observed in men and women" (p. 86). "A disposition to perversion is an original and universal disposition of the human sexual instinct" (p. 97).

When Adler (A1911i) used the term "psychological hermaphroditism," he pointed out: "Bisexuality indicates that two sexual impulses are inborn—an assumption that is avoided by use of the expression 'psychic hermaphroditism'" (p. 174). But Adler also abandoned this term, as Freud had done. Adler replaced it with "masculine protest," a term he introduced in his above-mentioned paper. Adler (A1911i) held that the masculine protest ensues from psychic hermaphroditism (p. 174). In the neurotic man the masculine protest takes the form of wanting to demonstrate that he is a "real man"; in the neurotic woman, it takes the form of fighting the notion of being "only a woman." In other words, neurotics of both sexes are fighting the feminine aspects of themselves—that is, femininity in the sense of the gender stereotype of weakness and inferiority—and are aspiring to the male-gender stereotype of power and dominance. Paradoxically, both sexes may do this by masculine or feminine means. This was Adler's "psychological hermaphroditism." A woman may attempt to conquer through stressing her femininity as well as through denying it. Likewise a man may attempt to conquer through feminine means. Adler reports from a male homosexual patient who commented on his ability to seduce men: "The power that I exert on men fills me with ecstasy." Male homosexuals stay away from women from fear of being dominated by them.

It should be mentioned that Adler (A1933b) later also expressed himself on somatic hermaphroditism, stating: "There are genuine hermaphrodites with whom it is really difficult to say whether one is dealing with girls or boys. They can decide for themselves what use they make of their hermaphroditism" (p. 199). The work of Money has shown that the outcome in such cases is indeed a matter of human decision, mostly that of the parents and ultimately also that of the individual involved. In general, hermaphrodites will form their gender identity in accordance with their sex assignment and rearing, and will adhere to it. Where this is not the case, it is due to uncertainty of sex of assignment. To quote Money and Ehrhardt (1972): "Hermaphroditic children who eventually decide that they were wrongly assigned, and request reassignment, typically have a biography of uncertainty as to their sex of assignment" (p. 153).

Concomitant to Freud's theory of innate bisexuality are the assumptions of (1) an innate homosexual component, (2) latent homosexuality, and (3) the virtual impossibility of treating homosexuality. In the following pages we shall discuss how Adler dealt with and rejected the above three views and how they are met by modern psychoanalysts. As a fourth point we shall mention that the questioning of these concepts is only a part of today's questioning of Freud's entire metapsychology in psychoanalytic circles.

347

Homosexual component. Adler dismissed as untenable seven arguments for the innateness of homosexuality in the form of "innate homosexual components of the sex drive." Freud's assumption of bisexuality led him to believe that the sex drive itself is bisexual, having components of either sex. These would lead to homosexual and heterosexual behavior, respectively. The homosexual components could be repressed, like the heterosexual ones, resulting in neurotic symptoms, or could perhaps be sublimated. Or they could lead directly to "abnormal sexuality." From such reasoning Freud (1905) pronounced: "Neuroses are, so to say, the negative of perversions" (p. 31); hysterics are "negative perverts" (p. 102).

Freud's main evidence for the homosexual component were homosexual fantasies and dreams. Adler, rejecting this entire idea, considered such evidence but "an arrangement of the individual . . . to be understood only as attempts to support presumed homosexuality, from which one can infer that the dreamer is not very sure of it." More about this below, in the section on "Training and Self-training."

Rado (1940) concurs in forcefully rejecting Freud's evidence. "The idea that these so-called masculine and feminine manifestations are the direct expression of a constitutional component of the opposite sex is unwarranted. . . . A fantasy, even though influential in attitude or behavior, may or may not be the expression of a particular constitutional component." Rado adds the striking illustration: "Inspired by birds, man has dreamed for millennia of flying under his own power, but no one has ever suggested that this implied a flying component or predisposition in his constitution" (p. 185). This is preceded by the general refutation: "A homosexual component has been assumed, on the basis of the concept of bisexuality, to be present in every individual. It is not pleasant to have to admit that a closer scrutiny reveals no less than six major flaws in this procedure" (p. 184).

Latent homosexuality. The homosexual component, as long as it remains dormant, would be Freud's "latent homosexuality." Without using the term, Adler referred to this when he rejected Freud's assumption that a repressed homosexual libido component "existed as inclination and fantasy perhaps in all neurotics." In a second *de facto* reference, Adler considered it a misinterpretation to take a person's rejection of homosexuality "as betraying a struggle against one's own homosexual tendencies." This is an "attempt . . . to increase the number of homosexuals by exactly those who are opposed to it." Freud (1917a) had stated: "In every single neurotic, evidence of homosexual tendencies is forthcoming, and a large proportion of the symptoms are expressions of this latent inversion. Those who openly call themselves homosexuals are merely those in whom the inversion is conscious and manifest; their number is negligible compared with those in whom it is latent" (p. 27).

Recently, Salzman (1965) has rejected with particular force the concept of latent homosexuality. Referring to B. S. Robbins, Salzman (1965) distinguishes between latency as *"dormancy,* that is, the presence of a fully developed and matured function in an inactive state (e.g., the hiberating bear and portions of our memory), or *potentiality,* that is, the possibility that some state . . . may develop" (pp. 235–36). While the second use of latent homosexuality is taken for granted, the term is used strictly in the first sense. This use, however, is based "on anatomical and physiological fallacies" and is "detrimental in a scientific and humanistic sense" (p. 244). Therefore, Salzman recommends, unless the concept can be validated, "the term be completely abandoned" (p. 246).

Bieber (1965) cleverly turned Freud's phrase around when he stated, "Most men are not latent homosexuals; rather, all homosexuals are latent heterosexuals" (p. 253).

Deplorable consequences. Freud's assumption of an innate homosexual component creates the belief that homosexuality, once it has developed, is unalterable. Adler pointed this out, noting: "Homosexuals who complain about their 'unfortunate disposition' generally do very little about it. They rather conclude from their futile efforts that they cannot be saved. . . . On the other hand [there are] those who pride themselves on being 'different.'" It must be understood that "the homosexual has been misguided through general human weakness of thought [and] his argumentation is advanced by a frequent scientific myth."

These considerations are also shared by Rado (1940). "The vague notion of biological bisexuality and the incredibly loose manner in which it has been used in psychoanalysis have had deplorable consequences. . . . The idea that he is up against a homosexual component in his constitution has often produced in a patient needless discouragement or panic, if not more serious complications" (p. 186).

Ovesey (1954) notes that Freud's assumptions "excluded homosexuality from the neuroses and also, at least theoretically, from the realm of psychoanalytic therapy, since only neuroses were believed susceptible to psychoanalysis" (p. 128). Beyond this, "The classical constitutional approach can do great damage. The interpretation of overt homosexuality as an expression of inherent bisexuality is discouraging enough, but to explain dependency and power strivings to a heterosexual patient on the same basis can be catastrophic" (p. 139).

Proceeding from his concept of bisexuality, Freud assumed further a normal homosexual phase of development in early adolescence. This view has found so much credence that one of the definitions of homosexuality in Webster's Third International Dictionary is, "A stage in normal psychosexual development occurring during prepuberty in the male and during adolescence in the female during which libidinal gratification is sought with members of one's own sex" (Perloff, 1965, p. 44). The damaging suggestion exerted by such wide permeation of this fallacious idea of Freud's is deplored by Salzman (1974b) in the following: "The strength of the Freudian impact on our culture is manifest in the way an individual turns these [adolescent] doubts [about adequacy] into concerns about potency and then possible homosexuality. . . . The adolescent is the most probable victim of such misconceptions and distortions, and his doubts can too easily be viewed as evidence of homosexuality, thereby reducing his heterosexual capacity, producing a serious vicious circle" (p. 206).

Metapsychology. Freud's concepts of an innate homosexual

350

component and latent homosexuality are part of his general approach of physicalistic reductionism. This was formulated in his metapsychology with its three aspects: the *dynamic,* referring to his entire instinct theory; the *topographic,* referring to the distinctions among the unconscious, the preconscious, and the conscious, to which later the distinctions among the id, the ego, and the super-ego was added; and the *economic,* referring to the concepts of psychic energy, cathexis, and countercathexis, and the way in which psychic energy is distributed and discharged. We have shown elsewhere (Ansbacher, 1974a) that Adler's complete critique of Freud, of which the present is only a part, amounted to a critique of Freud's entire metapsychology.

Today there is a broad movement in psychoanalytic circles to abandon Freud's metapsychology and to retain his clinical theory only. To give a few expressions of this movement: George S. Klein (1973) finds metapsychology incompatible with and "irrelevant" (p. 107) to clinical psychoanalytic practice where one meets and interprets in terms of "purpose, function, accomplishment" (p. 111), intention and meaning. Although Freud considered his metapsychology "the most fundamental level of explanation" (p. 102), Klein would abandon it completely and reconstruct the entire psychoanalytic theory from what actually takes place during the psychoanalytic hour. Leon J. Saul (1972) writes: "Most of metapsychology I believe could be and in fact is being abandoned, and this is freeing the field so that analysts do not feel constrained by the libido theory and can become more open-minded observers" (p. 10). Peterfreund (1975), after stating that metapsychology "from the very first . . . was almost completely unacceptable" (p. 536) to him, singles out the concept of "ego" as an "empty tautology" (p. 538). He finds that the concepts of ego and id are used in such a way that "one cannot truly distinguish between them" (p. 542), and that "psychoanalytic theory has . . . given the ego all the attributes of the person" (p. 542). This is quite similar to Adler's (A1956b) observation regarding the id when he wrote: "Even if one believes one has dislodged the self [person] from the unconscious, or from the id, in the end the id

351

behaves mannerly or unmannerly like a self [person]" (p. 176). Judd Marmor (1968) declared categorically: "The cumbersome metapsychological superstructure that Freud erected . . . —notably his theory of instincts, of libido, of the tripartite structure of the psyche, and of psychic energy—has become obsolete" (p. 6). "Psychoanalytic theory will not only move farther away from Freudian metapsychology but will gradually begin employing more and more of the common language of the other behavioral sciences: the language of adaptation, learning theory, communications, and information theory" (p. 11).

Such utterances are today still considered to show "scientific independence and courage . . . refusal to be bullied by convention or dogma or prevailing opinion" as Smith (1973, p. 97) stated in reference to Klein. From this, one may estimate Adler's courage and stature when he confronted Freud personally with a rejection of the entire instinct theory and its concomitants, even before Freud had written his papers on metapsychology, while Freud (1905) believed, "The theory of the instincts is the most important . . . portion of psychoanalytic theory" (p. 34n).

Sexuality in the Service of Personality

Adler's system is indeed a "human psychology in holistic terms," to use Marmor's phrase (p. 104). This implies that a person's sexuality will be dominated by his personality, his style of life. This principle applies also to sexual disorders, which Adler counted among the neuroses. Thus Adler states: "We derive the understanding of any sexual abnormality from an understanding of the whole person, not vice versa, as Freudian psychoanalysis teaches." "The patient acquires the neurosis that he feels corresponds best to his fictional goal and corresponding life plan." The problem in sexual disorder, including homosexuality, becomes the description and understanding of the respective life style and its development, and its possible modification.

352

Expression of the life style. The term "life style" represented to Adler the ideas of the individual as a self-consistent unity, an actor and creator rather than a mere object and reactor, and his goal directedness—all these as they manifest themselves concretely in the unique individual case. Life style includes the person's conception of his goal of success, his opinion of himself and the world, and his characteristic way of striving for his goal. Life style is thus an integral part of Adler's humanistic psychology (see Ansbacher, 1971b).

Adler (A1956b) equates life style variously with self, ego, a man's own personality, the unity of the personality, individuality, individual form of creative activity, the method of facing problems, the whole attitude to life, and other terms (p. 174). "The unity in each individual—in his thinking, feeling, acting, in his so-called conscious and unconscious—in every expression of his personality, we call the 'life style' of the individual. What is frequently labeled the ego is nothing more than the style of the individual" (p. 175).

The organic functions are also dominated by the style of life. "This is notably the case with the lungs, the heart, the stomach, the organs of excretion, and the sexual organs. The disturbance of these functions expresses the direction that an individual is taking to attain his goal. I have called these disturbances the organ dialect, or organ jargon, since the organs are revealing in their own most expressive language the intention of the individual totality. The dialect of the sexual organs is especially expressive" (A1929c, p. 156).

The view of personality dominating sexuality has since been reiterated by Rado and by Marmor among many others. Marmor (1974) states: "Patterns of sexual behavior always reflect personality patterns and problems" (p. 89). Marmor (1977) adds that "modern physiology leans more heavily toward the interrelationship of organ systems in their functioning rather than of individual organs," and that Franz Alexander's "vector theory" offers "a more sophisticated adaptation of Adlerian views about how organ systems operate within the body on a receptive, retentive, and discharge basis." Marmor (1968) also introduced a term similar to life style when he wrote about a "transactional life-system"

353

(p. 9). Before him Rado, in a particularly "Adlerian" statement, introduced a term functionally equivalent to life style, which he used to express the influence of personality on sexuality. Rado (1949) wrote: "The child's experiences in the family group lay the foundations of what will later emerge as his Established Pattern of Psychodynamic Adaptation (EPPA). This includes the individual's attitudes toward cooperation and competition, his proneness to domination or submission, his aspirations, social fears, and resentments. This lasting adaptive organization has of course profound bearings on the individual's sexual behavior as well" (p. 107).

Adler's conception of sexuality, including sexual disorders, as subject to the total personality, the life style, is one aspect of a holistic theory that sees man as (1) culturally rather than instinctually determined, (2) part of social units, (3) creative and importantly self-determined, and (4) teleological (goal-oriented). Some of the support Adler's theory has received on these counts are shown in the following pages.

Cultural determination. Adler introduced his concept of "masculine protest" as a move away from an instinct theory of personality toward a theory of cultural psychology. Today this reorientation has been so widely followed that Salzman (1968b) could say: "Instinct theory is largely outmoded as a biological model for the comprehension of personality development, and the view of sex as an instinct limits the understanding of its role in human behavior" (p. 125), a statement documented by fifteen references. "The tendency to move from an instinctual framework to a more culturally oriented perspective in personality theory has been reflected in a number of alternative theories regarding infantile sexuality, homosexuality, female sexuality, and sexual deviations. These approaches take into account the scientific developments in psychology, anthropology, sociology, and ethology over the past fifty years" (p. 125). Adler took this decisive step toward a culturally oriented personality theory several years before the beginning of this period.

Man as part of social units. Adler's cultural orientation, together with his holistic approach, included the conception of the individual as part of larger social units and the necessity

354

to study him as such rather than as an isolated being. Adler (A1926d) had stated: "Individual Psychology regards and examines the individual as socially embedded. We refuse to recognize and examine an isolated human being" (p. ix). Later Adler (A1936j) added: "The field of investigation of Individual Psychology is the relationship, carried out in actions, of a peculiarly stylized individual to problems of the environment" (p. 244). Adler's (A1956b) definition of "environment" transpires from his description of the mother's function as being to awaken the child's social interest, then spread it from herself toward the father, and turn it "to the social life around the child, to the other children of the family, to friends, relatives, and fellow human beings in general . . . until it includes the whole of our human society" (p. 373).

Marmor (1968) considers the emergence of such holistic-social thinking the most important development of recent times. "The revolutionary change that has been taking place in psychodynamic thought in the latter half of the twentieth century has been . . . a shift from the closed system of the individual model to an open-system module in which the individual's functioning is always examined in the context of his group or field situation. Thus, while Freud's conceptual framework was . . . individual-centered . . . in advanced psychoanalytic circles today the focus of psychopathology is . . . in the individual's system of relationship, his family, his small groups, his community, his society" (p. 4).

Creativity and dialectical self-determination. Yet Adler was not a cultural determinist. Beyond heredity and environment Adler (A1956b) assumed as decisive "the existence of still another force: the creative power of the individual. We have been impelled to attribute to the child creative power, which casts into movement all the influences upon him and all his potentialities, a movement toward the overcoming of an obstacle. . . . The individual is thus . . . the artist of his own personality" (p. 177). "Heredity only endows the individual with certain abilities. Environment only gives him certain impressions. These abilities and impressions . . . are the bricks that he uses in his own 'creative' way in building up his atti-

355

tude toward life" (p. 206). The meaning a person gives to life "is built up in his style of life and runs through it like a strange melody of his own creation" (p. 181).

The necessity for attributing to man creative ability is today well expressed and supported by Arieti (1975). He states, for example: "The image that the child has of himself does not consist of reflected appraisals from parents or family members but of what the child did with those appraisals. In the same way, the image that he has of his parents and siblings . . . is not a mirror reproduction but rather a subjective interpretation. . . . Our self-image is not created exclusively by others but also by ourselves. We are among our own creative forces" (p. 41).

Arieti considers this an important insight for a patient if he is ever to stop blaming others and take on some responsibility for his own future. Adler (A1956b) had forcefully expressed the same thought: "The life plan of the neurotic demands categorically that if he fails, it should be through someone else's fault and that he should be freed from responsibility" (p. 27). Adler considered resistance encountered in psychotherapy directed exactly against this insight. "Every therapeutic cure, and still more any awkward attempt to show the patient the truth, tears him from the cradle of his freedom from responsibility and must therefore reckon with the most vehement resistance" (p. 271).

To express the individual's active participation in the creation of his world, Adler (A1964a) quoted from Pestalozzi (1746–1827): "The environment molds man, but man molds the environment" (pp. 28 and 321). This sentence, used also by Karl Marx (1818–83), became one of the key phrases of dialectical materialism. Today Marmor (1974), who is also convinced of man's active participation, uses this sentence again, one time modified as: "Man shapes his institutions, but he is also shaped by them" (p. 421). On another occasion when he used the modification: "Circumstances are changed by men as much as men are changed by circumstances" (p. 141), Marmor made the point that "Freud's theoretical limitations . . . flow . . . from the fact that his materialism was mechanistic instead of dialectical"

356

(p. 131). By contrast, Adler's approach was dialectical, as discussed earlier, and like Marmor today, Adler (A1964a) found fault with Freud as being "wholly confined in a mechanistic conception" and using "a mechanistic principle for the explanation of mind and psyche" (p. 218).

Goal orientation (*teleology*). The concept of creativity leads directly to that of goal orientation, or teleology. Adler (A1956b) stated: "The creative power is teleological. It expresses itself in striving after a goal, and in this striving every bodily and psychological movement is made to cooperate" (p. 92). "Individual Psychology insists absolutely on the indispensability of finalism for the understanding of all psychological phenomena. Causes, powers, instincts, impulses, and the like cannot serve as explanatory principles. The final goal alone can" (p. 92). This is in direct opposition to Freud (1937), who held from his mechanistic and reductionistic position that "in the psychological field the biological factor is really the rock bottom" (p. 357).

Adler's position on this issue also is supported by "progressive psychoanalysts" of today, members of the Academy. Rado (1969) stated: "We examine behavior first from the point of view of means to an end. . . . The question is, 'What is its purpose?' . . . The organism is seen to do its own goal searching, goal finding, goal pursuing, and goal attaining. . . . The organism's own expectancies enter as components into the causal mechanism of its behavior" (p. 8). Rado (1949) considered this viewpoint indispensable "for the understanding of sexual behavior. . . . Teleology has become a methodological principle" (p. 124). Arieti (1972) concurs with such words as: "The will of man becomes a cause of action. . . . Teleological causality is added to deterministic causality . . . a causality compatible with free will" (p. 51). Marmor (1974) also arrives at the conclusion: "We can postulate that human beings, consciously or unconsciously, usually operate with a hierarchy of plans, some of which are concerned with long-term goals, others with short-term goals" (p. 179).

The many uses of sex. The preceding in turn leads to the understanding that sex can become a means to many different

357

ends, rather than being a prime mover on its own accord. This is practically the burden of Adler's main argument with Freud. While Freud saw many different behaviors motivated by sex, Adler recognized the many different purposes that may motivate sexual behavior. When this takes place more or less unconsciously, Adler speaks of "the dialect of the sexual organs" (p. 353 above). To Adler it was "strange that Freud, a connoisseur of the symbolic in life, was incapable of resolving the symbolic in the sexual apperception, to recognize the sexual as a jargon, as a *modus dicendi*."

Sex is especially often in the service of power striving, thus disturbing love relationships. As we have seen, it may turn into "prestige politics" or may become a means of revenge against one's partner, as when falling in love with a third party.

Within the Adlerian framework Shulman (1967) identified quite informally twenty-one different uses of sex. The six principal socially constructive uses are: reproduction, pleasure, feeling of belonging, sharing or co-operating, consolation, and healthy self-affirmation. Seven less important constructive uses are: encouragement, relaxation, distraction from unpleasant stimuli, physical and emotional closeness, general stimulation, a gift, and a way of getting acquainted. On the socially destructive side are the remaining eight, namely, use for mischief, distance, domination (power), the reward value of suffering, demonstrating success or failure, vanity, revenge, and proving abnormality (as in homosexual urges). This last group are, of course, the neurotic and sociopathic uses characterized by lack of social interest. The reader may easily extend this inventory.

Recognition of the many uses of sex is acknowledged by Salzman as part of "modern psychoanalytic theory." At the same time, the "causative influence" of sex is minimized. Salzman (1974a) writes: "Most sex behavior in man is not motivated by procreative needs, or even exclusively for the erotic pleasure or release of gonadal tension. Sex activity serves a wide variety of purposes in the service of fulfilling man's other needs, such as power, control, anger, etc., and also the expression of tender, affectionate feelings. . . . The direction of interest in the past thirty years is toward a fuller understanding of sex, while minimizing its etiological and causative influence" (p. 264).

Earlier, Salzman (1968b) had given the following *de facto* affirmation of Adler's position: "Sex activity may be the background for exerting power and control over others" (pp. 125–26). "Sex can become an active agent in the manipulation of human relationships. . . . It can be the grounds on which battles for power, prestige, envy and jealousy, generosity or meanness are fought. . . . Since sexual satisfactions usually depend on the co-operation and willingness of the partner, sex can be used to withhold or deny satisfaction or to administer favor or largesse to another person. Problems, conflicts, and interpersonal struggles in any area of human functioning are apt to express themselves in sexual behavior" (p. 130).

Infantile sexuality. As mentioned earlier, with regard to infantile sexuality Adler (A1905a) immediately asked: For what purpose has nature equipped the infant with sexuality? And his answer was: For the purpose of "leading the child to the things of the outside world and to initiating relations with the culture."

The interpretation of infantile sexuality given by today's critics of a simple libidinal interpretation is very similar. Salzman (1968b) anticipates that, as data accumulate, "most infantile behavior will be recognized to be related to nonlibidinal needs. . . . The infant is involved in developing skills relating to survival and interpersonal security. Exploratory activities relating to his own body are preparatory to expanding his knowledge and skill in achieving mastery of himself and his environment. The special interest in the genitals may derive from their particular accessibility in the male, or because of their profusion of nerve endings and the self-sentient capacity of genital play. Such play, however, does not differ in any substantial way from the manipulation of other body zones" (p. 128).

The occurrence of penile erections in male infants had generally been the chief evidence for the existence of infantile sexuality. Yet such erections can now be explained differently.

Chodoff (1966a), in his extensive critique of Freud's theory of infantile sexuality, points out that research of REM (rapid eye movement) sleep had found a very high correlation between it and penile erection. Such erections may then "represent simply another of the nonspecific expressions of this altered metabolic state. It may have no more specific sexual significance than, say, the hypotonia that also occurs in connection with REM sleep" (p. 512).

While Adler's initial explanation of infantile sexuality may have sounded somewhat far-fetched, it appears that he was nevertheless right in principle as far as penile erection is concerned in that what looks as a sexual reaction when adult standards are applied, is in the infant not necessarily sexual in its significance.

Distance from the Other Sex

Adler defined sexual disorders in a simple behavioral or operational way in terms of what actually takes place. They constitute a distance from the normally to be expected partner of the other sex. "All sexual deviations—homosexuality, sadism, masochism, masturbation, fetishism, etc.— . . . have in common . . . an increased psychological distance between man and woman."

While generalizing here regarding all sexual deviations, Adler mentions homosexuality first. In his writings as a whole he also gives homosexuality most of his attention and does not always make a clear distinction between it and other deviations. This will also be reflected in our comments.

Directional definition. As seeking distance or "retreat" from the other sex is a directional term, it is of interest that the term recently suggested by the American Psychiatric Association board of trustees to replace the term homosexuality, namely, "sexual orientation disturbance," is also directional. Robert L. Spitzer (1974) who proposed the term explained that it refers to "individuals whose sexual interests are *directed* primarily toward people of the same sex and who are

360

either bothered by, in conflict with, or wish to change their sexual orientation" (p. 12, italics added).

While both terms being directional are primarily descriptive, there is the difference in naming the direction. Spitzer's direction is *toward* individuals of *the same sex*, Adler's, *away from* individuals of *the other sex*. In Adler's naming, a dialectical reflection is added to the simple observation, consistent with his general dialectical approach. Thereby Adler adds an explanatory aspect to the mere description and achieves a direction which is applicable to all sexual disorders, not only homosexuality. He thus provides a comprehensive and simple theory for all sexual disorders.

The direction in sexual disorders as "away from" is part of Adler's understanding of the ideal sexual norm as closeness to and co-operation with a partner of the other sex. Moving away from, or seeking distance, on the other hand, implies, as it generally does, low valuation, unfriendliness, hostility, fear, or some other negative attitude regarding the person from whom one moves away. It precludes any assumption of a primary attraction to the same-sex partner or to disordered sexual behavior as such.

Heterosexuality as the norm has also been asserted by Bieber et al. (1962). Attributing spontaneous homosexuality to fear of the other sex, although in different terms than Adler (see pp. 387–88 below), Bieber argues: "Any adaptation that is basically an accommodation to unrealistic fear is necessarily pathologic; in the adult homosexual, continued fear of heterosexuality is inappropriate to his current reality. We differ with other investigators who have taken the position that homosexuality is a kind of variant of 'normal' sexual behavior" (pp. 303–4).

Various determinants of distance. If we take heterosexuality in the sense of close contact with the other sex as the norm, any distance from the other-sex partner in sexual activity, be it physical or psychological, becomes a deviation, although there are large differences, depending on the circumstances. We may distinguish three types:

1. Sexual-distance behavior may be a cultural phenomenon, as in the case of pederasty in ancient Greece. Such homosex-

uality would have no personal significance, although it did, according to Adler, reflect a culturally sanctioned poor relationship between the sexes.

2. Physical distance from the other sex may in our culture be imposed from the outside, as in military or prison situations, between young people of opposite sexes, or by the general difficulty of life. In these instances homosexuality would be transitory and resorted to as a second-best. Yet even under these circumstances not everybody would engage in homosexuality, so that personal factors may also be involved.

3. The distance from the other sex may be sought by an individual on his own, be self-imposed, reflecting negative motivation toward the other-sex partner individually or generically. This type is Adler's main concern.

Although Adler did not actually name these three types, he made the respective distinctions, acknowledging different reasons, for example, for homosexual behavior. His decisive statement on the complexity of the problem of homosexuality was: "Homosexuality, the result of psychological factors, shares with these a characteristic that is much too little appreciated: It is in itself ambiguous and can be understood in its significance only in reference to its time and the particular individual."

The relativity of homosexuality and the existence of various kinds of homosexual behavior have also been noted by Salzman (1962). He stated that altogether, "It would be more desirable to speak of homosexual behavior rather than homosexuality. This would . . . allow for a more operational statement about homosexual behavior. . . . We could visualize a continuum from the most extreme to the least evident homosexual behavior. . . . This approach would also allow for the phenomenon of homosexual behavior as a situational problem" (p. 204). We consider this completely in line with Adlerian thinking.

Homosexuality in ancient Greece. To illustrate Type 1 homosexuality, Adler used the well-known example from ancient Greece, where it took the form of pederasty, love of boys by adult men. Freud (1905) had used the Greek phe-

362

nomenon in support of his theory of bisexuality. A boy was chosen as love object because he "combines the characters of both sexes; there is, as it were, a compromise between an impulse that seeks for a man and one that seeks for a woman. . . . Thus the sexual object is a kind of reflection of the subject's own bisexual nature" (p. 10).

For Adler the important factor was that Greek pederasty, being socially sanctioned, also included social values, and was, thereby, one might say, normalized. The man was to the boy not only a lover but also a teacher, protector, inspirer. The man was married, and the boy was expected to get married later on. Thus the relationship was integrated into the general social process. It was for the boy, as Adler points out, "a preparation for heterosexual love and for comradeship." Within this framework it is understandable that, as Stoller (1974) noted, "many Greek writers represented homosexuality as ennobling and normal" (p. 604).

But why did the culture institute and sanction this form of homosexuality? Adler saw in self-imposed homosexuality fear of being overpowered by the other sex and, as one of the safeguarding devices, retreat from the other sex and depreciation. He believed that the same dynamics were at work when Greek culture institutionalized pederasty. It occurred "at a time of increasing emancipation of women, which raised their self-esteem" and caused men "to doubt their privileged position." It was "man's masculine-protest-type answer," an attempt at "a reduction of woman's value."

Two current authors, Gordon R. Taylor and Saul H. Fisher, confirm that woman suffered degradation at the time of pederasty, although they believe that it was instituted *after* society had changed from an original matrilineality to patrilineality—that is, after woman had lost her dominant role—whereas for Adler it was a countermeasure against woman's ascendency. Taylor (1965) speaks of a myth of "the gradual establishment of male dominance after a period of female dominance" (p. 159). Fisher (1965) finds, "that, in the Homeric period, the absence of pederasty coincided with the more elevated status of women, whereas in the historic period the prominence of pederasty coincided with the degraded sta-

363

tus of women" (p. 171). These authors agree with Adler on the contemporaneousness of pederasty with a reduced status of woman, yet do not mention any possible intrinsic dynamic relationship.

Present-day situational factors. The form of homosexuality that frequently occurs when the sexes are separated by external force for a length of time, Type 2, is noted by Adler only briefly. "Homosexual relations are almost regularly furthered . . . by opportunity and strict supervision in prisons, institutions, boarding schools, military barracks, or at home," also "on long sea voyages." Adler adds in this connection, "Homosexuality is also frequently connected with drug addiction."

Adler believes that these and other special forms of homosexuality "are really compatible only with our conception. . . . Our view places into the proper light the freechoice factor in this behavior, which, to be sure, appears to be mitigated by the individual's apparent freedom from responsibility for it."

Going on from here, and probably with the example from ancient Greece in mind, Adler observed, "In times when women step more vigorously into the foreground of public life, the large army of cowardly men prefer to increase the distance from the female sex and resort among other safeguards also to homosexuality." A similar conclusion has recently been drawn by Lawrence J. Hatterer, a psychiatrist specializing in the treatment of homosexual men, who was reported as saying, "Woman's liberation will bring out the latent insecurities of some men and push them toward homosexual outlets" (Brody, 1974).

Regarding the incidence of homosexuality, it may be surprising that Adler, writing over fifty years ago, found that "large sections of the population are not true to their sexual role" and that "the number of sexual deviates appears to be on the increase, in rural districts and large cities alike," with "children, adults, and older people" being involved. This account from a different time and place lends more credence to the Kinsey figures, which startled the world, even as the Kinsey figures support Adler. Kinsey (1953) reported that by the age of forty-five about 28 per cent of women and 50 per cent of the men had made some homosexual response, while about 13 per cent of women and 37 per cent of the men had had homosexual experience to orgasm (p. 487).

Adler also noted "quite a few" cases of mixed homosexuality and heterosexuality—that is, bisexuality in the current usage of the term—and considered "occasional and partial homosexuality very widespread among both sexes." Such bisexual behavior has today again attracted attention, as growing, although still a minor phenomenon (Brody, 1974).

Childhood homosexual behavior. One form of Type 2 homosexuality in which the distance from the other sex is imposed from the outside is homosexual behavior in childhood and adolescence. Some of Adler's statements on this point are: "The problem of the so-called natural development of sexuality is not as simple as psychoanalysis teaches. . . . Keep in mind that no childhood offense is considered as serious and punished as severely than development toward the sexual norm." "For boys . . . it is much easier to turn through mutual masturbation to homosexuality than to turn to normal sexual behavior." While these young people would prefer normal heterosexual intercourse, this "is much more strictly forbidden and is usually so severely punished that, in view of the dangers connected with it, the early-maturing youngsters are deterred from the other sex. Obviously, these early signs are inadequate evidence of innate homosexuality." "There is immeasurable horror when a child behaves in the normal sexual way. Thus what we observe in children again and again must be regarded as influenced by external circumstances. We do not know what development sexuality would take if we would not, and would not have to, set up barriers against it."

Today Marmor (1965) concurs that "such behavior may be the expression of transitory and exploratory sexual interests among adolescents and preadolescents in a society that prohibits them from the heterosexual explorations they would prefer" (p. 3). Regarding punishment for heterosexual behavior in childhood, Bieber (1965) found in his study of male homosexuals that "the recall of unusually harsh punishment when caught in heterosexual experimentation" was indeed "not uncommon" (p. 253). We would add that such punishment did not "cause" them to become adult homosexuals and that this development was ultimately still the individual's own "choice." Most children who were punished for early heterosexual activity and who even turned subsequently to homosexuality probably did not "choose" to remain separated from the other sex once the outside barriers were removed.

Homosexuality as Neurosis

In Types 1 and 2 of homosexual behavior the distance from the other sex is imposed from without. In Type 3—homosexuality proper—the distance is imposed from within, and it is here that Adler speaks of neurosis, compulsion neurosis in particular.

The concept of homosexuality as neurosis also finds acceptance today. Ovesey (1954) briefly reviews the challenges by modern psychoanalysts of Freud's concept of homosexuality as the opposite of neurosis (p. 107) and states that finally "the reclassification of homosexuality as a neurosis . . . opened pathways to psychotherapy" (p. 129). Furthermore, Karen Horney, Clara Thompson, and Harry Stack Sullivan all pointed out "nonsexual elaborations" of homosexuality "that had to do with dependency, aggression, competition, domination, and submission" (p. 130)—quite Adlerian concepts. Salzman (1968b) writes: "The crucial question for psychological theory is which comes first, the sexual difficulties [from homosexuality to premature ejaculation] or the neurotic problem. Freud postulated the primacy of the sexual complication, but more recent psychoanalytic theorists lean toward the notion that the sexual complications are the consequence rather than the causes of disordered human relationships" (p. 130). "If homosexuality is viewed as a symptom of a wider personality disorder rather than a specific syndrome, it is then possible to study it in its broad social and psychological context" (p. 137).

Structure of compulsion neurosis. In general, Adler considers the overt compulsive symptom a secondary phenomenon, while the individual's primary compulsion originates in a social demand from which he wants to gain distance or that he approaches with a "hesitating attitude," from fear of failure. The compulsive thought or action is really a "countercompulsion," a device, an arrangement, to safeguard a distance from the problem with which the individual is faced, or at least to gain time before meeting the problem. Generally, "the patient himself recognizes the thoughts as foolish. But, foolish as they may be . . . they are completely suited as a means for the neurotic to disengage himself from those tasks that he is afraid to fulfill."

The problem to be evaded is related by Adler (A1931f) to the three main life problems, "social living, occupation, or love" (p. 136). It represents the primary "compulsion of a social order" that "the patient, through his prestige policy, answers with a countercompulsion, and thereby removes" (p. 136, editors' translation). "When the compulsion neurotic is on sure ground, he advances, unimpeded by obsessive ideas; he solves his task. Only in a certain sector of his life . . . is he particularly inclined to prevent defeat by proceeding to a secondary theater of operations (*sekundärer Kriegsschauplatz*), eliminating the compulsion of life by a countercompulsion" (pp. 115–16).

Adler offers this interpretation to replace the misconception that "the compulsive idea or compulsive action is charged with compulsion and rises occasionally from nowhere to seize upon its victim, as an 'ego-alien' demonic power, removed from normal thinking" (p. 120). Adler credits Freud for having recognized the compulsive symptom as a secondary phenomenon, although he believed the primary force to be instinctual rather than purposive. "Freud certainly does not support an anthropomorphizing conception of compulsion—provided we transform his language (anal, sadistic, guilt feelings) into what we already know (lack of social interest, inferiority feeling, striving for superiority)" (p. 120, editors' translation). These last three characteristics refer to the neurotic disposition concept, which will be discussed below.

367

Compulsion neurosis as prototype. In the final revision of his original paper on compulsion neuroses Adler (1918b) applied its structure to neurosis in general. "The usual forms of compulsion neurosis are the compulsions to wash, to pray, to masturbate, moral compulsive ideas of all kinds, compulsion to brood, etc. . . . We can considerably extend the field . . . since we find the same mechanism also in . . . nocturnal enuresis, neurotic refusal to eat, compulsive hunger, sexual deviations, etc." (pp. 134–35). Furthermore, "The distinction from neurasthenic, hysterical, and anxiety-neurotic symptom complexes is often very vague; alcoholism, drug addiction, etc., are closely related; impulsive insanity, impulsive actions, compulsive self-accusations, certain stereotyped behavior, and psychotic depressions manifest a similar structure" (p. 141). Adler (A1956b) also sees in compulsion neurosis an obvious "relationship to paranoia" (p. 306).

To quote from the present volume: "There is little difference, psychologically speaking, whether the neurotic, when faced with the problem of marriage and love, points to the difficulty of earning a living, the responsibility regarding children, the unfitness of the other sex, his own inferiority; or whether he interposes between himself and his partner a proof of illness, hysteria, a compulsion neurosis, a phobia, impotence, compulsory masturbation, a psychosis, or a sexual deviation."

Thus it becomes quite evident that for Adler compulsion was the prototype of the neuroses. Leonhard Seif (1926), prominent coworker of Adler, stated: "One could call virtually any neurosis a 'compulsion neurosis'" (p. 509).

Here Salzman (1968a) again offers support for Adler's view, stating: "The obsessive-compulsive personality type is today's most prevalent neurotic character structure. . . . Freud used the hysteric as the paradigm of his conceptualization. . . . There is now good reason to believe that . . . the obsessive defense mechanism provides the most widespread technique for enabling man to achieve some illusion of safety and security in an uncertain world" (p. vii). And while Adler (A1931f) described "the life style of the compulsion neurotic" (p. 137) in terms of striving for godlikeness and

368

the hesitating attitude, for Salzman (1968a) the obsessive or compulsive individual is likewise characterized by grandiosity and omniscience, but also by indecision, doubt, and ritual, through which he "avoids the awareness of imperfection, fallibility, and humanness" (p. viii).

Homosexuality as compulsion. Adler (A1918a) speaks specifically of "the compulsion of homosexuality." Like any compulsion neurosis, it does not originate in the symptom, "but in the compulsive diversion of normal relationships in which the individual anticipates certain defeat and before which he stands as before an abyss" (p. 134).

But there is a difference. In the ordinary compulsion the individual is, as mentioned, typically very much aware of the foolish nature of his actions—such as washing his hands, the innumerable ways of wasting time, etc.—and consciously would like to stop them. In homosexuality the individual may want to change, but may also accept his behavior as an unalterable fact, supported by various "scientific myths." Probably on account of this difference, Adler (A1918a) spoke initially only of "the analogy of homosexuality with compulsion neurosis" (p. 131). We shall return to this later. Since, as mentioned, Adler saw a relationship of compulsion neurosis to paranoia, homosexuality was also linked with paranoia, as in the third case of this book.

Salzman (1968a), consistent with his understanding of compulsion neurosis and its importance, speaks of homosexual thoughts also in a very Adlerian way, not as "evidence of latent or repressed homosexual desires" but as possibly "defensive devices designed to distract and displace attention from a significant problem" (p. 29). Salzman (1968b) defines homosexuality as "a manifestation of some failure in personality development in which an individual compulsively prefers and becomes exclusively involved in sexual relations with the same sex" (p. 137).

Substitute satisfaction. To the extent that homosexuality offers satisfaction, Adler sees it, like all sexual deviations, as a substitute for normal sexual behavior, providing, like all of them, substitute satisfaction. Depending on the circumstances, a girl may, for example, early in life develop a substitute goal

369

for a male partner. "Forced into a direction away from men . . . the natural ultimate goal of human sexuality changes into a substitute goal (*Ersatzziel*). This . . . manifests fear of men, indifference, or aversion, or has a masculine tendency and leads to a masculine role in sexual life as well as in the whole modus vivendi." Altogether, "The simplest and most comprehensive formula for understanding homosexuality may be: Homosexuality is a miscarried and misunderstood substitute (*Notbehelf*)." In this, homosexuality does not differ from neurosis in general, in which Adler (A1912a, p. 187) sees the emergence of a "substitute goal" when the individual sees danger that the original goal cannot be reached.

The view of homosexuality as a substitute is also shared today. Bieber (1965) arrived at the conclusion: "The homosexual adaptation is a substitute alternative brought about by the inhibiting fears accompanying homosexuality" (p. 254). Salzman (1968b) regards sexual deviations as "compromise attempts to achieve as much satisfaction in sex activity as is consistent with the anxiety surrounding activity," which makes it unnecessary "to postulate 'polymorphous perverse' beginnings of sexual activity" (p. 140). Stoller (1975) concurs, "One will understand the origins of perversion best if one views it as blighted heterosexuality" (p. xvii).

"Normal" homosexuality. To what extent did Adler recognize that a homosexual may, aside from his homosexuality, function otherwise quite normally? Adler (A1918a) deals with this in the following: "The homosexual presents a faultless picture of a neurotic, except that his neurosis is not clearly expressed because he has narrowed his radius of activity through his homosexuality as much as the neurotic does only through his neurosis. In such a small circle neurotic symptoms often do not show up much. By eliminating aggravating conditions, the homosexual has as a rule succeeded in arranging his life so that he can either meet it quite adequately, or at least follow it more easily than one of heterosexuality, which continuously brings a person in contact with all the problems, demands, and difficulties of social life. Nevertheless, one finds in many homosexuals whose radius of

activity is not too narrow serious symptoms, primarily compulsions" (p. 126).

This position of Adler's by which one could define normal homosexuality as a tolerable level of neurosis seems to be borne out by available knowledge of nonpatient homosexuals. As suggested by the following five sources, they function quite normally, yet seem to be somewhat more neurotic than nonpatient heterosexuals.

1. Evelyn Hooker (1965) observed from male homosexuals that the "one-night stand"—that is, sex "without obligation or commitment"—is "one of the most standardized and characteristic patterns of social interaction" (p. 95). "Wherever homosexuals meet, the expectation that sex can be had without obligation or commitment is a stable, reproducible, standard feature of their interaction" (p. 97). Such lack of obligation and commitment is generally considered a sign of poorer mental health.

2. Kurt Adler (1967) expresses the opinion that "within the homosexual group itself fellowship and social interest are at an extremely low level" (p. 67).

3. Manosevitz (1970), in a study of twenty-eight nonclinical male homosexuals and twenty-two heterosexual controls, found that among the homosexuals 75 per cent "consulted with a physician, psychiatrist, psychologist, or other counselor regarding illness or personal problem," against only 27 per cent among the controls. And of the homosexuals, 46 per cent obtained psychotherapy for a median length of twelve months, against only 9 per cent of the controls.

4. Saghir and Robins (1973) compared nonpatient homosexuals (eighty-eight men and fifty-seven women) with heterosexuals (thirty-five men and forty-three women). They found among the homosexual men significantly more "feminine identification . . . more psychotherapy, seeing a physician more often during a depression, greater dropping out during the college years and . . . greater number of full-time jobs" (p. 132). There also were trends of "greater oversensitivity, greater problems with alcohol, greater use and abuse

371

of non-prescription drugs, a greater number of suicide attempts . . . and greater likelihood for being fired from a job" (pp. 132–33). Among the homosexual women, "significantly more identify themselves as masculine, abuse alcohol, and drop out from college" (p. 293), although "like homosexual men, they usually show little impairment of function" (p. 294).

5. Weinberg and Williams (1974) studied large numbers of nonclinical homosexual men in the United States and smaller numbers in Holland and Denmark, and found them less happy than controls. The societal reactions theory that homosexuals appear less well adjusted due to the harassment by a hostile society, was not supported. Although Denmark and Holland presumably have a social climate more tolerant of homosexuality, the samples from these countries appeared just as "maladjusted" as the American samples (pp. 151, 267–69).

These studies seem to warrant the minimum conclusion that normal, nonclinical homosexuals are generally not as healthy mentally as normal controls. This does not contradict Marmor's (1975) conclusion from such studies that the stereotyping of all homosexuals as neurotically disturbed "is quite unwarranted" (p. 1517).

The preceding results are almost exclusively about men and cannot necessarily be generalized to women. "Normality" may be greater among female homosexuals. For example, Siegrid Schäfer (1977) in a comparative study in West Germany, found among female homosexuals a prevalence of real love and faithfulness, which was in sharp contrast to her findings among men. From this she concluded that male and female homosexuality are "two entirely different phenomena." These findings are in line with earlier informal observations. In partial explanation, we may refer to Clara Thompson, as quoted by Marmor (1965), who noted that "Women in general are permitted greater physical intimacy with each other without social disapproval than is the case with men" (p. 14).

372

Other Sexual Disorders

Sadism and masochism. Sadism and masochism, the obtaining of sexual pleasure by administering or receiving pain, respectively, were considered by Adler, like homosexuality, to be compulsion neuroses. From the start Adler (A1908b) rejected the general understanding of the sexual aspect as primary and the cruelty but an admixture. Instead, when he still expressed himself in terms of drives, he considered sadism and masochism a confluence of two forces of equal strength, the sex drive and the aggression drive (p. 23). Eventually, the aggressive, respectively submissive components became primary, with the sexual drive only added, although as "an enormous reinforcement."

Sadism is explained by Adler as the seeking of power in an easy way by persons lacking the necessary courage to meet the real problems of life. Sadists are looking for easy triumphs, "the semblance of power, of a secret, often unconscious supermanliness in a situation of uncontested superiority." The sadist is in fact "the triumphant vanquished." Such paradoxical or dialectical interpretation, in addition to being based on keen observation, always carries within itself the components for a reconstruction of the situation through the therapist, the basis for a psychotherapeutic change.

Masochism also is seen by Adler as an expression of the universal upward striving, again a paradoxical, dialectical formulation. "In every person are traits of defiance and obedience, cravings for domination and submission, which serve the striving for significance." "Even . . . in masochism, there is always a compensatory line upward, as when in flagellation the individual seeks a ridiculous justification in thoughts of penance." In actual masochism, "The partner falls under the dictates of the masochist." Thus the masochist becomes the "vanquished conqueror." Adler (A1928k) asserted: "I have always maintained that there is no genuine masochism as described in the literature. To clarify this statement let me add that the masochist experiences his superiority by forcing his partner's actions upon the partner" (p. 149n). As with regard to "feminine traits in men, homosexuality, impotence," etc., "the ultimate purpose is always the domination of others" (p. 29). Adler then believed there was no true masochism and that it would be better called "pseudomasochism" (p. 129n).

As on other issues, so also with regard to masochism, Salzman (1960) is quite in accord with Adler, stating that it "may yet be an attempt at mastery" (p. 185). Salzman 1962) writes further: "In the process of self-degradation the individual . . . manages to escape real responsibility for his actions and to present a justifiable excuse for his failures. The process allows him to manipulate and exploit others through his display of utter powerlessness . . . his suffering" (p. 235). "Freud interpreted this behavior as a need to fail, but the ego psychologists have emphasized the element of the 'need to succeed'" (p. 237).

Dialectics of suffering and weakness. The dialectical conception of suffering or weakness as a neurotic means of conquest is applied by Adler (A1928k) also to various nonsexual contexts. Obedience, submission, and humility in general may become means "to capture and conquer the other" (p. 5). "One of the core points of nervous dynamics [is] the heroism of the feeling of weakness." Adler (A1910b) speaks of "a dialectical change" (p. 209) when children with great inferiority feelings use their physical weaknesses "as weapons . . . to secure a certain domination over the environment" (p. 210). In his paper "Defiance and Obedience," Adler (A1910d) stated that "according to the law of dialectics" (p. 86) "the child . . . may seek to gain his final triumph through passive behavior, submission, and honest and dishonest obedience. . . . For the most part we find mixed cases in which traits of obedience and defiance run side by side" (p. 87).

In recent times Jay Haley (1969), under the heading "The Surrender Tactic" (p. 38), has expressed very similar thoughts. To quote: "There is an old saying that you cannot defeat a helpless opponent . . . your blows are unreturned, you can only suffer . . . doubt about who is the victor. This tactic has been proved effective by weeping wives and by anxious parents who find that helplessness will enforce their directives more tyrannically than giving orders" (p. 39). It is also used, for example, in the army. "The lowliest private can win in a power struggle with his highest superior if he merely does more than he is told. . . . His superiors will be both furious and incapacitated since they cannot punish him for doing what he is told" (p. 40). The tactic of weeping was also singled out by Adler (A1956b), who gave it the nickname "water power." He considered it "an extremely useful weapon for . . . reducing others to a condition of slavery" (p. 288).

In general, Haley (1963) noted: "The helpless behavior may influence the other person's behavior as much, if not more, than the authoritarian behavior" (p. 10). Altogether, "the crucial aspect of a symptom is the advantage it gives the patient in gaining control of what is to happen in a relationship with someone else" (p. 15). Haley thus confirms not only Adler's understanding of masochism but also of neurotic symptoms in general.

Fetishism. With regard to fetishism we want to refer to a review of psychoanalytic literature and case study by Nagler (1957), who accepts Rado's adaptational approach. Nagler finds that among traditional psychoanalysts "fetishism is still a defense against castration anxiety by denial of the penisless mother, which leads, mechanically, to a splitting of the ego" (p. 724). For Freud (1940), "The fetish was created with the intention of destroying the evidence for the possibility of castration, so that fear of castration could be avoided" (p. 117).

Adler found "fetishism, like all other deviations . . . an expression of an inferiority feeling and the attempt to compensate in an erroneous direction, guided by personal experience and training." This general view of Adler's is approached by Nagler (1957) when he states: "Fetishism is not merely a narrow aspect of psychosexual development . . . but is a segment of a way of living" by one with an "abysmally low self-esteem" (p. 737). Nagler's case was also "very eager to impress [others] that he was a 'real man'" (p. 736).

There is, however, a crucial difference between Adler and Nagler regarding their understanding of the relationship to the partner. Nagler believes that "the fetishist seeks slavishly in fantasy to win favor and acceptance. . . . He serves the woman adoringly . . . to gain her love . . ." (p. 739). Adler creates a more consistent and dialectical construction that furthermore again points to possible therapeutic intervention. His crucial statement is, "We believe it is more important to consider what happens to the sexual partner. . . . Through the displacement of the sexual accent onto the fetish, the sexual partner experiences disparagement, becomes devalued." The outcome is "an alleviation of the fetishist's fear and feeling of weakness toward the other sex."

Sexual dysfunction—organ dialect. Adler considered all kinds of sexual dysfunction, impotence, frigidity, premature ejaculation, etc., forms of "organ dialect." "While the patient's words, his thoughts and desires express his longing, his body, his sexual organs, speak another language, expressing his cowardliness." But before arriving at this judgment, "We must, of course, exclude as causes of sexual failure certain organic disorders, such as diabetes and peculiar types of kidney trouble that hinder normal sexual functioning, as drug addiction and chronic alcoholism also frequently do" (A1932m, p. 56).

Body functions in general are, according to Adler (A1929c), "dominated by the style of life." "This is notably the case with the lungs, the heart, the stomach, the organs of excretion, and the sexual organs. The disturbance of these functions expresses the direction that an individual is taking to attain his goal. I have called these disturbances the organ dialect, or organ jargon, since the organs are revealing in their own most expressive language the intention of the individual totality" (p. 156).

About the sex organs in particular, Adler wrote: "The dialect of the sexual organs is especially expressive. . . . In practically every case the patient expresses by a disorder of sexual functioning, a stoppage, hesitation, or escape in the face of the three life problems. . . . Most cases of impotence that I have known concerned patients faced with the problem of marriage. Ejaculatio praecox . . . invariably goes with a very poor social adjustment. . . . In women the same dialect appears as vaginism . . . signifying the woman's aversion either to a certain man or to men in general. Besides this active avoidance, there are the passive forms of sexual rejection, frigidity, and a display of passivity" (p. 157).

A rather complete discussion of the problem of impotence from the Adlerian viewpoint was provided in a small book in German by Rudolf Dreikurs (1931). It dealt with the subject under the headings: Impotence and Personality, Conflict in Love, Impotence as a Means of Escape, Symptomatology [doubt of one's manliness, fear of commitment, fear of sexuality], and Therapy, including sixteen illustrative cases. There is also a brief statement on frigidity by Dreikurs (1973, pp. 201–3) in English.

The paradoxical nature of organ dialect was described by Adler (A1929c) in the opening quotation of this section, and again in the following: Sexual dysfunctions "are all signs of a determination to exclude actions that the individual is apparently willing to perform" (p. 50). Both the fact of organ dialect and its paradoxical nature have today been recognized independently, although in forms slightly different from Adler's. Thomas S. Szasz (1961) speaks of "body language" as a "protolanguage" (p. 126) used "whenever people feel unable . . . to prevail over the significant objects in their environment" (p. 130). Paul Watzlawick et al. (1967) regard the neurotic symptom in general as a form of communication of the order: "It is not I who does not (or does) want to do this, it is something outside my control—for example, my nerves, my illness, my anxiety, my bad eyes, alcohol, my upbringing, the Communists, or my wife" (p. 80). According to Jay Haley (1963), the symptom, although it "may represent considerable distress" (p. 15), offers the patient the advantage that he may communicate something, and even exert a certain amount of control, without having to take the responsibility for his action (pp. 17–19).

All this is well within Adler's (A1956b) theory that

symptoms serve as alibis and excuses (pp. 265–66). He also explains the concomitant suffering to which Haley refers. The symptoms would lose their alibi function and power "if the patient were to be happy in his neurotic actions. Therefore, he suffers."

Anorexia nervosa may be regarded as one form of organ dialect. Although not a sexual dysfunction, it is mentioned here because Freud (1918a) considered it an expression of "aversion to sexuality" (p. 588). Adler believed it was "perhaps always initiated by the masculine protest in rejection of the feminine role." And in accordance with his preference for concepts from the social scene, Adler (A1925a) named it "neurotic hunger strike," stating about such cases: "We are dealing with girls who already as children had tested the value and significance of the 'hunger strike' as a means of attaining power" (p. 212). It is an "artifice of the weak. . . . Impulses toward revenge are always present, as is tyranny over the other family members" (pp. 212–13).

Today, a considerable consensus of opinion on the subject, as reviewed by Hilde Bruch (1973, p. 3) comes quite close to Adler, and rejects the Freudian view of anorexia as "an expression or repudiation of sexuality, specifically of 'oral impregnation' fantasies" (p. 2). Instead, Bruch considers the main issue to be "the struggle for control . . . the frantic desire for a sense of personal identity, competence, and effectiveness" (p. 4). This being the case, "the traditional psychoanalytic approach has been singularly ineffective, as has been reported by many" (p. 13). Bruch's treatment method is guided by the recognition that "the core issues" are "deficits and failure in active self-awareness and the conviction of being the helpless product of others" (p. 14).

Prostitution. As part of the total picture of sexuality, Adler also deals with prostitution. He considers a girl's "inclination toward prostitution and exaggerated polygamous tendencies . . . manifestations of the aversion to the feminine role," a form of masculine protest. Prostitution is determined neither by economic need and misery, nor by excessive sensuality. Rather, on "the premise of woman's inferiority" the girl secures for herself through prostitution "the significance that is elsewhere denied." She finds satisfaction in being able to solicit like a man while at the same time degrading the male to "the dependent means of her livelihood." Thus the real prostitute will keep on pursuing her trade even after all financial necessity has disappeared.

Adler's description has been largely confirmed in a study by Harold Greenwald (1958) based on interviews of twenty nonpatient call girls, "the aristocrats of prostitution" (p. 1). On the economic factor, "eighteen of the twenty girls reported that they had chances either to marry or become the mistresses of wealthy men . . . but that they were unwilling or unable to avail themselves of these socially more acceptable solutions" (p. 142). Regarding sensuality, Adler had noted that with her clients "the prostitute lacks any sensual excitement," while on the other hand "she favors homosexual relationships surprisingly often." Greenwald (1958) found that half of his sample were totally frigid in their private lives, eighteen of the twenty girls were without sexual feelings in relation with their clients (p. 135), and "fifteen of the girls admitted having had homosexual relationships" (p. 118). As to feelings of inferiority and their compensation, Greenwald noted, "All of these girls seemed prey to feelings of worthlessness" (p. 121), which they were trying to overcome by their ability to attract men and have them pay well. One girl stated simply: "Being a call girl helped me overcome my inferiority complex" (p. 117).

Yet this is far from a satisfactory way of living. A composite picture of the nonpatient call girl, constructed by Rowena Ansbacher (1958) from Greenwald's data, shows her as "unhappy, lonely, unable to trust anyone, beset with feelings of insecurity and worthlessness, and taking to drink or drugs. She is bored, restless, and lazy. She is resentful and rebellious against her next of kin, and takes this out in her relations with men, all of whom, collectively, she sees as a predatory enemy. She is unsure of her sexual role and of what she is altogether. She wants to indulge herself and to have all the advantages of life without any of its chores or responsibilities" (pp. 192–93). This description of the normal, nonpatient call girl is quite in line with what one would expect from the Adlerian viewpoint and justifies Adler's (A1956b) classification of "neurotics, psychotics, criminals, drunkards, problem children, suicides, perverts, and prostitutes" as failures in life, which he attributes ultimately to lack in social interest (p. 156).

VI. SEXUAL DISORDERS: CLINICAL ASPECTS

For Adler the ideal normal mental order is one of co-operation among fellow men striving for an ultimate higher development of humanity. This includes an ideal individual sexual order of co-operation between two members of the two sexes. All mental disorder has its roots in lack of co-operation in which an individual is concerned with his own interests to the exclusion of the larger context of which he is a part. Sexual disorder would be a lack of co-operation with the other sex, generically or individually.

Our discussion has right along been in accordance with this consideration. We have shown that sexual disorder is a self-imposed distance from the other sex and can be regarded as a form of neurosis. In the present section we shall at first be concerned with the question, Who will resort to the neurotic, nonco-operative form of meeting the sexual problem? The question requires a threefold answer: (1) The individual prone to sexual disorder will, according to Adler, be neurotically disposed in general. (2) The individual who chooses sexual disorder as the main symptom, or method of coping, including especially homosexuality, will additionally have experienced discouragement from the other sex, or discouragement or uncertainty about his own sexual role. (3) In order actually to engage in sexually disordered behavior, the individual will have trained in that direction.

The remainder of this section will be concerned with treatment.

Neurotic Disposition

The neurotically disposed individual shares with the normal individual the general unitary dynamic principle of all forms of life—a movement toward growth and expansion. This forward urge is conceptualized in ideals, expectations, and goals of success. This lets the individual experience his present situation as one of relative inferiority. "In comparison with unattainable perfection, the individual is continuously filled by an inferiority feeling and motivated by it" (A1956b, p. 117).

Normally, inferiority feelings are positive factors. "To be a human being means to have inferiority feelings. One recognizes one's own powerlessness in the face of nature. One sees death as the irrefutable consequence of existence. . . . This inferiority feeling acts as a motive for productivity, as a motive for attempting to overcome obstacles, to maintain oneself in life" (A1964a, p. 54n). "Inferiority feelings are the cause of all improvements in the position of humanity. Science itself, for example, can arise only when people feel their ignorance. . . . Indeed, it seems that all our human culture is based upon feelings of inferiority" (A1956b, p. 117).

Increased inferiority feelings. The key to the neurotic disposition is an inferiority feeling in the face of normal tasks, normal goals to be achieved, which is so strong that the individual believes he cannot cope with the task. He will not have the courage to meet the task head-on, and instead will try to bypass it. There are of course reasons for such increased inferiority feeling. At first Adler traced it to organ inferiorities; then he added the situations of the neglected and the pampered child. Yet it is never the situation by itself that is decisive, but how the individual responds to it. The situation provides only probabilities for increased inferiority feelings and discouragement to develop. In such individuals "activity and preparation for life has thus been impaired. . . . They have lost faith in themselves and remain . . . the 'nervously disposed persons.' "

In sexual deviation the inferiority feelings are primarily rel-

381

ative to the other sex—in men, "a feeling of inferiority in relation to the overrated power of the female"; in women, "the feeling of feminine inferiority in relation to the male, who is felt to be the stronger."

High, self-centered goals. Increased inferiority feelings may in an overcompensatory fashion lead to unrealistically high, self-centered goals. Such persons may seek "to cover up the inferiority feeling with a fictive superiority complex. . . . The nervous person dictates to his environment the rules of its conduct and more or less limits his co-operation" (A1964a, p. 56). Adler (A1956b) speaks of "the low self-estimation of the child who feels inferior, and the over-life-size goal that may reach as high as godlikeness. Between these two points there rest the preparatory attempts, the groping devices and tricks, as well as the finished readinesses and habitual attitudes. It is from these that the . . . goal, which is actually hidden, may be inferred" (A1956b, p. 245).

"The normal person does not have a superiority complex. He does not even have a sense of superiority. He has the striving to be superior in the sense that we all have ambition to be successful; but so long as this striving is expressed in work it does not lead to false valuations, which are at the root of mental disorder" (A1956b, p. 260).

Underdeveloped social interest. Increased inferiority feelings make a person feel short-changed and experience the world as hostile, with the result that "interest in one's own person is strengthened while interest in others dwindles" (A1912a, p. 25). "The striving for personal superiority and the nondevelopment of social interest are . . . not two mistakes that the individual has made; they are one and the same mistake" (A1956b, pp. 240–41). Such persons strive on the socially useless side of life (pp. 254–55). They have "a false attitude toward all life problems . . . in regarding these demands as merely personal, private affairs and overlooking the common relationships and general implications" (A1956b, p. 243).

It is the lack of social interest that leads to actual failure. "All failures—neurotics, psychotics, criminals, drunkards, problem children, suicides, perverts, and prostitutes—are failures because they are lacking in social interest. They approach the problems of occupation, friendship, and sex without the confidence that they can be solved by co-operation" (A1956b, p. 156), as quoted in part earlier.

Regarding sexual disorders, Adler (A1964a) sees these as attempts to solve the sexual problem in a self-centered way, without sufficiently developed social interest or social feeling. "Lack of social direction in the sexual function plays the chief role in all sexual deviations and in all psychological disturbances of sexuality" (p. 105). Beyond this, sexual deviates are "deficient in deeper comradeship, mutual benevolence, and common effort. . . . There is little inclination to 'play the game' toward men as well as women." Homosexuality specifically is considered "a failure in education to become a fellow man." "The homosexual shows little communal spirit, hardly the kind of good will toward others through which the bond of unity among men can be tied. . . . He has not developed into a partner of society."

Depreciation tendency and oversensitivity. Increased inferiority feeling and a self-centered goal of superiority often lead to the "depreciation tendency," "which finds an analogy in the fable of the fox and the sour grapes." It is an effort to raise one's own self-esteem by disparaging the other person, or the normal goal that one considers unattainable. Adler (A1912a) considered increased inferiority feeling and the resulting depreciation tendency "the two important poles of any neurotic attitude" (p. 164), a dialectical conception.

All sexual disorders, as they represent degrees of distance from the other sex, can be understood as analogies of telling the partner of the other sex, "I don't need you," or, as in fetishism, "Parts of you or some paraphernalia are more important to me than you." "Through the displacement of the sexual accent onto the fetish, the sexual partner experiences disparagement, becomes devalued," as quoted earlier. Adler refers to depreciation and disparagement also in connection with sadism and masochism, sodomy, and three of his cases of homosexual orientation. In summary, "The tendency to depreciate the normally to be expected partner is never lacking, so that, if one looks carefully, traits of hostility and fighting against him or her stand out as essential in the posture of the deviate."

Complementing his tendency to depreciate others, the neurotically disposed is very sensitive to disparagements by others. While noting that he was not the first to have recognized "oversensitivity," Adler (A1956b) takes credit for having observed that it always occurs when "the patient considers himself neglected, hurt, small, or besmudged" (p. 290). It is to be traced to "the oversized inferiority feeling" that "leads to egotistical self-considerations and self-reflections" (A1964a, p. 54n). Persons with sexual disorders are, according to Adler, generally "oversensitive, overambitious, and defiant."

Exogenous factor. As stated earlier, the symptom arises as a "countercompulsion" (p. 125) against a social demand for which the individual feels unprepared; it interposes a distance between himself and this task, as a "secondary theater of operations" (p. 126). This demand is the "exogenous factor." If the surrounding conditions were so favorable to the neurotically disposed that he would never be put to test, he would not come to an actual crisis. "The exogenous factor, the proximity of a task that demands co-operation and fellowship, is always the exciting factor of the symptoms, the behavior problem, the neurosis, the suicide, the crime, the drug addiction, and the sexual deviation" (A1956b, pp. 297–98).

An understanding of the exact nature of the exogenous factor—which is always related to the three basic problems of social living, occupation, and love—becomes of great importance in therapy. "We must understand the relationship of this unique individual to the problem he is facing. We must regard two sides, and learn how this individual moves in relation to the external problem, how he endeavors to master it" (A1933b, p. 188, new translation).

Unity and diversity of mental disorders. The preceding represents a unitary theory of mental disorder, in keeping with Adler's unitary dynamic theory and general holistic approach. Mental disorders, the failures in life, are mistaken ways of meeting life problems, by people with increased inferiority feelings (which may be covered up), excessively high

384

personal goals of superiority, and underdeveloped social interest—which Adler, in time, increasingly emphasized. Without changing this unity, Adler eventually discriminated among failures along two lines: (1) degree of activity, and (2) degree of acceptance of social requirements.

(1) The less active are the potential neurotics, the more active the potential criminals. When Adler (A1956b) added the "pampered life style" to the concept of the neurotic disposition, it meant the individual's expectation of "quick fulfillment of his wishes" (p. 242). This may be limited to merely "expecting everything from others," in which case not much activity is required, as in the potential neurotic; or the pampered life style may be found in combination with the realization that to achieve one's ends greater activity is required, including the active taking from others what one wishes, as in the potential criminal (p. 421; A1935l, p. 139).

Quite apart from this distinction, the pampered life style must not be understood as necessarily the result of a pampering situation, as the term would imply. It is ultimately the individual's own doing. According to Adler (A1956b), "The pampered style of life as a living phenomenon is the creation of the child. . . . It can be found occasionally in cases where we cannot speak of pampering, but where, on the contrary, we find neglect. . . . It should not be read into the attitude of the mother or the grandmother" (p. 242).

(2) All mental disorders show deficiency in social interest. But they differ in the extent to which the individual acknowledges the social obligation. This is greatest in the neurotic. He has the best intentions, only that he does not perform. "Neurotic behavior can be expressed in two words: 'Yes—but'" (A1956b, p. 302). By "yes" the neurotic acknowledges the common sense, an expression of social interest, whereas the "but" carries the full weight of his symptoms, which prevent him from realizing his intentions.

The psychotic, on the other hand, has cut himself off from the common world. Other forms of mental disorder in which the individual "openly withholds his contribution from the community are . . . suicide, crime, alcoholism, and active sexual deviation" (A1936k, p. 73). This difference between neurosis and sexual deviation was alluded to earlier, when we noted that the compulsive neurotic would typically like to stop his compulsion, whereas the homosexual may well accept his behavior as an unalterable fact (p. 129).

Predisposing Background Factors

Factors involved in the development of the neurotic disposition in general are organ inferiorities, being pampered, or being neglected or hated as a child (A1956b, p. 368). They are likely to result in increased inferiority feelings, unrealistic self-centered compensatory goals, and lack of social interest. Presently we shall discuss (1) pampering and neglect as they pertain to sexual disorder, and the additional relevant factors of (2) uncertainty of one's sexual role, (3) the domineering mother, and (4) the tyrannical father. In a boy the last two are extremely discouraging for the approach to the other sex. The domineering mother raises serious doubt of ever being able to prevail in confrontation with a woman; the tyrannical father raises doubt of ever growing into a "real man" like his father, which also disturbs the boy's courage toward the other sex. This will be followed by (5) an examination of the Schreber case.

Pampering and neglect. Adler (A1918a) found homosexuals often to have been pampered or neglected children. "Both types grow up in lonesomeness, do not have sufficient ability to co-operate, and succumb to the first best relationship (*Bindung*) that flatters them. The mother or the lack of a mother made the development of social interest more difficult for them" (p. 127).

In the present selections we find further: "Pampering may become the occasion for avoidance [of the other sex] from fear never again to achieve similar warmth," and "Sexual deviations probably always betray the misconception and the style of life of a pampered or neglected child." Homosexuality running in families is attributed by Adler to an erroneous family tradition, "especially if pathological pampering or great severity have been passed on for some time."

Uncertainty of sexual role. As mentioned earlier, Adler considered uncertainty of one's sexual role a basic factor in all psychopathology, and accordingly attributed great importance to teaching children their sexual identity. Homosexuality in particular originates from "the attempt to change one's sexual role," or as modified in a later edition, "the uncertainty of one's sexual role." Adler writes, "A striking uncertainty regarding his sexual role . . . [is] the main condition in the prehistory of the homosexual."

This observation is today widely supported. Marmor (1965) states: "For a homosexual adaptation to occur, in our time and culture, psychodynamic, sociocultural, biological, and situational factors must combine to (1) create an impaired gender-identity, (2) create a fear of intimate contact with members of the opposite sex, and (3) provide opportunities for sexual release with members of the same sex" (p. 5). "Impaired gender-identity" takes the first place, while the other factors also agree with Adler. Gender identity and gender role are today's equivalents for Adler's sexual role.

Adler's early hypothesis of uncertainty of one's sexual role as an important factor in mental disorders in general has recently been supported by Money and Tucker (1975): "Your sense of yourself . . . your identity—is the essence of you, and at the core of it lies your sense of yourself as male or female, your gender identity. It is . . . the anchor of your emotional health" (p. 5).

Domineering mother, fear of woman. Adler observed that among men who had a domineering mother, "surprisingly many make a great detour around women, as if inoculated with bitterness and unable to have confidence in a female." "Sons of strong-willed, masculine mothers are deeply imbued with a fear of the female. . . . Their distrust grows to the point where they become sexually incompetent." The son of such a mother also "will evade competition with men . . . and usually be inclined to evade the problem of love and marriage." Such mothers are likely to be married to a weak husband (who in turn becomes an ineffectual father), to be frigid, and to have difficulties with their female physiological functions.

(1) *Similarity with modern psychoanalytic observations.* Adler's characterization of the male homosexual's mother largely anticipates the findings of Bieber and others (1962). Bieber (1965) describes the homosexual's mother as dominating, overprotective, and often seductive. "She demands undue attention and solicitude . . . is usually . . . sexually frigid . . . babies her son . . . and hinders his participation in the normal activities of boyhood, presumably out of concern for his welfare. . . . As a wife, she is almost always inadequate . . . dominates her husband, whom she minimizes. . . . The husband is usually detached" (p. 250). As Adler mentioned that homosexuals "grow up in lonesomeness," so Bieber (1965) notes that "The prehomosexual boy is not a member of a peer group . . . he tends to be an isolate" (p. 252). And as Adler noted that some homosexuals were rejected children, so does Bieber mention, "In a few cases, the mother is seemingly detached, rejecting, and overtly hostile to her son" (p. 250).

(2) *Differences from modern psychoanalysis.* One can easily understand how a small boy through unpleasant experiences with his mother or other females may acquire a generalized negative attitude toward all women. The boy acquires "a fear of the female" in general. But Bieber (1965) limits this to "fear and aversion to female genitalia" (p. 253). Ovesey (1965) also speaks of "a fear of the female genitalia" as "defense against castration anxiety" (p. 221). Ovesey and Person (1973) attempt an explanation through calling on still further Freudian concepts. "The answer lies in the intensity of the vagina dentata fantasy. . . . It is this fear that is mobilized by erotic interest in the mother during the Oedipal phase and displaced to her vagina" (p. 61).

Here we see that "modern psychoanalysis" is in certain respects still quite Freudian, reductionistic, and speculative. We ask, How could fear of the female be reduced to fear of the female genitalia? This can certainly not be conceived in operational terms. Under what circumstances could such a fear be acquired? It can only be an inference, or at best be based on a report from an adult. In this case it could be considered as merely symbolic for fear of women as such, with the female genitalia functioning as a *pars pro toto*.

Tyrannical father. The father's "absolute authority within the family" may destroy the boy's self-confidence that he will ever be a man like his father. "The child may not even have enough self-confidence for any solution. But someday he will make a virtue of necessity and in secret defiance of his father's dominance disappoint the latter's reasonable expectations and destroy them. Thus the child finally succeeds after all in being triumphant over the paternal 'tyrant.' "

Adler (A1912a) makes this more explicit in terms of the masculine-protest concept. "The masculine protest of the neurotic includes the older compensating will to power, which even revalues the sensations and may turn pleasure into pain. This follows from the quite frequent cases where the direct attempt to behave manly meets with great resistance and uses a detour: The female role is valued more highly, passive traits are reinforced, masochistic, passive homosexual traits appear by which the patient hopes to gain power over men or women. In short, the masculine protest uses feminine means. . . . This apperception according to the schema male-female brings the sexual jargon into the neurosis, which must be taken symbolically and resolved further, and urges the eroticism into a direction that fits the core of the personality" (p. 23).

The Schreber case. Masculine protest with feminine means became the basis for an Adlerian interpretation of the Schreber case. Schreber (1903) had suffered from paranoia, including delusions of having been transformed into a woman with female sexual feelings. From this case and others Freud (1911) drew his well-known conclusion that in paranoia "the really operative factor . . . lies in . . . the homosexual components" (p. 445).

The Adlerian interpretation, by Shulman (1959), points

389

out that in his delusional conversion into a female, Schreber finally attained a most exalted position. Formerly he had a very high self-centered goal, but "must have always doubted his masculinity" and "was much concerned with the question of superiority-inferiority, expressed in the antithesis masculine-feminine. . . . During the early part of his illness, he tried to 'act like a man,' but the 'voices' decried his lack of manliness" (p. 150). Eventually it was God who transformed Schreber into a woman, and this was "a beneficial act for the whole universe because he will give birth to a new race of humans to repopulate the world" (p. 151). Shulman quotes from Schreber: "I would like to meet the man who faced with the choice of either becoming a demented human being in male habitus or a spirited female, would not prefer the latter" (p. 151). The homosexual or better transsexual delusions can then be readily explained as serving Schreber's exalted self-centered goal of superiority. The Schreber case becomes one of masculine protest, with the individual "striving for masculine power through feminine means" (p. 147).

Adler (A1912a) himself mentioned the Schreber case only once, very briefly, when he stated: "Following Schreber's biography Freud has described a very clear case of dementia in which psychological hermaphroditism [which includes masculine protest with feminine means] can be easily recognized" (p. 129).

Since Shulman's interpretation it has become known through Schatzman (1971), who refers also to W. G. Niederland, that Schreber's father was an extreme home tyrant, one of Adler's background factors for male homosexuality. As to the paranoia, from which Schreber suffered primarily and which Freud considered a defense against homosexuality, Adler (A1914d) held that this will originate "from situations of some kind of degradation" (p. 186). To such Schreber seems indeed to have been exposed through his tyrannical father. The new knowledge of Schreber's background thus lends further support to Adlerian theory.

390

Training and Self-training

Adler minimized the direct influence of heredity on any form of behavior, stressed social factors, and maximized the individual's own interpretation of his situation in reference to his goals, based on his own creative power. Thus he emphasized the acquisition of behavior. Rather than "learning," he chose the term "training" (which, incidentally, is the same word in German), meaning preparation for a particular performance. One trains actively to achieve a certain goal. And as Adler (A1956b) considered the individual "the artist of his own personality" (p. 177), he frequently used the term "self-training."

Adler (A1924m) declared: "Every phenomenon in human life is the result of training. Nothing can have come into existence suddenly; everything must have been prepared. Every phenomenon of a person is connected with his earliest history. . . . In some persons the training becomes so evident that it is openly visible, through their posture, or handwriting. What we call arrangement of a symptom is a matter of training. . . . The training occurs not only in the presence of others; the patient trains also when he is alone and avails himself of his fantasy. This is seen most clearly in dreams. . . . We will have a different attitude when we know we are dealing with a person who is training than if we think the behavior is due to a childhood influence or a trauma" (p. 39).

Also in reference to scholastic achievement, Adler (A1929b) considered training, not innate intelligence, the decisive factor. For example, whether a child will do well in composition will depend on whether he practiced at home to express his thoughts. "How competent children and adults have trained, and how the failures in life have trained, is a vast area yet to be explored. . . . Here lies the point of attack against the myth of general aptitude. The better-trained children will later seem more gifted in the sense of the myth. Those who trained less, or more poorly, will be described as not gifted" (pp. 106–7). Minimizing innate intellectual differences short of feeble-mindedness, Adler (A1929c) illustrated the importance of the right training method by the example of Charlemagne. Charlemagne was considered unable to learn to read or write "from sheer lack of talent for such things! Now, with the development of educational method, no normal child finds these tasks beyond it" (p. 5). All this is of course quite in line with recent educational philosophy and policy regarding minority and other underprivileged children.

Normal sexual training. In much the same way did Adler (A1929c) think that a person's sexuality, which he generally designated by "love," was also essentially based on training and self-training. "Love is a necessary life task for which an early preparation is needed, and training for love is an integral part of one's education for life. Both normal love and all its deviations, such as homosexuality, are a matter of training and education" (p. 44).

Unfortunately, training is often not of the right kind. Adler (A1929d) wrote: "Our education is certainly too strict. . . . Instead of preparing boys and girls as if for sin, it would be much wiser to train the girls better in the feminine and the boys in the masculine role of marriage—but train them both in such a way that they would feel equal" (p. 120). As matters stand, "Most persons are less well prepared and less well trained [for the question of love] than for the other questions of life" (p. 123).

As to self-training for sexual relations, Adler found this "a continuous ongoing process," especially during adolescence. "In thoughts, on the street, in the theater . . . there are constant stimulations that help the inclination toward love and marriage to prevail." "Undoubtedly a person continuously trains for the sexual role and the sexual ideal he has before him. The sum of this training cannot be overestimated: It includes his gait as he walks on the street, his associations with the other sex, the comparison of himself with others of his own sex, etc."

This position of Adler's has in recent years found strong support. Money and Ehrhardt (1972) concluded from Money's well-known work with hermaphrodites: "Nature has ordained a major part of human gender-identity differentiation to be accomplished in the postnatal period. It then takes place, as does the development of native language, when a prenatally programmed disposition comes in contact with postnatal, socially programmed signals" (p. 18). Money and Tucker (1975) repeat: "You attain your gender identity/role in much the same way you attain speech" (p. 88). Some of the evidence was obtained from pairs of hermaphrodites who were matched physiologically and sociologically as closely as possible and differed only in the sex to which they were assigned at birth and in which they were reared. These individuals were found to have so completely identified with their assigned sex that the ordinary person meeting them socially would have no clues as to their physiological hermaphroditism. Money (1976) believes that for postnatal gender-identity formation the period up to the age of five or six years is decisive. Regarding homosexuality, Money remarks, although somewhat indirectly, that due to this postnatal further "programming," errors in gender identity can be made and that this "puts a great deal of responsibility on adults—parents and others who take care of children."

By contrast, Freud's theory of psychosexual development, based as it is on instinctual development, is increasingly questioned. According to Chodoff (1966), "The entire Freudian psychosexual sequence is not a regularly occurring and normal development but constitutes, rather, a pathological formation symptomatic of serious disturbances and hypersexualization of intrafamily relationships" (p. 517). To Adler (A1956b) the Oedipus complex, for example, had always been "but a figure of speech," and the thoughts connected with it but "the result of wrong upbringing . . . always found only in pampered children" (pp. 375–76).

Training in sexual disorder. Sexual disorders like normal sexual development are for Adler the outcome of training and self-training. "No sexual deviation without training" (A1933b, p. 125). In fact, the book from which most of the present Chapters 5 to 7 on sexual disorders is taken carries the subtitle *Erotic Training and Erotic Retreat,* which was also the title of a paper presented by Adler (A1928c) at the First International Congress of Sex Research (Berlin, 1926). In the Preface to the book, Adler (A1930d) stated: "The emphasis is on the significance of training within the frame of the style of life. . . . Homosexuality represents a training from childhood on of a discouraged person to evade the normal solution of the problem of love, excluding the possibility of defeat through the exclusion of the opposite sex" (pp. v–vi).

Adler gives the example of a male homosexual looking at girls. "This was only to train himself in denial, in order firmly to establish his distance from the female sex, and to learn how to drop relationships quickly after they had barely begun." In general the homosexual "diverts his attention continually from the other sex toward his own sex. This is the most important way toward schematization or mechanization of homosexuality."

The training for homosexuality, like the life of a homosexual, is not easy, as Adler (A1918a) describes in the following: "It is so infinitely more difficult to be a homosexual than to be normal that this alone gives one an idea of the immense effort required to go through life as a homosexual. This effort can indeed be observed in every deviate, in the way of his deductive thinking, in his conception of men and women, and in his experiences. And we see his stepwise preparations, the cunning technique that he has acquired to attain a unified presence that cannot be easily shaken. Especially the countless mixed cases that represent the majority of homosexuals show us the stepwise development of homosexuality and how it took very special efforts to leave the normal direction and narrow life sufficiently to leave more room for homosexuality. Specifically, it is often touching to observe how a person hypnotizes himself step by step, forcing the thought upon himself that he is not made to be normal. His arguments are often so flimsy that one must be accustomed to the jargon of homosexuals to remain calm. I know some men who are externally absolutely inconspicuous, yet emphasize some small detail about themselves such as a larynx that is not sufficiently

394

manly, or that their beard is not as thick as that of others, etc." (p. 125).

Fantasy, dreams, and early memories. Adler regarded dreams, fantasies, and early memories not as disguises for repressed unconscious primary processes, as Freud did, but as thinly veiled expressions of the individual's general line of movement, as part of his style of life. They are "preparations" for actions to be taken by the individual, or, as Adler often called them, devices of "training."

Regarding dreams and fantasies in homosexuality, we are quoting from Chapter 5: "Some authors [take these] as evidence that homosexual development is innate and unavoidable. This is a daring but incorrect assumption . . . which contributes greatly to a general strengthening of homosexuality. . . . Dreams and fantasies indicate an arrangement of the individual and not established facts—a demand, not a condition (*ein Sollen und nicht ein Sein*). . . . The dream is a working hypothesis . . . and has the function of a training. Thus homosexual dreams and fantasies, insofar as they do not represent other relationships of life in terms of sexual dialect, are to be understood at the most as attempts to support presumed homosexuality—from which one can infer that the dreamer is not very sure of it."

Early recollections suggestive of homosexuality are likewise often taken as evidence for its innateness. Yet such recollections generally tend "to falsify events in favor of the life plan," and, whether objectively true, partly true, or only fantasy, may serve as training devices. Adler (A1929b) relates one of his own early recollections as an example. As a child on his way to school he had to cross a cemetery. Although the other children thought nothing of it, he was always uneasy about it. One day he stayed behind and walked alone back and forth across the cemetery until he felt he was rid of his fear. As an adult he learned one day, much to his surprise, that there was no cemetery on the way to school; the story was a fantasy mistaken for a fact. Adler concludes: "This fantasy of mine was not useless; it belonged to my psychological training. It contributed to my facing the problem of death much more firmly and not so timidly" (p. 63).

Independent vs. *dependent variable.* Thus early incidents in a person's life history pointing toward homosexuality were taken by Adler not as evidence for its innateness but as evidence for self-training. Thereby Adler turned these incidents from outcomes of heredity—that is, from *dependent variables*—into parts of the individual's intentions, and in this sense *independent variables,* with the full-fledged deviation as the outcome, the dependent variable. This change illustrates the complete reversal of thinking for which Viktor Frankl (1970) gives Adler credit: "What Adler achieved was no less than a Copernican switch. No longer could man be considered as the product, pawn, and victim of drives; on the contrary, drives form the material that serves man in expression and action" (p. 12).

Here again Adler's theory is capable of accommodating new developments. Behavior therapy of homosexuality had previously succeeded only with bisexuals, not with pure homosexuals (Feldman and MacCulloch, 1971). This was changed when sexual fantasy was made the independent variable. Abel and Blanchard (1974) taught the patient "to change his fantasies directly" (p. 468), replacing the view of "deviant fantasy as a dependent variable . . . occurring because of . . . an independent variable, the inaccessible instinctual sexual drive" (p. 468). Although no controlled studies are yet available, the authors believe from case reports that such methods are effective. "The behavioral approach has given sexual fantasy the critical position of an independent variable to be altered directly as treatment." Consequently, it will be important to scrutinize "fantasy as the pivotal process leading to deviant behavior" (p. 474).

As far apart from each other as Adlerian psychology and behavior therapy are in actual treatment methodology of sexual deviation, still Adler's understanding of fantasy as a device by which the patient *trains* himself for deviation provides a theoretical opening for a therapeutic intervention that *retrains* for heterosexuality by replacing homosexual with heterosexual fantasies. This is a cognitive change, and Adlerian therapy is largely one of cognitive change.

Cognition is today considered the independent variable also

in the wider field of psychotherapy. Rensberger (1977) reports that neurosis is attributed to self-centered, immature thinking rather than immature emotions, and that depression, likewise, is understood as a phenomenon of "illogical thinking patterns" and is accessible to "cognitive therapy."

Psychotherapy

Adlerian psychotherapy has generally been described as consisting of four overlapping phases: (1) establishing and maintaining a good relationship with the patient; (2) gathering data from the patient for understanding his life style; (3) interpreting the patient to himself, providing insight; (4) reorientation and re-education (Alexandra Adler, 1946; Dreikurs, 1973; Ansbacher, 1974).

Further comprehension may perhaps be afforded by dealing with phase 1 as part of the larger concept of *encouragement, affective aspect;* combining phases 2–4 under *cognitive aspect;* and adding *technical aspect,* formerly included in phase 4. The first two aspects are more descriptive of what the therapist attempts to accomplish—namely, increase in courage, and recognition and elimination of mistakes. In the third aspect the emphasis is on what the therapist actually does, specific techniques he uses.

We have briefly described the rationale of Adlerian counseling and psychotherapy above. A survey of all aspects of therapy as practiced by contemporary Adlerians has been published by Arthur G. Nikelly (1971).

Encouragement, Affective Aspect

For Adler encouragement is the basis of psychotherapy, consistent with his conception of increased inferiority feeling as the core of psychopathology (pp. 381–82 above). "Increased inferiority feeling goes hand in hand with inadequate development of courage" (A1933b, p. 160, new translation),

397

where courage in turn can be defined as activity plus social interest. The patient is a discouraged person.

State of discouragement. A state of "discouragement" is Adler's equivalent of anxiety as the basis of psychopathology. This designation has the advantage of having a positive polar opposite, "courage," as the basic ingredient of mental health. The discouragement-courage pair is consistent with Adler's general dialectic orientation. With anxiety, on the other hand, mental health can be described only as absence of pathology, consistent with a medical model.

In discouragement, the patient lacks the courage to strive on the socially useful side. But striving for success and the maintenance of his self-esteem he does, as according to Adler's supreme law of life, "The sense of worth of the self shall not be allowed to be diminished" (A1956b, p. 358). So the patient strives on the socially useless side where "successes," although pseudosuccesses or substitute satisfactions (p. 130), are more easily and safely attained. Such lack of courage applies even where on the surface no inferiority feelings can be discerned, as is generally the case in character disorders. Then the patient must be shown through his life history and recollections how he became discouraged from striving on the socially useful side.

As we have seen, sexual disorders are forms of discouragement particularly in reference to the other sex. Important general characteristics of homosexuals are "inability to co-operate, excessive ambition, extreme caution or existential cowardliness (*Lebensfeigheit*), and great discouragement regarding socially necessary demands" (A1918a, p. 126). For Adler, the problem of treatment becomes essentially how "to change an adult coward into a courageous human being." Eventually he qualified his statement on cowardliness, acknowledging, "In other fields, such as sports, war, adventure, etc., as well as in homosexual attacks, courage and insolence may become evident" (A1918a, p. 126), and to this extent acknowledged normality among homosexuals.

Activation of social interest. With courage as activity plus social interest, encouragement includes development of social interest. "Social interest is the most important part of our education, treatment and cure" (A1929d, p. 7). When one feels solidarity with others one has more courage in facing life problems than in isolation. Adler (A1933b), considers courage "but one side of social interest" (p. 194). "Courage and confidence grow from [favorable] contact with the environment" (p. 146). "Lack of social interest expresses itself in open or hidden lack of courage" (p. 78). Consequently, criminal activity "must not be mistaken for courage" (p. 142). In fact, criminals are cowards, typically attacking totally defenseless victims. "Courage is found only on the side of life that advances the community" (p. 72). Referring to all forms of guidance, Adler considers it "the task of the educator, teacher, physician, and clergyman to raise social interest and thereby raise courage" (p. 26).

Adler (A1956b) sees psychotherapy as "an exercise in co-operation and a test of co-operation" (p. 340), which begins with the therapist extending social interest to the patient. His task is "to give the patient the experience of contact with a fellow man, and then to enable him to transfer his awakened social interest to others. This . . . is strictly analogous to the function of the mother" (p. 341), whose twofold function is "to give the child the completest possible experience of human fellowship, and then to widen it into a life attitude toward others" (p. 372). If the mother has failed in this, the task is likely to fall much later to the psychotherapist. "His is a belated assumption of the maternal function" (p. 341). "What the Freudians call transference . . . apart from sexual implications . . . is merely social interest" (p. 343). Altogether, the successes of other schools are due less to their methods "than when they happen to give the patient a good human relationship with the physician, or above all, encouragement" (p. 343).

Process of encouragement and training. A first and indispensable step toward encouragement is then a good relationship between the therapist and the patient. In the most general sense, encouragement is the imparting of a more optimistic world philosophy in which the patient sees himself more objectively as a fellow human being among others, with general human frailties that must be accepted. More specifically, a person's self-esteem and courage are raised by recognition of his existing competencies and skills, and by training in further skills.

We must also "recognize the specific discouragement the patient shows in his life style; we must encourage him at the precise point where he falls short in courage" (A1931b, p. 49). From a holistic viewpoint, the improvement of any function or condition would be encouraging for the individual as a whole, especially if he was discouraged by this particular insufficiency. For example, in his Preface to a book on plastic surgery, Adler (A1936c) tells that when he was once asked, "What is the most important thing in life?" he replied, "What you don't have," meaning, what you experience as a discouraging deficiency. If this refers to a person's looks, "I naturally cannot belittle the importance of one's appearance," and successful plastic surgery can certainly be encouraging. In this sense also the results of behavior therapy can be expected to have a general effect of encouragement. And behavior therapy in turn avails itself of encouragement through positive reinforcement.

Encouragement is particularly indicated in the treatment of sexual disorders. "Without encouragement . . . any success is precluded." Therapy must aim "toward a more courageous approach to life and society."

Noting that some sexual dysfunctions may arise from "deep-rooted technicalities," Adler also mentions specific training. Such training is difficult because it means to "catch up with the training that in normal persons plays such an enormously important role. . . . We obviously need some invention to raise poorly trained persons to a better level of training without doing harm to them and society. Undoubtedly the method plays the decisive role here." It would seem that thereby Adler left an opening for modern sex therapies such as described by Kaplan (1974), Masters and Johnson (1970), and Barbach (1975). Perhaps sexual surrogates (Jacobs, Thompson, and Truxaw, 1975) could also be included—provided they would act in a professional manner so as not to do any harm. Relationships with prostitutes, which in Adler's day were apparently often recommended in cases

400

of impotence, he considered antitherapeutic. "Escape into prostitution is cheap and cowardly . . . and advances the inferiority feeling."

Cognitive Aspect

The cognitive aspect of therapy takes up most of Adler's didactic efforts, as is well shown in the present writings, including the case discussions.

Uncovering and changing goals. Adler (A1913a) considered "uncovering the neurotic system . . . the most important component of therapy, because it can be maintained . . . only as long as the patient succeeds in withdrawing it from his own critique and understanding" (p. 28). What Adler "uncovers" are mistakes—of interpretation, goals, and resulting self-training. "We are always able to draw attention to errors only, and never to innate defects, to the possibility of a cure, and to equality with others" (A1956b, p. 342), an important therapeutic advantage.

When Adler presented the masculine protest, he included the treatment of homosexuality, obviously pointing at Freud, whose concept of bisexuality precluded the possibility of treatment. Adler proposed that the dynamic of "avoidance of the feared woman" must be uncovered and made conscious. "Thereby the biased overgrowth of 'feminine and masculine traits' will disappear and the childish valuation give room to a more mature world view." Additionally, psychotherapy must uncover and undo the patient's antisocial line and exaggerated goal of personal superiority and "destroy it as a firmly established utopia." The concept of the patient's "utopia" has today been expanded upon by Watzlawick et al. (1974), who, similarly to Adler, arrived at the conclusion, "It is the utopian premise that things *should be* a certain way that requires change, and not the way things *are*" (p. 61).

The "uncovering" described does actually not present new "facts." It is rather a new interpretation—that is, it brings to bear "an alternate frame of reference" (Levy, 1963) to fa-

401

cilitate change. As we shall see below, the patient must learn to "resee the world."

Methods of understanding the life style. The understanding of the patient's life style, his total personality, is based on data provided by him. Among such, Adler (A1956b) found the following most valuable: "The most trustworthy approaches to the exploration of personality are given in a comprehensive understanding of (1) the earliest childhood recollections, (2) the position of the child in the birth order, (3) childhood disorders, (4) daydreams and night dreams, and (5) the nature of the exogenous factor that causes the illness. All the results of such an investigation, which also include the attitude toward the physician, must be evaluated with the greatest caution and their course must always be examined for consistency with other findings. In this way we will succeed in obtaining a faithful picture of the self-consistent life style of an individual, and in comprehending in the case of failure the degree of his deviation, the nature of which always turns out to be a lack of the ability to make contact" (pp. 327–28). These approaches are discussed in the various books by Adler. Summaries of his position and further developments are to be found with regard to points (1) in Mosak (1958), (2) Shulman (1962), and (4) Shulman (1969).

The understanding so arrived at is conveyed to the patient, getting him to make it his own, and thus giving him insight.

Training and cognitive reorganization. Consistent with Adler's emphasis on training for behavior, including normal and abnormal sexual behavior, psychotherapy is understood as a process of re-education, where initial insight is followed by training and retraining. As early as 1907, Adler stated: "Therapy consists primarily in strengthening certain psychic fields through a kind of psychic training. . . . During and after the treatment, the patient masters material that was entirely strange to him before. . . . From an unwitting pawn of circumstances, he becomes a conscious antagonist or sufferer of his fate" (Nunberg and Federn, 1962, p. 95). In a later statement Adler (A1918b) held that the very co-operation with the physician on which psychotherapy is based "is to be understood as a training" (p. 141).

To a large extent the training is one of teaching the patient

402

to see the world, his situation, and himself differently—that is, bring about nothing less than a general cognitive reorganization. "The patient will have to resee the world and alter his old private view to bring it more into harmony with a 'common view' of the world" (A1956b, p. 254). "The cure or reorientation is brought about by a correction of the faulty picture of the world and the unequivocal acceptance of a mature picture of the world" (p. 333). "The fault of construction," of which the individual has not been aware, "is discovered, and a reconstruction is accomplished" (A1930a, p. 22).

The contents of this educative process would consist in explaining to the patient his life style, including his hidden goal and basic mistake, as Adler understood these. In the case of sexual disorders this would be very much like their discussion in the present volume, especially as found in the case histories.

The following from Adler (A1964a) may serve as a summary of his conception of psychotherapy: "The cure must consist of reconciling the patient with the problems of life. He must be made to see the defects in his life style and develop his social interest, important elements of which are active social contribution and a generally courageous attitude to life" (p. 138, new translation).

Technical Aspect

Of the first two aspects much is contained in the present volume. But on specific techniques to induce therapeutic change we find directly only that psychotherapy requires "greatest tactfulness and most subtle means." This is quite representative of all of Adler's writings. Two small volumes by him (A1928a, A1930e), *The Technique of Individual Psychology*, contain case discussions much like those in the present volume. The problem of specific techniques in the sense of tactics and strategies was presumably to be dealt with in a third volume of that series, under "technique and position of the counselor" (A1930e, p. 14). But this volume never appeared. Instead there is only a paper "The Technique of Treatment" (A1932l), which begins with Adler's frank admission: "If you don't ask me, I know it; when you ask me, I don't know it. This happens to every one of us when he is asked to speak about technique. For years I have been occupied writing about it—I hesitate, not because I don't know it; it has become automatic with me. But a description founders in that here nothing can be formulated into rules. Here the artistic side of Individual Psychology shows itself most clearly" (p. 192).

Ultimately psychotherapy is of course an art; yet certain techniques can be identified from Adler's writings beyond the limits he gives. In Adler's time one was not yet ready to focus on tactics and strategies as such. Freud and Jung, even more than Adler, also confined themselves to more general considerations.

Today, identification and systematic consideration of techniques used by Adler have been greatly aided by the work of Rychlak (1968, 1973), Haley (1963, 1969), and Watzlawick et al. (1967, 1974), among others, to whom we previously had occasion to refer. It is of interest that the last two belong to the Mental Research Institute group, Palo Alto, which advances a communication theory of psychotherapy, as set forth originally by Ruesch and Bateson (1951), which is in many ways close to Adlerian theory.

All of Adler's special techniques are related to his general holistic and dialectical approach.

Reframing. Technically the process of psychotherapy can be well described as one of "reframing." Watzlawick et al. (1974), who introduced the term, explain: "To reframe means to change the conceptual and/or emotional setting or viewpoint in relation to which a situation is experienced and to place it in another frame that fits the 'facts' . . . equally well or even better, and thereby changes . . . the meaning attributed to the situation, and therefore its consequences" (p. 95).

As mentioned earlier, what Adler at first called "uncovering" is truly a new interpretation, bringing to bear "an alternate frame of reference." Adler (A1927f) introduced this concept in the following, but he actually mentioned it only on a few occasions. "The neurotic has, of course, a notion of the

404

frame of reference (*Bezugssystem*) of normal life. . . . Yet
. . . he behaves according to another frame. Here then we
have two frames of reference . . . the normal . . . which includes all logic and reason, and . . . the neurotic, a private
frame of reference. An example of such a private frame of
reference would be a very pampered child whose behavior
. . . requires that everything should be handed to him on a
platter and that there should always be someone at his service" (p. 251)—the patient's utopia mentioned above. In the
present volume we find: "The task of Individual Psychology
is to replace the neurotic frame of reference with one of fellowship, and this is tantamount to encouragement."

While Adler generalizes here in accordance with his theory
about a neurotic or private vs. a normal frame of reference,
concretely the problem of reframing differs in each particular
case.

Humor and reframing. Humor is discussed in psychotherapy most often with regard to its affective qualities, and
Adler (A1956b) used it in this sense consistently. But beyond this he used jokes to demonstrate the possibility of changing the frame of reference and thereby finding the solution
for a problem. "I have always found it an immense advantage
to keep the level of tension in treatment as low as possible,
and virtually developed it into a method to tell almost every
patient that there are jokes altogether like the structure of his
peculiar neurosis, and that therefore the latter can also be
taken more lightly than he does" (p. 346). Adler (A1964a)
listed among the requirements for a psychotherapist, "trained
sagacity and ingenuity, a jovial attitude . . . blessed with
cheerfulness and good humor . . . also extreme patience and
forbearance" (p. 201).

In a paper on neurosis and jokes Adler (A1927f) wrote:
"If we employ the view of the private frame of reference of
the neurotic, we find that the neurosis and the joke have similar
characteristics. While the listener uses a normal frame of reference, the one who tells the joke suddenly introduces a new
frame of reference, which . . . shows the matter in an entirely
new light. . . . What happens, is a sudden split according to
two points of view. The essential part of the joke is this dual
frame of reference, and here we see the relationship with that

other device, the neurosis. . . . But a joke can only be good if the two frames of reference appear to have approximately equal general validity. . . . The neurosis is rather to be compared to a poor joke, because its particular frame of reference appears . . . invalid. . . . We have always been inclined to use jokes to clarify his error to the neurotic. In this way we can show him that he has a second frame of reference . . . and that he tries to bring his problem in line . . . with this false system. Here is a main point of attack of therapy" (p. 252).

Walter O'Connell (1975) has described the humorist as one who "moves well in the world of existential paradoxes" (p. 187), and the function of humor in psychotherapy as a tutoring "in moving across many frames of references" (p. 188). O'Connell follows this with examples of the use of humor in psychotherapy, especially by Adler.

Consideration of context. With Adler reframing was most often consideration of the context (*Zusammenhangsbetrachtung*), that is, consideration of a particular symptom in the context of the patient's style of life, and of the patient's situation in its full social context. The former was advanced by Adler's general holistic orientation, the latter particularly by his concept of social interest. Loss of the larger context is characteristic of the neurotic's frame of reference. Adler (A1956b) speaks of "the narrowness of the 'abnormal' frame of reference" within which "the adaptation to new life problems, and demands of the day are excluded" (p. 279). Such "exclusion tendency" is seen clearly in homosexuality (p. 424). "Successful treatment is possible with all kinds of means, but especially with insight into the deeper context and encouragement, the great advantage of Individual-Psychological treatment."

To see a situation in its larger context is also objectively the better approach, because a person's behavior does indeed affect his social environment just as the latter is an important factor in influencing his behavior. "It is an irreparable mistake to tear symptoms from their natural context and to regard them in isolation. Such procedure presently still generally practiced in the psychology of the neuroses is like taking one note from a melody and regarding it by itself. To understand nervous phenomena we must keep firmly in view their socially given and socially effective context." The similarity with the standpoint of Gestalt psychology is notable.

Conflict resolution. Reference to a larger frame is the dialectical approach to conflict resolution. It is the synthesis on another level of discourse, leaving the original thesis and antithesis behind. Adler applied this principle consistently to "intrapersonal" as well as interpersonal conflicts.

Indecision or ambivalence, which can be seen as an inner conflict, was interpreted by Adler by moving from the subjective to an objective level of discourse. When an individual is undecided, the objective outcome is that nothing will happen, the status quo will be maintained. From this outcome Adler inferred the meaning of indecision to be maintenance of the status quo. With this interpretation Adler reconstructed the situation for the patient. Now seeing the situation differently, the patient may more easily get out of his indecision, in one way or another. "The psychological structure of indecision is . . . not two different goals, but a single goal, and that is, 'But stay!'" (A1956b, p. 232). A pertinent passage from the present volume is: "All apparently contradictory impulses of the neurotic—love and hatred, defiance and obedience, dominance and submission, sadism and masochism, activity and passivity, homosexuality and heterosexuality—are only means to reach the fictive final purpose of over-all superiority. With this explanation, however, their antithetic character disappears!" Similarly, Adler approached the problem of abortion not so much from the viewpoint of the woman, but from a broader viewpoint, the welfare of the child who is involved.

The outstanding example of an interpersonal problem situation that Adler reframes by placing it into a larger context is marriage. He first restructures it from a problem of one person into one of two persons. It is a task for two. Then he broadens the context still much further by declaring it not a private matter of the two persons involved, but through the possibility of children, a matter concerning the community and humanity at large. Adler construes marriage as an event of social significance.

Dialectical interpretation. Adler (A1912a) noted that

407

pairings of opposites, such as below-above, form one category so that "the thought of each of the pair antithetically includes the other" (p. 127). But the person is most often not aware of the imp. d antithesis in many of his thoughts. Thus it is of great help in psychological interpretation if the therapist listens to the patient and observes him dialectically—that is, asks himself what opposites could be paired with certain statements and actions of the patient. Such dialectical or bipolar conception has considerable implications for redefinition or reframing, which may be considered the essence of psychotherapy.

Thus, a dream of flying, of being above, may point to a position and feeling of inferiority from which the dreamer wants to escape. Adler (A1912a) interprets a girl's dream of "walking in my sleep and stepping on everybody's head" (p. 219), on the basis of the context in which the dream occurred, as meaning: As one steps on my head, so will I step on other people's heads. Two examples from the present volume are: The person who considers himself "too good for any occupation" may in fact consider himself "not good enough." A girl's fear of being attacked may be an expression of "pure vanity."

Regarding dialectical interpretation of actions, Adler (A1956b) liked to tell the story: "Once when Socrates saw a sophist with his robe full of holes, he said to him: 'Young man of Athens, your vanity peeps from the holes in your robe!' Unassumingness and vanity side by side!" (p. 232). Self-inflicted harm is linked by Adler with attempts to hurt others (pp. 323–24). A further, simple example is eating difficulties in children, which suggest emphasis on eating by significant adults.

A comprehensive statement of dialectics is: "While the patient regards one point, we must look at the other. He looks at his obstacles; we must look at his attempt to protect his fictive superiority and rescue his ambition" (A1964a, p. 199). This reinterpretation means a shift from causality to purposiveness, as well as a shift in the stimulus-response pair from the stimulus or passive side, to the response or active side, a technique applied throughout Adlerian psychotherapy. When the individual would tell what happened to him, or what the other person did, Dreikurs (1972) particularly would ask consistently, "And what did you do about it?" (pp. 205, 211, 215).

Further specific examples of Adlerian dialectical interpretation are given by Mosak and Gushurst (1971). Dependency is interpreted as controlling others, placing them in one's service; guilt feeling, as pleading for acquittal; any self-accusation, as excuse from accepting responsibilities; and flattery of the therapist, as preparation for knocking him down later; etc. All this is related to Adler's basic dialectical interpretation of the symptom as a device by which the patient protects his self-esteem within the frame of his mistaken style of life.

Paradoxical communication. Since the human mind functions dialectically, human beings are capable of "paradoxical communication" (Watzlawick et al., 1967, pp. 187–229)—that is, expressing contradictory messages simultaneously. More specifically, in paradoxical communication one end of a bipolar construct is expressed overtly, while on another level and unknown to the person the opposite end is also expressed. From this viewpoint the patient's statements and actions, which are interpreted dialectically, can be understood as the patient's paradoxical communications. Although Adler did not formulate this concept, he described it, for example, when he stated that in the case of impotence the patient's words express one intention, whereas "his sexual organs speak another language."

Since the patient hides the contradictory part of his communication from his awareness, Adler speaks of "self-deception," by which the patient frees himself from responsibility. The neurotic will blame his parents, fate, looks, education—anything, because his life plan "demands categorically that if he fails . . . he should be freed from personal responsibility" (A1956b, p. 270). Watzlawick et al. (1967) express the same thought: "Communication theory conceives of a symptom as a nonverbal message: It is not I who does not (or does) want to do this, it is something outside my control—for example, my nerves, my illness, my anxiety . . . or my wife" (p. 80).

As the neurosis or the symptom carries this message paradoxically, it is likely to withstand direct attack. It is, however, amenable to paradoxical communication on the part of the therapist. This technique has been used by many psychotherapists and under many different names (see Watzlawick et al., 1967, pp. 239–40). We like the name "paradoxical intention" of Frankl (1960), meaning a therapeutic intervention intending the opposite of its overt meaning. An excellent example was given by Fay (1977) in the following brief interchange: Patient: "I am really worthless." Therapist: "Yes, you are." Patient: "I know what you are trying to do. It's a trick, but it won't work." Therapist: "It's interesting that when you say you are worthless, it doesn't sound ridiculous or like a trick, but when I say the same thing, it does."

The most universal application of the therapeutic paradox is "prescribing the symptom" (especially, Haley, 1963). This technique was frequently used by Adler. When a patient complained, "There is nothing I like doing," Adler (A1956b) would direct him to "refrain from doing anything you dislike" (pp. 346–47). To a patient characterized by indecision and finally asking, "What shall I do?" Adler would say, "Do for a few months more what you have been doing! Above all, don't do anything rash!" (Wexberg, 1927, p. 101).

Mozdzierz et al. (1976) have described the history and dynamics of the paradox in Adlerian psychotherapy as applied dialectics and have identified twelve types of paradoxical intervention. While such interventions are "seemingly self-contradictory and sometimes absurd," they are "always constructively rationalizable," and "join rather than oppose symptomatic behavior while containing qualities of empathy, encouragement, and humor, leading to increased social interest" (p. 169).

Prevention

From his conviction that homosexuality is the result of faulty early training and self-training, it follows that Adler gave much thought to primary prevention. "Our findings give

410

us much more ground for advocating the prophylaxis of homosexuality than its therapy, which is exceedingly difficult." "The elimination of homosexuality . . . is a problem of the education of children." Adler's outline for such prevention is simple enough. "In the nursery the most important demands will be not to deprive the child of his courage, not to keep him in the dark regarding the problems of his future life, and to establish from the start his sexual role as fixed and unalterable," where actually only the third demand is specific to homosexuality.

As Adler's theories of psychopathology and psychotherapy in general were learning theories, including self-training, he considered prevention always possible. He wrote special papers on the prevention of neurosis and the prevention of delinquency (A1935h, A1935i). Prevention would address itself to the early acquisition of a courageous, co-operative, responsible approach to the problems of life and avoidance of the opposites. From this general concern stemmed Adler's interests in sex education for children (pp. 332–34 above) and premarital and marital counseling (pp. 334–38 above), where he formulated the problem into: "What can we do to prevent errors in love relationships?"

Beyond merely writing on the subject, Adler engaged on a large-scale effort of prevention through the Vienna school system. He reasoned that if adult mental disorders can best be prevented by correcting any early mistake in outlook of the child, then it is important to work through the schoolteachers, through whom theoretically every child can be reached. Thus Adler embarked upon teaching teachers, and at the Pedagogical Institute of the City of Vienna lectured over the years to many hundreds of them. He also established and conducted with his coworkers the numerous child-guidance clinics that were described earlier.

Advice to a Young Social Worker

On several occasions we pointed to Adler's flexibility and nondogmatic attitude despite some contrary-sounding statements. He would warn his audience: "Don't blindly believe

411

any 'authority'—not even me!" or state: "We assign only limited value to general rules and instead lay strong emphasis on flexibility and empathy into nuances," or: "We do not believe that we have . . . pronounced the last wisdom."

It was not Adler's main purpose to prove a theory. His purpose was to help specific, concrete individuals. Thus the one point that remained fixed with him was the regard for the welfare of the individual in harmony with the welfare of humanity. Adler (A1956b) saw his Individual Psychology "connected with all great movements through the common urge . . . toward a higher development of humanity and the welfare of all" (pp. 463–64).

Adler's lack of dogmatism and fresh approach to each particular problem is most characteristic for him as practitioner and human being. In reference to sexual disorders, where he often sounds particularly dogmatic, this ultimate open-mindedness is well illustrated by the following anecdote, with which we are concluding this essay. The anecdote is told by Elizabeth H. McDowell (1977) from the mid-1930s, when Adler was professor at Long Island College of Medicine in Brooklyn, now Downstate Medical Center, State University of New York, and she was a social-work student in New York. She writes:

"Among my more rarefied clients was a very personable, highly intelligent young man of twenty-one who 'lived in sin' with an older man. . . . At my supervisor's suggestion that we take advantage of Dr. Adler's presence I wrote up the case of John and sent it to Dr. Adler, asking for his treatment advice. He granted me an interview. . . .

"Adler glanced down for a moment at my report . . . then looked at me over his glasses: 'You say this John is a homosexual?'

" 'Oh yes,' I replied.

" 'And is he happy, would you say?'

" 'Oh yes,' I replied.

" 'Well,' leaning back in his swivel chair and putting his thumbs in his vest, 'why don't we leave him alone? Eh?'—adding a few words about how little was known about the sexual deviate."

412

BIBLIOGRAPHICAL-
HISTORICAL COMMENTARY

Comments on the history of Adler's writings included in this volume, and related matters, should add to an appreciation of the material itself and knowledge of Adler the man. Rather than dispersing such comments throughout the essay they are gathered here in one place.

I. SOCIOLOGICAL AND THEORETICAL WRITINGS

Chapter 1, "The Myth of Women's Inferiority," is a new translation of "The Relationship Between the Sexes," Chapter 7 in Adler's most popular book, *Understanding Human Nature* (A1927a). Although published later than most of the other material in the present book, these sociological thoughts most likely preceded Adler's psychological concepts. We believe his psychological system could not have become "the first in the history of psychology that was developed in . . . a social-science direction" (Murphy, 1949, p. 341) had Adler not started with sociological and educational problems.

If Adler did not write on these matters at any length before 1927, it is probably because they did not become his main professional concern. But he frequently interspersed his views in papers on related topics, or made them known at meetings. Those who knew Adler personally were well acquainted with these views. Edward Hitschmann, one of Adler's adversaries in the Vienna Psychoanalytic Society, commented on Adler's "personal relations with academic psychology, as well as with pedagogy, socialism, and the feminist movement," giving these as explanations why Adler rejected the pre-eminence that Freud attributed to sexuality (Nunberg and Federn, 1974, pp. 155–56). The occasion for a more systematic presentation of his views on the woman question arose for Adler in the popular lectures on which *Understanding Human Nature* is based.

Chapter 1's Appendix, "The Problem of Abortion," is a paper by Adler (A1925i), which is here translated for the first time. It was reprinted the following year by Margaret Hilferding (1926), Adler's first woman follower, at the end of a booklet on birth control. At that time decline of the birth rate below reproduction level was "a grave concern of the population experts of all civilized countries and all political parties" (p. 10), so that the advocate of birth control also warned against "the refusal to have children" (*Flucht vor dem Kinde*). Some of this concern seems to be reflected also in Adler's paper. Interestingly, as of 1977, fifty years later, the birth rates in East and West Germany are again below the reproduction level.

Chapter 2, "Masculine Protest and a Critique of Freud," presents material from 1910 to 1912. With the exception of Sections 2 and 3, it appeared in the first volume of collected papers by Adler and his colleagues, *Heilen und Bilden* (Healing and Educating), edited by him and Carl Furtmüller (A1914a). The subtitle, *Medical-educational Papers,* changed in subsequent editions to *Foundations of Pedagogy for Physicians and Educators,* expresses Adler's acceptance of an essentially educational rather than a medical model of psychotherapy. These selections are presently published for the first time in full-length translation. Previously only translated excerpts had been available (A1956b). These papers were originally presented and discussed at the weekly meetings of the Vienna Psychoanalytic Society, of which Adler was a member since its modest beginnings in 1902. Adler was one of the four younger men whom Freud invited then for weekly discussions of problems of neurosis.

Minutes of the Vienna Psychoanalytic Society. Beginning

with 1906, the proceedings of the group were recorded and have been published as the *Minutes of the Vienna Psychoanalytic Society* (skillfully edited and translated by Nunberg and Federn, 1962–75). These *Minutes* are of great help for a fuller understanding of Adler, in that he often presented important ideas in an informal introduction to a paper or as a remark in a discussion, such as can be found nowhere else.

The original credit for the *Minutes* goes to Otto Rank. Introduced to Freud in 1906 by Adler (Jones, 1955, p. 8) as a promising young man, Rank was given the job of recording secretary of the small group, a job he filled until 1915, when he was drafted into the Austrian Army. Rank carried out his function in an exemplary fashion, leaving an invaluable document.

Chapter 2, Section 1, is Adler's original paper on the masculine protest, entitled "Psychological Hermaphroditism in Life and Neurosis" (A1910c), with two enlightening points from the *Minutes* (A1910n) added: (1) In replacing "aggression drive" with "masculine protest," Adler explains that the former, as a drive, is a *biological* conception, whereas he now considered only a *psychological* conception, "in terms of cultural psychology," as suitable. (2) This change raises the issue of determinism vs. freedom.

Sections 4 to 7, a critique of Freud's concepts of sexuality and repression, are Adler's presentations before the Vienna Psychoanalytic Society on January 4 and February 1, 1911, which led to the separation by Adler and his followers. The events leading up to these meetings were the following: In October 1910 Adler presented a case in which he found "the patient filled with masculine protest . . . the motive force in her entire life: the avid desire to be 'on top'" (Nunberg and Federn, 1974, p. 18). Adler noted also "the wish to be 'on top'" (p. 46) in children's vocational choice. To such observations Freud replied: "Adler, with his usual masterly skill, has shown the pedagogical and social settings of the case; on the other hand, his expositions require, as usual, psychoanalytic filling-out" (p. 22). Edward Hitschmann had commented: "Adler's approach is very different from ours" (p. 21). By November 1910 a point was reached where Hitsch-

415

mann moved "that Adler's theories be for once thoroughly discussed in their interconnections, with particular attention to their divergence from Freud's doctrine, so that there may be achieved, if possible, a fusion of the two views, or at least a clarification of the differences between them" (p. 59). Adler was willing to discuss the problem, but thought this could not be done easily. On Freud's suggestion it was then moved that "only one aspect of Adler's views be discussed . . . the relationship of the 'masculine protest' to the doctrine of repression" (p. 59). This led to Adler's presentations on January 4 and February 1, 1911, and ensuing discussions on February 8 and 22.

The Neurotic Constitution. In Chapter 2, the sections entitled "Antithetical Apperception" and "Critique of Freud's Libido Theory," respectively, are newly translated from *The Neurotic Constitution* (A1912a), Adler's most important book. The first shows the influence on Adler of the German pragmatist Vaihinger (1911b) and is essential for a full understanding of Adler's theory of human dynamics. The second is a good summary of Adler's critique of Freud's sex theory.

Adler (A1930o) considered *The Neurotic Constitution* "fundamental for Individual Psychology." "In this treatise I described the dependence of all psychic phenomena on the final goal of superiority. The pre-eminent role of the human feeling of inferiority, its compensations in good and bad directions, and other subordinate problems connected with these, were all expounded. The unity of the individual in his thousandfold variations was recognized as the proper subject matter of Individual Psychology, and the derivation of all symptoms and expressions from this unity—the later 'goal of life'—was established. At the same time, the decisive role of the first years of childhood in shaping the 'style of life' is explained, and, with this discovery, determinism in psychology suffers a breach at an important point. The individual *determines himself* when he takes any particular experiences or situations (often mistakenly) as the basis of his subsequent life" (p. 8).

Unfortunately, the existing translation of *The Neurotic Constitution* is quite inadequate. Even the title should actually

416

read *The Nervous Character,* and in the subtitle, *Individual Psychology* is erroneously rendered as *Individualistic Psychology*—exactly the opposite of what Adler stood for.

II. SEXUALITY AND THE INDIVIDUAL

The first section of Chapter 3 is a paper on sexual development (A1945b) published posthumously. It is included as the only paper in which Adler discusses the sexual function as such and from a developmental viewpoint. The fourth section, "Sex Education," is taken from *The Education of Children* (A1930a), a very good popular book translated from the German. While the original is unknown, the book was recently re-translated into German. The remainder of the chapter is from *The Problem of Homosexuality* (A1930d), which otherwise has supplied the material for Chapters 5 to 7, and will be discussed in connection with these chapters.

Chapter 4, "Love and Marriage," is taken from two sources. The first is a booklet entitled *Liebesbeziehungen und deren Störungen* (Love Relationships and Their Disturbances, A1926a), translated for the first time in the first four sections of this chapter. In the first section Adler presents love and marriage as a task, one of three life tasks, a conception always included in his writings from then on. The remainder of Chapter 4 is from *What Life Should Mean to You* (A1931b), another popular book, which appeared originally in English. It was edited by Alan Porter, an associate professor of English at Vassar College, who also edited two books by the then Adlerian psychiatrist Olga Knopf (1932, 1935).

The Right Conduct of Life. The booklet Love Relationships and Their Disturbances appeared in a series entitled *The Right Conduct of Life: Popular Essays on the Education of Men and Women According to the Principles of Individual Psychology.* This series, founded and edited by Sofie Lazarsfeld, was one of four or more such series designed to bring the work of Adler and his followers to the people.

A Preface to this series by Adler (A1926bb) tells in its

brevity a great deal about Adler, the man convinced of the great usefulness of his psychology and dedicated to the striving of humanity for a better future. Because this interesting document has not been published in translation before, we are citing it here in full.

"A body of knowledge serves its purpose if it makes its important results alive. This applies particularly to Individual Psychology because it instructs in self-understanding, understanding of others, independence, and encouragement. It is so committed to general usefulness that its development takes it to the broad masses of the people. Its foremost task is to establish among them a firm basis for a sound, optimistic view and conduct of life, promoting the welfare of all. Born from good common sense, it returns to the people in purified and practically applicable form what it has received from them. It feels at one with the noblest striving and the most sublime, peaceful ideals of humanity freed from hatred. Its scientific insights have found in the editor [Sofie Lazarsfeld] an enthusiastic and popular representative. My coworkers and I wish these popular essays their deserved success and the widest public distribution, because we have the firm conviction that along our way a happier lot for humanity can be found.—Dr. Alfred Adler."

The Book of Marriage. A year before the booklet on love relationships, Adler (A1925b, A1926aa) had written a chapter "Marriage as a Task" for a symposium volume, in which he expressed some of the same thoughts. The volume was *The Book of Marriage: A New Interpretation by Twenty-four Leaders of Contemporary Thought,* edited by Hermann Keyserling (1925). Among the contributors were psychiatrists Beatrice M. Hinkle, Carl G. Jung, Ernst Kretchmer, and Alphonse Maeder; writers and poets Havelock Ellis, Ricarda Huch, Thomas Mann, Rabindranath Tagore, and Jacob Wassermann; and Rabbi Leo Baeck.

Keyserling (1880–1946) was a philosopher who tended toward mysticism and stressed self-actualization. He believed, "What a person does is totally indifferent; what counts is the spirit in which he does it. He who acts according to his deepest nature necessarily acts correctly, no matter what im-

418

pression his action may make on others" (quoted after Schmidt, 1934). Adler (A1926aa) quite disagreed with this, making at the outset of his contribution the noteworthy opposing statement, showing himself clearly as the pragmatist and operationalist. He wrote: "It is quite immaterial what a person thinks, feels, or wants by his performance. Only the accord of his act with the requirements of evolution can vindicate him. [One who plants trees] creates for the community and for posterity, even if in so doing he considers only his own well-being" (pp. 363–64).

III. SEXUAL DISORDERS

Chapters 5, 6, and 7, and Chapter 3, are almost exclusively a new and partly original translation of *Das Problem der Homosexualität: erotisches Training und erotischer Rückzug* (The Problem of Homosexuality: Erotic Training and Erotic Retreat, A1930d). Like several of Adler's books, it is a collection of previous publications. These are in the order in which they appear in the book, A1917b, A1929c, and A1926h, i, j, g, e, and f.

In Chapter 6 the last section, "Prostitution," is from Adler's collection of papers "Practice and Theory of Individual Psychology" (A1920a), one of the very few papers in that volume not previously published. It was apparently addressed to a socialist audience, because Adler speaks regretfully of visits to prostitutes by "comrades" (*Volksgenossen*), an appellation used among socialists.

The Problem of Homosexuality. The first edition of this collection (A1917b) consisted of an essay on homosexuality and four case histories. Interestingly, it appeared in English translation (A1914i) three years before the original. The explanation is probably that the German version was delayed by the outbreak of World War I (1914–18) which disrupted all nonwar activities. This assumption is supported by two circumstances: (1) the monograph had been announced early in 1914 as forthcoming; (2) the English translation does not include the fourth case, which Adler had encountered during his wartime service as a physician in the Austrian Army.

Bethe's Handbook. The 1926 publications enumerated above appeared originally in the encyclopedic and prestigious *Handbuch der normalen und pathologischen Physiologie* (Handbook of Normal and Pathological Physiology), a work of eighteen volumes edited by Albrecht Bethe and others. Adler's articles represented six out of ten entries in the section "Sexual Activity and Sexual Relationships" in Volume 14.1. The editor of this section was Arthur Kronfeld, friend and supporter of Adler's Individual Psychology in Berlin and chairman and organizer of the most successful Fifth Congress of Individual Psychology in Berlin, 1930. The editors of the *Handbook* stressed the organismic approach, stating in their brief introduction to Kronfeld's section: "There is increasing realization in our time that it is impossible to consider physiological and psychological phenomena isolated from each other. In Kronfeld's general summary this inseparability is convincingly expressed."

Early interest in Adler. "The Homosexual Problem" by Adler (A1914i) was his first title to appear in English, as early as 1914. But his works were altogether quickly introduced in this country. The important G. Stanley Hall of Clark University studied *Heilen und Bilden* (A1914a), in seminars with his students as soon as it appeared and invited Adler for a lecture series, which was, however, obviated by the outbreak of the war (Ansbacher, 1971a). The translation of *The Neurotic Constitution* (A1917a), with an Introduction by William Alanson White, was published three years later. And during the same year Smith Ely Jelliffe supplied a translation of Adler's monograph on organ inferiority (A1917c).

An autobiographical statement. In Chapter 7, Case 5, dated 1926 by its footnote, was not published prior to 1930. Cases 6 and 7 had been published in English (A1929c, pp. 92–95 and 141–42) before they appeared in German.

Case 6, "Disappointment in Women," interests us further. We note that paragraphs 3 and 4 (pp. 243–44) are a digression from a case of agoraphobia to another case. The

420

digression illustrates the point that the memory of a better relationship to the father than to the mother may mean disappointment in the mother, with resulting preference for the father. Adler only barely indicated that this was a digression to another case, introducing it with, "One man said . . ." (A1929c, p. 92), without marking its end. Moreover, the German edition replaced "one man" with "the patient" (A1930d, p. 52), thereby completely obscuring the digression. We were told, however, that such tacit combining of case material was within prevailing practice.

But in this instance the two cases are actually quite incompatible. In the digression, we have a boy who actively intervenes in situations, or at least takes a very definite position. He is "very much upset" by a certain behavior of his mother; was considered being rough toward his mother; and praises his father with, "You were brave like a soldier!" The case of agoraphobia, on the other hand, remembers being "in love with a schoolmaster," and having been "seduced by a boyhood friend into mutual masturbation." This describes a much less spontaneous, passive boy, one who does not take responsibility and blames someone else, quite in contrast to the first boy. This difference becomes immediately plausible when we learn to our surprise that the first boy is Adler himself and the recollections are autobiographical. In a little-known paper Adler (A1930o) gives all three recollections as his own. Adler's recollections are discussed in the essay (pp. 263–66).

REFERENCES

There are three lists of references: (1) to Adler, (2) by Adler to other authors, and (3) by the editors to other authors.

1. *References to Adler.* This list includes all references to Adler, made by himself or by the editor. The items are identified by "A," the year of first publication, and a letter, following the master bibliography of Adler in *Superiority and Social Interest* (A1964a, pp. 397–420). In those items from which the text includes a quotation, the original source is followed by the source from which the quotation is actually taken, where this applies. Page references in the text thus may refer to this second source.

There are eleven books by Adler in German (including one as co-editor and one as co-author). Ten of these have been published as paperbacks by the Fischer Taschenbuch Verlag between 1972 and 1977 under the competent editorship of Professor Wolfgang Metzger and have been supplied with excellent introductions by him. These books are A1907a, A1912a, A1914a, A1920a, A1928a, A1929b, A1930d, A1933b, A1933c, and one not referred to in the present volume. The eleventh book (A1927a) was included in this series six years earlier, in 1966, with an introduction by Oliver Brachfeld. Most of these volumes are provided with unusually extensive subject indexes which have been of great help in the preparation of the present volume and for which we are very grateful. If we have nevertheless not referred to these paperbacks, it is for the consideration that the student will most likely have access to the hardcover editions, but not the paperback, through his library.

2. *Adler's References to Other Authors.* Adler was generally very sparse with references. Most of those included in the present writings were supplied by him with his contributions to the Bethe *Handbook* (see p. 420), apparently on request from its editors. Nearly all these references were in various degrees incomplete and were completed by the present editors as far as possible. English translations are cited where such could be readily found.

3. *Editors' References to Other Authors.* We considered it helpful to keep Adler's and the editors' references to other authors distinct.

REFERENCES TO ADLER

A1905a Das sexuelle Problem in der Erziehung (The sex problem in education), *Neue Gesellschaft* (Berlin), 1, 360–62.

A1905b Drei Psycho-Analysen von Zahleneinfällen und obsedierenden Zahlen (Three psychoanalyses of ideas of numbers and obsessive numbers), *Psychiatrische und neurologische Wochenschrift*, 7, 263–66.

A1907a *Studie über Minderwertigkeit von Organen* (Study of organ inferiority). Vienna: Urban & Schwarzenberg [Trans.: A1917c].

A1908b Der Aggressionstrieb im Leben und in der Neurose (The aggression drive in life and in neurosis), *Fortschritte der Medizin*, 26, 577–84; as reprinted in A1928n, pp. 33–42.

A1908e Die Theorie der Organminderwertigkeit und ihre Bedeutung für Philosophie und Psychologie (The theory of organ inferiority and its significance for philosophy and psychology), *Universität Wien, Philosophische Gesellschaft, Wissenschaftliche Beilage*, 21, 11–26; as reprinted in A1928n, pp. 24–33.

A1908f Zwei Träume einer Prostituierten (Two dreams of a prostitute), *Zeitschrift für Sexualwissenschaft*, 1, 103–6.

A1909a Über neurotische Disposition: zugleich ein Beitrag zur Ätiologie und zur Frage der Neurosenwahl (On neurotic disposition: a contribution to the etiology and problem of choice of neurosis), *Jahrbuch für Psychoanalyse und psychopathologische Forschung*, 1, 526–45; as reprinted in A1928n, pp. 59–75.

A1909d On the psychology of Marxism, *Minutes of the Vienna Psychoanalytic Society;* Vol. 2, *1908–10*, ed. H. Nunberg and E. Federn (New York: International Universities Press, 1967), pp. 172–74.

A1910b Über den Selbstmord, insbesondere den Schülerselbstmord (On suicide, especially among students), *Diskussionen des Wiener Psychoanalytischen Vereins;* Vol. 1 (Wiesbaden: Bergmann), pp. 44–50; as reprinted in A1928n, pp. 206–11.

A1910c Der psychische Hermaphroditismus im Leben und in der Neurose (Psychological hermaphroditism in life and neurosis), *Fortschritte der Medizin*, 28, 486–93; as reprinted in A1928n, pp. 76–84.

A1910d Trotz und Gehorsam (Defiance and obedience), *Monatshefte für Pädagogik und Schulpolitik*, 2, 321–28; as reprinted in A1928n, pp. 84–92.

A1910f Die psychische Behandlung der Trigeminusneuralgie (The psychological treatment of trigeminus neuralgia), *Zentralblatt für Psychoanalyse*, 1, 10–20; as reprinted in A1930p, pp. 52–67.

A1910n Psychic hermaphroditism, *Minutes of the Vienna Psychoanalytic Society;* Vol. 2, *1908–10*, ed. H. Nunberg and E. Federn (New York: International Universities Press, 1967), pp. 423–28.

A1911a Die Rolle der Sexualität in der Neurose (The role of sexuality in neurosis); in A1928n, pp. 92–100.

A1911b "Verdrängung" und "männlicher Protest": ihre Rolle und Bedeutung für die neurotische Dynamik ("Repression" and "masculine protest": their role and significance for the neurotic dynamics); in A1928n, pp. 100–9.

424

A1911c Über männliche Einstellung bei weiblichen Neuroti-
kern (On masculine attitude in female neurotics), *Zentralblatt für Psychoanalyse*, 1, 174–78; as reprinted in
A1930p, pp. 74–78 plus new pp. 78–97.

A1911d Beitrag zur Lehre vom Widerstand (Contribution to
the theory of resistance), *Zentralblatt für Psychoanalyse*,
1, 214–19; as reprinted in A1930p, pp. 97–103.

A1911h Some problems of psychoanalysis, and discussion,
Minutes of the Vienna Psychoanalytic Society; Vol. 3,
1910–11, ed. H. Nunberg and E. Federn (New York:
International Universities Press, 1974), pp. 102–11
(pp. 102–5, abstract of A1911a; pp. 105–11, discussion).

A1911i The masculine protest as the central problem of neurosis, and discussion, *Minutes of the Vienna Psychoanalytic Society;* Vol. 3, *1910–11*, ed. H. Nunberg and E.
Federn (New York: International Universities Press,
1974), pp. 140–58, 168–77.

A1912a *Über den nervösen Charakter: Grundzüge einer vergleichenden Individual-Psychologie und Psychotherapie*
(The nervous character: fundamentals of a comparative individual psychology and psychotherapy) (Wiesbaden: Bergmann), 4th ed., A1928k. [Trans. A1917a.]

A1912h Das organische Substrat der Psychoneurosen: zur
Ätiologie der Neurosen und Psychosen (The organic sub-
stratum of the psychoneuroses: on the etiology of the
neuroses and psychoses), *Zeitschrift für die gesamte
Neurologie und Psychiatrie*, 13, 481–91; as reprinted in
A1930p, pp. 161–70.

A1913a Individualpsychologische Behandlung der Neurosen
(Individual-Psychological treatment of the neuroses), *I.
Jahreskurse für ärztliche Fortbildung*, ed. D. Sarason
(Munich: Lehmann), pp. 39–51; as reprinted in
A1930p, pp. 21–35.

A1913d Individualpsychologische Ergebnisse bezüglich
Schlafstörungen (Individual-Psychological conclusions

regarding sleep disturbances), *Fortschritte der Medizin,* 31, 925–33; as reprinted in A1930p, pp. 116–23.

A1913f Der nervöse Charakter (The nervous character), *Sozial. Monatsschrift,* 19; as reprinted in A1928n, pp. 130–39.

A1913g Individualpsychologische Bemerkungen zu Alfred Bergers *Hofrat Eysenhardt.* (Individual-Psychological comments on Alfred Berger's *Hofrat Eysenhardt*), *Zeitschrift für psychologische Medizin und Psychotherapie,* 5, 77–89; as reprinted in A1930p, pp. 189–99.

A1914a [Editor with Carl Furtmüller] *Heilen und Bilden: ärztlich-pädagogische Arbeiten des Vereins für Individualpsychologie* (Healing and educating: medical-educational papers of the Society for Individual Psychology) (Munich: Reinhardt); as in 3rd ed., A1928n.

A1914f Soziale Einflüsse in der Kinderstube (Social influences in the nursery), *Pädagogisches Archiv,* 56, 473–87.

A1914h Die Individualpsychologie, ihre Voraussetzungen und Ergebnisse (Individual Psychology: its assumptions and results), *Scientia,* 17, 74–87; as reprinted in A1930p, pp. 1–11.

A1914i The homosexual problem, *Urological and Cutaneous Review, Technical Supplement,* 2, 278–94.

A1914k Das Problem der "Distanz": über einen Grundcharakter der Neurose und Psychose (The problem of "distance": a basic trait of neurosis and psychosis), *Zeitschrift für Individualpsychologie,* 1, 8–16; as reprinted in A1930p, pp. 68–73.

A1914m Lebenslüge und Verantwortlichkeit in der Neurose und Psychose: ein Beitrag zur Melancholiefrage (Life lie and responsibility in neurosis and psychosis: a contribution to the problem of melancholia), *Zeitschrift für Individualpsychologie,* 1, 44–53; as reprinted in A1930p, pp. 170–77.

A1914p Nervöse Schlaflosigkeit (Nervous sleeplessness), *Zeitschrift für Individualpsychologie,* 1, 65–72; as reprinted in A1930p, pp. 110–16.

A1916 Die Frau als Erzieherin (Woman as educator), *Archiv für Frauenkunde* (Würzburg), 2, 341–49.

A1917a *The neurotic constitution: outline of a comparative individualistic psychology and psychotherapy*, trans. B. Glueck and J. E. Lind, Introduction by William A. White (New York: Moffat, Yard).

A1917b *Das Problem der Homosexualität* (The problem of homosexuality) (Munich: Reinhardt).

A1917c *Study of organ inferiority and its psychical compensation: a contribution to clinical medicine*, trans. S. E. Jelliffe (New York: Nervous and Mental Diseases Publishing Co.).

A1917d The homosexual problem, *Alienist and Neurologist*, 38, 268–87.

A1918a Über die Homosexualität (Homosexuality), in A1930p, pp. 123–34.

A1918b Die Zwangsneurose (Compulsion neurosis), in A1930p, pp. 134–42.

A1918e Bolschewismus und Seelenkunde (Bolshevism and psychology), *Internationale Rundschau* (Zurich), 4, 597–600.

A1919a *Die andere Seite: eine massenpsychologische Studie über die Schuld des Volkes* (The other side: a social-psychological study on collective guilt) (Vienna: Leopold Heidrich).

A1920a *Praxis und Theorie der Individualpsychologie: Vorträge zur Einführung in die Psychotherapie für Ärzte, Psychologen und Lehrer* (Practice and theory of Individual Psychology: introductory lectures in psychotherapy for physicians, psychologists, and educators) (Munich: Bergmann), 4th ed., A1930p. [Trans. A1925a.]

A1920c Die Individuelle Psychologie der Prostitution (The Individual Psychology of prostitution), in A1920a, pp. 228–36; as reprinted in A1930p, pp. 230–38.

A1921 Wo soll der Kampf gegen die Verwahrlosung einsetzen? (Where should the fight against waywardness begin?) *Soziale Praxis* (Vienna); as reprinted in A1928n, pp. 139–42.

A1923b Danton, Marat, Robespierre: eine Charakterstudie (Danton, Marat, Robespierre: a character study), *Arbeiter-Zeitung* (Vienna, December 25), 17–18.

A1924a Die Strafe in der Erziehung (Punishment in education), *Arbeiter-Zeitung* (Vienna, June 14), 12.

A1924m Training? (Training?), *Internationale Zeitschrift für Individualpsychologie*, 2(6), 39.

A1924n Kritische Erwägungen über den Sinn des Lebens (Critical considerations on the meaning of life), *Internationale Zeitschrift für Individualpsychologie*, 3, 93–96.

A1925a *The practice and theory of Individual Psychology*, trans. P. Radin. (London: Routledge & Kegan Paul; reprinted, Totowa, N.J.: Littlefield, Adams, 1968).

A1925b Die Ehe als Aufgabe (Marriage as a task), *Buch der Ehe*, ed. H. Keyserling (Celle: Chapman) [trans.: A1926aa].

A1925c Unerziebarkeit des Kindes oder Unbelehrbarkeit der Theorie? Bemerkungen zum Falle Hug (Uneducability of the child or incorrigibility of the theory? Comments on the case of Hug), *Arbeiter-Zeitung* (Vienna, March 5), p. 6.

A1925g Diskussionsbemerkungen zum Vortrage des Prof. Max Adler (Discussion of the lecture by Prof. Max Adler), *Internationale Zeitschrift für Individualpsychologie*, 3, 221–23.

A1925i Erörterungen zum Paragraph 144 (Discussion of paragraph 144 [making abortion illegal]), *Internationale Zeitschrift für Individualpsychologie*, 3, 338–40.

A1926a *Liebesbeziehungen und deren Störungen* (Love relationships and their disturbances) (Vienna, Leipzig: Moritz Perles).

A1926d Geleitwort (Preface), *Individuum und Gemeinschaft* (Munich), No. 1, ix–xi.

A1926e Psychische Einstellung der Frau zum Sexualleben (Woman's psychological attitude to sex life), *Handbuch*

428

der normalen und pathologischen Physiologie, ed. A. Bethe et al. (Berlin: Springer), Vol. 14 (1), pp. 802–7; as reprinted in A1930d, pp. 89–97.

A1926f Psychosexuelle Haltung des Mannes (Man's psychosexual attitude), *Handbuch der normalen und pathologischen Physiologie,* ed. A. Bethe et al. (Berlin: Springer), Vol. 14 (1), pp. 808–12; as reprinted in A1930d, pp. 98–106.

A1926g Pubertätserscheinungen (Puberty phenomena), *Handbuch der normalen und pathologischen Physiologie,* ed. A. Bethe et al. (Berlin: Springer), Vol. 14 (1), pp. 842–44; as reprinted in A1930d, pp. 85–89.

A1926h Homosexualität (Homosexuality), *Handbuch der normalen und pathologischen Physiologie,* ed. A. Bethe et al. (Berlin: Springer), Vol. 14 (1), pp. 881–86; as reprinted in A1930d, pp. 56–65.

A1926i Sadismus, Masochismus, und andere Perversionen (Sadism, masochism, and other perversions), *Handbuch der normalen und pathologischen Physiologie,* ed. A. Bethe et al. (Berlin: Springer), Vol. 14 (1), pp. 887–94; as reprinted in A1930d, pp. 67–78.

A1926j Sexualneurasthenie (Sexual neurasthenia), *Handbuch der normalen und pathologischen Physiologie,* ed. A. Bethe et al. (Berlin: Springer), Vol. 14 (1), pp. 895–99; as reprinted in A1930d, pp. 78–84.

A1926k Die Individualpsychologie als Weg zur Menschenkenntnis und Selbsterkenntnis (Individual Psychology, a way to understanding of human nature and oneself), in *Du und der Alltag: eine Psychologie des täglichen Lebens,* ed. J. Neumann (Berlin: Warneck).

A1926o Vorrede (Preface) in H. F. Wolf, *Strategie der männlichen Annäherung* (Vienna: Ilos Verlag; Amsterdam: Bonset, 1969), pp. 9–14; trans. *The male approach* (New York: Covici-Friede, 1929), pp. vii–xi.

A1926q Die Ehe als Aufgabe (Marriage as a task), *Internationale Zeitschrift für Individualpsychologie,* 4, 22–24.

A1926aa Marriage as a task, in *The book of marriage: a new introduction by twenty-four leaders of contemporary thought*, ed. H. Keyserling (New York: Harcourt, Brace), pp. 363–72.

A1926bb Geleitwort (Preface), in *Richtige Lebensführung: volkstümliche Aufsätze zur Erziehung des Menschen nach den Grundsätzen der Individualpsychologie*, ed. Sofie Lazarsfeld (Vienna: Moritz Perles), unnumbered series, p. 3.

A1927a *Menschenkenntnis* (Understanding human nature) (Leipzig: Hirzel) [trans. in A1927b].

A1927b *Understanding human nature*, trans. W. B. Wolfe (New York: Greenberg; reprinted, New York: Fawcett Publications, 1954).

A1927f Zusammenhänge zwischen Neurose und Witz (Relationships between neurosis and jokes), *Internationale Zeitschrift für Individualpsychologie*, 5, 94–96; as trans. in A1956b, pp. 251–52.

A1927g Weiteres zur individualpsychologischen Traumtheorie (More on Individual-Psychological dream theory), *Internationale Zeitschrift für Individualpsychologie*, 5, 241–45.

A1928a *Die Technik der Individualpsychologie*, Vol. 1. *Die Kunst, eine Lebens- und Krankengeschichte zu lesen* (The technique of Individual Psychology, Vol. 1. The art of reading a life- and case history.) (Munich: Bergmann) [trans. A1929a.]

A1928c Erotisches Training und erotischer Rückzug (Erotic training and erotic retreat), in *Verhandlungen des l. Internationalen Kongresses für Sexualforschung, Berlin, 1926*, ed. M. Marcuse (Berlin, Köln: Marcus & Webers), Vol. 3, pp. 1–7.

A1928f Kurze Bemerkungen über Vernunft, Intelligenz und Schwachsinn (Brief comments on reason, intelligence, and feeble-mindedness.) *Internationale Zeitschrift für Individualpsychologie*, 6, 267–72, trans. in A1964a, pp. 41–49.

A1928k *Über den nervösen Charakter: Grundzüge einer vergleichenden Individual-Psychologie und Psychotherapie* (The nervous character: fundamentals of a comparative individual psychology and psychotherapy), 4th ed. (Munich: Bergmann).

A1928m Psychologie der Macht (Psychology of power), in *Gewalt und Gewaltlosigkeit: Handbuch des aktiven Pazifismus,* ed. Franz Kobler (Zurich: Rotapfel-Verlag), pp. 41–46, trans. in *Journal of Individual Psychology* (1966), 22, 166–72.

A1928n [Editor with C. Furtmüller and E. Wexberg] *Heilen und Bilden: Ein Buch der Erziehungskunst für Ärzte und Pädagogen* (Healing and educating: a book of the art of education for physicians and educators), 3rd ed. (Munich: Bergmann).

A1929a *The case of Miss R.: the interpretation of a life story,* trans. Eleanore & F. Jensen (New York: Greenberg).

A1929b *Individualpsychologie in der Schule: Vorlesungen für Lehrer und Erzieher* (Individual Psychology in the school: lectures for teachers and educators) (Leipzig: Hirzel).

A1929c *Problems of neurosis: a book of case histories,* ed. P. Mairet (London: Routledge & Kegan Paul; reprinted, New York: Harper & Row, 1964).

A1929d *The science of living* (New York: Greenberg; as reprinted, Garden City, N.Y.: Doubleday Anchor Books, 1969).

A1930a *The education of children,* trans. Eleanore and F. Jensen (New York: Greenberg; reprinted, Chicago: Henry Regnery, 1970).

A1930d *Das Problem der Homosexualität: erotisches Training und erotischer Rückzug* (The problem of homosexuality: erotic training and erotic retreat), 2nd ed. (Leipzig: Hirzel).

A1930e *Die Technik der Individualpsychologie,* Vol. 2, *Die Seele der schwererziehbaren Schulkinder* (The technique of Individual Psychology, Vol. 2, The soul of difficult schoolchildren) (Munich: Bergmann).

A1930f [and Associates] *Guiding the child on the principles of Individual Psychology* (New York: Greenberg).

A1930j Nochmals—die Einheit der Neurosen (Once more —the unity of the neuroses), *Internationale Zeitschrift für Individualpsychologie*, 8, 201–16.

A1930n Die Grundbegriffe der Individualpsychologie (The basic concepts of Individual Psychology), in *Handwörter-buch der Arbeitswissenschaft*, ed. F. Giese (Halle a/S: Marhold Verlag), Vol. 1, pp. 2428–437; as trans., Fundamentals of Individual Psychology, *Journal of Individual Psychology* (1970), 26, 36–49.

A1930o Something about myself, *Childhood and Character*, 7(7), 6–8.

A1930p *Praxis und Theorie der Individualpsychologie* (Practice and theory of Individual Psychology), 4th ed. (Munich: Bergmann).

A1931b *What life should mean to you*, ed. A. Porter (Boston: Little, Brown; reprinted, New York: Putnam Capricorn Books, 1958).

A1931f Zwangsneurose (Compulsion neurosis), *Internationale Zeitschrift für Individualpsychologie*, 9, 1–16; as trans. in A1964a, pp. 112–38.

A1932m Failures in sex, *Modern Psychologist*, 1(2), 55–60.

A1933b *Der Sinn des Lebens* (The meaning of life) (Vienna, Leipzig: Passer [trans. A1938a]).

A1933c Religion und Individualpsychologie (Religion and Individual Psychology) in E. Jahn and A. Adler, *Religion und Individualpsychologie: eine prinzipielle Auseinandersetzung über Menschenführung* (Vienna, Leipzig: Passer), pp. 58–92; as trans. in A1964a, pp. 271–308.

A1934i Zur Massenpsychologie (Mass psychology), *Internationale Zeitschrift für Individualpsychologie*, 12, 133–41.

A1935l Vorbeugung der Neurose (Prevention of neurosis),

Internationale Zeitschrift für Individualpsychologie, 13, 133–41.

A1935m Die Vorbeugung der Delinquenz (Prevention of delinquency), *Internationale Zeitschrift für Individualpsychologie*, 13, 197–206; as trans. in A1964a, pp. 253–68.

A1936c Introduction, in M. Maltz, *New faces—new futures: rebuilding character with plastic surgery* (New York: R. R. Smith, p. vii).

A1936j Das Todesproblem in der Neurose (The death problem in neurosis), *Internationale Zeitschrift für Individualpsychologie*, 14, 1–6; as trans. in A1964a, pp. 239–47.

A1936k Symptomwahl (Choice of the symptom), *Internationale Zeitschrift für Individualpsychologie*, 14, 65–80.

A1936n Love is a recent invention, *Esquire* (May 1936), pp. 56 and 128; as reprinted in *Journal of Individual Psychology* (1971), 27, 208–12.

A1936p Report on question period following lecture at Conway Hall, May 11, 1936, *Daily Mail* (London), May 12, 1936.

A1937g Ist der Fortschritt der Menschheit möglich? wahrscheinlich? unmöglich? (Is progress of mankind possible? probable? impossible?), *Internationale Zeitschrift für Individualpsychologie*, 15, 1–4; as trans. in A1964a, pp. 23–28.

A1938a *Social interest: a challenge to mankind*, trans. J. Linton and R. Vaughan (London: Faber & Faber [orig.: A1933b]; reprinted, New York: Putnam Capricorn Books, 1964).

A1945b The sexual function, *Individual Psychology Bulletin*, 4, 99–102; as reprinted in A1964a, pp. 219–23.

A1956b *The Individual Psychology of Alfred Adler: a systematic presentation in selections from his writings*, ed. H. L. and Rowena R. Ansbacher (New York: Basic Books; reprinted, New York: Harper & Row, 1964).

A1964a *Superiority and social interest: a collection of later writings*, ed. H. L. and Rowena R. Ansbacher (Evanston, Ill.: Northwestern University Press).

ADLER'S REFERENCES TO OTHER AUTHORS

Note: For nontechnical authors, and for technical authors where no specific work is mentioned, see the Index.

Allers, Rudolf. *Psychologie des Geschlechtslebens.* Munich: Reinhardt, 1922.

Aschner, Bernhard. *Die Konstitution der Frau und ihre Beziehungen zur Geburtshilfe und Gynäkologie.* Munich: Bergmann, 1924.

Asnaourow, F. *Sadismus und Masochismus in Kultur und Erziehung.* Munich: Reinhardt, 1913.

Bachofen, Johann J. *Das Mutterrecht: Eine Untersuchung über die Gynekokratie der alten Welt nach ihrer religiösen und rechtlichen Natur.* Stuttgart: Kreis & Hoffmann, 1861 [*Myth, religion, and mother right.* Princeton, N.J.: Princeton University Press, 1967].

Bebel, August. *Die Frau und der Sozialismus.* Stuttgart: Dietz, 1885 [*Woman and socialism.* New York: Socialist Literature Co., 1910].

Birstein, J. "Mitteilungen aus der Kinderpsychologie," *Zentralblatt für Psychoanalyse und Psychotherapie* (1913), 4, 81–84.

Bloch, Iwan. *Beiträge zur Ätiologie der Psychopathia Sexualis.* Dresden: Dohrn, 1902; 2 vols.

Boissier, F., and Lachaux, G. Perversions sexuelles à forme obsédante, *Archives de Neurologie,* Oct. 1893.

Bühler, Charlotte. *Seelenleben der Jugendlichen,* 2nd ed. Jena: Fischer, 1923.

Cramer, August. Die Beziehungen des Exhibitionismus zum Strafgesetz, *Ärztliche Sachverständigen Zeitschrift* (Berlin), 1897.

Deutsch, Helene. *Psychoanalyse der weiblichen Sexualfunktionen.* Leipzig: Internationaler Psychoanalytischer Verlag, 1925.

Ellis, Havelock. Die Psychologie des normalen Geschlechtstriebes, in A. Moll (ed.), *Handbuch der Sexualwissenschaften*. Leipzig: Vogel, 1912. (a)

———. Die Funktionsstörungen des Sexuallebens, in A. Moll (ed.), *Handbuch der Sexualwissenschaften*. Leipzig: Vogel, 1912. (b)

Epaulard, Alexis. *Vampirisme*. Lyon: A. Storck, 1902.

Eulenburg, Albert. *Sadismus und Masochismus*, 2nd ed. Wiesbaden: Bergmann, 1911 [*Sadism and masochism*. New York: New Era, 1934].

Fliess, Wilhelm. *Der Ablauf des Lebens: Grundlegung zur exakten Biologie*. Wien: Deuticke, 1906.

Freud, Sigmund. *Drei Abhandlungen zur Sexualtheorie*. Wien: Psychoanalytischer Verlag, 1923 [*Three essays on the theory of sexuality*. New York: Basic Books, 1962].

———. Zur Einführung des Narzissmus, *Gesammelte Werke*. Vienna: Psychoanalytischer Verlag, 1924 [On narcissism: an introduction. *Standard Edition*, Vol. 14, pp. 67–102].

Furtmüller, Carl. *Psychoanalyse und Ethik*. Munich: Reinhardt, 1912.

Haberda, Albin, in Casper-Liman (ed.), *Handbuch der gerichtlichen Medizin*. Berlin: Hirschwald, 1905–7.

Hall, G. Stanley. *Adolescence*. New York: Appleton, 1918.

Hall, G. S., and Smith, Theodate L. Showing off and bashfulness as phases of self-consciousness, *Pedagogical Seminary*, 1903, 10, 159–99. (a)

———. Marriage and fecundity of college men and women. *Pedagogical Seminary*, 1903, 10, 275–314. (b)

Heymans, G. *Die Psychologie der Frau*. Heidelburg: C. Winter, 1910.

Hirschfeld, Magnus. *Sexualpathologie*. Bonn: Marcus & Weber, 1922.

———. *Jahrbuch für sexuelle Zwischenstufen*. Stuttgart: Püttmann, n.d.

Hitschmann, Edward. *Freuds Neurosenlehre*, 2nd ed. Leipzig: Deuticke, 1913 [*Freud's theories of the neuroses*. New York: Moffat, Yard, 1917].

Hochsinger, Karl. Die gesundheitlichen Lebensschicksale erbsyphilitischer Kinder, *Wiener klinische Wochenschrift*, 1910, 23, 881 and 932.

Janet, Pierre. *Geisteszustand der Hysterischen*. 1894 [*The mental state of hystericals*. New York: Putnam, 1901].

Jung, Carl G. Die Bedeutung des Vaters für das Schicksal des Einzelnen, *Jahrbuch für psychoanalytische und psychopathologische Forschung*, 1909, 1.

——. *Jahrbuch für psychoanalytische und psychopathologische Forschung*, 1913, 4.

Kant, Immanuel. Anthropologie in pragmatischer Hinsicht (1798), *Gesammelte Schriften*, Vol. 7. Berlin: Reimer, 1917, pp. 117–333.

Key, Ellen. *Über Liebe und Ehe*, 15th ed. Berlin: Fischer, 1911 [*Love and marriage*. New York: Putnam, 1911].

Krafft-Ebing, Richard von. *Psychopathia sexualis*. Stuttgart: Enke, 1893.

Kronfeld, Arthur. *Über Gleichgeschlechtlichkeit*. Stuttgart: Püttmann, 1922.

Lasègue, Ernest C. Les exhibitionistes, *Union médicale*, Paris, 1877, 23, 709.

Liepmann, Wilhelm. *Psychologie der Frau*, 2nd ed. Vienna: Urban & Schwarzenberg, 1922.

Löwenfeld, Leopold. *Über die sexuelle Konstitution und andere Sexualprobleme*. Wiesbaden: Bergmann, 1911.

Marcuse, Max. Ein Fall von vielfach komplizierter Sexualperversion, *Zeitschrift für die gesamte Neurologie und Psychiatrie*, 1912, 9, 269–300.

Marcuse, Max (ed.). *Handwörterbuch der Sexualwissenschaft*. Bonn: Marcus & Weber, 1923.

Maschka, Josef (ed.). *Handbuch der gerichtlichen Medizin*. Tübingen: Laupp, 1881–82.

Mill, John S. *Die Hörigkeit der Frau*. Berlin, 1869 [*The subjection of women*. London: Oxford, 1966].

Möbius, Paul J. *Über den physiologischen Schwachsinn des Weibes*, 5th ed. Halle: Marhold, 1903 [The physiological mental weakness of woman. *Alienist and Neurologist*, 1901, 22, 624–42].

Moll, Albert. In Eulenburgs *Enzyklopädie*, 1908.

Müller, Robert. *Sexualbiologie*. Berlin: Marcus, 1907.

436

Reimann. Exhibitionismus eines nicht erweislich Geisteskranken, *Zeitschrift für Medizinalbeamte und Krankenhausärzte*, 1898.

Rohleder, Hermann. *Die Funktionsstörungen der Zeugung*, 2nd ed.

Sade, Donatien Marquis de. *Justine*. 1791.

Schirmacher, Käthe. *Die moderne Frauenbewegung*, 2nd ed. Leipzig: Teubner, 1905 [*The modern woman's rights movement*. New York: Macmillan, 1912].

Schrenk-Notzing. *Die Suggestionstherapie bei krankhaften Erscheinungen des Geschlechtssinnes*. Stuttgart, 1892.

Schwarz, Oswald. Das psychophysische Problem in der Sexualwissenschaft, *Wiener klinische Wochenschrift*, 1922, 35(11), 243–46.

———. *Psychogenese und Psychotherapie körperlicher Symptome*. Vienna: Springer, 1925.

Seif, Leonhard. Über die Bedeutung der Tendenz zur Konfliktlosigkeit im Leben und in der Neurose, *Internationale Zeitschrift für Individualpsychologie*, 1923/24, 2(2), 31–34.

Sellheim, Hugo. *Das Geheimnis vom Ewig-Weiblichen*, 2nd ed. Stuttgart: Enke, 1924.

Spranger, Eduard. *Psychologie des Jugendalters*, 4th ed. Leipzig: Quelle & Meyer, 1925.

Tandler, J., and Gross, S. *Die biologischen Grundlagen der sekundären Geschlechtscharaktere*. Berlin: Springer, 1913.

Tumlirz, Otto. *Die Reifejahre*. Leipzig: Klinkhardt, 1924.

Vaerting, M. *Wahrheit und Irrtum in der Geschlechterpsychologie*. Karlsruhe: Braun, 1923.

Vaihinger, H. *Die Philosophie des als ob*. Leipzig: Felix Meiner, 1911 [*The philosophy of "as if."* London: Routledge & Kegan Paul, 1924].

Weininger, Otto. *Geschlecht und Charakter*, 17th ed. Wien: Braumüller, 1918 [*Sex and character*. London: Heinemann, 1906].

Weinmann, Kurt. Selbstwertgefühl und dessen Störungen, *Internationale Zeitschrift für Individualpsychologie*, 1926, 4, 69–76.

Wexberg, Erwin. Rousseau und die Ethik, in A. Adler and C. Furtmüller (eds.), *Heilen und Bilden.* Munich: Reinhardt, 1914, pp. 187–206.

——. *Das nervöse Kind.* Vienna: Perles, 1926. (b)

——. *Individualpsychologie: eine systematische Darstellung.* Leipzig: Hirzel, 1928 [*Individual Psychology.* New York: Cosmopolitan Book Corp., 1929].

——. *Einführung in die Psychologie des Geschlechtslebens.* Leipzig: Hirzel, 1930 [*The psychology of sex: an introduction.* New York: Blue Ribbon Books, 1931].

Wexberg, Erwin (ed.). *Handbuch der Individualpsychologie.* Munich: Bergmann, 1926, 2 vols. (a)

Witt, Alexander. Ein Beitrag zum Thema "Sexuelle Eindrücke beim Kinde," *Zentralblatt für Psychoanalyse und Psychotherapie,* 1911, 1(4), 165–66.

EDITORS' REFERENCES TO OTHER AUTHORS

Abel, G. G., and Blanchard, E. B. The role of fantasy in the treatment of sexual deviation, *Archives of General Psychiatry,* 1974, 30, 467–75.

Adler, Alexandra. Individual Psychology: Adlerian School, in P. L. Harriman (ed.), *Encyclopedia of psychology.* New York: Philosophical Library, 1946, pp. 262–69.

Adler, K. A. Life style, gender role, and the symptom of homosexuality, *Journal of Individual Psychology,* 1967, 23, 67–78.

——. Power in Adlerian Theory, in J. H. Masserman (ed.), *Science and psychoanalysis,* Vol. 20. *The dynamics of power.* New York: Grune & Stratton, 1972, pp. 53–63.

Adler, M. Erkenntniskritische Bemerkungen zur Individualpsychologie (Epistemological comments on Individual Psychology), *Internationale Zeitschrift für Individualpsychologie,* 1925, 3, 209–21.

Adler, R. Das gemeinsame Studium [der Medicin von Frauen und Männern] und die Professoren. (Co-education in medicine and the professors.) *Dokumente der Frauen* (Wien), 1899, 1 (Jul.–Dec.), 289–93.

———. Kindererziehung in der Sowjetunion (The education of children in the Soviet Union), *Internationale Zeitschrift für Individualpsychologie*, 1931, 9, 297–309.

Adler, V. Bemerkungen über die soziologischen Grundlagen des "männlichen Protests" (Comments on the sociological foundations of the "masculine protest"), *Internationale Zeitschrift für Individualpsychologie*, 1925, 3, 307–10.

Ansbacher, H. L. The significance of the socio-economic status of the patients of Freud and of Adler, *American Journal of Psychotherapy*, 1959, 13, 376–82.

———. Rudolph Hildebrand: a forerunner of Alfred Adler, *Journal of Individual Psychology*, 1962, 18, 12–17. (a)

———. Was Adler a disciple of Freud? *Journal of Individual Psychology*, 1962, 18, 126–35. (b)

———. Sensus privatus versus sensus communis, *Journal of Individual Psychology*, 1965, 21, 48–50.

———. Love and violence in the view of Adler, *Humanitas* (Duquesne University), 1966, 2, 109–27.

———. Life style: a historical and systematic review, *Journal of Individual Psychology*, 1967, 23, 191–212.

———. The concept of social interest, *Journal of Individual Psychology*, 1968, 24, 131–49.

———. Suicide as communication: Adler's concept and current application, *Journal of Individual Psychology*, 1969, 25, 174–80.

———. Alfred Adler: a historical perspective, *American Journal of Psychiatry*, 1970, 127, 777–82.

———. Alfred Adler and G. Stanley Hall: correspondence and general relationship, *Journal of the History of the Behavioral Sciences*, 1971, 7, 337–52. (a)

———. Alfred Adler and humanistic psychology, *Journal of Humanistic Psychology*, 1971, 11, 53–63. (b)

———. Utilization of creativity in Adlerian psychotherapy, *Journal of Individual Psychology*, 1971, 27, 160–66. (c)

———. Adler's "striving for power" in relation to Nietzsche, *Journal of Individual Psychology*, 1972, 28, 12–24.

———. Adler's interpretation of early recollections: historical account, *Journal of Individual Psychology,* 1973, 29, 135–45.

——. The first critique of Freud's metapsychology: an extension of George S. Klein's "Two Theories or One?", *Bulletin of the Menninger Clinic,* 1974, 38, 78–84. (a)

——. Adler and Virchow: new light on the name "Individual Psychology," *Journal of Individual Psychology,* 1974, 30, 43–52. (b)

Ansbacher, R. R. Review of Harold Greenwald, *The call girl.* New York: Ballantine Books, 1958. *Journal of Individual Psychology,* 1958, 14, 192–93.

Arieti, S. *The will to be human.* New York: Quadrangle Books, 1972.

——. Psychiatric controversy: man's ethical dimension, *American Journal of Psychiatry,* 1975, 132, 39–42.

Arndt, W. B., Jr. *Theories of personality.* New York: Macmillan, 1974.

Bachofen, J. J. *Myth, religion, and mother right* (1861). Princeton, N.J.: Princeton University Press, 1967.

Barbach, L. G. *For yourself: the fulfillment of female sexuality.* Garden City, N.Y.: Doubleday & Company, 1975.

Bashkirtseva, M. *The journal of a young artist, 1860–1884,* trans. Mary J. Serrano. New York: Cassell & Company, 1889.

Bateson, G. A theory of play and fantasy: a report on theoretical aspects of the project for the study of the role of paradoxes of abstraction in communication (1955). In *Steps to an ecology of mind.* New York: Ballantine, 1972, pp. 177–93.

Bateson, G.; Jackson, D. D.; Haley, J.; and Weakland, J. H. Toward a theory of schizophrenia. *Behavioral Science,* 1956, 1, 251–64. As reprinted in G. Bateson, *Steps to an ecology of mind.* New York: Ballantine, 1972, pp. 201–27.

Bauer, R. A. *The new man in Soviet psychology.* Cambridge, Mass.: Harvard University Press, 1952.

Bebel, A. *Woman and socialism* (1885), trans. Meta L. Stern (Hebe). New York: Socialist Literature Co., 1910.

Beecher, W. Every stick has two ends, *Individual Psychology Bulletin*, 1946, 5, 84–86.

Bieber, I. Clinical aspects of male homosexuality, in J. Marmor (ed.), *Sexual inversion: the multiple roots of homosexuality*. New York: Basic Books, 1965, pp. 248–67.

Bieber, I., et al. *Homosexuality: a psychoanalytic study*. New York: Basic Books and Vintage Books, 1962.

Biller, H. B. Sex-role uncertainty and psychopathology, *Journal of Individual Psychology*, 1973, 29, 24–25.

Bodelsen, M. Thyra Boldsen, in *Dansk Biografisk Leksikon*. Copenhagen: Schultz, 1933–44, and P. Weilbach (ed.), *Kunstnerleksikon*. Copenhagen: Aschehoug, 1947–52.

Bonsal, S. The end of the strange career of "the red countess," New York *Times Magazine*, Oct. 8, 1911, p. 1.

Bottome, P. *Alfred Adler: a portrait from life*. New York: Vanguard Press, 1957.

———. Frau Dr. Adler (Mrs. Raissa Adler), *Journal of Individual Psychology*, 1962, 18, 182–83.

Bourdet, Y. Alfred Adler, in Dictionnaire biographique du movement ouvrier international, Vol. 1, *Autriche*. Paris, 1971.

Brennan, J. F. Upright posture as the foundation of Individual Psychology: a comparative analysis of Adler and Straus, *Journal of Individual Psychology*, 1968, 24, 25–32.

Broderick, C. B. The two faces of marital power, in Masserman, J. H. (ed.), *Science and Psychoanalysis*, Vol. 20, *The dynamics of power*. New York: Grune and Stratton, 1972, pp. 148–52.

Brody, J. Bisexual life-style appears to be spreading. . . . New York *Times*, Mar. 24, 1974.

Bruch, H. Anorexia nervosa, in A. E. Lindner (ed.), *Emotional factors in gastrointestinal illness*. Amsterdam: Excerpta Medica, 1973, pp. 1–15.

Chaplin, J. P. Dictionary of psychology, rev. ed. New York: Dell Publishing Company, 1975.

Chodoff, P. A critique of Freud's theory of infantile sexuality, *American Journal of Psychiatry*, 1966, 123, 507–18.

Credner, L. Verwahrlosung (Delinquency), in E. Wexberg

(ed.), *Handbuch der Individualpsychologie*. Munich: Bergmann, 1926, pp. 209–34.

De Beauvoir, S. *The second sex* (1949). New York: Knopf, 1953.

Deutsch, D. A step toward successful marriage, *American Journal of Individual Psychology*, 1956, 12, 78–83.

——. Group therapy with married couples: the birth pangs of a new family life style in marriage, *Individual Psychologist*, 1967, 4, 56–62.

Dolliver, R. H. Alfred Adler and the dialectic, *Journal of the History of the Behavioral Sciences*, 1974, 10, 16–20.

Dreikurs, R. *Seelische Impotenz* (Psychological impotence). Leipzig: Hirzel, 1931.

——. *The challenge of marriage*. New York: Duell, Sloan & Pearce, 1946.

——. Determinants of changing attitudes of marital partners toward each other, in Salo Rosenbaum and Ian Alger (eds.), *The marriage relationship: psychoanalytic perspectives*. New York: Basic Books, 1968, pp. 83–103.

——. Technology of conflict resolution, Family counseling, *Journal of Individual Psychology*, 1972, 28, 203–22.

——. *Psychodynamics, psychotherapy, and counseling: collected papers*, rev. ed. Chicago, Ill.: Alfred Adler Institute, 1973.

Ellenberger, H. F. *The discovery of the unconscious: the history and evolution of dynamic psychiatry*. New York: Basic Books, 1970.

Encyclopaedia Britannica, Matriarchy, 1973.

Engels, F. *Origin of the family, private property and the state* (1884), with Introduction and Notes by Eleanor Burke Leacock. New York: International Publishers, 1972.

Fay, A. Clinical notes on paradoxical therapy, *Psychotherapy*, 1976, 13, 118–22.

Feldman, M. P., and MacCulloch, M. J. *Homosexual behavior: therapy and assessment*. Oxford, Eng.: Pergamon Press, 1971.

Fisher, S. H. A note on male homosexuality and the role of women in Ancient Greece, in Judd Marmor (ed.), *Sex-*

ual inversion: the multiple roots of homosexuality. New York: Basic Books, 1965, pp. 165–72.

Frankl, V. E. Paradoxical intention: a logotherapeutic technique (1960), in *Psychotherapy and existentialism: selected papers on logotherapy.* New York: Simon & Schuster, 1968, pp. 143–63.

——. Tribute to Alfred Adler, *Journal of Individual Psychology,* 1970, 62, 12.

Freschl, R. August Strindberg's Corinna aus "Heiraten": eine psychologische Analyse (August Strindberg's Corinna from *Marriage:* a psychological analysis), *Zeitschrift für Individualpsychologie,* 1914, 1(1), 21–26.

Freud, S. The interpretation of dreams (1900), in *Standard Edition,* Vol. 4. London: Hogarth, 1953.

——. *Three essays on the theory of sexuality* (1905), trans. and newly ed. J. Strachey. New York: Basic Books, 1962.

——. The antithetical meaning of primal words (1910), in *Standard Edition,* Vol. 11. London: Hogarth, 1957, pp. 153–61.

——. Psychoanalytic notes upon an autobiographical account of a case of paranoia (dementia paranoides) (1911), in *Collected Papers,* Vol. 3. London: Hogarth, 1925, pp. 385–470.

——. On the history of the psychoanalytic movement (1914), in *Collected Papers,* Vol. 1. London: Hogarth, 1924, pp. 287–359. (a)

——. On narcissism: an introduction (1914), in *Standard Edition,* Vol. 14. London: Hogarth, 1957, pp. 67–102. (b)

——. Instincts and their vicissitudes (1915), in *Collected Papers,* Vol. 4. London: Hogarth, 1925, pp. 60–83.

——. *A general introduction to psychoanalysis* (1917), trans. Joan Riviere. Garden City, N.Y.: Garden City Publishing Co., 1943. (a)

——. Mourning and melancholia (1917), in *Collected Papers,* Vol. 4. London: Hogarth, 1925, pp. 152–70. (b)

——. From the history of an infantile neurosis (1918), in

Collected Papers, Vol. 3. London: Hogarth, 1925, pp. 471–605. (a)

——. Contributions to the psychology of love. The taboo of virginity (1918), in *Collected Papers*, Vol. 4. London: Hogarth, 1925, pp. 217–35. (b)

——. Some psychological consequences of the anatomical distinction between the sexes (1925), in *Collected Papers*, Vol. 5. London: Hogarth, 1950, pp. 186–97.

——. *Civilization and its discontents* (1929). London: Hogarth, 1946.

——. Female sexuality (1931), in *Collected Papers*, Vol. 5. London: Hogarth, 1950, pp. 252–72.

——. The psychology of women: Lecture XXXIII, in *New introductory lectures on Psycho-Analysis* (1933). New York: Norton, 1933, pp. 153–85.

——. Analysis terminable and interminable (1937), in *Collected Papers*, Vol. 5. London: Hogarth, 1950, pp. 316–57.

Freudenberg, S. Individualpsychologie und Jugendwohlfahrtspflege (Individual Psychology and social work with adolescents), in E. Wexberg (ed.), *Handbuch der Individualpsychologie*. Munich: Bergmann, 1926, pp. 367–81.

——. *Erziehungs- und heilpädagogische Beratungsstellen* (Child-guidance and remedial teaching clinics). Leipzig: Hirzel, 1928.

Friedan, B. *The feminine mystique*. New York: Norton, 1963; as reprinted, New York: Dell Publishing Company, 1964.

Friedmann, A. Das Frauenproblem der Gegenwart (The woman problem of the present), *Internationale Zeitschrift für Individualpsychologie*, 1936, 14, 94–104.

Furtmüller, C. Die psychologische Bedeutung der Psychoanalyse (The psychological significance of psychoanalysis), in A. Adler and C. Furtmüller (eds.), *Heilen und Bilden*. München: Reinhardt, 1914, pp. 168–86.

——. Alfred Adler: a biographical essay, in A. Adler, *Superiority and social interest*. Evanston, Ill.: Northwestern University Press, 1964, pp. 307–94.

444

Greenwald, H. *The call girl: a social and psychoanalytic study.* New York: Ballantine Books, 1958.

Grünbaum-Sachs, H. Frauenbewegung und männlicher Protest (Woman's movement and masculine protest), *Internationale Zeitschrift für Individualpsychologie,* 1926, 4, 88–90.

Haley, J. *Strategies of psychotherapy.* New York: Grune & Stratton, 1963.

———. *The power tactics of Jesus Christ, and other essays.* New York: Grossman, 1969.

Hammel, L. New York *Times,* Apr. 29, 1974, p. 40.

Hilferding, M. *Geburtenregelung: mit einem Nachwort von Dr. Alfred Adler: Erörterungen zum Paragraph 144* (Birth control: with a postscript by Dr. Alfred Adler: Comments on paragraph 144). Wien, Leipzig: Moritz Perles, 1926.

Hooker, E. Male homosexuals and their "world," in J. Marmor (ed.), *Sexual inversion: the multiple roots of homosexuality.* New York: Basic Books, 1965, pp. 83–107.

Jacobs, M.; Thompson, L. A.; and Truxaw, P. The use of sexual surrogates in counseling, *Counseling Psychologist,* 1975, 5, 73–77.

Jones, E. *The life and work of Sigmund Freud,* Vol. 2. New York: Basic Books, 1955.

Kankeleit, O. V. Internationaler Kongress für Individualpsychologie in Berlin vom 26. bis 28. September 1930 (Fifth International Congress for Individual Psychology), *Archiv für Psychiatrie und Nervenkrankheiten,* 1931, 93, 261–336.

Kaplan, H. S. *The new sex therapy: active treatment of sexual dysfunctions.* New York: Brunner/Mazel, 1974.

Kaufmann, W. *Nietzsche: philosopher, psychologist, Antichrist,* 4th ed. Princeton, N.J.: Princeton University Press, 1974.

Kelly, G. A. *The psychology of personal constructs,* Vol. 1. New York: Norton, 1955.

———. Nonparametric factor analysis of personality theories, *Journal of Individual Psychology,* 1963, 19, 115–47.

Keyserling, H. (ed.). *The book of marriage: a new intro-*

duction by twenty-four leaders of contemporary thought (1925). New York: Harcourt, Brace, 1926.

Kinsey, A. C. et al. *Sexual behavior in the human female* (1953). New York: Pocket Books, 1965.

Klein, G. S. Two theories or one?, *Bulletin of the Menninger Clinic*, 1973, 37, 102–32.

Knopf, O. *The art of being a woman*, ed. Alan Porter. Boston: Little, Brown, 1932.

——. *Women on their own*, ed. Alan Porter. Boston: Little, Brown, 1935.

Krausz, E. O. Die Weiblichkeit in der Psychoanalyse (Femininity in psychoanalysis), *Internationale Zeitschrift für Individualpsychologie*, 1934, 12, 16–31.

Kronfeld, A. and Voigt, G. Der V. Internationale Kongress für Individualpsychologie (The Fifth International Congress for Individual Psychology), *Internationale Zeitschrift für Individualpsychologie*, 1930, 8, 537–50.

Landry, H. Philosophie, in S. Kaznelson (ed.), *Juden im deutschen Kulturbereich: ein Sammelwerk*, 2nd ed. Berlin: Jüdischer Verlag, 1959, pp. 242–77.

Lazarsfeld, S. Kleist im Lichte der Individualpsychologie (Kleist in the light of Individual Psychology), in *Jahrbuch der Kleist Gesellschaft*. Berlin: Weidemann, 1927.

——. *Wie die Frau den Mann erlebt* (How woman experiences man). Leipzig, Wien: Verlag für Sexualwissenschaft, 1931. In English: *Rhythm of Life: a guide to sexual harmony for women*, trans. Karsten and E. Pelham Stapelfeldt. New York: Greenberg, 1934.

——. Aus der Wiener Ehe- und Sexualberatung (Marriage and sex counseling in Vienna), *Archiv für Psychiatrie und Nervenkrankheiten*, 1931, 93, 333–36.

Leonhard, S. *Gestohlenes Leben: Schicksal einer politischen Emigrantin in der Sowjetunion* (Stolen life: the fate of a political émigré in the Soviet Union), 5th ed. Herford, Germany: Nicolaische Verlagsbuchhandlung, 1968.

Levy, L. H. *Psychological interpretation*. New York: Holt, Rinehart & Winston, 1963.

Lewin, K. *A dynamic theory of personality: selected papers*. New York: McGraw-Hill, 1935.

Lewis, S. *Main Street* (1920). New York: New American Library, 1961.

Lichtheim, G. *Marxism: an historical and critical study.* New York: Praeger, 1961.

Lief, H. I. Power in the family: a preface, in Masserman, J. H. (ed.). *Science and Psychoanalysis,* Vol. 20, *The dynamics of power.* New York: Grune & Stratton, 1972, pp. 117–19.

Lindsey, B. B., and Evans, W. *The companionate marriage.* New York: Boni & Liveright, 1927.

M. R. Kongress für Individualpsychologie: Der Sinn des Lebens. *Vorwärts* (Berlin), Sept. 26, 1930.

Mairet, P. Hamlet as a study in Individual Psychology, *Journal of Individual Psychology,* 1969, 25, 71–88.

Manosevitz, M. Early sexual behavior in adult homosexual and heterosexual males, *Journal of Abnormal Psychology,* 1970, 76, 396–402.

Marmor, J. Comments on "Adlerian psychology: the tradition of brief psychotherapy," *Journal of Individual Psychology,* 1972, 28, 153–54.

——. *Psychiatry in transition: selected papers.* New York: Brunner/Mazel, 1974.

——. Homosexuality and sexual orientation disturbances, in A. M. Freedman, H. I. Kaplan, and B. J. Sadok (eds.), *Comprehensive textbook of psychiatry,* 2nd ed., Vol. 2. Baltimore: Williams & Wilkins, 1975, pp. 1510–20.

——. Personal communication, Mar. 4, 1977.

Marmor, J. (ed.). *Sexual inversion: the multiple roots of homosexuality.* New York: Basic Books, 1965.

——. *Modern psychoanalysis: new directions and perspectives.* New York: Basic Books, 1968.

Maslow, A. H. Was Adler a Disciple of Freud?, *Journal of Individual Psychology,* 1962, 18, 125.

Masserman, J. H. (ed.). *Science and Psychoanalysis,* Vol. 1. New York: Grune & Stratton, 1958.

Masters, W. H., and Johnson, V. E. *Human sexual inadequacy.* Boston: Little, Brown, 1970.

———. *The pleasure bond: a new look at sexuality and commitment* (1975). New York: Bantam Books, 1976.

May, R. *Love and will.* New York: Norton, 1969.

McDowell, E. H., in G. J. Manaster, G. Painter, D. Deutsch, and B. J. Overholt (eds.), *Alfred Adler: as we remember him.* Chicago: North American Society of Adlerian Psychology, 1977.

McGuire, W. (ed.). *The Freud/Jung letters: the correspondence between Sigmund Freud and C. G. Jung,* trans. Ralph Mannheim and R. F. C. Hull. Princeton, N.J.: Princeton University Press, 1974.

Mill, J. S. *The subjection of women* (1869). London: Oxford, 1966.

Millett, K. *Sexual politics.* Garden City, N.Y.: Doubleday & Company, 1969; as reprinted, New York: Avon Books, 1971.

Minor, M. Ursachen und treibende Kräfte der Frauenbewegung im Lichte der Individualpsychologie (Causes and driving forces of the woman's movement in the light of Individual Psychology), *Internationale Zeitschrift für Individualpsychologie,* 1924/25, 3, 310–14.

Money, J. Interview. *APA Monitor,* June 1976, 10–11.

Money, J., and Ehrhardt, A. A. *Man and woman, boy and girl: the differentiation and dimorphism of gender identity from conception to maturity.* Baltimore: Johns Hopkins University Press, 1972.

Money, J., and Tucker, P. *Sexual signatures: on being a man or a woman.* Boston: Little, Brown, 1975.

Morgan, L. H. *Ancient society* (1877). New York: World, 1963.

Mosak, H. H. Early recollections as a projective technique, *Journal of Projective Techniques,* 1958, 22, 302–11; also in G. Lindzey and C. S. Hall (eds.), *Theories of personality: primary sources and research.* New York: Wiley, 1965, pp. 105–13.

———, and Gushurst, R. What patients say and what they mean, *American Journal of Psychotherapy,* 1971, 25, 428–36.

——, and Kopp, R. R. The early recollections of Adler, Freud, and Jung, *Journal of Individual Psychology*, 1973, 29, 157–66.

Murphy, G. *Historical introduction to modern psychology*, rev. ed. New York: Harcourt, Brace, 1949.

Mozdzierz, G. D.; Macchitelli, F. J.; and Lisiecki, J. The paradox in psychotherapy: an Adlerian perspective, *Journal of Individual Psychology*, 1976, 32, 169–84.

Nagler, S. H. Fetishism: a review and a case study, *Psychiatric Quarterly*, 1957, 31, 713–41.

Nietzsche, F. Thus spoke Zarathustra: third part (1884), in *The Portable Nietzsche*, ed. Walter Kaufmann. New York: Viking Press, 1968, pp. 260–343.

Nikelly, A. G. *Achieving competence and fulfillment*. Monterey, Calif.: Brooks/Cole, 1977.

Nikelly, A. G. (ed.). *Techniques for behavior change: applications of Adlerian theory*. Springfield, Ill.: Charles C. Thomas, 1971.

Nunberg, H., and Federn, E. (eds.). *Minutes of the Vienna Psychoanalytic Society*. New York: International Universities Press, Vol. 1, 1906–8, 1962; Vol. 2, 1908–10, 1967; Vol. 3, 1910–11, 1974.

O'Connell, W. E. *Action therapy and Adlerian theory: selected papers*. Chicago: Alfred Adler Institute, 1975.

Oppenheim, D. E. Der Kampf der Frau um ihre gesellschaftliche Stellung im Spiegel der antiken Literatur (Woman's struggle for status in the light of antique literature), *Internationale Zeitschrift für Individualpsychologie*, 1924/25, 3, 287–90.

Orgler, H. *Alfred Adler: the man and his work*. New York: Liveright, 1963.

Ottenheimer, H. Soziale Arbeit (Social work), in Kaznelson, S. (ed.), *Juden im deutschen Kulturbereich: ein Sammelwerk*, 2nd ed. Berlin: Jüdischer Verlag, 1959, pp. 825–57.

Ovesey, L. The homosexual conflict: an adaptational analysis (1954), in H. M. Ruitenbeek (ed.), *The problem of homosexuality in modern society*. New York: Dutton, 1963, pp. 127–40.

——. Pseudohomosexuality and homosexuality in men: psychodynamics as a guide to treatment, in J. Marmor (ed.), *Sexual inversion: the multiple roots of homosexuality*. New York: Basic Books, 1965, pp. 211–33.

——, and Person, E. Gender identity and sexual psychopathology in men: a psychodynamic analysis of homosexuality, transsexualism, and transvestism, *Journal of the American Academy of Psychoanalysis* 1973, 1(1), 53–72.

Papanek, H. Group psychotherapy with married couples, in J. H. Masserman (ed.), *Current psychiatric therapies*, Vol. 5. New York: Grune & Stratton, 1965, pp. 157–63.

Perloff, W. H. Hormones and homosexuality, in Judd Marmor (ed.), *Sexual inversion: the multiple roots of homosexuality*. New York: Basic Books, 1965, pp. 44–69.

Peterfreund, E. The need for a new general theoretical frame of reference for psychoanalysis, *Psychoanalytic Quarterly*, 1975, 44, 534–49.

Pew, M. L., and Pew, W. L. Adlerian marriage counseling, *Journal of Individual Psychology*, 1972, 28, 192–202.

Plottke, P. Über das Verhalten der schönen Krimhilde: ein individualpsychologischer Versuch (On the behavior of the beautiful Krimhilde: an essay in Individual Psychology), *Internationale Zeitschrift für Individualpsychologie*, 1947, 16, 112–22.

Powers, R. L. Myth and memory, in H. H. Mosak (ed.), *Alfred Adler: his influence on psychology today*. Park Ridge, N.J.: Noyes Press, 1973, pp. 271–90.

Racowitza, H. *Princess Helene von Racowitza: an autobiography*. New York: Macmillan, 1910.

Rado, S. A critical examination of the concept of bisexuality, *Psychosomatic Medicine*, 1940, 2, 459–67; as reprinted in J. Marmor (ed.), *Sexual inversion: the multiple roots of homosexuality*. New York: Basic Books, 1965, pp. 175–89.

——. An adaptational view of sexual behavior, in P. Hoch and J. Zubin (eds.), *Psychosexual development in health and disease*. New York: Grune & Stratton, 1949, pp. 189–213; as reprinted in H. M. Ruitenbeek (ed.),

The problem of homosexuality in modern society. New York: Dutton, 1963, pp. 94–126.

——. *Adaptational psychodynamics: motivation and control.* New York: Science House, 1969.

Rasey, M. J. *Toward maturity: the psychology of child development.* New York: Hinds, Hayden & Eldridge, 1947.

——. *It takes time: an autobiography of the teaching profession.* New York: Harper & Bros., 1953.

Rayner, D. Adler and his psychology: seen through his early memories. *Mental Health* (London), 1957, 16, 58–62.

Reinecke, A. Personal communications, Mar. 10 and 26, 1975.

Rensberger, B. Emotional disorders and mental illness: psychiatrists debate cause-effect relationship, New York *Times*, Apr. 7, 1977, p. A21.

Riegel, K. F. The dialectics of human development, *American Psychologist*, 1976, 31(10), 689–700.

Roazen, P. *Freud and his followers.* New York: Knopf, 1975.

Ruesch, J., and Bateson, G. *Communication: the social matrix of psychiatry.* New York: Norton, 1951.

Rühle-Gerstel, A. *Das Frauenproblem der Gegenwart: eine psychologische Bilanz* (The present-day woman problem: a psychological balance sheet). Leipzig: Hirzel, 1932; reprinted as *Die Frau und der Kapitalismus* (Woman and capitalism), ed. H. Jacoby. Frankfurt: Verlag Neue Kritik, 1973.

Rychlak, J. R. *A philosophy of science for personality theory.* Boston: Houghton Mifflin, 1968.

——. *Introduction to personality and psychotherapy: a theory-construction approach.* Boston: Houghton Mifflin, 1973.

Saghir, M. T., and Robins, E. *Male and female homosexuals: a comprehensive investigation.* Baltimore: Williams & Wilkins, 1973.

Salzman, L. Masochism and psychopathy as adaptive behavior, *Journal of Individual Psychology*, 1960, 16, 182–88.

——. *Developments in psychoanalysis.* New York: Grune & Stratton, 1962.

——. "Latent" homosexuality, in J. Marmor (ed.), *Sexual inversion: the multiple roots of homosexuality.* New York: Basic Books, 1965, pp. 234–47.

——. *The obsessive personality: origins, dynamics and therapy.* New York: Science House, 1968. (a)

——. Sexuality in psychoanalytic theory, in J. Marmor (ed.), *Modern psychoanalysis: new directions and perspectives.* New York: Basic Books, 1968, pp. 123–45. (b)

——. Modern psychoanalytic theory and practice in the neuroses: a review, *Journal of the American Academy of Psychoanalysis,* 1974, 2, 261–68. (a)

——. Sexual problems in adolescence, *Contemporary Psychoanalysis,* 1974, 10, 189–207. (b)

Saul, L. J. *Psychodynamically based psychotherapy.* New York: Science House, 1972.

Scarf, M. The man who gave us "inferiority complex," "compensation," "overcompensation," "aggressive drive," and "life style," New York *Times Magazine,* Feb. 28, 1971, pp. 10, 11, and 44–47.

Schäfer, S. *Psychologie Heute,* July, 1977.

Schatzman, M. Paranoia or persecution: the case of Schreber, *Family Process,* 1971, 10, 177–207.

Schmid, A. Zum Verständnis von Schillers Frauengestalten (Toward an understanding of Schiller's female characters), *Zeitschrift für Individualpsychologie,* 1914, 1, 72–80.

Schmidt, H. *Philosophisches Wörterbuch* (Philosophical dictionary). Leipzig: Kröner, 1934.

Schreber, D. P. *Memoirs of my nervous illness* (1903), trans. and ed. I. Macalpine and R. A. Hunter. London: Dawson & Son, 1955.

Schulhof, H. *Individualpsychologie und Frauenfrage* (Individual Psychology and the woman question). Munich: Reinhardt, 1914.

——. *Henrik Ibsen, der Mensch und sein Werk im Lichte der Individualpsychologie* (Henrik Ibsen, the man and his work in the light of Individual Psychology). Reichenberg (now Liberec), Czechoslovakia: Erich Spiethoff, 1923.

———. Zur Psychologie Strindbergs (On the psychology of Strindberg), *Internationale Zeitschrift für Individualpsychologie*, 1923/24, 2(2), 20–25. (a)

———. Strindberg und Ibsen als Frauenpsychologen (Strindberg and Ibsen as psychologists of women), *Internationale Zeitschrift für Individualpsychologie*, 1923/24, 2(2), 44–45. (b)

Seelbach, H. Verstehende Psychologie und Individualpsychologie: ein Vergleich der psychologischen Richtungen von Dilthey, Jaspers und Spranger mit der Individualpsychologie Alfred Adlers (Understanding psychology and Individual Psychology: a comparison of the psychologies of Dilthey, Jaspers, and Spranger with the Individual Psychology of Alfred Adler), *Internationale Zeitschrift für Individualpsychologie*, 1932, 10, 262–88, 368–91, 452–72.

Seif, L. Die Zwangsneurose, in E. Wexberg (ed.), *Handbuch der Individualpsychologie* (1926), Vol. 1. Amsterdam: Bonset, 1966, pp. 507–31.

Shulman, B. H. An Adlerian view of the Schreber case, *Journal of Individual Psychology*, 1959, 15, 180–92; as reprinted in *Contributions to Individual Psychology: selected papers*. Chicago: Alfred Adler Institute, 1973, pp. 140–55.

———. The family constellation in personality diagnosis, *Journal of Individual Psychology*, 1962, 18, 35–47; as reprinted in *Contributions to Individual Psychology: selected papers*. Chicago: Alfred Adler Institute, 1973, pp. 45–59.

———. The uses and abuses of sex, *Journal of Religion and Health*, 1967, 6, 317–25; as reprinted in *Contributions to Individual Psychology: selected papers*. Chicago: Alfred Adler Institute, 1973, pp. 81–90.

———. An Adlerian view, in M. Kramer et al. (eds.), *Dream psychology and the new biology of dreaming*. Springfield, Ill.: Charles C. Thomas, 1969, pp. 117–37; as reprinted in *Contributions to Individual Psychology:*

selected papers. Chicago: Alfred Adler Institute, 1973, pp. 60–80.

Simon, R. Alfred Adlers Bedeutung für die Strafrechtswissenschaften (Alfred Adler's significance for the judicial disciplines). *Internationale Zeitschrift für Individualpsychologie*, 1937, 15, 162–66.

Smith, S. Editor's note, *Bulletin of the Menninger Clinic*, 1973, 37, 97.

Sperber, M. *Masks of loneliness: Alfred Adler in perspective*, trans. Krishna Winston. New York: Macmillan, 1974.

Spitzer, R. L. The homosexual decision—a background paper, *Psychiatric News*, Jan. 16, 1974, 11–12.

Sprung, B. Personal communication, May 20, 1974.

Stoller, R. J. Sexual deviations, in Encyclopaedia Britannica, Macropaedia, 1974, Vol. 16, pp. 601–10.

———. *Perversion: the erotic form of hatred*. New York: Pantheon Books, 1975.

Szasz, T. S. *The myth of mental illness: foundations of a theory of personal conduct*. New York: Harper & Row, 1961.

Taylor, G. R. Historical and mythological aspects of homosexuality, in J. Marmor (ed.), *Sexual inversion: the multiple roots of homosexuality*. New York: Basic Books, 1965, pp. 140–64.

Thilly, F., and Wood, L. *A history of philosophy*, 3rd ed. New York: Holt, Rinehart & Winston, 1957.

Vaihinger, H. *Die Philosophie des als ob: System der theoretischen, praktischen und religiösen Fiktionen der Menschheit auf Grund eines idealistischen Positivismus* (1911) (The philosophy of "as if": A system of the theoretical, practical, and religious fictions of mankind based on an idealistic positivism), 3rd ed. Leipzig: Felix Meiner, 1918. This reference for passages not included in the English edition. (a)

———. *The philosophy of 'as if': a system of the theoretical, practical, and religious fictions of mankind* (1911), trans. C. K. Ogden. London: Routledge & Kegan Paul, 1924. (b)

Vleeschauwer, H. J. de. Kantianism, in Encyclopaedia Britannica, Macropaedia, 1974, Vol. 10, pp. 395–98.

Vorstand des Vereins für freie psychoanalytische Forschung. An die Leser, in *Schriften des Vereins für freie psychoanalytische Forschung.* München: Reinhardt, 1912, No. 1, pp. iv–v.

Watzlawick, P.; Beavin, J. H.; and Jackson, D. D. *Pragmatics of human communication: a study of interactional patterns, pathologies, and paradoxes.* New York: Norton, 1967.

——; Weakland, J. H.; and Fisch, R. *Change: principles of problem formation and problem resolution.* New York: Norton, 1974.

Weinberg, M. S., and Williams, C. J. *Male homosexuals: their problems and adaptations.* New York: Oxford University Press, 1974.

Wertheimer, M. *Fundamental issues in psychology.* New York: Holt, Rinehart & Winston, 1972.

Wexberg, E. *Individual Psychological treatment* (1927), 2nd ed., rev. and annot. B. H. Shulman. Chicago: Alfred Adler Institute, 1970.

Winetrout, K. Adler's psychology and pragmatism, *Journal of Individual Psychology,* 1968, 24, 5–24.

Wolberg, L. R. Tribute to Alfred Adler, *Journal of Individual Psychology,* 1970, 27, 16.

INDEX

457

First International Congress of
  Sex Research, 394
Fisher, Saul H., 363–64
"Fixating experiences," 146. *See
  also* Sexual disorders
Flagellation, 176, 373
Fliess, Wilhelm, 32, 33, 92 n, 146,
  191, 348, 408
Forehead, and homosexuality, 150
Forgetfulness, 65
Frankl, Viktor, 396, 410
Freschl, R., 276
Freud, Sigmund, 32, 37, 53, 68,
  69, 71, 77, 92 n, 146, 147, 150,
  153, 156, 171 n, 172, 177, 179 n,
  183 n, 185, 214, 254, 258, 274,
  280, 282, 286, 289–90, 291, 293,
  305–13, 314–15, 319–20, 323,
  327, 342 ff., 355 ff., 374,
  378, 390, 393, 399, 401, 404,
  414 ff. (*See also* specific theories); and ancient Greece, 362–
  63; critique of concepts on sexual disorders, 346–52; critique
  of libido theory, 48–51; as dialectician, 299–301; and fetishism, 375; and infantile wishes,
  50–51; "love series," 73; as psychologist of women's inferiority,
  276–78; sexual etiology metaphor, 49–50
Freudenberg, Sophie, 273, 274
Friedan, Betty, 277
Friedmann, Alice, 276
Friendship, 134. *See also* Society
Frigidity, 36, 65, 81, 88, 89, 133,
  164, 183–84, 186, 202, 287, 376,
  377, 379, 388
Fromm, Erich, 344
Frustration-aggression hypothesis,
  260–61
Furtmüller, Carl, 120 n, 255, 257,
  272, 342, 414

Games, 12, 20, 134, 154, 217–19,
  333
Ganghofer, case of, 70
General German Women's Association, 274
Genitals (*See also* Infantile sexuality; specific disorders, organs): fantasies of women with

masculine, 70; fear of female,
  388–89
Germany (Germans), 101,
  121–22, 149 n, 273–74, 328–29,
  372, 414. *See also* Berlin;
  Hitler, Adolf
Gestalt psychology, 407
Giant women, 70
Girls. *See* Children; specific disor-
  ders
Glocke, Die, 93 n
Glove fetishism, 42
Goals, 39, 231, 233, 250, 357, 382
  (*See also* specific disorders);
  and cognitive aspect of therapy,
  401–2; substitute, 369–70
Goethe, J. W. von, 85, 111, 119
Gonorrhea, 183
Governesses, 73
Grandeur, 40
Grandparents, 242–43
Greece, 156, 157–58, 361–62,
  363–64
Greenwald, Harold, 379
Grillparzer, Franz, 119
Gross, S., 92 n
Grünbaum-Sachs, Hilde, 276
Guiding image. *See* Life style
Guilt feeling, 39. *See also* specific
  disorders
Gushurst, R., 409

Haberda, Albin, 182 n
Hair, and homosexuality, 150
Halban, and hermaphroditism,
  32
Haley, Jay, 320, 374–75, 377–78,
  404, 410
Hall, G. Stanley, 100 n, 218,
  420
Hall, Radcliffe, 97
Hamlet, 39, 71–72, 305
Hammel, L., 333
Handbook of Pacifism, 272
*Handbook of the Science of
  Work,* 330
Handbuch der . . . Physiologie,
  420
Hands, and homosexuality, 150
"Hardening measures," 220, 222,
  224–25, 228
Harz Mountains, 329
Hatterer, Lawrence J., 364

Headaches, 40, 231
Hebbel, Friedrich, 118
Hegel, G. W. F., 294–95 ff., 301
Heilen und Bilden, 414, 420
Heraclitus, 301
Herder, and bride songs, 88
Heredity, 78, 149, 154–55, 250, 355, 391, 396
Hermaphroditism, 32–35, 36, 39, 40, 42, 44, 147, 192, 264, 285–86, 346–47, 392–93. *See also* Bisexuality
Heymans, G., 83 n
Hildebrand, Rudolph, 295
Hilferding, Margaret, 414
Hinkle, Beatrice M., 418
Hirschfeld, Magnus, 32, 92 n, 146 ff., 191
Hitler, Adolf, 269, 274
Hitschmann, Edward, 54, 413–14, 415–16
Hoch, Paul, 344
Hoche, A., 211
Hochsinger, Karl, 212
Holland, 372
Homer, 7, 118
Homosexuality, 32, 35, 41, 80, 96, 145–70, 264, 265, 346, 347, 348–52, 366–72, 386 ff., 392 ff., 406, 410–11; active creation, 159–67; cases, 205–47; critique of evidence for innateness, 150–55; and distance from other sex, 164–66, 205–10, 360–65 ff.; general considerations, 145–50; psychotherapy and, 167–68; social factors, 155–58; summary on, 168–70
"Homosexual Problem," 198, 420
Hooker, Evelyn, 371
Hormones, 147. *See also* specific hormones
Horney, Karen, 344, 366
Huch, Ricarda, 418
Humor, 405–6
Hunger, 368 (*See also* Appetite, lack of); "strike," 90, 378
Hutchinson's teeth, 212
Hymen, 186
Hyperesthesia, 185
Hypnosis, 172
Hypochondriasis, 42, 210, 212

Hypophysis, 190
Hypospadias, 33
Hysteria, 35, 103, 348, 368
Hysteron proteron, 52

Ibsen, Henrik, 72
Id, 312, 351–52
Ideal(s), 14, 49, 94, 115, 132–33, 250, 272. *See also* Art; Love and marriage
Iliad, 7, 118
Impotence, 73, 81, 133, 183, 187–93, 229, 230, 376, 377, 401, 409; rationale, 187–89; therapy, 190–93
Impregnation, 89. *See also* Pregnancy
Incendiarism, 172
Incest, 50–51, 56, 57, 108–9, 213
Indians, American, 262
Infantile sexuality, 315, 359–60
Infantile wishes, 50–51. *See also* Freud, Sigmund; Neurosis
Inferiority, 381–82 (*See also* Freud, Sigmund; Neurosis; Organ inferiority; Sexual disorders; specific disorders); myth of women's, 3–31
Inheritance, 6. *See also* Heredity; Matrilineality
Insecurity. *See* Masculine protest; Neurosis
Insomnia (sleeplessness), 68–69, 210, 231
Instincts, 352, 354. *See also* Freud, Sigmund
"Intermediates theory," 147
International Society of Individual Psychology, 235 n
Irritation, 81

Jackson, Donald D., 320, 344
Jacobs, M., 400
Janet, Pierre, 49, 146
Jealousy, 89
Jelliffe, Smith Ely, 420
Jerusalem, Wilhelm, 49
Job. *See* Occupation
Johnson, V. E. *See* Masters and Johnson
Jokes, 405–6
Jones, Ernest, 301, 308, 415

461

of the artist, 117–20; understanding task of marriage, 121–26
Löwenfeld, Leopold, 183 n

MacCulloch, M. J., 396
McDowell, Elizabeth H., 412
McGuire, W., 308
Maeder, Alphonse, 418
Mairet, Philip, 305
Mania, 181
Mann, Thomas, 418
Manosevitz, M., 371
"Man-women," 14
Marcuse, Max, 147 n, 230 n
Marmor, Judd, 341, 344, 345, 352 ff., 365, 372, 387
Marriage. *See* Love and marriage
Marx, Karl (Marxism), 255, 270 ff., 290, 301, 356
Maschka, Josef, 182 n
Masculine protest, 32–74, 218, 276, 280–313, 320, 346–47, 354, 390, 401, 415, 416 (*See also* Defiance; Sexuality); critiques of Freud's theories—Adler-Freud controversy, 48–51, 61–70, 305–9; dialectical dynamics, 292–99; facts of psychological hermaphroditism, 32–35; and Freud as dialectician, 299–301; Freud's reaction to critiques, 309–13; and homosexuality (*See* Homosexuality); importance, transitoriness of term, 281–84; and neurotic's antithetical apperception, 43–47, 302–5; psychological hermaphroditism (*See* Hermaphroditism); reinforcement of feminine lines, 39–40; sexual disorders and (*See* Sexual disorders); social origin of term, 286–88; social, psychological, and philosophical origins of other concepts, 289–92; structure of neurosis, 38–39; therapy, 42–43; two examples, 288–89; "will to power" and its misunderstanding, 284–85
Maslow, A. H., 309

Masochism. *See* Sadism/masochism
Masserman, Jules H., 344
Mass murder, 172
Master Builder, The, 72
Masters and Johnson, 327 ff., 336, 400
Masturbation, 55 ff., 65, 73, 80, 81, 89, 90, 94, 156, 157, 172, 183 ff., 219, 221 ff., 232, 244, 365
Mathematics, 7, 12, 246
Matriarchy, 6, 262–63
Matrilineality, 6, 263, 363
Maturity, 42, 403
May, Rollo, 326–27
Mechanisms, interest in, 218
Medicine, 8
Melancholia, 300
Menopause, 91, 164
Menstruation, 91, 164
Mental health, 253–54
Mental Research Institute, 320, 404
Metaphors, 303
Mill, John S., 83 n, 292
Millett, Kate, 276, 277–78, 319
Minor, Margarete, 276
Minutes of the Vienna Psychoanalytic Society, 414–15
"Misoneism," 46
Moebius, Paul, 7, 83 n, 191
Moll, Albert, 146, 148, 181 n, 182 n
Money, J., 285, 333, 347, 387, 392–93
Money, earning. *See* Occupation
Monogamy, 137–42, 262, 324. *See also* Love and marriage
Morgan, Lewis, 262
Morphinism, 157
Mosak, H. H., 266, 402, 409
Moscow, 267
Mothers, 16–17. *See also* Abortion; Birth; Children; Love and marriage; Matrilineality; specific disorders
Mouth, 41
Mozdzierz, G. D., 410
Müller, Robert, 92 n
Munich, 273
Murder, 172, 182, 241
Murphy, G., 413

464

Penis, 33, 55, 71, 76, 204–5, 310–11, 373. *See also* Erections; Masturbation; specific problems

Perloff, W. H., 350

Perry, Ralph Barton, 328

Person, E., 388

Personality, 110 n. *See also* Life style

Pestalozzi, on environment, 356

Peterfreund, E., 351

Pew, W. L., and Miriam, 337–38

Pfungst, and apes, 146

Philosophy, 291–92

Phimosis, 152, 219, 222

Phobia, 35

Plastic surgery, 400

Play. *See* Games

Pleasure, 52, 62. *See also* Sexuality

Plottke, P., 276

Poets, 117 ff.

Poisoning, 240–41

Politics, 105. *See also* Prestige

Pollutions, 41, 56 ff., 73, 90, 94, 183, 184–85

Polygamy, 88, 96, 198

Polymorphous pervert, 52

Porter, Alan, 417

Positivism, 306

Power, 320–21 (*See also* Inferiority; Masculine protest; Prestige; Sadism/masochism); as disturbance of love relationship, 110–12

Practice and Theory of Individual Psychology, 290, 419

Pragmatism, 306

Precociousness, 54–55; sexual, 62, 65

Predatory desire, 113

Pregnancy, 164 (*See also* Birth); abortion, 27–31, 261, 324

Premarital sex, 133. *See also* Abortion

Premature ejaculation. *See* Ejaculation

Prestige, 25, 121, 319–20, 339

Prickling sensation, 185

Prisons, 167

Private property, 6, 258, 262

Problem of Homosexuality, 417, 419–20

Procurers, 200

Promiscuity, 81, 262, 324

Prostitutes, 32, 59, 73, 81, 88, 94, 96, 103, 172, 186, 193–204, 209, 229, 231 ff., 314, 324, 378, 400-1, 419

Psyche. *See* Life style

Psychoanalysis, 341–46

Psychological hermaphroditism. *See* Hermaphroditism

"Psychological Hermaphroditism in Life and Neurosis," 415

"Psychological Significance of Psychoanalysis," 342

"Psychology of Power," 272

"Psychology of Women," 277–78

Psychosis, 47, 192, 199, 240, 385

Puberty, 94–95, 97–103. *See also* Adolescence; specific problems

Pubic hair, 150

Public opinion, 148–50

Punishment (*See also* Sadism/masochism): fear of, 40

Pythagorean tables, 43, 303, 304

Racowitza, Helena, 288–89

Rado, Sandor, 341, 343–44, 348, 349, 353, 354, 357, 375

Rank, Otto, 415

Rape, 172

Rasey, Marie I., 140

Rats, 191, 192

Rayner, D., 266

Reframing, 404–7

Regression, 51, 177

Reimann, and exhibitionism, 181 n

Reinecke, Adolf, 329

Relationship of the Sexes, 3 n

Religion, 236–37, 240, 322; Church councils, 7

REM sleep, 360

Rensberger, B., 397

Repression, 61–70, 254, 294, 309, 415, 416. *See also* Freud, Sigmund; Masculine protest

Rhythm of Life, 338

Rickets, 265

Riegel, Klaus, 301

Right Conduct of Life, 417–18

Roazen, Paul, 312–13
Robbins, B. S., 349
Robins, E., 371
Rohleder, Hermann, 92 n, 183 n
Roman History (Niebuhr), 291
Romantics, 175–76
Rops, Félicien, 118
Ruesch, J., 404
Rühle, Alice, 272, 276
Rühle, Otto, 272
Russia (Soviet Union), 268, 269, 330; Bolshevism, 256, 257, 271–72
Rychlak, Joseph F., 293, 295, 298, 299, 301, 306, 404

Sacher-Masoch, Leopold, 171
Sade, Marquis de, 171
Sadger, and homosexuality, 32
Sadism/masochism, 35, 38, 40, 42, 53, 70, 81, 96, 157, 171–79, 229, 373–75, 383
Safeguarding, 63, 291. *See also* Love and marriage; Sexual disorders; Sexuality
Saghir, M. T., 371
Salomon, Alice, 274
Salzman, I., 349, 350, 354, 358–59, 362, 366, 368–69, 370, 374
Sand, George, 14 n, 84
Saninism, 330
Satyriasis, 192
Saul, Leon J., 351
Scarf, M., 268
Scented Garden, 335
Schäfer, Siegrid, 372
Scharf, Sigmund, 231
Schatznan, M., 390
Schiller, J. C. F. von, 93 n
Schirmacher, Käthe, 83 n
Schizophrenia, 181, 241, 303
Schleirmacher, Friedrich, 119
Schmid, A., 276
Schmidt, H., 419
School. *See* Education and schools
Schopenhauer, Arthur, 8, 86, 191
Schreber, D. P., 310, 389–90
Schrecker, and recollections, 165

Schrenck-Notzing, 146, 147, 171
Schulhof, Hedwig, 276
Schuschnigg government, 273
Schwarz, Oswald, 147 n, 151
Sea voyages, 167
Seelbach, H., 323
Seif, Leonhard, 176, 189, 273, 368
Self-determination, 250–51. *See also* Creative power
Sellheim, Hugo, 83 n
Seneca, 291
Senile dementia, 181, 192
Senile homosexuality, 167
Sensitivity. *See* Oversensitivity
Servants, 73, 94, 233, 234
Sex organs, 53. *See also* Genitals; Organ inferiority; specific disorders, organs
Sexual anesthesia. *See* Frigidity
Sexual disorders, 41–42, 143–247, 341–412, 419–21 (*See also* specific disorders); clinical aspects, 380–412; consensual development, 341–46; critique of Freud, 346–52; distance from other sex, 360–65; dysfunctions, 183–92; sexuality in service of personality, 352–59
Sexuality, 75–103, 417–19 (*See also* Inferiority; Love and marriage; Sexual disorders; specific disorders, theories); Adlerian books, 338–40; development of the sexual function, 77–83; education, 332–34, 411; man's psychosexual attitude, 92–97; holistic, goal-oriented approach, 313–16; many uses of, 357–59; nondogmatic stance, 329–32; sex education and puberty, 97–103; woman's attitude toward, 83–91
Sexual Politics, 319
Sexual precocity, 62, 65
"Sexual Problem in Education," 314
Sexual surrogates, 400
Shoe fetishism, 42
Shulman, B. H., 358, 389–90, 402
Sickliness, 33, 40

467

468